W9-BVN-131

FINLAND
BERLIN
BALTIC SEA
HELSINKI
RIGA
LENINGRAD
WARSAW
Minsk
MOSCOW
GORKI
KIEV
Cheboksary
Kazan
Kharkov
Odessa
UNION OF SOVIET
SVERDLOVSK
DONETSK
Volga
Rostov na Donu
Ural
Don
Stalingrad
BLACK SEA
Astrakhan
Nalchik
CASPIAN SEA
Groznyy
Mahach Kala
TURKEY
TBILISI
ARAL SEA
Yerevan
Hatch Mas
Nakhichevan
BAKU
Syr Dar'ya
Krasnovodsk
TASHKENT
Ashkhabad
Bokhara
Samarkand
Dushanbe
IRAN
AFGHANISTAN

★ Capitols of Nations
Borders of Nations
Borders of Soviet Socialist Republics
Route of Travel During WWII

The political divisions and names shown here reflect those in effect when the events described in Fifty Russian Winters took place

Yana
Nizhnaya Tunguska
Angara
OCIALIST REPUBLICS
TOMSK
Omsk
Novosibirsk
Barnaul
Irtysh
Rubtovsk
Semipalatinsk
Ulan Bator
MONGOLIA
GOBI DESERT
Alma-Ata
CHINA

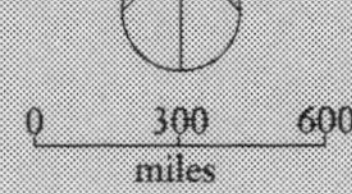

Fifty Russian Winters

An American Woman's Life in the Soviet Union

Margaret Wettlin

INTRODUCTION BY
HARRISON SALISBURY

John Wiley & Sons, Inc.
New York • Chichester • Brisbane • Toronto • Singapore

To my grandchildren,
Ted, Natasha, Andrei, and Paul.

This text is printed on acid-free paper.

First published in hardcover by Pharos Books.
Published in softcover by John Wiley & Sons, Inc.

Library of Congress Cataloging-in-Publication Data:

Wettlin, Margaret, 1907–
Fifty Russian winters : an American woman's life in the Soviet Union / Margaret Wettlin ; introduction by Harrison Salisbury.
p. cm.
ISBN 0-471-02877-0 (paper : alk. paper)
1. Wettlin, Margaret, 1907– . 2. Soviet Union—Politics and government. 3. Women authors, American—20th century—Biography.
I. Title. II. Title : 50 Russian winters.
DK268.W48A3 1994
947.084′2′092—dc20 93-43635
[B]

Printed in the United States of America

10 9 8 7 6 5 4 3 2 1

Acknowledgments

NO BOOK IS THE RESULT of a single person's endeavor—not, that is, if it reaches the public, as every author intends that his or her book shall. So I thank all those who contributed in any way to having this book published.

But there are those who made very personal contributions. First in point of time is Lev Kopolyev, Russian scholar and dissident who, while we were both living in Russia, managed to get the first part of my manuscript out of the country clandestinely when to do so legally was impossible. Second was Harold Minton, bereaved husband of my late college mate Helen Sewall; Harold offered me the moral and material support required to continue work on the book after I returned to the United States in 1980. A new friend made at that time, Carol Riddle helped me with typing and advice. The first friends to whom I read the most important chapter of my story were Joyce and Edward Espen; their understanding made easier the difficult task I was still in the process of performing. Unfortunately, Ed did not live to see manuscript into book. Neither did our mutual friend Esther Schafer, but Esther's daughter, Susan Rappaport, found me an agent and spared no effort or expense to see that my manuscript was given proper form and shown to the proper people. The first professional eye to focus on the manuscript was that of novelist Shirley Yarnall, who was assigned the task of reading it by my good agent Leona Schecter. Shirley's approval gave me grounds for hoping I had not labored in vain. So did the sympathy and dedication with which Hana Lane, my editor at Pharos Books, presided over the birth of the book.

To all these, my heartfelt thanks.

I almost wish I hadn't gone down that rabbit hole—and yet—and yet—it's rather curious, you know, this sort of life! I do wonder what *can* have happened to me. There ought to be a book written about me, that there ought! And when I grow up, I'll write one.

—Lewis Carroll, *Alice in Wonderland*

Contents

Introduction
by Harrison Salisbury

THE SAVAGE EVENTS of the last sixty years have almost wiped from our consciousness the great idealistic dreams which sprang from the Russian events of 1917.

The rise of Stalin, the ruthless purges, the infamous pact of Hitler and Stalin, World War II, the pervasive Cold War, and finally the titanic collapse of the Soviet system and communism as a form of society have buried the hopes of millions that a new day would arise in the world out of the fire of the Russian Revolution.

It is well that we pause a moment amid the exhilaration over the events of 1991 to look back upon a time when the future seemed bright and boundless not only in Russia but around the globe and especially in the United States.

Margaret Wettlin possessed that vision and it led her to Russia and transformed her life. She tells that story simply, courageously, honestly, and winsomely in *Fifty Russian Winters*. She went to Moscow in 1932 at a time when thousands of Americans were visiting the land of Lenin's Revolution, fell in love, and stayed, making her life beside her husband, Andrei Efremoff, a theater director.

She and Andrei were not political persons, never members of the Communist party, but they believed in the idyllic dream even long after common sense told them it was the cruelest of frauds. In a sense they *had* to believe or bring their lives to an end. They watched their friends, one by one, fall victim to the terror, telling themselves over and over that it could not be true, that it had to be a mistake. They could not bring themselves to believe that it was all too true, that the rot in the revolution had started at the top, and when they finally admitted to themselves the terrible truth it was too late. Like millions, they were trapped in the cage of lies that Russia had become.

Even after the death of Andrei, even after she had returned to her native Philadelphia and again was living a life in which it was possible to sleep without fear of the dread knock on the door at midnight, Margaret Wettlin remained silent. She was rightly fearful of the consequences of speaking frankly upon her friends and relatives still in Soviet Russia.

But with Mikhail Gorbachev and *glasnost* she finally decided to put her story on paper, and with the explosion which has torn out the roots of Communist dictatorship not only in Russia but across the world she consented to the publication of her book.

The virtue of Margaret Wettlin's tale is that it is simple and personal. She does not wallpaper over her feelings, her aspirations, her beliefs, her compromises, not even the fact that once she found herself trapped into becoming an informer for the secret police. But she tells, too, how she turned upon the monstrous agents and with the bravery of an honest heart told them she was finished with their dirty game. It could have cost her her life.

This is not a narrative of unrelieved anguish. There were bright and happy days, amusing times, the warm closeness of Russian friendships, the life the Russians constructed for themselves within the prison camp which their country had become.

In their first years Margaret and Andrei lived and worked in Outer Mongolia. No more primitive and exciting life could have been found within the bounds of the Communist Empire. (Outer Mongolia was nominally independent but almost totally under Moscow's influence and direction.) It was a little like living amid the mountains of the moon.

Nonpolitical as Andrei was, they escaped some of the worst terror because they were not members of the Party and Stalin's butchers concentrated on the Party and not the general public (unless they belonged to some vast category like the peasants of the Ukraine, returning prisoners of war after World War II, residents of particular areas about which Stalin had security concerns, or citizens of one minority or another whose loyalty he began to doubt).

Many works have professed to tell the story of "inside Russia." Margaret Wettlin lived inside Russia, kept her heart and mind and eyes open—and remembered.

PART ONE

Antebellum

one

Into the Rabbit Hole

I wonder if I shall fall right *through* the earth! How funny it will seem to come out among people that walk with their heads downwards! The antipathies, I think . . .

—Lewis Carroll,
Alice in Wonderland

MY COMPANIONS IN THE JET leaving London for New York settled themselves comfortably in their seats for the long night's journey over the ocean—removing a coat, requesting a pillow, a blanket. Not I. Every cell in my body had been tingling with excitement ever since I left Moscow. I was Mrs. Rip Van Winkle coming home to the old New World from the new Old World. Rip was away twenty years. I was away forty-two. Rip slept the time away. I lived it eventfully.

ON ENTERING THIS INCREDIBLE JET, this Leviathan whose like I had never seen before, this Pan Am Jumbo with over three hundred passengers in its belly, my foot touched American soil, so to speak, for the first time in nearly half a century. No wonder my heart was racing. As if to quiet it, Jumbo wheeled away from the airport building as smoothly as a cruising taxi, bouncing slightly over bumps and turning corners with a circumspection that gave no hint of its terrible intention. Once it reached the airstrip it became a raging beast, quaking in all its parts as it built up power for the takeoff, and when the takeoff began it was with a fury that should have torn it apart. But no, the roaring ceased, the quaking subsided, there was no more speed, we were floating in space. The death agony was over, and we had gone to heaven. Earth slumbered below, and never have I seen anything more enchanting than slumbering London as it tipped away from us in the dark of that December night. It was a garden of phosphorescent flowers in myriad configurations with fireflies darting among the flowers and snails weaving luminous trails on the paths. The beauty brought repose and reflection.

FORTY-TWO YEARS. I did not dream that so much time would elapse when I left New York on the S.S. *Colombia* in September 1932. In my bag were tickets for a month's tour of Soviet Russia, very little money, and a few letters of introduction, for I harbored the hope of finding a job that would keep me in Russia for a year.

When I asked my high school principal in Media, Pennsylvania, for a year's leave of absence "to study abroad" he willingly granted it, glad, I suppose, that his teachers wanted to improve themselves.

"And where do you intend going?"

"To Russia," I said. His face lengthened like a smear on a slide.

"How do I know you will not come back a Communist?" he asked.

How indeed! That was one of the reasons for my going, to find the answer to this question.

IT IS SAID that people do what they have to do. I would modify the statement. The mind recoils from the notion that a person is a mere straw adrift on the stream at the mercy of wind and wave. But it seems as foolish to assume that a person has complete control over his destiny as to assume that he has none.

I choose to think we are free to make determinative decisions that control succeeding events, much as the piers of a bridge determine the length and strength of the spans springing from them. The making of such a decision is an ordeal, it gives you no peace, it follows you like a hound at your heels, like an inescapable staring eye, until the happy day when, with a word like tempered steel, you cut yourself free and strike out for better or for worse along the new way.

Two such decisions stand at the beginning and end of my life: the first, my decision to go to Russia in 1932; the second, my decision to return to the United States in 1979. Everything that happened between these years is the long span of circumstances, events, and experiences I lived through in the Soviet Union.

In the center of them all is Andrei. Yet I almost missed meeting him, and when we did meet, the encounter was incidental, seemingly inconsequential. It took place in Moscow's Kamerny Theater on November 9, 1932, on the eve of my leaving Russia.

Yes, I was leaving. I had been here two months, had lived out my original visa issued in the United States as well as the extension granted me in Moscow, and now I had to go. I had been offered a job here but I could not take it as a tourist. I had to leave the country and be invited back by the Soviet government; if they wanted me badly enough, they would issue me a worker's visa at a foreign consulate. And so I was going to Finland the next day. My fate hung in the balance. So distraught was I at the prospect of having to use my return ticket to New York that when Robert, an American living in Moscow who had brought me to the theater that evening of November ninth, met a Russian friend in the lobby and briefly presented him, "Peg, this is Andrei," I scarcely noticed the man, grunted an acknowledgment, and went back to my uneasy thoughts.

I desperately wanted to stay in Russia for a year. My two months had been too short a time to give me a real insight into the essence of living under socialism, but that was only to be expected—tourists never get more than a superficial view of a country, its shapes and colors. I had tried hard to absorb the new Russia's shapes and colors, and in doing so had been rewarded with occasional glimpses under the surface. How could I go away without expanding these glimpses?

My efforts to get a job enabling me to do this had run up against exasperating obstacles. The first month had yielded no success at all. Then I met Evelyn Rogers, a young French teacher from New Zealand who, I soon learned, had come to Moscow with the same purpose as my own. One day when I was feeling particularly frustrated in the matter of making job contacts, Evelyn gave me the telephone number of a man from the People's Commissariat of Education.

After that, most of my mornings were spent in going to his office. On leaving my hotel I would cross the bridge over the Moscow River to a streetcar stop at the foot of Red Square. Boarding a car was no mean physical feat in those days. Passengers spilled over not only onto the steps but even onto the narrow ledge encircling the back of the car. You fought your way aboard with friendly assistance. The young men fanning out in various degrees of horizontality from a one-hand grip on the upright between entrance doors, would support you with their free arms until you got a foothold; then, pushed from behind, you became part of the human paste being squeezed toward the front exit. In such congestion it was impossible to reach the conductor, so fares were passed overhead and tickets were returned by the same aerial route. The aisle was full of noises, the all-pervading one being the *"Vwe Vwikhoditye?" "Vwekhoditye li vwe?"* Could such vaporosity mean anything as downright as "You getting off here?" It did. Or take the name of the stop *Sifsikh Vrazhik.* To a foreign ear such sounds seem fashioned of froth and spume. But there were others: "*Stóy!*" shouted a woman to the motorman when he was about to start up before she had extricated herself, and "*Perestan!*" barked a girl to a man who was taking advantage of the close quarters. Good hard plosives that brought you up as sharply as "Stop!" or "Don't!"

THE BUILDING IN WHICH Comrade Friedman at the People's Commissariat of Education had his office was on the A Circle (Moscow is built on two concentric circles with Red Square the pivotal point). The office was bare: bare walls except for The Portrait (of Lenin, of course), bare floors but for a desk and two upright chairs. The only indulgence was in telephones; a battery of them stood between me and Comrade Friedman. He was smallish, with black hair and eyes and the fat cheeks that give a false impression of general corpulence. His English was of the "How you do" variety but adequate to let me know he had a job to offer. A teacher was needed in an American school near Gorki (formerly Nizhni Novgorod) on the Volga. The school was for the children of Ford engineers and workers who were here on contract to help launch a Soviet automobile plant patterned after the Ford plant. The Soviet plant site, including the "American Village" housing these workers, was called Autozavod ("*auto*" for "automobile"; "*zavod*" for "factory".) I understood that I was needed there immediately, but such esoteric conversations were held over the telephones, such mysterious levels were consulted, such a labyrinthine course pursued, that I feared my tour would be over before the conditions for getting the job were formulated. At last Comrade Friedman came out with an unequivocable statement:

The first condition for staying was leaving.

That is why I was going to Finland on November 10th, 1932, and why, on the eve of my departure, I had no eyes for Andrei in the Kamerny Theater.

I had done my best to avoid making this trip to Finland. In the first place, I could not afford it. In the second, once out of Russia I could not be sure of getting back. I had appealed for help to a Bulgarian Communist staying in our hotel. He told me to wait; having access to men in high places, he thought he could have my tourist visa exchanged for a worker's one without my leaving the country. This was welcome news. Even if he did not succeed, I would have time to see more of Moscow, and so I had decided to wait.

In foreign cities, fellow countrymen inevitably gravitate toward one another. I soon began to meet Americans living in Moscow. Robert, who took me to the Kamerny that night, was one of them. An American engineer of Russian descent and Communist persuasion, he was a victim of the Depression who had come with his wife and their two children to work for the Soviets because there was little hope of finding work in the States. His hobby, like mine, being theater, we sometimes indulged in it together. Another such American was Gerald, a young filmmaker who had come to study under Eisenstein at the Moscow Institute of Cinematography. Still another was Gerald's friend Arthur, a New York Communist teaching English at the Foreign Language Institute. These two introduced me to the first Russian girl to become my friend. She was Olga Polyenova, and she remained my friend until the day of her death in 1976. Her father, Vasili Polyenov, had been an eminent artist of aristocratic birth; her mother, related to Stanislavsky, was of the rising merchant class.

"Much better stock, the merchant," said Olga. "More life in them." Olga spoke the Oxford English she had learned from governesses in childhood. Now she earned her living by conducting a drama circle at a Moscow factory. She showed no discontent with her lot. Her staging plays with factory workers was a continuation of her family's staging plays with peasants on the Polyenov estate before the revolution. Her family had maintained close ties with the peasants, devoting much time to teaching and cultivating them, and so when the revolution came and mobs of irate peasants burned and plundered rich estates, the Polyenov peasants defended their benefactors' lives and property.

The four of us—Gerald, Arthur, Olga, and I—went to the theater together once a week. Not the Monday, Tuesday, Wednesday week I was used to, but a new Soviet six-day week of unnamed days—just first day, second day, third day—and no common rest day; everyone was assigned whatever rest day was convenient for the enterprise where he or she was employed. This kept factories and offices working without interruption. It also kept families and friends from enjoying weekends together. This may have been a contributing factor for going back to the universal seven-day week later in the thirties.

There were a great many theaters in Moscow, and all of them were sold out for every performance. This was a surprise; play-going was a luxury in America. "How can they afford it?" I asked Gerald.

"Tickets are cheap, cost next to nothing," he said.

Precisely nothing is what they cost us. The minute Gerald, Arthur, or I poked a head in at a box office and it was perceived (easily) that we were foreigners, we were turned over to the manager, who received us as honored guests and ushered us to reserved seats gratis.

All playgoers are required to check their coats before entering concert and theater auditoriums in Russia, and this made me painfully aware of my foreign clothes, modest though they were, among shapeless cotton skirts, sagging cotton sweaters, darned and shiny and made-over woolen dresses sometimes incongruously embellished by a fichu of genuine old lace that had survived political upheaval. Footwear was mostly sneakers, but one also saw high-laced boots and antiquated pumps with long pointed toes and egg-cup heels. No jewelry. Jewelry was taboo. Jewelry was bourgeois. And by this time most of it had been exchanged for food coupons in the Torgsin (Foreign Trade) stores operating on a gold and foreign currency basis, for food was scarce in Moscow. Indeed, I often wondered what Russians ate. There were no restaurants or tearooms except in the hotels for foreigners. In my wanderings about the city I had often dropped into food stores. I could not have bought anything even if I had wanted to because food was rationed, but I certainly did not want to buy those blue gobs of meat wrapped in bloodstained newspapers, or those eggs whose stench came through the shells, or those candies glued into a solid chunk by the jam fillings oozing out of them.

FOOD AND CLOTHES were scarce, but they were scarce for everybody. That, I concluded, made it easier to bear; nothing for anybody today, everything for everybody tomorrow. A new world was in the making. New values. New relationships. New art.

NEW THEATER certainly. The bottles were as new as the wine, and of all shapes and colors: Meyerhold's Theater, divested of curtain (a startling innovation in those days) and with constructionist scenery that made the stage look like a Kandinsky abstraction; Okhlopkov's Theater, the first professional theater-in-the-round; Tairov's Kamerny Theater, more modestly radical; Stanislavsky's Moscow Art Theater, which in one way or another had sired all the others. At that time Moscow was the Mecca of playgoers throughout the world, for nowhere else were such exciting things being done. The audiences may have looked dowdy, but they were partaking of intellectual fare far in advance of the times. They found it stimulating, judging by the animated arguments and discussions they engaged in when, during intermissions, they walked round and round in one big circle out in the foyer.

WHEN THE PLAY WAS OVER Gerald, Arthur, Olga, and I would walk back to her house at Nikitsky Gates for supper and our own discussions. There I was introduced to one of those baleful congeries known as a communal apartment. Little did I think that I would live in one myself in five years. In the old days the Polyenovs' Moscow apartment had occupied the entire second floor of this house. After the revolution only one room of it was left to Olga; the rest was parceled out to total strangers.

We followed her into a long, dusty, windowless, airless corridor—a no-man's-land flanked by shut doors, dimly lighted by an unshaded low-watt light bulb. Space between the doors was stacked with overflow furniture and tools. A bicycle was suspended from the ceiling. Trunks were piled high with nondescript bundles. Interstices were filled by a snow shovel, a washbasin, a samovar pipe. At the end of the corridor, to the left, was the kitchen, with seven tables on which seven primus stoves let out a dreadful roar and smell of kerosene when seven dinners were being cooked simultaneously. Directly in front was the common toilet. To the right of it was the common bath. Still further to the right was Olga's room.

She switched on the light, and there we were in a little oasis of comfort and culture. Sweeping the books off the center table, Olga pulled it up to her studio couch that fitted cozily into a nook formed by a corner of the room at one end and a wardrobe placed at right angles to the wall at the other. A strip of handblocked linen was tacked around the wall of the nook as a background for pillows and small paintings by her father and his friends Serov, Levitan, Surikhov, and other prominent painters of the late nineteenth and early twentieth century. She sat herself in a carved oaken chair brought from the Polyenov estate on the Oka River. Now the estate belonged to the government and was maintained as a museum dedicated to her father's memory. Olga and her brother and sisters were allowed to spend their summers on the top floor of the main house and in the little houses on the property formerly occupied by their servants.

When we had seated ourselves at Olga's table, Arthur produced cheese from the Torgsin store and a bottle of wine, and Olga contributed some of those gummy candies as sugar substitute for our tea.

At one of our discussions I mentioned having met Maurice Hindus. I had looked up from dinner in the hotel dining room one evening to see him standing in the doorway. I recognized him at once from the photos on the jackets of his books and from having heard him lecture in Philadelphia. In those days, anyone interested in Russia had read Maurice Hindus. His most popular book was *Black Bread and Red Coffins*. The title indicates his appreciation of the hardships the Russians were undergoing, but he was sympathetic with their cause. He himself was of Russian origin and knew the language, which meant he had wider opportunities than most correspondents to make direct contact with Russians and hear their views. I thought he could help me better than anyone else to understand what I was seeing.

"And did he?" asked Arthur.

"He tried to. He took me for a walk after dark and we peered into basement windows and saw people sleeping on the floor in rows."

Arthur bristled. "Did he tell you *that* was communism?"

"Not exactly. But he told me enough to let me know his views have changed. He was angry. He said he was through with this country. He said he couldn't forgive them for what they were doing to the peasants."

"And what did he say that was?"

"He said they were taking the land away from them."

"Nobody's taking the land away," Arthur snorted. "They're collectivizing it, so that agriculture can be mechanized."

"Well, the peasants don't seem to want it. He said they were running away from the farms, driven away by hunger. I saw them in railroad stations in Leningrad and here."

"That's all the fault of the *kulaks*, the rich peasants. They're sabotaging collectivization, killing off the cattle and destroying the crops. They're even killing the people sent out by the Party to explain why it's necessary to change to large-scale farming."

"But Louis Fischer seems to agree with Hindus." I brought in Louis Fischer thinking his opinions would carry weight. Hindus was, after all, a popular writer. Fischer was more serious. He was said to be writing ponderous tomes on Soviet Diplomacy. His name was respected, as was his presence in any gathering—his dark, brooding presence. He had a bulky form, and I seem to remember him walking down the street all hunched over, hands plunged deep in coat pockets, mind plunged deep in thought. He had a Russian wife and two (was it two?) sons. I visited them at a later date. Theirs was a very simple, distinctly intellectual ménage, not at all like the homes of most correspondents, where it was clear on entering that they were milking the best of two worlds. All the goodies of the West were on their shelves and in their Frigidaires and many Russian antiques and objets d'art were in their rooms, bought for a pittance from people in dire straits.

"Louis Fischer agrees with Hindus?" asked Arthur in some surprise. "I wouldn't expect him to. What did he say?"

"Nothing much. He didn't go into it. Just shook his head and said, 'Go home, little girl, go home.' Portentously."

"And are you going?"

"Not if I can help it."

But could I? October was coming to an end, and so was my money. At this point my Bulgarian friend broke the news that his efforts had been in vain—I would have to go abroad to obtain a worker's visa.

I chose Finland as the nearest country, and the cheapest.

Since I still had a few days left before my extended visa expired, my friends easily persuaded me to postpone my departure until after the November seventh celebration of The Great October Revolution (the oddity of celebrating the October Revolution in November is explained by the Soviet adoption of the Gregorian calendar used in the West in place of the Julian calendar used in Russia until the revolution).

THROUGHOUT THE WEEK before the seventh I had been awakened at night by the roar of tanks practicing for the parade through Red Square, and of marching columns of Red Armymen singing at the top of their voices. On the very morning of the "Enormous Jubilee," I woke up to the sound of music coming from loudspeakers posted citywide—not martial music, but choruses of vague indefinable harmony that flowed along the streets and rose to my hotel window.

At eight o'clock on the morning of November seventh Gerald and Robert called for me. We went out into the music and the snow and the tide of people that had engulfed Moscow streets. We walked about a mile to Robert's factory, where we found the workers forming a column that was to join innumerable other columns that would pour through Red Square for hours and hours until all Moscow had saluted its leaders standing in the rostrum on top of Lenin's mausoleum.

At the factory we witnessed much hand-shaking and back-slapping, enjoying a goodly share of it ourselves. There was no sign of the suspicion and alienation of foreigners that the future was to bring.

Robert's associates offered us tea and cheese sandwiches. "America!" they cried enthusiastically, as if the country itself had come to make them a bow.

"What is your nationality?" they asked me.

I thought they knew. "Why . . . American."

"That's no nationality," they replied deprecatingly. "That's just where you live. Are you English, German, Irish? (glancing at my red hair)."

I turned to Robert. "Tell them that American *is* a nationality. It's neither English nor German nor Irish, but all of them mixed together."

While we were discussing this, for they were not easily convinced, along came the boy responsible for lining us up in ranks of ten. The march to Red Square went in fits and starts, for the columns funneling into the square were city-wide coordinated, and we had now to stand and wait so as not to get there too soon, now to run and catch up.

Like our neighbors as far as the eye could see, we joined hands to form a big circle and danced and played games to keep warm while waiting. Every quarter-mile of column had its own band, but everybody sang and clapped for the folk dances in the teeth of the band music, the resulting cacophony outdoing anything conceived by the most far-out composer. There were Russian dances, and the Ukrainian *hopak* with much squatting and kicking, and the Caucasian *lezginka.*

In the middle of a game or a dance somebody would cry out, "*Bezhim!*" ("We're running!", which is to say, "We're off!"), at which the circle disintegrated amid shouts and shrieks, everybody reached for his neighbor's hand, and the column went tearing off down the street to catch up.

The march through the square was orderly, with all heads turned to the mausoleum on the right.

"Which is Stalin?"

"There. See? In the middle. Waving."

"Voroshilov on his left?"

"And Budenny. Couldn't miss him with those mustaches."

We were through the square in a trice. It was already afternoon, and we went to Olga's for our holiday dinner. Special rationing had seen to it that no family lacked flour for making *piroshki* and vodka for making toasts.

That evening everybody was in the streets again, this time to see the sights. The First Five Year Plan had been completed, and blazing signs covering the entire facade of buildings explained what this meant.

There were cascades of light resembling water spilling over dams, and figures telling how much electricity these dams would produce. There were furrows of light representing new lands tilled, and charts giving the number of acres and percentage of increased harvest. There were eruptions of light standing for steel pouring out of blast furnaces, and graphs showing the growth of the country's steel output.

All shop windows on central streets were turned into exhibition stands. They displayed artists' sketches of settings for new plays, and architects' drawings for the new plants, schools, kindergartens, theaters, provided for by the next Five Year Plan.

Temporary stages had been erected on the city's numerous squares where street crowds were entertained by leading actors from Moscow theaters. Puppet shows for the children competed with slapdash political skits showing bloated capitalists brought to dust by worker-champions. All the city was a stage for the enjoyment and edification of the populace.

THE NOVEMBER CELEBRATION of 1932—the extent of it, the elaborateness of it, the exuberance and splendid extravagance—offered me more than shapes and colors. It was charged with vitality. It was youthful. Its face was turned to the future. I was lucky to have arrived in Russia at the tail end of a period of revolutionary fervor that lasted, with diminishing force, from 1917 to 1936 and was succeeded by one of such ignominy that it blotted out the memory of its vibrant antecedent. My own children, born later, are skeptical of my testimony, attributing it to my being a foreigner unable to grasp what was actually going on. There may be a modicum of truth in this. But only a modicum. The evidence is there. Today's young Russians are inclined to look upon this evidence as fabricated, because so much that is dished up to them is fabricated. Or they use today's standards to deprecate achievements that were valid by earlier standards. Or they shrug off these achievements as inconsequential in the light of what followed. But I must bear witness to this vibrant period because it alone reveals the extent to which hopes were betrayed, and it explains behavior, my own in particular, that is otherwise inexplicable.

NONE OF THESE CHANGES could possibly have been foreseen on November 9, 1932. When Robert phoned and invited me to the theater that evening I answered sharply, "I can't go. I'm leaving tomorrow. I've got to pack."

A little gasp of incredulity came over the wire. "You mean you're leaving the country, perhaps forever, and you want to spend your last night *packing*?"

I got his point.

We were late in arriving at the theater, and the meeting with Andrei in the lobby made us even later. The last warning bell sounded as we stood in line to check our coats. That night's performance was part of an international theater festival. Again foreigners were paid special attention. There were some French, and a few Germans, and here was this Andrei from . . .

"Mongolia," said Robert.

An usher appeared and hurried us to seats in the director's box.

"Mongolia . . ." I began when we were seated, but just then the lights went out.

In the first intermission Tairov, the director, invited the foreigners into his office for tea. The office, with its massive mahogany furniture, its velvet curtains, its thin china teacups, suggested a Henry James drawing room. And Tairov in no way resembled a stage director serving the new masses. His portly figure was sheathed with sartorial perfection. I cannot say with assurance that he wore a sardonyx intaglio on his index finger or that he dallied with a gold watch fob, but the mind supplied these details as complementary to the whole.

Andrei brought me tea and Robert acted as interpreter. I observed Andrei for the first time in Tairov's office. He was not very tall, five-feet-ten or thereabouts. Bald, with a black fringe brushed straight back from his temples. Roman nose. Crooked smile. Nice, on the whole, but . . . I don't suppose anybody could have pleased me that night, poised as I was between going and coming. Besides, I couldn't talk to him. He had no English and I had accumulated, oh, about two hundred Russian words that I hadn't yet learned to fit together properly. But I didn't want to appear impolite, and so:

"Mongolia . . ." I murmured, searching my mind for its place on the map.

"North of Tibet, west of China," supplied Andrei. I understood him. Anyone who has studied a foreign language and has listened to the sound of it for any length of time, knows that the ability to understand comes sooner than the ability to speak.

"Ever heard of the Gobi Desert?" Robert asked me.

"Um . . . something about dinosaur eggs?"

"That's it. Well, the Gobi's in Mongolia."

The only thing I knew about Mongols was that they were Orientals, and this man certainly was not.

"You, in Mongolia—biologist? Archeologist?" I asked Andrei.

"No, I'm a stage director," he replied. That was weird—a Russian stage director in the Gobi Desert. I said as much to Robert, who passed it on to Andrei.

"Not in the Gobi," he smiled, "although I found a very talented young fellow for my studio in the Gobi."

"Studio?"

"We've opened a studio in Ulan Bator to train actors for a national theater."

"Even United States—no national theater."

"Well, we're going to have one in Mongolia. You'll see it in another two or three years."

"*I* see it?" Enticing, but hardly realistic.

During the second intermission Andrei led me out to join the people walking round and round in the foyer in the way of Russian audiences. On the wall hung a map of the world, charting with little flags the course of the Kamerny Theater's recent tour of South America.

For want of anything better to do I traced on it another journey: from New York to Moscow; and Andrei still another: from Ulan Bator to Moscow. Together we had covered some 15,000 miles, he moving in one direction, I in the opposite, to converge here in the Kamerny Theater.

"Your home—Moscow?" I asked.

"I was born and raised here."

"Why you go Mongolia?"

He did not attempt to tell me, knowing serious answers could not be contained in the Russian he cut down to my size.

"You must come to Mongolia. You must see it."

"Tomorrow I go away. Leave Russia."

"But you will come back?"

"Maybe yes, maybe no."

"You want to come back?"

"Very."

"Then you will."

The audacity of this young man with the bald head and the Roman nose! I found it amusing, and at the same time it pleased me. It was not wishy-washy. It showed character. And it fitted in with my own idea of controlling one's destiny by the making of determinative decisions. The trouble in this case was that while the decision to come to Russia had been mine, the decision to stay here did not rest with me. I might be able to impose my will on another person but not on the Soviet state.

"May I take you home after the play?" Andrei asked.

"No, Robert take me."

Robert would take me not home—home was thousands of miles away; he would take me back to the New Moscow Hotel for my very last night before I set out for—could it be home? No. I must not admit even the possibility of such a disaster. I must fortify myself with some of Andrei's confidence that a person gets what a person wants.

two

Finnish Interlude

> . . . the East's gift,
> Is quick and transient . . .
> While Northern thought is slow and durable.
> —Robert Browning,
> *Bells and Pomegranates*

WHEN, ON THE TENTH OF NOVEMBER, I retraced, in the opposite direction, the journey I had made in September from Helsinki to Leningrad, my mind was occupied with weighing my chances. Why, I asked myself, should the Soviets add another mouth to their overtaxed ration list? On the other hand, the school in Autozavod had to be adequately staffed, and I seemed to be the only person asking for the job. But the school was functioning without me; it could go on doing so; the country was facing shortages in fields more important than teaching, especially teaching the children of foreigners who were here today and gone tomorrow. On the other hand, it was a matter of prestige for the Soviets to demonstrate their principle of having children taught in their native tongue by qualified teachers. I was qualified. But there were excellent Russian teachers of English. . . .

So I argued with myself, back and forth, as I gazed out the train window at the shine of sun on snow, at pine trees with fluffy white fur growing all along their boughs, at a black filigree of birches and aspens against a sapphirine sky. How different, this, from the September scene. Then we had crossed dark fields blurred with rain and punctuated with log-cabin villages where we caught sight of an occasional peasant, formless in quilted jacket, perched on the edge of a flat cart, legs swinging over the side, hands loosely holding reins draped over the back of a skinny nag. In November I saw this same peasant as our train swept past a road-crossing to the jangle of a warning bell on lowered gates. This time he was ensconced in straw on a sledge drawn by the same skinny nag; he was still a shapeless bundle, now wearing a sheepskin coat instead of a quilted jacket, and with a fur cap clapped to one side of his head, the earflaps sticking out at different angles like donkey ears.

The two months since my arrival in Russia and the journey back to Finland had dulled my senses to the striking contrast between the Russian and the Western scene. On leaving America, I knew I was going to a country impoverished by war and revolution, but I was in no way prepared for the shock of the crossover from Western Europe to Soviet Russia. The transition from one European country to another is undramatic: a change of tongue and manner, slight deviations in food and clothes—nothing drastic. All in one key, so to speak. Here was a sudden transition to a minor key. More. To the five-tone scale. From the immaculate Finnish border station with its lunch counter stocked with cheese, cold cuts, Danish pastries, and its air filled with the heavenly smell of percolating coffee, our group of foreign tourists had found itself transported to a barnlike Soviet border station with an atmosphere as stark as the premises. Armed guards hovered in the background and from the walls bearded and mustached faces stared past us: Marx, Stalin, Lenin, Voroshilov. No American grins here. The men in the photographs seemed intent on telling us how real, how earnest, life was. The food on display at the lunch counter was just as forbidding: fly-specked open sandwiches, this one with a bit of cheese dried and curling at the edges, that one with stringy salt fish. Thin tea in thick glasses.

An eight-hour journey had delivered us to the Leningrad railroad station, so solidly padded with human bodies that we could hardly make our way out. The air was foul with the smell of damp sheepskins and raw herring. People were shouting, scolding, snoring, against a background of buoyant music coming over the intercom. Suddenly the music was interrupted by the announcement of a train departure. It had the same effect on the supine bodies that a probing stick has on an anthill. They scurried away dragging homemade wooden suitcases and gargantuan bundles. No sooner were they gone than other bodies poured in to take their places like water filling the hollows left by dislodged pebbles. Travel was expensive in America. How could these ragged people afford it? Where were they going in such droves? Where coming from? Why?

Our group of foreign tourists was guided gingerly around the edges of this camping ground and out into the station square where four Lincoln limousines were waiting in the rain to take us to our hotel.

The hotel was as cold and uncomfortable as the weather, and there were no good meals to cheer us, only cold meatballs and tepid tea. Not even a warm bed to take refuge in, only a cotton blanket and clammy sheets.

If the halls and palaces Intourist whirled us through in the three days of our Leningrad stay looked shabby, what could be said of the houses lining the streets? They could hardly have been in a worse state of disrepair if the city had been undergoing siege since the revolution. The drizzling rain was augmented by drippings from disjointed rain pipes. Paint was peeling, plaster· chipping. Every window of these houses held displays of soup pots and cabbages; evidently the double windows required by this cold climate served the populace as refrigerators.

Hard as it was to dampen my spirits, they were pretty soggy after Leningrad. I was eager to move on, to put the dreariness behind me and find shapes and colors that pleased.

I found them. Moscow met us with sunshine. With limousines, too, which carried us away from a station as solidly padded with bodies as the Leningrad one, along the Sadovaya Circle with trees wearing autumn foliage, down the steep cobblestoned Tverskaya, and up the gentler slope leading into Red Square. As we made the ascent, St. Basil's Cathedral rose into view like a ship over the horizon. Shapes fantastic and colors galore. I had hoped for the exotic, here it was. Equally exotic was the Kremlin to the right of St. Basil's. The churches rising behind its crenelated walls were, in their austerity, the exact opposite of St. Basil's: white, four-square, pilastered, with onion domes of pure gold. We moved out of the square and down to the Moscow River with all this loveliness reflected in its waters. Our hotel was across the river, and the room assigned to me looked out upon the river, the churches, the Kremlin walls.

This was the happy beginning of two months that presented a challenge I longed to accept. But I could not accept it if the Soviets did not accept me. That is why I was on my way to Finland—to see if they would invite me back.

AS SOON AS I reached Helsinki I reported to the Russian Consulate where I was informed they not only had no worker's visa for me but they had not even heard of me. I would have to wait while they made inquiries.

Very well, I would wait. Delay did not present catastrophic financial difficulties because the American dollar was soaring in value in the Finland of those days. I got myself a room and bath in Helsinki's best hotel for fifty cents a night and ate sumptuous dinners in the hotel's empty dining room for the same price. After Russia's penury, Finland's stores bursting with food and clothes spelled opulence. This, I was to discover, was an illusion.

As a teacher interested in progressive education, I thought the best use of my time would be to visit Finnish schools. Under the influence of Dr. Lucy Wilson, I had experimented with advanced methods in Media High School. Dr. Wilson was a well-known Philadelphia educator, principal of South Philadelphia High, whose advanced thinking had led South American countries to seek her council in methods of teaching and curriculum-building. Every year she made trips to the Soviet Union, which had adopted the most avant-garde school system in the world. On her return from these trips she gave slide-lectures on what she had seen. It was at a reception in her honor after such a lecture that I met her. When I confided to her the adventure I was contemplating, she invited me to come to her home to talk about it. She encouraged me, said she thought I could get a job in Russia if I had a command of needed skills. Could I sew? Could I type? The best bet, of course, was teaching English. Did I know how to teach English to foreigners? She offered me some books that would help me.

Following her guidelines, I prepared myself.

I thought of Dr. Wilson and her precepts when I went to visit Helsinki schools. I found nothing progressive there. No coeducation, even in the lower grades. The little girls in the first English class I visited were all dressed alike in starched white pinafores. They sprang to their feet as if manipulated by strings when the teacher and I entered the room, and they stayed on their feet until the teacher signaled them to sit down. The teaching was mostly by rote. The children chanted words and phrases in unison, and when the lesson was over they all sprang to their feet again and sang an English ditty in unison.

At the end of the day the teachers invited me to have tea with them. Knowing that I had just come from the Soviet Union, they looked at me in awe, as at one who had survived an unspeakable ordeal.

"Was it awful?" asked a nervous young woman in the cautious voice one adopts when the subject may be too painful to broach.

"Not at all," I said brightly. This provoked a tightening of lips and a shifting of postures. "I mean . . . it was interesting."

"What, for instance?" A girl with flaxen hair and clear blue eyes strained toward me.

Before I could open my mouth, I was cut off by another voice, a shrill one, "I don't suppose you were there very long."

"No, only two months," I admitted.

"And living in a hotel all the time."

"Yes."

"And shown only show places."

This series of accusations (for the tone was patently accusatorial) was made by a middle-aged woman who spoke English with an Oxford accent and wore a lofty look that put her authority out of reach. My feeble effort to elaborate, "Well, I was able to—" was swept away by, "You could not possibly get a true picture in that time and those circumstances."

"I know," I said. "That's why I hope to go back."

The ladies could hardly have been more aghast had I confided to them my intention of jumping off the church steeple that very afternoon. Silence ensued. Then the authoritarian took over again. "You must not go back, my dear." Her voice was patronizing now. "You are young and uninformed. You have no idea of the atrocities being committed inside that country—*my* country. I am a Russian, my husband was Russian Ambassador to Finland at one time. I *know* what is going on. You must not go back."

"Have you been there recently?" I ventured.

"Heaven forbid!"

"Well, quite a few years have passed since the revolution."

This must have seemed ungrateful, not to say impertinent, considering the concern for my welfare she had displayed. She snapped back like a rubber band. "Quite a few indeed! Years of bloodshed, starvation, violence, outrage! I can see you have been hoodwinked. Oh, they are clever at that, with their propaganda and subterfuge! Swallow it if you like, you will live to rue it! Go back if you like—and if they let you. They are not anxious to have foreigners see things from the inside."

This was dismissal. The tea party was over from that point, though we toyed with our spoons with lowered eyes until we could decently escape. No one accompanied me out.

I was walking briskly down the street when I heard my name called. It was the flaxen-haired girl. She fell into step beside me and turned an agitated face to me.

"I'm so sorry," she said. "I don't want you to think we're all like that. We're not, really. Not so narrow-minded and pigheaded. I'd hate to have you go away with only this impression of us. Would you come to see me? I live with my aunt. I think you would like her. She's an actress."

"I'd love to."

"And our schools . . . what did you think of this one?"

I believe I raised an eyebrow.

"Our schools aren't all like this either. When you come to see us, I'll show you an experimental school. Private, of course. My little brother goes to it."

THIS GIRL, whose name was Aini, lived on the outskirts of Helsinki where houses stood in the fir forest. She took me directly to the school, which occupied one of those delightful Scandinavian wooden houses with steep roofs and deep eaves and many chimneys signifying the comfort of fireplaces or big tiled stoves. There were no classrooms in this school—not, that is, in the sense of desks in serried ranks facing a blackboard. This was just a home with lots of books in it and rugs to sit on and sheds outside, one of them a workshop and laboratory, another a storehouse for skis and skates and sleds. I didn't attend any lessons because the pupils were off on an excursion with their teachers that day, but I was shown the school's program and I talked with the owner, a cultivated Englishwoman who spoke nothing but English to her charges, as well as giving them regular lessons in grammar.

It was a nice school. Not unique—similar schools could be found in most countries, but only in small quantities. Only private schools. Only for privileged children. It cost a lot of money to attend a school like this.

The Soviets had made modern methods the basis of nationwide free and compulsory education. The few schools I had seen there made me think they might have gone overboard with their innovations considering the country's lack of highly trained teachers and of all kinds of equipment, from pencils to school buildings. I hoped it would work.

We went from the school to Aini's home, where her aunt was waiting for us. Over the lunch table she looked at me with eyes as blue and inquiring as Aini's. She was a middle-aged woman with manners that in no way bespoke the actress, although her trained voice and carefully preserved figure did. Beneath her composure I sensed a store of controlled energy that told me she must have played Ibsen's Nora beautifully in her youth and could probably play her just as beautifully now.

She put an elbow on the table and said bluntly, "Tell me what you have seen in the Soviet Union."

I could only tell her about Moscow, not having taken a step outside the capital after I entered it. I warmed to the subject as our neglected lunch cooled and, in an effort to be objective, I fear I overstressed the dark side. My secret sympathies must have come through, however, for when I finished she sighed and said, "I thought so. We are given terrible distorted accounts here. Everybody in Finland trembles at the mention of Russia. We have had our taste of revolution, they say. Russia is—what you call it?—the incubus. We are a country of small shopkeepers, isn't it? They fear revolution. They want their neat wives to make them good meals and knit them warm socks, and on Sundays they want to put on dark suits and white spats and walk with their wives and greet their neighbors and see if their neighbors' suits are made of cloth as good and their spats as spotless. Dear God! What have they brought us to? I have been all over the world, to your America, too, and now I cannot go anywhere. There is no money in Finland now. You see it is so, isn't it? Mostly, I want to go to Russia, especially after I hear what you say. At least they *do* something there. We just hang on. Hang on to what? Knitting and white spats? Bah! Russia is just a few hours away and I cannot afford to go there. Am I a free woman? A free artist? They say there is no freedom in Soviet Russia. In Finland no law says I cannot go, but I could just so be in prison. They say it is dangerous to go to Russia. Is it dangerous?"

"Well, I was only there for two months."

"They want us to believe their goblin tales. They believe them—the shopkeepers do. And nobody contradicts them. Nobody goes there from here and nobody comes here from there, just a few tourists, and what do they say? Bad food, no clothes, no toilet paper, bad plumbing. Such low minds. And the goblins grin and say *See*? Oh, if I was young I would go and see for myself. Money would not stop me. You, for instance, you have much money? But you are from America, such a rich country."

"The higher the climb, the harder the fall," I said, thinking of the trouble our rich America was in.

"No doubt, no doubt," she said when I had expounded. "Yes, the whole world is in dreadful state. Something must be done. Some operation must be performed on society, and that hurts, isn't it? Everybody is afraid. Everybody." She paused as if contemplating the direful implications of that fear; then, rousing: "No, you must go back to the Soviet Union. You must go back and stay until you really know, then come and tell us. We will be waiting for you."

On the following day, my fifth in Finland, the Soviet consul issued me a visa giving me the right to go back and work in Russia. I immediately left Helsinki, foolishly fearing that the men at the travel agency who had spent hours trying to dissuade me from going back might, by fair means or foul, send me home.

three

Origins

> Man's search for meaning is the primary motivation in this life and not a 'secondary rationalization' of instinctual drives.
>
> —Victor Frankl,
> *Man's Search for Meaning*

WITH JOYOUS RELIEF I arrived at the foul-smelling Moscow railroad station, climbed over the bodies and bundles on the floor, and took a bus to Robert's house. He and his wife, Leah, knowing I was practically broke, had offered, in the event of my return, to put me up until I left for Gorki, and from there for the factory town of Autozavod. There were no guest rooms in Moscow apartments, but I could sleep on the couch in the dining room.

I had brought Leah a new dress, and their two kids some mechanical toys. While Leah was trying on, and the kids were trying out, Robert came home from work.

"Peg!" he exclaimed. "So you did get back!"

"As you see," I replied with a grin.

"Well, good! Someone's been asking for you."

"Who?"

"Andrei."

"Andrei?"

"The man you met at the Kamerny Theater, remember? From Mongolia."

"Oh, yes. Of course." I hadn't given him a thought since we met.

"Let's ask him over. Can we give him some dinner, Leah?"

The conversation at the table was mostly about Finland, Andrei recalling having been taken there on a holiday as a child, I making valorous attempts to say it in Russian, Robert laughing boisterously as I floundered and fell, Andrei picking me up gently but not setting me right. He didn't then and he didn't thereafter; he would hand me words but let me use them as best I could.

When dinner was over I helped Leah wash up, then she went to put the children to bed and I rejoined the men. It wasn't long before Robert got up from the table.

"You two don't have to go to work in the morning, but I do, so I'll turn in if you don't mind."

With that he pushed off, leaving the two of us stranded on the little island picked out of darkness by the lamp hanging low over the table. I busied myself with a cigarette until I was ready to meet Andrei's gaze. I was a little wary of him and his audacity.

"It took you longer to get your visa than I expected," he said.

"I think—never. Never come back."

"You told me you wanted to come back."

"I want, yes. Want is little."

"Want is big," he said, a flicker of amusement lighting eyes I had thought were brown but now saw were green. Green flecked with brown.

"Big, yes," I said. "Not big enough."

"Well, you are here," as if his point were made; then, "What brought you here?"

"At Robert? No money for hotel."

"Not to Robert's, to Russia."

That was a big order even in English. I could have said, in my pidgin Russian, that I came because I was interested in socialism. His rejoinder would certainly have been "Why?" "Because better, maybe." And again "Why?"

To answer this I would have had to begin at the beginning and go through all the steps that had led to my coming to Russia. I was incapable of doing this for Andrei at that time, but through the years he learned, piecemeal, the whole story, which was . . .

I WAS ONE OF three children, an older sister, Helen, a younger brother, Dan, and I. All three of us were born in Newark, New Jersey. Father, of German descent, was a pharmacist with postgraduate work in therapeutics that brought him to within two years of becoming a doctor. He was thwarted in this by an early marriage and the advent of children.

His first job was at Holzhauer's Drug Store on the corner of Broad and Market Streets, the hub of downtown Newark. Well do I remember the store and the fascinating window displays Father arranged, for he had an artistic bent and enjoyed doing things with his hands. I can still see him bending over the dining room table of an evening, the tip of his tongue between his teeth as he concentrated on drawing charts and illustrations and making models showing the origin, processing, and use of various drugs.

My memories of early childhood in Newark are happy ones. For the life of me I cannot discover those Freudian phantoms planted in the subconscious in childhood to bedevil adulthood. There was no alcoholism in our family, no child abuse, sexual or otherwise, no rigid religiosity.

There was music. Mother had a contralto voice trained by a Mme. Hunt, who gave annual recitals at which Mother performed in evening dress and black satin slippers trimmed with jet beads. I would steal into her bedroom to admire those slippers and try my skill at walking on high heels. Mother was a member of the Newark Choral Society; she took me to their concerts, the most memorable of which was a performance of the *Messiah* with Geraldine Farrar as soprano soloist. Sunday evening musicales in our parlor became a feature of our life to which I looked forward with delight until Stephen Foster's songs became part of the program. I was so distressed by "My Old Kentucky Home" that I burst into tears and fled the room. Everyone found this behavior in a six-year-old so amusing that the following Sunday the song was repeated just to tease me. I screamed my anger and was put to bed for it.

We owned a big house and lived in the first-floor apartment, renting out the second and third floors. "Uncle" Fred from the third floor would take me on his knee and draw such amazing pictures that I wanted to become an artist like him. "Uncle" Ralph from the second floor grew roses in the elevated garden (ten steps up) behind the house. Further back, Father raised vegetables and kept a few chickens. At Eastertime he hid eggs among the rosebushes for us children to find. "Aunt" May, Ralph's wife, had a pleasing soprano voice and used to sing duets with Mother on those Sunday evenings.

The music came to an end, as did the pictures and the roses and the Easter eggs, when Father left Holzhauer's. I don't know why he did it. Mother always said it was the mistake of his life. Doc Holzhauer, she said, adored Father and, having no son of his own, would most certainly have left the store to him. But Father wanted to strike out on his own. So off he went to White Plains, New York, and opened not a drugstore as you might expect, but an ice cream parlor. Had it been a drugstore it would probably have come to the same bad end because even that long ago the expansion of the patent medicine industry was reducing prescription drugs to a minimum and turning drugstores with their soda fountains, lending libraries, and gift shops into enterprises differing little from haberdasheries and grocery stores—in a word, *business*, and if there was one bump missing on Dad's phrenological chart it was the bump of business acumen. The ice cream parlor as I remember it was bare and white, not the cozy corner that would have invited matrons to come in and gossip over a fudge sundae and young people to flirt over a chocolate soda. In two years the venture failed, leaving us in a yawning hole. We came back to Newark and lived with Aunt Jessie (mother's sister) and Uncle Al while Mother went through a weepy pregnancy. I shudder to remember her breaking down in the middle of singing "The Lost Chord" with Uncle Al at the piano. She left the room sobbing, one knee giving way under the weight of her belly like a broken spring so that her gait was step, shake; step, shake; step, shake.

That year was a nightmare for me in more ways than one. Aunt Jessie had a cleanliness phobia that made her strew the entire kitchen floor with newspapers when the iceman came, and wash the change he gave her when he left. Accordingly, she was always on the track of a little girl who cut paper dolls out of fashion magazines, leaving snippets on the floor, and who spent less than five minutes wiping her feet on the doormat when she came home from school. Dad spent his time taking care of Mother and looking for a job. By the time he found an acceptable one my brother Dan was a year old.

The job Father found was that of a salesman for the Upjohn Pharmaceutical Company, and it took us to Haddonfield in south Jersey. The move was fortunate for me. As a city child I had had little contact with nature. Haddonfield was a superior version of suburbia. Its Quaker founders, the Haddon family, had received the land indirectly from King Charles II, as the name of the main street, King's Highway, testifies. Its public buildings were largely colonial in architecture, its homes mostly Victorian. We moved into one of these big Victorian houses across the street from the school I attended.

The town was girdled by woods where a dammed-up stream formed a pool to swim in in summer, to skate on in winter. The Methodist Church, to which our family immediately transferred its Newark membership, thrust its square belfry into the sky only five minutes away from our house if you cut across a vacant lot between it and the railroad.

One of my most poignant memories is of crossing the tracks and the lot with Dad on an early Christmas morning, the ground glittering with snow, the sky with stars, to join other parishioners and set out to sing carols under dark Methodist windows that lighted up at the sound of our singing; hall lights went on too, and front doors were opened to invite us in for coffee, but we waited until we got back to the church for our coffee and doughnuts.

An idyllic two years in Haddonfield ended with my graduation from elementary school and the move to Philadelphia, a move made in the hope that I would get a better education in a big city than a small town could offer. My parents were particularly concerned about my education because my sister had finished only seven grades. She was retarded in an unusual way, perhaps the result of a bad case of scarlet fever suffered in infancy that may have damaged her endocrine system, stunting her mental and physical growth. She was shorter than average and never experienced puberty, never matured as a woman. She read a lot, had a sweet voice and disposition, and was Mother's constant, loving, and helpful companion. I offered her no companionship; in fact, I was ashamed of her, as many people were ashamed of retarded or demented relatives in those days. People show more understanding today, and that only deepens the guilt I feel for my neglect of Helen.

Our move to Philadelphia entailed Father's dropping his job with the Upjohn Company and becoming a pharmacist for Liggett's Drug Stores. I don't think he had been a very successful salesman anyway. For one thing, he had no car, and how many doctors can you interview in a day without one? For another, he had no pushing qualities. If a doctor said, "No thanks, I don't want your pills," I can see Dad picking up his hat apologetically and making for the door. I'm sure he felt uncomfortable hawking wares.

Since Mother's ambitions exceeded Father's salary, we took a house in Philadelphia beyond our means, hoping to make up the difference by renting rooms. This was not as simple as my parents had thought; too often the rooms were empty. Worry hung like a pall over our house. It sickened me to see Mother sitting in the dusk, rocking, back and forth, back and forth, a woeful look on her face and no lamp lighted, as if she enjoyed the gloom. No less distressing was Father's pumped-up cheeriness when he came home from work:

"Any news, Mother?"

"No news."

"Well, I guess it's too soon to get answers from the last ad."

So it went, day after day, week after week, month after month, with short intervals when somebody rented the second-floor-front or the third-floor-back but never all four rooms at once. We sank deeper and deeper in debt until we were entrapped, unable to pay and unable to move.

By my senior year we had five permanent lodgers who were boarders as well; Mother had agreed to feed them so that she could apply the extra money to paying off the debt. Little time did Mother have now to sit in the gloaming with the woeful face I turned my eyes away from. At six o'clock on Monday morning she and Dad would go down into the basement laundry and work the washing machine, which was nothing more than a round wooden tub on a swivel which Father, firmly grasping the upright peg serving as handle, would swing to and fro, swishing the dirt out of countless loads of the boarders' wash and our own. After that there was the wringing out and the hanging up, the ironing, the making of beds, the sweeping and scrubbing, the buying of food, the baking, the roasting, the stewing, the serving.

I could not but pity Mother for the drudgery forced upon her when she became a boarding-house mistress, but she pitied herself more than anybody else pitied her. She was not staunch in adversity. She crumbled. Her bottled-up misery gave her red eyelids. She tried to be brave, indeed she accepted with extraordinary courage the moil and toil of this degrading life. Degrading was what she found it. Her pride was mortally wounded. She felt ashamed, disgraced, déclassée. She put on face in front of the boarders and then we, her family, rejoiced to catch glimpses of her former charming self. But such efforts were only in defense of her pride; she could not sustain them. She sought no one's society. She did not even go to church because she didn't have the proper clothes to go in.

Father was staunch. His values were unlike Mother's. He cared nothing for what the Joneses had and even less for what they said. There was nothing exceptional about his mind or his talents, but much that was exceptional about his disposition. Like the millions and millions of the unsung, he walked the labor treadmill from youth to old age, always thinking it would get him somewhere. It never did, but this did not make him bitter or vindictive, nor did it dull his love of life, which sprang from little pleasures such as raising lettuce and radishes, mending a broken step, talking to a neighbor over the back fence or to a customer over the prescription counter. He looked defeat straight in the eye, never deceiving himself but never thrown off his balance by it. It was as if he wore a built-in gyroscope that made him steady in adversity.

Mother's brooding over what had been and, even more, over what might have been, did more to turn "home" into "house" than the presence of boarders did. I spent most of my time in school. School was my escape.

WEST PHILADELPHIA HIGH did not disappoint my parents' expectation that it would offer me a superior education. The school was not coeducational. Its enormous building, covering an entire city block and accommodating between two and three thousand students, was divided in two by bricks and mortar: boys in the west, girls in the east, and never the twain should meet. Back in those days when male supremacy was hardly challenged, this enabled us girls to achieve leadership that would most certainly have been usurped by boys if the school had been coeducational. In that respect it was a training ground for entering the Woman's Movement in later years.

West Philly had high academic standards sustained by a choice faculty, some of whose members held doctorates in their subjects. A modern foreign language, as well as Latin, was required of all who chose the Academic rather than Commercial Course. But in addition to studies, there were so many extracurricular activities that every student was offered an opportunity to test and develop her talent for sports, acting, debating, writing, music, or whatever.

All too quickly passed our four years at West Philly. Suddenly graduation was upon us. Commencement is another name for it, and indeed I looked forward to the new life awaiting me, whatever it was to be, for at that time I had no prospects of going to college, although I was determined to do so.

One hot afternoon in June 1924, just before graduation, I was late coming home from school. Housewives were sitting on porches, fanning themselves as they waited for their husbands to return from work. Dust had resettled on the steps and sidewalks they had hosed down early in the morning. Plants in porch boxes looked limp and thirsty. So did the husbands who, one by one, appeared from around the corner where the trolley-car stop was. They carried their jackets over their arms and tugged at their ties the minute they reached their porch steps.

I had been delayed that afternoon by a consultation with Miss Mathews, our English teacher, about a speech I had written and was to deliver as class president at commencement exercises the following week. We had made additions and corrections and she had given final approval, so my mind was not occupied with this speech as I walked home, but with another of an entirely different order, the bidding of farewell to the assembled student body. It was to be a fun speech, to make the girls laugh—not a difficult thing to do at our age. I often resorted to silly speech-making as compensation for not being good at games. I would have preferred winning popularity by popping the basketball into the bucket with breathtaking precision, or by driving the hockey ball down the field to a sure goal. Incapable of performing such feats, I earned my reward by being a rowdy cheerleader and an antic orator.

Before I knew it I came to our street, Sansom Street. "Evening, Mrs. Walters." "Hello, Gloria." Our house. What was that on the doorpost? I ran up the steps. A sign . . . a sheriff's notice . . . a sale . . . on July sixth . . . at auction . . . for the payment of debts.

I was struck as immobile as Lot's wife. There I stood without a thought in my head, empty as a cracked seedpod. Just stood. Until an eye rolled toward me from behind a neighbor's rubber plant, and another from behind a curtain, and another from Jane's turned head on the last porch in the row. I sprang into the house. Mother was sitting on our living-room stairs. Helen was cowering in a corner. The boarders hadn't come home yet. The table wasn't set. No dinner smells came from the kitchen.

"Does Dad know?" I asked.

"I called him. He's coming," said Mother faintly.

He came very soon, paper-pale but with a firm set to his mouth. When he had gotten all the facts from Mother, he asked, "Where's Dan?"

"Next door."

"With Mrs. Garfield?"

"Yes."

Father disappeared. Presently he came back holding my little brother by the hand. Then he did a surprising thing. He locked the front door and pulled down the window shade. He beckoned us to come around him. He got down on his knees. He prayed, "Help us, Lord." I looked at his face. It was as tight as a clenched fist, folded in on itself, pushing through to something I couldn't see. Then it relaxed. He got up. He pulled up the shade. He unlocked the door. "Well, Mother," he said. "I guess we want some dinner." Mother went into the kitchen and Helen followed her. I began setting the table.

The boarders had become our friends. After putting their heads together, Don Donaghy, a reporter for *The Philadelphia Bulletin*, told Father that if we could manage to move into another state unapprehended, the arm of the law would find it more difficult to reach us. The next morning Father went to Haddonfield, and when he came back he told us to quietly pack our things. Two days later our house showed no change on the outside: The curtains still hung at the windows, the porch furniture was in place. Inside, the two upper stories were dismantled and the furniture was stacked on the first floor, barring free passage from room to room. The boarders found new quarters but they did not abandon us. They came back and helped Father move the heavy things.

In the dark of midnight, with only the stars and street lamps as witnesses, a van drove stealthily up to our house. In half an hour it was as stealthily loaded and drove away with all our furniture and us inside. Not a word did we speak, not a whisper, Mother did not even cry. At any moment we could have been intercepted and arrested. By the turns and the time I followed our course: over Forty-sixth to Chestnut, down Chestnut to Broad, north on Broad to Market, east on Market to the river. To the river, to the river! With every minute my blood coursed faster. To the river! Would there be a ferry at so unearthly an hour? There was not. We would have to wait. We waited, listening to the water lapping against the wharves, to a workman dragging a chain over loose planks. A car stopped behind us. The driver shuffled over to our driver and chatted with him. We waited. It seemed forever until we heard a voice of authority say, "You can start loading that boat over there now." Our driver started up the engine; the driver behind started up his; we began moving. I felt the little dip as we passed from landing to boat, then an acceleration taking us through the passage to the front of the boat. Stop. Weights were pushed in front of wheels to keep us from slipping into the river. The other car stopped behind us. *Now* why didn't the boat go? Go, go! We waited. At last the low throb of the boat's engines sent a tremble through the deck, the cars, the people. As if we were not trembling enough! The churning of water behind us said we were moving. We were crossing the river, crossing the Delaware. From Pennsylvania to New Jersey. Bump! The ungainly ferry was nudging its way between the piles separating one wharf from another. Bump! We were there. We had escaped.

In the dark of night, like thieves, like felons, we had escaped the law. We had escaped justice.

* * *

IN MY FAREWELL SPEECH to the student body I jocularly took leave of the mock felicities of this beloved school: the hot roast beef sandwiches that had nourished us for four years, the ponies on which we had trotted through our Latin lessons, the drop-leaf arms on study-hall chairs that were wont to collapse under pressure. The longer I spoke the more vividly in my mind rose the picture of what had happened to my family, something shameful, gross, ignoble. What if even a few of these girls were to learn the truth about me? Perhaps they already knew. In two days word could have gotten around. Maybe they were not laughing with me but at me: "Have you heard?" "At midnight?" "Wow!" "D'ya suppose they wore masks?"

I broke off in the middle of a sentence and dashed off the stage. Instantly Miss Hill, our class sponsor, was at my side. "A fine time you chose to break down, young lady! If you can't control your feelings we'll have to find someone else to make the commencement address." And off she stamped, all six feet of her, leaving me to plummet down, down, into my own particular slough of despair.

HADDONFIELD FRIENDS HAD FOUND us a house along the railroad, so in the few remaining days before graduation I commuted between Haddonfield and Philadelphia, and I continued to do so when, in the fall, I entered the University of Pennsylvania on a scholarship from West Philly High.

Once more I found myself in the countryside. Seated on the floor of my attic room, elbows on the low windowsill, I spent many a midnight hour looking toward the woods and gazing up at the sky. After so lacerating an encounter with reality I was even more prone than most adolescents to seek for meanings and values transcending those of the cruel world. Communion with nature offered me rare moments of awe and ecstasy. But these alternated with moments of terror. The terror was within me, deep-crouched in my subconscious. At times I would draw it forth with masochistic recklessness and let it have its way with me. The terror said that I must die. What did it mean to die? To be put in a coffin and carried away with people watching and I not seeing. To be put in the ground and left to rot, and I not feeling. Total darkness, total insentience. Extinction. Forever. I strained my imagination to the breaking point to grasp so dread a concept. I could not accept it. I was too young, too alive, to accept extinction. If I were born for extinction I would be born soulless. Flesh, bones, blood, brain, but no soul. Soul? What was the soul? A figment of a cringing mind. I sought help. I read Carlyle's *Sartor Resartus*, Plato's *The Death of Socrates*, Emerson's essays. I read Wordsworth and Browning. Spinoza.

I held long sessions with Dr. Sloan, pastor of our church, an inspired preacher, distinguished from most preachers by his depth and breadth of understanding and the fervor of his dedication. He did not dismiss my purgatory pains as the exaggerated fantasies of youth. Patiently he considered them and offered the balm of faith, admitting that the acceptance of faith was one of two possible choices: neither was "right" or "wrong." But the rewards of each were easily assessable. Nor did he press dogma on me; I must choose what appeared reasonable to my intelligence. The soul? The soul was not the figment of a cringing mind, it was that part of me that rejected the idea of extinction, that saw beauty in a rose, evil in injustice, and strength in love. Were these things less real than graves and coffins?

Deeply engraved on my memory is a vision of Dr. Sloan in the pulpit, his leonine head thrown back, a rapt expression on his face as he says in a hushed voice vibrant with emotion: "Man dwarfs the stars."

That was a striking thought and one I longed to hear: Man not a clod doomed to extinction but Man the vessel of divinity sharing the immortality of divinity.

So overpowering was my conversion that I believed I had a calling. I would become a Methodist preacher. I would stir men's hearts, I would give them hope as Dr. Sloan had given me hope.

In a burst of romantic enthusiasm I went to confide my intentions to my parents who were sitting in the little living room of our hateful house where every few minutes in summer the Atlantic City Express went screaming past, its whistle warning of a turn in the road half a mile away.

My parents received the news with joy. Father's eyes beamed with a quiet light; it was enough for him that I should want to do this, however much he doubted the reality of it. His skepticism was well founded.

At the age of eighteen one's mind does not congeal; every new influence works a change in it. I was attending the university now, and its influence would be strong, prolonged, and directed in the opposite direction from the one Dr. Sloan had given my thinking.

One of the first blows aimed at my faith was dealt at a freshman lecture in General History. The professor went to the blackboard and drew a circle with two radial lines describing a narrow wedge which he labeled *Science*, the rest of the circle *Religion*.

"As the wedge of Science widens it crowds out Religion."

That was the beginning of my materialistic education. The entire climate of the university with its determinist approach to history and its behaviorist approach to psychology was inimical to an idealistic world view. By the end of my junior year I was a confirmed agnostic. No longer did I suffer the pains of doubt and query that had plagued my earlier years. Mysteries were the yet unexplored, the unknown but the knowable. Man still dwarfed the stars, but now because the stars, like everything else in the universe, were his laboratory for converting the unknown into the known. The enormousness of the task magnified man's image of himself while, paradoxically, his materialistic outlook shrank his image to that of a mechanism akin to the mechanisms he was investigating: an atom among atoms in a finite world that looked for nothing beyond itself. Such an outlook made his pursuits more disinterested, his endurance more heroic. The emancipated individual was guided by neither fear of, nor hope in, an afterlife; only by the proud consciousness that he had emerged through endless eons of mutation and selection as *homo sapiens*, the Olympian among creatures, the only one capable of purposefully changing the world. The acceptance of responsibility for changing it into a world more just gave a meaning to life that compensated for meaning lost with the loss of religious faith.

Now, if ever, the world was in need of change. The Great Depression was upon us. Banks were crashing. Once-affluent heads of families and pillars of society were throwing themselves out of five-story windows. Unemployment was widespread. People were frightened and confused. Even before the crisis many had become disappointed with the results of the "War to End War," with the League of Nations that was to have made good this slogan, and with an economic system that forced war veterans to peddle apples for a living and a significant part of the population to live in Hoovervilles, shantytowns. The skepticism and cynicism of the times were reflected in Hemingway's heroes, who roamed the world in quest of something to fill their vacuous lives, and in Scott Fitzgerald's golden youth, who found distraction in the titillations of high life.

But there were others who were looking for solutions. Scott Nearing was one of them. When I entered the university he had already been dismissed from the faculty for openly espousing socialism, but his name was a banner for many of the students. In economics classes we learned the principles of socialism. The tendency was toward the repudiation of these principles, but the very denial of an idea involves the statement of it, and I, who had never heard radical ideas before, felt that new planets were swimming into my ken. As a female I was flattered that George Bernard Shaw dedicated his *Guide to Socialism* to the Intelligent Woman. It looked as if he and the Webbs and the Fabians were the only ones making sense in this crumbling world. They and Oswald Spengler, whose *Decline of the West* offered rich nourishment for my simplistic belief that the sun was setting in the west only to rise in the east. What I did not choose to accept then was that the new socialist culture was but an aspect of Spengler's Faustian culture, the decline of which he envisaged as taking place slowly throughout the next millennium. I chose to see socialism as a complete and immediate transvaluation of values marking the end of one era and the beginning of the next.

The east, where the sun appeared to be rising, was Russia, a land always held to be mysterious but never more so than in its socialist aspect. Conflicting were the reports that came from there. Some saw it as an erupting volcano burying the world in red lava; others saw it as a funeral pyre from which the New World would arise like the Phoenix Bird. It was the hope of universal peace; it was the beginning of universal carnage. It would emancipate women; it would destroy womanhood. It would put an end to racial and religious prejudice; it would fan the flames of bigotry.

Above everything else it was the first socialist country in the world, and I believed I was a socialist. I was not an activist for the cause. The only contribution I had made was to vote for Norman Thomas in the presidential election of 1928. I did not like reading books on political and economic theory and had not read any of them—not Marx, not Engels, not even Adam Smith. What I did like to do was to learn from life experience, to do and see for myself. Who were these Russians who had taken upon themselves the task of building a new society? For better or for worse, their revolution had rocked the world.

And so in the very living room in which seven years earlier I had announced to my parents my intention to become a Methodist preacher, I now announced to them my intention of going to Socialist (and atheist) Russia.

I read the shock of my announcement on their faces. Mother's eyes grew dark with fear. Father's gaze remained steady, but it sharpened with disapproval.

"Have you given this step proper consideration?" he asked.

"Oh, yes. It's only for a year. Only for a month if I don't get a job there."

"Do you realize where you are going? What do you know about Russia?"

"Very little."

"From all I have been able to find out it's a very rough country. Are you prepared for the physical hardships you'll be confronted with?"

"I think so."

He paused. He wanted badly to deter me, and, knowing him as I did, I could not question his selflessness; he loved me and was afraid for me. At last he came out with, as a last hope, "It will cost you ten years of your life."

The solemnity of the pronunciation irritated me. I responded with flippancy: "A fair exchange: ten years of puttering about for one year of going it full blast."

The matter was never discussed between us again and on the morning of September 13, 1932, he was on the dock along with my friends, waving to me where I stood on the deck of the S.S. *Colombia* as a band played and tugs slowly pulled the ship away from its moorings in New York harbor and my heart turned handsprings with the rapture of this adventure that was to last a month for sure and—please, God, may it be a year!

THIS, THEN, IS THE STORY Andrei asked me for that night at Robert's dinner table. I could not give it to him in full because I could hardly ask for a glass of water in Russian at the time. But I did manage to convey the most essential elements of my life. We worked hard at the task. Every evening after this first one at Robert's, Andrei would call for me and take me to his father's apartment in Vorotnikovsky Lane, only a short walk from Robert's house. There we labored with dictionaries, pencils, and a notebook to draw pictures and write words in, for Andrei knew some French, whose kinship to English is most apparent in writing. I suffered moments of such frustration that it took relentless prodding on Andrei's part to make me go on. I did go on, however; we both did, on and on for two weeks.

four

Commitment

> My true love hath my heart, and I have his,
> By just exchange one for another given:
> I hold his dear, and mine he cannot miss,
> There never was a better bargain driven:
> My true love hath my heart, and I have his.
> —Sir Philip Sidney,
> "The Bargain"

ANDREI NIKOLAYEVICH, Andrei's father, was a stout old-world gentleman who wore a little tuft of whisker under his lower lip. He seemed taken aback when Andrei introduced me, but he accepted me graciously, resolving, no doubt, that I was just further evidence of the madness of a son who preferred the stage to a practical profession like his own, which was medicine. He always retired to his own room with Maria Vasilyevna, his second wife, leaving the dining room to Andrei and me. It was a pleasant little room, the walls hung with pictures, the double windows with heavy curtains to keep out drafts. In this room I learned all I needed to know about Andrei.

The two passions of his life were nature and the theater. In earliest childhood, on summer vacations in the country, he had driven his mother to distraction by running off to the woods in the morning and coming back at nightfall, bringing with him strange insects to be cared for and studied, or woodland flowers to be planted in his garden.

Andrei's mother had died five years before I appeared on the scene. He spoke of her lovingly and with regret that he, unlike his brother, Dmitri, had not been an attentive son during her last years when she and Andrei's father had separated and she was living alone.

In the middle of telling me about her he went into another room and brought out of some strongbox a bit of paper yellowed and crumbling with age. It was a letter written by his maternal grandfather to the nuns of an Old Faith convent in the Ukraine, asking them to take into their charge his little girl, Daria, who had just lost her mother from consumption and would soon lose her father from the same illness.

They did take her when her father died a little later, and they reared her in the fundamentalist branch of the Russian Orthodox Church, to which she was devoted to the day of her death.

Andrei told me that on graduating from the gymnasium (as Russian secondary schools were known before the revolution) he had entered Moscow University, but his heart was not in it. He had cut classes to attend matinees of the Moscow Art Theater, whose performances he never tired of seeing over and over.

He was seventeen when the October Revolution took place. The sense of freedom and release it brought prompted him to leave the university and join the Griboyedov Studio, an offshoot of the Moscow Art Theater. It was there that he fell in love with Alla, a fellow student, and married her. That was ten years before I met him. He told me he had loved her, still loved her, but she was no longer his wife. He had left her. That was all he said, that he had left her, and since he did not volunteer further information, I did not ask for it. He said Alla was still in Mongolia, having gone there with him three years before, but they had been living apart for over a year. The candor with which he told me this, and the ease, as if it had no bearing on our relationship, I found disquieting. But so were other things—the assurance, for instance, with which he made sweeping assertions: "If you want to, you will." I attributed these strange attitudes to the Russian character and tried not to let them intimidate me.

At one of our sessions I looked up to see a vision of delight framed in the double doors of the dining room. It was a small and fragile young woman with the oval face and long neck of the Virgin in Russian icons. And oh, the eyes, the long gray eyes filled with tranquility.

Her lips smiled at Andrei but the expression of the eyes hardly changed. He got up and went to her and they left for a while, talking together in the other room, and then he was seeing her out.

"She—who?" I asked when he came back.

"Sonya. She was my brother Dmitri's wife."

"No more wife?"

"Not his."

"Pity."

"She has a new husband. Georgi. An artist. He is our friend."

"Our?"

"Dmitri's and mine."

"Dmitri—he hurt she left him?"

"Badly."

It was only after several years that I learned how very badly Andrei's brother had been hurt when Sonya left him.

I met Dmitri two years after I met Andrei, and then it was in Mongolia where he was Chief Engineer in charge of building the country's first power plant. One day when he was lighting a cigarette I noticed that the top phalanx of the little finger on his left hand was missing. Andrei had told me that in youthful revolutionary zeal Dmitri had chosen to be an electrician so as to become a member of the working class. I supposed he had received the injury in an accident at that time. When I said as much to Andrei he gave me a quizzical smile.

"Why? Isn't that how it happened?" I asked.

"No, it isn't," said Andrei enigmatically. I sensed a story and had to hear it.

"Then tell me how it happened," I said.

He lifted his eyebrows and inclined his head.

"Can't you tell me?"

"Why not? Of course I can."

"Then do."

He looked embarrassed.

"Oh, come on, Andrei."

"All right," and he leaned forward in his chair, his hands clasped between his knees, and assumed an entirely different tone. "Have you ever read Tolstoy's *Father Sergius*?"

"No, I haven't."

"It's the story of a monk who is tempted by a beautiful woman who intentionally comes to his retreat in the woods to seduce him."

"Does she succeed?"

"Almost. At the most agonizing moment in the struggle between his vow and his temptation, he picks up a knife and cuts off his finger."

I let out a gasp.

"You mean . . . ?"

"Not that Dmitri suffered for the same reason that Sergius did; Sonya never trifled with Dmitri's feelings. But he loved her to distraction, and when he could stand the hurt of her leaving him no longer he, like Sergius, tried to quench mental anguish with physical pain."

That evening in Andrei Nikolayevich's apartment when I first met Sonya, Andrei told me that one of the reasons Dmitri had gone to

Mongolia was to get away from her, to escape the torture of her proximity. He took their little girl with him—Vyeta. Sonya didn't want him to. Andrei said he and Sonya had been talking about Vyeta in the other room, about how she was, and what she was doing, and how Dmitri was.

Sonya was to become a conspicuous thread woven into the fabric of my life with Andrei.

TIME WAS PASSING quickly. We had stolen two weeks from the carrying out of our duties, but we could not go on doing that. As the number of stolen days approached their limit, it became clear where our exchange of confidences was taking us. I found interminable the intervals between Andrei's seeing me home one night and calling for me the next. I was falling more and more under his spell. No other man of my acquaintance had ever pleased me so. I had dreamed of marrying a musician, having set my heart on a life associated with art, and music was the form of art to which I was most attuned. But all the arts are one at the source; the main thing was that Andrei was an artist, albeit of the theater. And an impassioned artist. An impassioned thinker, too, with strong likes and dislikes which for the most part were congenial to my own. And he was a dreamer who believed in the future, as could only be expected of one with his buoyant disposition and infrangible optimism.

All this was true, but—he could not even speak my language, and our backgrounds could hardly have been more different. Why, then, was I so sure that he was the man who most answered my needs?

I could not ignore the physical attraction we felt for each other. But this alone could not have held us together for thirty-six years of extraordinary vicissitudes.

I have answered this question in different ways at different times in my life, but never so satisfactorily as when, forty-eight years later, in 1980, after I had left Russia for good, it was again brought to mind by an experience in Wanamaker's Department Store.

Among the odd jobs by which I had earned my board-and-keep while a university student was that of a salesgirl in Wanamaker's, surely the most beautiful department store in the world. Its central court, with the tall bronze eagle in the middle of it, is surrounded by tier upon tier of balconies, one of which supports the organ that plays the opening and closing and noonday of the store. The winter of my return offered me the poignant experience of revisiting old places, one of the first of which was Wanamaker's. I set out for it alone on a late Saturday morning. As I pushed through the revolving doors I heard the organ playing. I rushed up to the third floor where from the west balcony I could look across the court and see the console and the organist. He was playing a Mendelssohn fugue. Its intricate harmonies rose out of the golden pipes and soared above them, up into the vault that seemed very close to heaven. A few other people stood at balustrades on other floors listening as I was listening, while down below shoppers hustled through the aisles jostling one another, examining gloves and scarves, studying price tags, digging into the depths of voluminous handbags for credit cards. The hum of merchandizing hung below the music filling the upper air.

That was it. That was Andrei. He was a dweller of the upper air. His spirit never descended—no, not even when life itself pressed our noses to the ground. It was my early, almost immediate perception of this, that made me so sure.

And now the time to part had come, me to go east to the Volga, he to go much farther east to Asia, to the city of Ulan Bator, erstwhile Urga, from which Genghis Khan and his Mongol hordes set out to conquer the world in the thirteenth century.

"It will not be for long, only until spring," said Andrei. "I will come for you in May and bring you back to Moscow."

May. And this was only the beginning of December.

"Will you go away with me for a few days before we part?" he asked.

A little shock went through me. Among the rights I demanded for the emancipated woman was the right to enjoy sex without traditional fetters. I believed in free love and had practiced it. I found it disappointing. At this moment I dreaded nothing so much as that my relationship with Andrei would become just another "affair." Frantically I sought defense against it.

"I want a child," I said.

I might have slapped him in the face, so white and still did he become.

After an endless pause he said, "Last year I told Alla I would leave her if she had another abortion. She had it. I left."

KSENYA STEPANOVNA, a Ukrainian peasant woman who was in Mongolia visiting her son, a friend of Andrei's, had given Andrei permission to use her house in a village near Poltava if he wanted a rest in the country.

So it was to this village we went.

An overnight train journey brought us to Kharkov, then capital of the Ukraine, where we visited a Torgsin store to buy provisions for our little stay, forewarned that we would not be able to buy food anywhere except in Torgsin stores. While Andrei exchanged Mongolian *tugrics* for ham and cheese, I watched the shoppers. Among them were "has-beens" easily recognized by the good quality of the old clothes they were wearing. There were peasants, too, who were trading for food the wide gold wedding bands they favored, and ex-merchants giving up heavy gold watches and chains.

Presently my eye fell upon a young boy standing at the door with outstretched hand. He was all of a grayness—gray rags, gray face, gray glance that hung uncertainly in the air, floating on currents rather than propelled by will or desire. He hardly resembled a human, was like something that has mildewed in a sunless hole. The outstretched hand said he was hungry but he was not gaunt. He was fat. No, bloated.

"What . . . ?" I asked Andrei in horror.

"Come," he said. When we were outside he explained: "He is starving. It is too late. He mustn't eat now, it would kill him. A doctor might be able to save him, but I doubt it."

We took a local train to the country. We rode in a hard little wooden car. Rows of double-decker bunks at right angles to the windows lined one side of the off-center aisle; little collapsible tables with seats at either end lined the other side. At such a table Andrei and I sat down. The car was filled with peasants in sheepskins and felt boots, any one of whom might have been the *muzhik* who haunted Anna Karenina. They all had bulky sacks and bundles with them, all were talking, all were smoking *makhorka*, that fiercely pungent home-grown Russian weed smoked in a "goat's leg," a kind of pipe made by rolling newspaper into a long narrow cone, bending it in the middle, filling the wide end with *makhorka*, putting the other end in your mouth. The *makhorka* was a godsend; its mordant smell helped stifle the stench of the toilet at the rear end of the car.

After a few hours of near-asphyxiation we arrived at our village. Oh, the blessing of the fresh air into which we stepped! It was December, a southern December. Mild as the weather was, snow was coming down slowly, softly, enhancing the silvery light of late afternoon. The snow scattered splendor upon the bare trees and the thatched roofs and the fields that stretched away and away, merging with the sky like a still sea. We stood agaze for a few moments, feasting our lungs on this heavenly air, our eyes on the gleaming beauty. Then a peasant stepped up and spoke to Andrei; then we were walking toward a waiting cart with straw in the bottom of it; then Andrei and I were sitting in the straw and the peasant was flicking his whip and we were jouncing over the ruts of a dirt road with the snow coming down slowly, softly, settling on our hats and collars and eyelashes.

The hut we stopped in front of and which was opened for us by our driver consisted of one square room. Its main feature was a big whitewashed stove with a sleeping bunk built into it. In front of the stove and under the window was a bed with four enormous pillows in embroidered linen slips piled one on top of another at the head. As for the rest, there was a long table with wooden benches on either side of it, another bench at the door with two pails of water on it, and a little wooden cupboard. That was all. In anticipation of our coming someone, perhaps our driver or his wife, had made a fire in the stove and left us a supply of firewood.

"Russia," I said, taking it in.

"No," said Andrei. "The Ukraine."

We had a lovely tea by candlelight: ham and cheese and French pastries and sweet Crimean apples, all from the Torgsin store. When it was over, I was wriggling with discomfort.

"Andrei . . . where? . . ."

"Where? . . . Oh."

He put me into my coat and opened the door.

"There," he said, with a sweep of his hand wide enough to take in the universe.

"But . . ."

He shut the door behind me.

I explored.

No privy? No privy.

Well, there was not exactly a crowd milling about me, and there were bushes, and it was dark. But when daylight came? And me with my undersized bladder, an abomination that had always contrived to put me in the most painful and humiliating situations from the time when, at the age of five, I was taken for Sunday afternoon walks in the park and suffered agonies of fear as to what the policeman would do to a little girl who wet her pants, down to those blushful moments when as a student I had to rear up as on stilts and leave the room in the middle of a lecture on German philosophy.

I chose the biggest bush.

* * *

ON THE FOLLOWING DAY visitors began coming. The villagers wanted to hear about their neighbor, Ksenya Stepanovna, who had gone so far away to see her son. She had written to them about Andrei—not, obviously, about me. I was a surprise package, the more surprising for my exotic wrappings, but they paid me little notice, merely took their tea from me and turned to Andrei while I retired into a corner and listened to a tongue which presented only one comprehensible word in a hundred. My recollection is mostly of bearded men sitting with hands crossed on their walking sticks, talking gravely and in a meandering fashion. Andrei meandered along with them and looked a little alarmed by what they told him, I thought, and he seemed to be trying to explain something to them. They listened attentively, as villagers do to city folk, but they looked no less grave when they went away. In and out they came, all day long, this day and the next, sometimes with their beshawled wives, who kept repeating the name of Ksenya Stepanovna. She must have been quite a personage in this community.

When all of them had gone, I asked Andrei what the talk had been about.

"These people are in trouble, Margarita," he said. "There is hunger."

"With these great fields?"

"You cannot eat fields."

"But what fields give?"

"Fields give if *you* give. If you sow them. If you have seed for sowing."

"No seed?"

"They say so."

"Why? Our farmers put away. . . ."

"They have nothing to put away. They have not even enough to feed themselves and their cattle."

"Why?"

"It's a long story. They are killing and eating their cattle."

"Is it because collect . . . collectivi . . ."

"Collectivization? Largely, I suppose. It's always hard to introduce any new thing. Like potatoes, remember? Here as in Ireland."

"Maybe—too soon?"

Andrei shrugged his shoulders. "What can we do? You see how few young people there are here. All have gone away."

"Why?"

"To get an education, to become engineers, to work in factories. Who's going to feed the country? These old men? Machines have to do it. But machines can't work on little plots of land."

On the evening of the third day we were invited to visit Arkadi Petrovich, Ksenya Stepanovna's cousin. The house to which the old man conducted us was a thatched and whitewashed cube similar to the one we were living in except that inside it was divided in two so as to share the space with the fowl who clucked petulantly when they were disturbed by our entering.

We were greeted by his wife. She had prepared for us by getting out a bottle of homemade cherry wine and making dumplings (out of what priceless stores of flour!) stuffed with cherries—the famous Ukrainian *vareniki.* The men sipped at their words as sparingly as at their wine while the wife and I, for very different reasons, fell into the patriarchal pattern of sitting silent in the presence of the men.

When, after an hour or so of such communion, Andrei and I got up to go, the old man pulled on his sheepskin, picked up his staff, lighted a lantern, and we stepped out into starlit space. There must have been objects around—barns, bushes, trees—but I remember nothing but the vastness and emptiness of the scene. Sounds of singing came from far away.

"The next village," said Arkadi Petrovich.

The sounds rose and fell—phantom, ephemeral music, the articulate spirit of the night. Slowly and without speaking we walked over the new-fallen snow. When we reached our hut, Arkadi Petrovich merely bowed good night, as if speech were a desecration. Andrei and I stood together at the door watching the lantern light bob away.

We still stood there when it was gone, just the two of us in this white immensity of space, in this world without end, with the ghostly music rising and falling like diaphanous veils borne on the air. The music made the silence. Even our breathing seemed suspended by the awesome beauty of the night. Not only of the night, but of Andrei and me too, for beautiful we were in our oneness with the snow, the stars, the music, and the silence. Once more I was filled with the reverence I had known as I sat on the floor in front of my attic window and gazed at the sky above the Haddonfield woods. How long ago that had been! B.C., "Before the Circle"—the circle drawn on the blackboard that had put me straight as to the place of religion in our scientific age. And now here it was again, that feeling of awe and wonder inspired by beauty and shared this time by the one above all others I wished to share it with. Or did Andrei share it? I stole a glance at him. His fur cap was pushed off his forehead, his head was thrown back, and around his lips and eyes I could see the tension lines of concentration. I waited until he felt my gaze, when he turned to me, and from the deep shadow of his brows, now that his head was lowered, his eyes gave back the radiance they had absorbed from the sky. He put out a hand and drew me to him.

God, how I loved this man! He was Robert to my Elizabeth, but I had no wish to count the ways, for my love encompassed every possible way. His face. I studied it now in the starlight and my forefinger ached to trace once again, as I had learned to do, his classic profile, beginning with the brow, descending to cross the high bridge of his nose, then down along the curve of the ridge that ended in a little rise at the tip from which the nostrils winged back to the bone structure; still down over a short upper lip to an irregular mouth that made a crooked smile, from the mouth a dip inward emphasizing the outcurving of the chin whose cleft was only deep enough to define the two sides of the face, the two cheeks sloping down from high cheekbones. Ah, I could have gazed on that face forever!

After a while the cold began to seep into our cuffs and collars. "Let's go inside, Margarita."

The room was warm. We lighted candles. We took off our coats and Andrei poured water for me to wash my hands and face and I poured water for him. I took two of the gigantic pillows in their red-and-black-embroidered slips off the bed and put them on the table. Andrei laughed.

"Better not let one of the villagers see you do that," he said.

"Why?"

"A pillow on a table is a bad omen. I guess it's because the dead are laid out on tables."

I removed the pillows to a bench. I tugged at my boots; they wouldn't come off, Andrei had to pull them. He latched the door. I blew out the candles. The silvery light of the stars coming through the little window drew a cross on the bed.

Good night.

five

Autozavod

The vitality of thought is in adventure. . . . Ideas won't keep. Something must be done about them. When the idea is new, its custodians have fervor, live for it, and, if need be, die for it.
—Alfred North Whitehead,
Dialogues

I HAVE BEEN FORTUNATE on two counts. First, because I went to the Soviet Union in the early thirties and therefore witnessed the end of an extraordinary period of creative activity animated by revolutionary fervor. It was not a halcyon period; far from it. But its turbulence was caused by the conflict of the new and the old, a conflict that lent excitement to the daily experience and conferred a sense of participation in history-making.

My second piece of good fortune was that I met Andrei Efremoff and joined my life to his. Andrei was a representative of the old Russian intelligentsia whose distinction springs from the circumstances of Russian history rather than from any inherent difference separating them from Western intellectuals of the nineteenth century. These circumstances made them more deeply introspective, more soul searching, more concerned with the common destiny and the mystery of life, attributes reflected in the works of nineteenth-century Russian writers, eminently Tolstoy and Dostoyevsky.

While the West was evolving ever more democratic forms of government in the aspiration toward social justice, Russia retained the rigid autocracy required to hold in thrall its serf population. This was not the thralldom of developing industrial populations in which industrialization itself provided the masses with forms of organization through which they could gradually achieve emancipation. This was serfdom, an incongruous hangover of feudalism in the modern world.

Until 1861 Russian peasant serfs were bound to the land, were obliged to cultivate their masters' holdings, could be bought and sold, and their private lives were at the mercy of their owners. In this way they resembled the black slaves of America, but with the enormous difference that while the black slaves represented only about 12 percent of the population and this minority an imported people of a different race, the Russian serfs represented almost two-thirds of the native population at the time of emancipation. Russians in thrall to Russians, shackled to their bondage by imposed poverty and ignorance.

It was this iniquitous relationship that molded the quality of Russian thinking in the nineteenth century. The finest members of the privileged classes could not live in such a relationship without a deep sense of guilt. It was they who staged the revolt of the Decembrists in 1825, directed less against serfdom than against the autocracy, which they meant to supplant with representative government. The uprising was led by members of St. Petersburg's military aristocracy. It was easily crushed; six of the ringleaders were publicly hanged and the rest were exiled to Siberia. But the Decembrists set an example of heroism and self-sacrifice that was to inspire a growing movement of opposition to the monarchy whose most heinous crime was its support of serfdom.

In the dark days of Nicholas I's reign (which began in 1825) the leadership of this movement passed into the hands of middle class intellectuals who knew that reform could be effected only by an informed public demanding change. In magazines and newspapers, strictly censored and periodically shut down by the authorities, the voices of such liberal thinkers as Hertzen, Belinsky, and Chernyshevsky were heard, calling upon the people to free the serfs and initiate social and political reforms. Hertzen was banished from the country, Chernyshevsky spent long years in Siberian exile, Belinsky died young. The labors of these men and others of similar conviction brought telling results. Radical ideas penetrated the universities, from which young men and women emerged to join populist groups that went into the countryside to teach the peasants, or political groups that went into the factories to teach the workers. Thousands of young people from the upper classes sacrificed wealth and privilege to improve the lot of the masses. All of this was in the face of vicious persecution by the government, even in the reign of reformist czar Alexander II, by whose decree the serfs were freed in 1861. His assassination by radicals, (including Lenin's older brother, who was executed for it) only unleashed a fierce wave of repression that led to the abortive revolution of 1905, the Social Democratic revolution of February 1917, and the Bolshevik revolution of October 1917.

Andrei's father, Andrei Nikolayevich, early orphaned, received the education of a *feldsher* (a doctor's assistant), but his unusual gifts and liberal sympathies motivated him to organize a national Feldsher's Union that brought him considerable reputation. He actively supported the revolution of February 1917; yet when in October the Bolshevik revolution supplanted the Social Democratic one, Andrei Nikolayevich accepted it as inevitable and even expedient insofar as it answered the needs of the time. I never heard him or his numerous friends decry the October Revolution.

This, then, was the intellectual heritage and family background that made Andrei support the revolution with all his heart. However thorny revolution's path, he saw it as the only way out of the dark forest. He did not argue the theory of revolution—he was not a political scientist or political economist. He accepted it as an artist for whom it meant freedom from a stultifying social order. He was a visionary. His view of the revolution was that of his beloved poet, the Russian symbolist Alexander Blok who, in *The Twelve*, envisioned twelve Red Guardsmen (suggesting the twelve Disciples) marching through a Petrograd blizzard into the future, trailed by the mangy hound of the displaced bourgeoisie, seeking the enemy in dark houses and deserted alleys:

> On they march with steady tread,
> Hungry mongrel at their heels,
> And at their head—Jesus Christ,
>   Invisible in storm,
>   Invulnerable to harm,
> Pearls and diamonds at his feet,
> Roses white upon his brow,
>   Banner ceaseless glowing,
>   Blizzard ceaseless blowing.

I was more than ready to accept Andrei's views. I too had no theory of revolution. But experience had prepared me. I wore the scars of that nocturnal escape from justice that had turned my parents into lawbreakers. How could I revere the laws they broke, knowing Mother's and Father's integrity and the excruciating effort they put forth to live within the law? I saw at first hand the suffering a market-oriented society can inflict on those who are inept at playing its games. Its games. Stocks, credit, speculation, profit, money. Money above all. I had come to despise a plutocracy that sorted people according to their incomes. Even children. Jimmy-the-banker's-son and Rosey-the-charwoman's-daughter. Rosey might be bright, but she would never be invited to Jimmy's birthday parties. A stone-cold edifice, our society, and not very sturdy. The Great Depression had rocked it to its foundations, making its very pillars crack. There must be some flaw in its construction. I had come to the Soviet Union looking for a better design. The one they were using here pleased me: weight distributed more evenly, a broader base, loftier arches, warmer lines. And I liked the enthusiasm of the builders and their capacity for self-sacrifice in realizing their dream. So Andrei had little trouble in converting me. Not only to an acceptance of the revolution, but to his entire world outlook, which was idealistic. Uninterested in creeds and dogmas, he was essentially a mystic. His solitary visits to the woods in childhood had left him acutely aware of the marvel and mystery of nature and of his being part of it. That came to full flower in his studio days. He recognized a power beyond imagining in all things, from the tiniest leaf to the movement of the stars. This recognition and the joy of life it engendered retrieved for me the sense of the holy my mechanistic university education had taken away.

December was drawing to a close when Andrei and I parted, he to teach actors in Outer Mongolia, I to teach children in Autozavod on the Volga. Our arrangement was that he would come in the spring and take me back to Moscow.

When Andrei first heard I was being sent to the automobile plant near Gorki, he exclaimed, "Why, that's where Annushka is! Annushka is my cousin and her husband is vice-director of that plant." Andrei showed his fondness for his cousin Anna by always calling her Annushka.

Let me digress for a moment to briefly explain the nice variations on Russian names that foreign readers of Russian novels find so confusing. There is, in Russian, a middle ground that covers the space between the formal salutation "Mrs. Smith" and the more casual one, "Jane." This middle ground is the *patronymic*—first name plus father's name: Anna Mikhai*lovna* (feminine ending) meaning "Anna, daughter of Michael"; Ivan Petr*ovich* (masculine ending) meaning "Ivan, son of Peter." The *patronymic* is what schoolchildren use when addressing their teachers, and other people use when addressing acquaintances and those from whom they are respectfully distanced. In addition to this convenient middle form there are suffixes that carry emotional coloring. "Ann*ushka*, you darling!" makes the name endearing. "Ann*ka*, you beast!" makes it abrupt, reproving, or jocularly familiar. It is these name variations, so meaningful in Russian, that drive foreign readers berserk.

Andrei wrote to Anna as soon as he learned where I was going so that I would have someone besides school authorities expecting me. I remember that when he saw me off at the low oriental-looking Kazan Railroad Station in Moscow, he went directly to the KGB* office that is to be found in every railroad station and told them who I was and where I was going and asked them to see that this odd craft afloat in foreign waters be guided safely to harbor.

Thus I found myself relayed from station to station by KGB officers, most of them young and genial, who knocked at the door of my compartment whenever the train made a long stop to check my papers and ask if everything was all right and did I want anything.

The train brought us to the Gorki station the next morning, and to my surprise I was met by an Intourist guide even though I was no longer under the jurisdiction of Intourist. I assumed this was in answer to Andrei's request. She (the guide) put me into a car and we drove away over bumpy roads across flat fields, white and empty and—dear me, what was that? The carcass of a horse! And that? The carcass of a cow! Was it a Russian custom to dispose of dead animals by leaving them at the roadside?

When I drew the guide's attention to it, her lips tightened and she looked inscrutable, which led me to think this must be further evidence of the havoc wrought in the countryside by the peasants' resistance to collectivization.

In an hour or so we turned off the main road and headed for not an industrial site—there was not so much as a factory chimney to be seen—but a sprawling settlement of wooden houses, mostly two-storied and so rough-hewn that the whole looked like a frontier settlement. The barrenness was unmitigated by a single tree. This was the American Village connected with Autozavod.

Hardly had we drawn up in the middle of the village when a young woman came running to meet us. She gave me a big American smile, and she spoke New York English with a Russian accent. The camel's hair coat she was wearing might well have come from Bonwit's, and

*KGB is the acronym by which the Soviet secret service is known today. For the reader's convenience we will call it that throughout, although when first organized after the revolution it was called the Cheka, later the GPU (until 1934), then the NKVD, the MVD, and now the KGB (Committee of State Security).

her brown felt hat was the peer of the black Stetson I had treated myself to in a reckless moment. There was authority in the way she dealt with me. She was, it turned out, the Commandant of this American Village. As she led me to the house I was to live in, she told me her name was Shura, nickname for Alexandra. She and her husband were Russian-American Communists who were repatriating. She had come here first with their little boy, Vova. He was to be one of my pupils. Her husband was expected to arrive in a month or so. I was not to suppose it was only Americans who lived in this village with their families. There were also Russian engineers who had studied at the Ford plant and at American universities, and—see that big house over there?—that was where top executives lived. (That, then, was where I would find Annushka, I thought.)

The house I was to live in was indistinguishable from its neighbors. We entered a front door that went down right to the ground, no step or porch to introduce it, and heaven only knows how it got pushed open after a heavy snow. We climbed a dingy stairway to the second floor, and there a room was awaiting me in the apartment on the right. The other room of this two-room apartment, Shura told me, was occupied by a Ford mechanic.

"And his wife?" I asked.

"No, he's alone," she said.

I think my face did not reflect the undulation of surprise that passed over my stomach at the prospect of sharing a two-room apartment with an unknown gentleman. That was still the age of innocence, or rather a transitional age leading to the present one in which no undulations are caused by notices posted on college campuses: Wanted: an apartment mate, male or female.

"You must be hungry," said Shura when I had put my bag down and washed my hands. "I'll take you to the canteen and then to the school principal."

The canteen was a low building full of the good smell of wood fires and offering the standard refreshment of thin tea in thick glasses, gummy candies to sweeten it, and *piroshki* with meat fillings. Delicious I found it, especially in the company of this Russian-American who was so anxious that I should appreciate and understand and accept.

From the canteen, we went to the schoolhouse. The principal was a stocky, middle-aged woman with a masculine haircut and a masculine stride, whose English said she had lived long in America but was not American (or necessarily Russian, perhaps Polish or Jewish?). She greeted me warmly and showed me the school's four classrooms, two on each side of a central corridor whose walls were bright with posters of Red Armymen, red flags, red hammers and sickles, the whole pervaded by the faint aroma of toilets. Then she took me into the office and presented me with history and arithmetic textbooks translated from the Russian for these English-speaking children.

"You don't have to come to work tomorrow," she said. "Get settled in, look through the books and make some lesson plans. And since the next day is the school's Rest Day, you'll have two holidays before you begin. Not bad, eh? And oh, yes, I believe they told you you would teach the third grade. Sorry, but it will be third and fourth together because there aren't many children in this American village and only three teachers—Rosalie, you, and me."

Rosalie came into the office where we were sitting when the janitor jingled a little handbell announcing the end of classes.

"Greetings," she said without a smile when we were introduced. One word was enough to tell me she was American.

"Where are you from? What city?" I asked.

"Detroit." And with that she turned her back on us to deposit some papers in a desk drawer; then, "Good luck," as she whisked out of the door.

One would expect more from a girl with that flawless complexion, that short uptilted nose that was gaiety itself, and those fair tendrils of hair that escaped from under the red bandanna Russian working women affected in those revolutionary days. I was exceedingly curious as to who she was and how she had gotten here.

The next morning I was awakened by hearing the Ford mechanic moving about in the kitchen. Poor guy. He had to go out into the midnight gloom and freezing temperature of this December morning. Thank goodness I didn't have to. When the mechanic banged the front door I made a little excursion out of my warm nest to switch on the light, scurried back, snuggled in, waited for the chill to pass, reached for the Intourist guidebook with maps of the Soviet Union in it, and began tracing the route taking Andrei to Mongolia—if he had left last night as he had expected to. Moscow, Gorki—why, yes, he would pass right next door to me, might be passing this very morning, this very minute. I gave this thought pleasurable consideration for a while before proceeding on his way: Kazan . . . Sverdlovsk . . . Novosibirsk . . . Irkutsk . . . a southerly swerve around the lower shores of Lake Baikal . . . Ulan-Ude. I tried the exotic names on my tongue. What were the towns like? Would I ever see them? Andrei had promised to take me with him next year. Visions of anticipated delights rose in my mind one after another, each new one richer than the last, until I drowsed off and the visions were supplanted by equally delightful dreams from which I awoke to the light of day.

I made myself a glass of strong tea in the mechanic's teapot and sat down with my textbooks. It was well past noon when the doorbell rang. Shura had come to take me to the canteen.

"Who is this Rosalie?" I asked as we went down the stairs.

"Isn't she pretty?"

"Gorgeous."

"She's from Detroit."

"I know."

"She came here with her father and mother, Communists both."

"And Rosalie?"

"Active in the Young Communist League. Very active indeed."

Outside it was too cold to take our noses out of our scarves so we stopped talking until we reached the vestibule of the canteen.

"How old is she?"

"Rosalie? Twenty-seven."

"I don't believe it! She looks like a child."

"And is she tough!"

"Not just solemn?"

"No, *tough*. A Party girl. Absolutely dedicated and full of vigilance. Watch out."

"For what?"

"Don't let her catch you teaching the kids the wrong things. Well, I'll be going. Got to feed Vova."

"Wait. Is she married?"

"Oh, yes."

"To whom?"

"One of our Russian engineers. I'll come for you this evening and take you to Martha's. Good-bye."

"Who's Martha?"

"You'll see."

Inside the canteen I sat down at one of the long tables covered with oilcloth. Presently from the kitchen area emerged a figure made bulky by layer upon layer of clothing buttoned into a white smock and with a woolen shawl framing a peasant girl's florid face. She made for me with a dish of cabbage soup in one hand and a plate holding two mini-meatballs and a mound of macaroni in the other. She was the waitress and this was my dinner.

"I've never seen you before," she said. "You new?"

"*Da.*"

My articulation of the syllable spoiled everything. She decided we couldn't communicate and said no more while I ate my soup—just stood and watched. When I began on the meatballs, she had another go at it, this time adopting an approach as to a child or an imbecile. I was soon to become used to linguistic maltreatment—either having separate words flung at me like stones or being shouted at as if I were deaf.

"Boots—American?" she shouted, pointing to my feet.

"Finnish. Ski boots." I was proud of them. They were of tooled leather and had turned-up toes.

"No good. Cold. Must have . . ." and she held out a foot encased in a felt boot whose primitive form reminded me of a child's drawing: just a cylinder spreading out at the bottom into a roundness of heel and toe: *valenki.*

I got up to go.

"*Schastlivo,*" she said.

"*Schastlivo,*" I returned boldly. She grinned as if the baby had said "Mama" for the first time.

I found the Ford mechanic in the hall of our apartment when I got back.

"Hello," he said. "They say *you're* an American, too."

"I am."

"Detroit?"

"No, Philadelphia." I entered my room. He followed me in and sat down on my only chair. It creaked under him. He was big.

"Working at the plant?"

"No, teaching school."

"You come all the way from America to teach school here? What's-a-matter? Out of a job?"

"No, I just wanted to see what it was like."

"Listen, I been here six months. I can tell you all about it. It's no good."

"What's no good?"

"This place. See what they eat? Rotten cabbage and frozen potatoes. Sure, I get fed better, I get Insnob. Know what that is? Food for foreigners. I'm a Ford worker, see? I was making good wages at Ford's till they laid me off. Outta work for over a year and when I heard they was looking for skilled workers to come here—I'm a first-class mechanic—I signed up. Goddamn fool I was."

"Well, you got a job, didn't you?"

"So what? I lived better over there as an outtawork than here putting in eight hours a day. Tried their hamburgers? Give you the gripes. And a person wants a little fun sometimes, don't he? See a movie at least. Oh, they show you a movie once in a while, but who wants it? Nothing but war and revolution. If there's a girl in it, she's all done up in a leather jacket and high boots. Wouldn't know she was a girl if she didn't have a braid down her back. But a Chinaman's got that too." He grinned at his witticism. "What's your name?"

I told him.

"Sounds like home. I'm Charlie. Charlie Slonsky."

"Russian descent?"

"Polish. But I'm American, you bet. Hundred percent. Hooray for the red, white, and blue. What the hell did you ever come here for? You a Commie?"

"No."

"That's good. Most of the Americans who come here are Commies. Serves 'em right, let 'em have it—the rotten butter 'n eggs!"

"Sorry, Charlie, but I've got work to do," I said. "We'll talk another time."

He took himself off, not very graciously, and a few minutes later I heard him bang out of the apartment. I did sit down to the lesson plan and worked on it until darkness told me the day was done. That was when Shura called for me.

"Put on your things. I want you to meet Martha."

"She American too?"

"Yes."

"I'm not really interested in meeting all these Americans. That's not what I came to Russia for."

"You knew you were coming to the American Village, didn't you?"

"Yes, but at a Soviet plant."

"Martha's like Rosalie: married a Russian engineer. In Detroit, when he was studying at Ford's. But Martha's not a Communist. She's an artist."

That was interesting, but, "Isn't it rather late to go visiting?"

"Seven o'clock."

"Oh."

It was time, I should think, for me to get used to the long winter nights. These were the very longest, just before the winter solstice.

"Those boots," said Shura, looking down at them and shaking her head as the waitress had done. "It's thirty below. You've got to have *valenki*. I'll get you some tomorrow."

The wind had died down, but the cold made you catch your breath. We walked quickly to another square wooden house with a downright entrance door. We climbed dark stairs. The apartment door was opened to us by a tall thin girl with drooping shoulders and drooping wisps of yellow hair.

"Come in." Her half-smile showed teeth that were a little too prominent. "You're Peg? Shura told me about you."

"And me about you—a little," I said. Her pale blue eyes did not light up with enthusiasm, nor did her voice lose its languor.

The room she showed us into was dimmed by silk scarves thrown over lampshades. There were low couches in it and an oriental rug that began at the ceiling, slid down the wall, folded out to cover the couch, folded down to the floor, and folded out again to be walked on. Martha folded herself up against the pillows on this couch and Shura and I sat on another couch facing her.

"Where's Boris?" asked Shura.

"At the plant, of course."

"When will he come home?"

"You never know. Maybe ten, maybe eleven."

The words fell with a sodden thud that was absorbed by a pause. Shura broke the silence by asking Martha what she did with herself all day long.

"I've been given a job by the plant. To design a trademark."

"Great!" said Shura zestfully. "See? Jobs for everybody here, even artists." Martha winced.

"Could you show us some of your sketches?" I ventured.

"I've turned them all in."

"Oh, I didn't mean the trademark. You paint, don't you?"

"Not much. There's a little thing I did," pointing to a picture hanging over the door. "The river. And that other—a village about a mile from here. But I don't find this place inspiring. Terribly drab. And cold. And I have to keep house—cook and clean and go to the store."

Here was Shura's chance. "I'll find you a maid. No trouble. Almost any of the village women would be glad to come—get Insnob food and money besides. Shall I look for somebody?"

"Heavens, no!" To my surprise Martha could be roused. "I've had my fill of Russian maids. They're simply *filthy*, they don't even know what it *means* to be clean, they never see a corner, they wouldn't bend down to go *under* anything for twice their wages, they leave food around, they don't *clean* the toilet, they mess it up by throwing left-over soup in it—can you believe it? No more maids, thanks!" The flare of energy was spent and Martha sank back against the pillows again. Shura and I sank back too, figuratively, and left it at that.

"How long have you been here?" came a weak little voice from Martha's direction.

"Here or in Russia?" I asked.

"In Russia."

"About three months."

"I've been here for over a year." She might have been announcing that she had a terminal illness. "Can you get used to it? The dirt, I mean. I can't. I couldn't in France either—I lived in France for six months before coming here. This is worse."

Boris came in while we were having tea. Good looking. Twelve hours at the plant had left their mark on him, but he greeted his Marfochka brightly in an effort to balance the scales against her gloom.

"So you are going to teach here, Peg? Good. Marfochka will have a friend. Marfochka sits home too much. Maybe you will go skiing with her? You don't know how to ski? Marfochka neither, so you learn together. Yes, yes, you can learn, Marfochka. You can."

It was clear that Martha's coming here was a catastrophe. She deserved sympathy, but my compass was so south to her north that compassion could not straddle the distance between us.

We left, Shura and I, when we decently could. We did not speak for a while. I think Shura was upset. "I had no idea she was like that," she said at last. "I don't see much of her—only at the store or a movie."

"You don't have to apologize," I said.

"I thought you'd be friends."

"I'll go skiing with her."

This day had presented much to give me pause. It looked as if I really was going to meet only Americans here. I was disappointed.

These and related thoughts occupied my mind as I walked back from the canteen the next morning. Suddenly I was stopped by the sight of a man's figure outlined against the snow. Something familiar about it. That jauntily tipped beaver cap. The slow, deliberate step. And yes, as the image rapidly grew with his advance, those green eyes narrowed above the turned-up collar.

"Andrei!"

"Margarita!"

"How . . . ?"

"Jumped the train at Gorki."

He took my arm and turned me around and made for the road leading to the woods. In our elation we fairly ran. The snow on this road had been packed smooth between drifts by trucks that brought workers back and forth from outlying villages. Not a living creature was in sight, not a man, not a bird, not a mouse or a rabbit, only the two of us rushing as if about to take wing. By the time we reached the woods we had no need to bury our noses in our scarves, instead we put up our faces to catch the sun's warmth.

"How long?" I asked.

"All of today and all of tonight."

"Tomorrow you go?"

"That is light-years away."

Plumes of vapor brushed our faces when we talked. We walked back more slowly, blinded by noonday's gleam and glitter. The sun's rays splintered to iridescence on the ice and threw shadows as blue as the sky.

We reached the rough houses of the village in half an hour. When we entered my apartment, there stood the mechanic pulling on his sheepskin. He could not have looked gruffer. Andrei eyed him curiously as he mumbled a civility. The mechanic replied with a grunt and flung out of the door. Andrei stared at the slammed door and shrugged his shoulders.

"Who is he?"

"He lives here."

"Here? In this apartment?"

"*Da.*"

"Alone?"

"With me. I mean—he there (pointing to his room), I here (opening the door to my room)."

We went inside. Andrei surveyed the iron bedstead, the one chair, the rickety desk, his own snapshot pinned up on the wall, then he went out and inspected the unheated kitchen.

"I phoned Annushka and told her we would come about noon, but I see there is urgent business to be done," he said.

The urgent business took us to Shura's house, where he and she had an amiable conversation that ended in Shura's promising to find me new quarters.

"Tomorrow, then?" Andrei said to her as we were leaving.

"Yes, tomorrow; I will make arrangements this evening. I'm sure the Papernos can spare her a room, but I must speak to them first. They're at the plant now."

Once more we crossed the village, this time on our way to the executives' house which was also wooden and two-storied, as crudely fashioned as the other houses, but long, extending in two wings on either side of the front door. We were admitted in a cloud of vapor by a rotund woman with a kerchief tied under her chin and an apron tied around her middle who was obviously the "houseworker" in this community of housewives. At the mention of Anna Mikhailovna's name she bounced away to call her.

Anna appeared quietly, smilingly. Sort of no-color. Pale hair, paler face, a bun in the nape of her neck, a smile that wavered like the light of a loosely screwed-in bulb.

"*Ochen rada*," she murmured when Andrei introduced us. The smile strengthened, and the eyes curled warmly when I came back with "*Ya tozhe*." She had supposed I knew no Russian at all. That is why, she said as she led us into the dining room, she had invited Vera Abramovna to join us. Vera Abramovna knew English perfectly.

Vera Abramovna rose as we entered.

"I very much like English," she said to me. "English literature. Galsworsy, Jeck London, Teckeray. I very, very much like English literature. I take English courses in Moscow. Here?—What is here?" she said, casting a scornful glance about the room we were in, one of those impersonal rooms shared by people in temporary association. There was a square table in the middle, six straightbacked chairs, a sideboard with nothing on it but a small plaster cast of Lenin, a picture calendar hanging lonelily on the wall. None of the women living here looked upon this as home. I was to learn that they were only here to take care of husbands appointed by the Party to high posts in this hinterland, husbands they rarely saw but for whom they waited at all hours with soup on the fire and kettles on the hob so that they could minister to the men's needs at whatever odd moments of day or night they might appear for a meal and a nap. The wives' homes were in Moscow where their children were, where their hearts were.

"Have you seen Jhenya?" Anna asked Andrei. Jhenya was her son. "Grusha says he's studying too hard. Doesn't eat regularly. Doesn't get enough sleep."

"Grusha's just an old nanny who can't bear to see her baby grow up," Andrei consoled her. "Jhenya's old enough to take care of himself now."

"No he's not. At eighteen boys don't know how to take care of themselves. Especially Jhenya. He's like his father. All or nothing."

"Don't worry about him."

"Will you look him up when you get back?"

"I'm not going back—not soon," said Andrei.

"Ah, yes. You told me. Well, I'll be going back myself for a week in February. Anatoli's been summoned by the Central Committee. Thank goodness for these summonses. Without them I'd never see my boy."

Vera Abramovna turned to me. "Moscow now for us is like for Chekhov's three sisters. How long must we stay here? Our husbands, they cannot last long this way. Too much work, too much. Sergei Diakonov, he is Director, he fainted in his office two weeks ago. Bi-i-ig man." Her gesture indicated a barrel chest. "Now he is gone to a sanitorium, but when he comes back he will kill himself again."

Meanwhile, tea and the standard cheese and bologna sandwiches were served. I gasped when my lips made contact with the scalding-hot bitter-strong tea Russians serve at home.

"Water," I sputtered. "Water. You may, please?"

A little gust of laughter shook Anna. "*MozhNO*," she corrected. "Not *mozhESH*."

Andrei's green eyes flickered. "You *could* say it that way."

"Perhaps, but . . ."

"She'll learn soon enough. Let's enjoy it while it lasts."

"Shame, shame," expostulated Vera Abramovna. "I will teach her." She turned to me. "You are here now to live. You must know Russian good. I will teach you. I will teach you Russian, you will teach me English, yes?"

"Oh, gladly."

Andrei and I did not stay long. We did not want to impose our presence on a work-weary husband who might come home unexpectedly and find us there. My moving into a new apartment was excuse enough to cut our visit short. As Anna saw us to the door she made no effort to conceal her amusement at discovering her cousin attached to so unlikely a lady as an *Amerikanka*. Andrei and I laughed too, as if all three of us were in on a big joke.

When we got back to my room I asked Andrei to tell me more about Anna, Annushka, Anna Mikhailovna.

"Her parents who?" I asked Andrei.

"You'd be surprised," he said. "Her father was a country gentleman from the Tula province, a loveable rake who woke up one fine day to discover that wining and wenching had exhausted his modest inheritance. At that point his wife left him for the stage. Left him and her three children. How do you like that? Left Annushka, aged thirteen, with two little boys to bring up—twins and both deaf mutes."

"Deaf . . . ?"

"Deaf," pointing to his ears. "Stone deaf. One of them died soon after that. Annushka mothered the other, a sweet mooing child. Now he works at the School for the Deaf in Tula. His wife is head of the school. Also deaf. A pretty woman, fair and round in the Russian way. Quite a touching love story."

"And Anna? Her love story?"

"I'm not sure she had one. Oh, she got married. She was only seventeen when she met Anatoli. He was an engineer and a revolutionary. She admired him. She married him. Love him? What does a provincial girl of seventeen know about married love? She hardly sees him. First he was away fighting, came home for brief visits from battlefields far and near. When the fighting was over, he was given a big Party job in Moscow. Now he has *this* big job. It's hard for a man to be married to a cause and a wife at the same time. Some men, anyway."

The next day Andrei left in the car Anna sent to take him to the Gorki railroad station, and I moved in with the Papernos. This was a great improvement.

Samuel Paperno was a Russian who years before the October Revolution had escaped from political exile in Siberia and gone to America. There he became a lawyer, and in later years he was legal consultant at the Soviet headquarters in Detroit while Russian engineers were being trained in the Ford way of running an automobile plant. When the Detroit headquarters closed down, Paperno came with his wife and seventeen-year-old daughter, Eleanor, to help with the opening of the Autozavod plant. His wife soon went back to the States, but Eleanor, who had just finished high school, found it a great adventure to live in the Village and work in one of the plant's laboratories for a year until she entered a university either here or back home. She was knowing beyond her years and with a keen sense of humor that made her a delightful companion. She would have found it a great joke if I had told her her father had tried to climb into my bed, the old goat. Well he did try, and I didn't tell.

The Papernos enjoyed a luxurious apartment for these parts: a big common room, two bedrooms, and a sun parlor that became my room. Its double windows with a continuous row of radiators beneath them kept it comfortable except when the thermometer went to thirty degrees below zero (centigrade). These windows looked out upon a low line of hills and woods above the Oka River. The room was bright when there was brightness outside. The frost patterns on the panes made the daintiest of lace curtains. I had a comfortable couch and a big solid desk at which most of my free time was spent writing letters, keeping a journal, and studying Russian. Often while sitting there I would gaze out of the window and see strange sights. Once an old woman, bent double under the load of fagots on her back, emerged from the dark forest like a witch out of a fairy tale, and I held my breath for fear Hansel and Gretel would appear and she would set off after them. Often I saw younger women in *valenki* and full-skirted sheepskins walking wonderfully erect to balance the pails of river water (reached through a hole in the ice) swinging from opposite ends of long wooden yokes slung over their shoulders. And there was the ubiquitous *muzhik* on his low sledge driving a horse festooned with the hoarfrost of its breath and its sweat.

Together with our maid, Marusa, we made a congenial household (Paperno and I easily dismissed the little incident of the bed). Marusa was a characteristic village type, cheerful and imperturbable on all occasions. She attached no importance to forgetting to give us a message left by a caller or to being an hour late with the dinner because her girlfriend had dropped in to see her. "*Nichevo!*" ("It's nothing!") she would say with a disarming smile.

It was the ordinary Russian's *nichevo* attitude that drove poor Miss Meyers to distraction. Miss Meyers was a Russian-American spinster who had been in charge of the office at Soviet headquarters in Detroit. Sharing Paperno's devotion to the Communist cause, she had come here with him to organize office work at the Autozavod plant. She was a prim, thin-lipped little woman, eminently efficient in all things.

"But it's ridiculous!" she would fume. "Why have I invested so much Soviet money in American filing cabinets if they insist on shoving scraps of paper away in desk drawers and then spending hours looking for them? And typing? They won't take the pains to learn the touch system, say they can do it quicker with two fingers. I had to have a special order signed by the plant director—the *director*, no less!—forcing secretaries and typists to use the touch system. Do you think it helped? It did not. They do a drill half-heartedly while the teacher is looking and go back to their two fingers when her back is turned."

Of course. They were all Marusas, and could I get Marusa to put water in pots while they stood waiting to be washed? What for? To save cleaning time? *Nichevo.* She was in no hurry.

One day I walked with Marusa to her village about a mile away. The open door of the village church suggested that a service was being held. Marusa refused to go inside with me: that would have identified her with the old women who, with the exception of a grandchild held tightly by the hand or a wobbly old man pressing a fur cap to his chest, made up the small group of worshipers I observed from a shadowy corner pricked by the light of a few thin tapers. The congregation was standing up (for the Orthodox Church does not humor the faithful with the comfort of seats), but now and again they would throw themselves on their knees and bump the floor with their foreheads. The priest and his assistant intoned the liturgy in ancient Slavonic, a tongue as incomprehensible to these Russian Orthodox peasants as Latin is to Irish Catholic peasants. Slowly the fumes of the swung censer curled up into the low dome of this country church, deadening the smell of old sheepskins and unabashed farting.

As for my teaching, I fear I did not take it as seriously as Rosalie took her communism. It was but a bridge to carry me over to the month of May. Never before had I taught little children, and I had no intention of making it my profession. I would muddle along somehow and hope no young lives were ruined by a short term of muddling. The kids themselves looked upon their life here as a strange interlude to be played out like a game. Shura's son, Vova, was different. He had been told he had come for good, but I'm sure the idea had not sunk in. He was, after all, only ten years old. A smart little boy was Vova, and charming with his cap of black curly hair and big black eyes with long lashes sticking out all around like the lashes children draw around eyes.

When school was over, it was Vova and his gang who escorted me to the canteen, Vova doing most of the talking: Had I been to the river yet? Where did I come from—Philadelphia? He bet there were no skyscrapers there like in New York where he lived; his father was coming from New York soon and bringing him some new skis.

Far more important to me than my teaching was my contact with Russians in the American Village. I had feared it would never take place, but Vera Abramovna began regularly coming to me in the evening for English lessons. She had acquired so much knowledge of the language that I had only to let her talk and read aloud so as to gain confidence and fluency.

I usually met her at the entrance to our house, which was through the kitchen, and I held her books as she stamped the snow off her boots and unwound the shawl from around her head and shoulders. We would stop in the common room on our way to my sun parlor to chat a little with the Papernos, then take our places on either side of my big desk.

"It is so strange not to be a working woman," she remarked plaintively one evening as she arranged pencil, notebook, and *The Forsythe Saga*. "Always I worked. Now my husband thinks I must rest. I worked special hard when he was studying. Studying for a higher education. He graduated the Economics Institute. Before that he knew only war—war, war, war. World War I. Revolution. Civil War. No time for education. Ah, you think that *is* education? I suppose so." She reached for a cigarette—or rather a *papirosa*, the Russian cigarette with a cardboard mouthpiece which was the only kind you could get in Russia in those days. She smiled. "Yes, of course. Everything is education. But war is very terrible education." As she lighted up she left the stain of her rouged lips on the cardboard. Her bright red lips and her soft brown eyes were striking points of color against ivory skin. "When he went back to school—to the Institute—he got so little a government stipend that we lived mostly on what I earned. He studied all day at the Institute, all evening in the library. All day I worked in an office. No time for pleasure. Still I attended English courses. I very much like English. And I saw my friends and sometimes we had parties. I like parties." Her girlish smile belied the middle-aged look of her figure. "When my husband finished the Institute I was very tired. So that is why when he was sent here to take charge of plant's finances, he said I must not work, I must rest. And here I am. I rest." It didn't sound happy. "I rest. I walk. I read English books. But I *skuchayu*—I am lonely, homesick—for Moscow and my friends there. I like to dress up, but our life does not have a place in it for such. Now I find I do not care so much about my nails manicured, my hair set."

She avoided speaking about what was happening in Russia. She dismissed the subject with a shrug of her shoulders. "Life is hard," was her only comment. But her experience of present hardships was always offset by memories of the Civil War when in her native town of Kiev she had witnessed murder and plunder and rape. "Now that is over. Now we think about future," she said. "But I have a strange feeling. I feel I will not live to see it. Never before I feel like this. Now I know deep down here (pointing to her chest), I know I will not live long." She paused. Then with an embarrassed laugh, she picked up *The Forsythe Saga* and began reading to me. She did not find it easy to speak of private things.

Another time she talked about her husband. "I worry about him," she said. "He is very jolly and he is not sick, but I know how tired he is. No relaxation. Our men, they have no life, only work, and we their wives also die for their work. Every night he is at the plant till ten, eleven, twelve. Even later, till early morning sometimes when they have meetings. Even on Rest Days he goes to the plant."

The next lesson found Vera in a lighter mood. "We had a good party on Rest Day. At the School for Red Army Automobile Mechanics. I danced and danced. I'm getting too fat, I must be thin like American women; then I can dance and still have breath to breathe with." She pulled in her belly and thrust out her ample bosom. I caught the gleam of a gold tooth in the side of her mouth when she laughed—a third point of color: eyes, lips, tooth. "Yesterday our plant returned the invitation. They gave a big dinner at our plant's restaurant. But I was very angry. They did not invite wives. I went to the head of the restaurant and complained. He was very sorry. It did not depend from him. Still I said he must repay me for insult. He gave me two cakes. So all the wives at our house had apple cake for supper."

"I hope you didn't save any for your husband," I said.

"I know. I shouldn't do it. But he is so like a little boy."

On a February evening of strangulating cold I had to defrost her at the door. When I had rubbed the stiffness out of her hands with snow and pulled away the stuck folds of her shawl to discover her face, I was shocked to see how weary she looked. There were black circles under her eyes and drooping lines about her mouth. The usual animation of her greeting was lacking.

"You know," she said when we were seated at the desk, "I don't think I will be here much longer. No, no, I mean exactly here, in Autozavod."

"You're moving away?" I knew it could not be back to Moscow, for then she would have rejoiced.

"There is new government policy," she said. "They are sending the best men to the *kolkhozes*—the collective farms. There is much trouble on the farms. They say my husband may be sent."

"Does your husband know anything about farming?"

"He lived in the village but he is not a farmer. His father had a little store."

"You wouldn't think he would be the best person to send."

"It is political work. He is good organizer. He must organize the *kolkhozes*. If they say he is the person to do it, he must go."

"How would you like that?" I asked, ill disguising my consternation.

"I suppose it doesn't matter," she said with sad resignation.

"And your husband? Would he mind?"

"He does not care. Work is work, one place, another place, all the same." Vera lighted a *papirosa*. She reached for the books, her red lips smiling. "You think our life is hard, yes?"

THESE EVENINGS of teaching English to Vera Abramovna were preceded by afternoons of learning Russian from our next door neighbor. Eve was her name, and she was a great respecter of rules and regulations, one of which was that a person must get fresh air and exercise.

So in the early afternoon, the warmest part of the day, we would preface our lesson with a walk, during which we spoke English. Her husband was one of the chief engineers at the plant and had spent much time in Detroit. Eve had been there with him and had acquired a haphazard sort of English full of surprises, such as calling me "Margarita-thing," the suffix "thing" evidently taking the place in her mind of the endearing Russian suffix "-ochka," "Margaritochka."

"You read of the great trial, Margarita-thing? No? My poor girl, you must practice reading the paper. I will help you. You see, you must know politics. You go backward. You must read the paper."

Eve was one to take things into her own hands. She was brisk and brusque, as different as possible from the soft, reflective Vera. Eve's eyes were dark, too, and very handsome, but in a hard shining way, the whites like porcelain and the lashes framing rather than shading them. "Tomorrow we begin, we will read *Pravda*." The trials of saboteurs were just beginning. Saboteurs in industry, *kulaks* on the farms; the first flashes of lightning and rumble of thunder on the horizon. "You see how it is going, Margarita-thing? This Russian engineer who is head of the—how you call it?—the *electricheski station*—he already for ten years was in this station in the Ukraine, and first he was just—what you say?—head over just part of it—yes, a foreman. But he was a good worker, and you know how it is in Russia now. He goes up and up and soon he is director of the *electricheski station*. He is not a Party member, but he is in position to know many secrets. So now he tells in his—what you call it?—yes, testimony—you see he was on trial because of an accident at the plant—so in his testimony he tells everything. Everything, Margarita-thing. Now everything is clear. Absolute! He is not interested in money, no, but he is an absolute enemy of our Soviet government." Eve pronounced this with the decisiveness of a proclamation.

"You cannot understand how this could be if he is not interested in money? Oh, Margarita-thing, I understand. You see, he has been doing maybe from childhood so. Maybe it is not even that he comes from very rich people, but only that he cannot understand Russia's new life. You see? It is very hard. He is a good engineer, I suppose. And you know how was the life before the revolution—all those good things. An engineer, he had his nice home and servants, he goes to Europe. And now things are very different. Take a man like my husband. He is a Party member for ten, maybe fifteen years. Nobody could think he is not a good Communist. He is a good engineer too—a *young* engineer, but at the plant, I suppose so, they make out of him a first-class engineer. But see how we live. And don't forget, Margarita-thing, we are better off than most people. We are the developed people. Then there are the ones who have it harder and harder. And then the peasants who suffer very much. But even if we are better off than most, just see how hard it is, not only because sometimes there is no meat and no milk, but it is not easy to work in the plant. Now you see there are two classes, the old engineers who want to do it old-stylish, and the new engineers who want to do it new-stylish. You see? Sometimes my husband comes home and he is so terrible sick when his work is spoiled. But always he sees how things are going. He sees what will be in future. Always, he finds an excuse. He understands everything. This engineer at the *electricheski station*, he wants to live now. To hell with the future! Then how can he be happy to go without meat, without milk, to live with his family in one room? His wife wants this and that. Of course, Margarita-thing! It is not easy to live this life. A person has to be strong. Very strong." She stressed the word by thrusting out her chin and clenching her fist.

"People have suffered so long—you cannot even *think* how people have suffered. But always we must build and see the future. We must build a new life or we cannot be happy. Take myself and Mrs. MacLain" (wife of one of the American engineers). "It was hard for her to leave America, and always when she would walk down the street and would see me, she would start crying, 'What shall I do? There is no butter. There is no meat. My apartment is cold.' But see she had a big apartment, not like our two rooms for my husband, my boy, and me. She had better food from the foreigners' store. But always she was unhappy and couldn't understand why I was happy. And so she left her husband here and went back to America. She didn't love her husband, I suppose so, because when she was here she didn't lose her husband, only she lost her nice apartment.

"Oh, Margarita-thing, this is for strong people, and Russia is strong! You see how it is now? A few years ago Russia could say to Europe only, 'Please don't touch me. Please leave me alone.' But now, even if it would be very hard for Russia to go to war, she is not afraid. She is ready for everything!" Her black eyes flashed as if she were about to loose a restive horse she had mounted.

THESE CONTACTS—with Anna, Vera Abramovna, and Eve—dispelled my fear of meeting only Americans in the American Village. True, these people could not be called "average Russians." The men, whom I saw through the mirror of their wives, represented the top echelon of Bolsheviks, those who had made the revolution and were now totally involved in building a new nation based on principles never before incorporated into government. They had no model to copy, no experience to fall back upon, and all the odds seemed to be against them: a country impoverished by war, deserted by a large section of the professional class, threatened by discontent within and enmity without, burdened by a backward population whose character, molded by history and tradition, was ill-adapted to the pragmatic demands of industrialization. But the "dictatorship of the proletariat" implies industrialization, and industrialization was the new nation's only hope of survival among the industrial giants whom it dared to challenge.

I saw these men and their wives at Autozavod as true heroes. Much has been written about the heroism of the people of Leningrad during the blockade in World War II. The people of Leningrad were not heroes, however valorously they endured their sufferings. They were victims. They were trapped in the city. No other choice was offered them. A hero is one who chooses to sacrifice himself for something he holds dearer than his own life, be it the life of another, or a cause, or a cult. For me, the entrapping of the citizens of Leningrad was a war crime. Rome was declared an open city to preserve its people and its treasures. Had Leningrad been declared an open city it would not have meant the capitulation of the country. The Soviet Union lost all its western provinces to the invaders, it almost lost Moscow and did indeed lose Kiev, capital of the Ukraine. But this did not mean defeat. All its cities and provinces were taken back. And nothing would have spurred Russians to victory like the outrage of losing Leningrad, their most venerated city.

But this is mere speculation and beside the point. The point is that the men at the head of the plant in Autozavod had made their choice. And their wives had made theirs, for no one compelled them to be there. They chose to stand by their men, sacrificing themselves to keep the fires going so that their husbands could have hot baths and hot food and guarded rest when they needed it most sorely. Love prompted the wives' sacrifice and elevated them to the pedestal of heroism on which their men stood.

THUS, IN TEACHING, studying Russian, writing at my desk, tumbling about on skis with Martha, talking things over in the common room after dinner, time moved forward. The days lengthened with astonishing rapidity after the New Year. The frosts of February, the most severe of the entire winter, gave way to the vacillations of March, whose blizzards today and thaws tomorrow made it impossible to know where you stood until April came in with determined tread and put her blight on the snow; it turned livid and wasted away, leaving the plains piebald, the roads slushy, the hillsides gashed by torrents. The sun, which had eagerly sucked up the vapors of its own making, was satisfied at last; it shone forth with warmth and brilliance, the torrents stopped plunging and wound their way down the slopes with a sweet murmur, and many birds sang. Spring had come, bringing Andrei with it.

He arrived unannounced as he was to do again and again over the years; it was a compulsion with him, a desire to punctuate life's prose with exclamation marks. Like a gust of wind he blew into our common room on a May evening, flushed of face, radiant of eye, wearing top boots and leather jacket and a considerable layer of road dust. This new image of him jounced me out of my wits; I could not introduce him to my friends for I had suddenly forgotten his last name. This was a jolly beginning which he followed up by extracting a bottle of vodka from the tangle of socks and shirts and notebooks and Mongolian trinkets in his rucksack. We had a gay little party before he and I retired to my sun parlor, now moon parlor—no, truly sun parlor, for the days were lengthening to the summer solstice and it was indeed the sun outshining the moon that bathed the earth in a pale luminosity that even now lasted far into the night and would soon all but extinguish the night. He told me and I told him and he told me and I told him while the nightingales sang frenziedly in the woods down by the river, and by the time the telling was over the mysterious light had faded into darkness and revived again, no longer mysterious but shot through with the golden beams of a new day.

That new day was the only one Andrei could spare me for leave-taking. I had no scruples about ending my teaching so abruptly; the school year was practically over and it had never been a serious school year. Saying farewell to the friends I was leaving behind in this barren outpost was harder. I read more misery than envy in Annushka's eyes when we said good-bye, and in Vera Abramovna's too, even in the doughty Eve's. In deference to their feelings I suppressed my own exuberance, which was induced less by the prospect of going to Moscow than by that of going to Mongolia with Andrei. That was the high adventure awaiting me!

six

Mongolia

In Xanadu did Kubla Khan
A stately pleasure-dome decree:
Where Alph, the sacred river ran
Through caverns measureless to man,
Down to a sunless sea.
—Samuel Taylor Coleridge,
"Kubla Khan"

THE HIGH ADVENTURE was postponed. Andrei went back to Mongolia in August alone, leaving me in Moscow in his father's care. I did not understand why. His explanations were vague and mysterious—something about the international situation. I did not understand why, if Mongolia was not a war zone, he could not take his wife with him. Was it because I was not legally his wife? We had not registered our marriage because we found it unimportant, recognizing, as we did, that true marriage was the declared and dedicated union of two who loved. As soon as we got back from our honeymoon in the Ukraine, Andrei had divorced Alla by simply writing a declaration of divorce and submitting it to ZAGS (the office for the Registration of Civil Acts). That is all that was required of either husband or wife in those early days of Soviet law.

When I suggested to Andrei that our marital status might be the reason for my being left behind, he shrugged off the idea with a little laugh; we could remedy that in a wink if we wanted to, he said; did I want to? I did not. I prided myself on being the emancipated woman.

One thing disturbed me. Whenever I asked Andrei to be specific about the international situation he became evasive. Was the international situation merely an excuse? Was there another reason? Horrid suspicions entered my mind. I knew that Alla, Andrei's first wife, was still in Mongolia; Andrei had told me so. He had also told me, in those first days of our acquaintance, that he loved her even after he left her. Did he love her more than he loved me? Had I been too credulous?

Had the language muddle led me to draw false conclusions? Had I staked my life on a fantasy? I was ashamed of these suspicions and denied every one of them, but they plagued me. I drove them away in the daytime by accepting a heavy workload at the Institute of Foreign Languages, teaching English four hours a day. But at night the dance of the demons kept me awake.

The winter dragged on in aching uncertainty. I tried to hide my feelings from my father-in-law, and I think I succeeded. One day he urged me to join the apartment-house cooperative in which we were living and of which he had been a founding member at the end of the twenties. "Don't let Andrei know you're joining," he warned. "He's an arch enemy of owning anything, but that's all poppycock. It's impossible to get an apartment in Moscow and he'll be only too glad to have one when you and he start a family." So I sold my typewriter and some American clothes for a down payment and joined the cooperative without telling Andrei.

Andrei Nikolayevich and Maria Vasilyevna were as attentive to me as to a daughter. I gradually became much attached to Maria Vasilyevna, attracted as much by her personality as by her looks. Her figure was wasted by a heart disease that gave her a cough and nervous little gestures reflecting the unpredictable flutterings of a sick heart. She spent most of the day lying down with a book (she was a voracious and discriminating reader). Sometimes she would have Lyalya, her housemaid's three-year-old daughter, lie down beside her. She would read to the child and teach her her letters. No longer able to do housework herself, she kept a strict eye on her housemaid to see that everything was scrupulously clean and the household well ordered, down to the placing of Andrei Nikolayevich's house slippers in the hall at precisely six o'clock every evening, by which time the kasha kernels had been roasted and cooked to a perfection of fluffiness. Andrei Nikolayevich never had to wait for his dinner. Ill as she was, Maria Vasilyevna was beautiful in an Audrey Hepburn way—long neck, high cheekbones, skinny body, but with dark eyes set deeper than Hepburn's light ones. Her health deteriorated as the winter of 1933–34 drew to a close and in March she died. Andrei Nikolayevich was devastated. He needed Andrei for support.

In 1934, as in 1933, he came back from Mongolia in May, just as overwhelmingly, if not as boisterously. He gave his father what comfort he could, and as for me—well, one by one the demons slunk away under the steady light of his green-brown eyes. The first announcement he made was that he and I were leaving for Mongolia as soon as I could wind up my teaching at the Institute.

We left at the beginning of June. To make this journey a second honeymoon Andrei bought not just first-class tickets, but tickets in the International Car of the Trans-Siberian Express. Our compartment was a private room in which we spent seven days speeding eastward across a vast country in which everything was outsize: the mountains, the Siberian rivers, the endless forest called the taiga, the dreary plains, the four-hundred-mile-long Lake Baikal into whose waters, clear as if distilled, we could gaze from the window of our compartment and see the fish darting, for the train skimmed the lake's edge, sometimes precariously on a ledge carved into the sheer cliffs girding it on the south.

After leaving the train at Ulan-Ude, capital of Buryat Mongolia (a Soviet republic), our route was directly south some three hundred miles to the border of Outer Mongolia. There being no railroad in Outer Mongolia in those days, we had to make the rest of the journey by whatever means of transportation we could find. Several days of impatient waiting on my part and persistent effort on Andrei's ended in his finding the driver of a food truck bound for Kyakhta, the Soviet border town, who agreed to let us ride with him. And so with the sun and wind on our faces and the vagabond's abandon in our hearts, we rode on top of rice and flour sacks in the back of the truck, stopping to spend a night in a peasant's one-room cottage, sleeping on the floor with our heads just missing the stove and our feet not missing the prone bodies of the housewife and her daughter. We were up and off at dawn, riding down, down, according to the compass, up, up, according to the altimeter, for Outer Mongolia is a high plateau. At Kyakhta we took leave of our taciturn driver, crossed the border to Altan Bulak, and resumed our journey in the cabin of an oil truck, one of a fleet of four bound for Ulan Bator, the Mongolian capital. It took us three days of perilous riding to reach it. Indescribably beautiful were the low mountains through which we passed. Nothing in the landscape was static, all as vibrant as a Matisse canvas, the wind-blown clouds sending pale shadows scudding over steppe and slope.

There were no roads except those worn into the terrain first by camel caravans, then by fleets of trucks, so that our progress was constantly being interrupted by having to tow one another out of boggy stretches or dig rocks away from wheels while fording rivers. The truck drivers were of the stuff buccaneers are made of, adventurers of the great open spaces, a tight-knit clan united as much by the loyalty required for survival as by their common love of derring-do.

We spent two nights in way stations. The first station was one big room with wooden bunks built into the walls and long candlelit tables down the middle. The drivers, Mongols and Russians, mingled genially; they all seemed to know one another and they certainly knew the "mistress of the inn," whom they pestered with complaints and advances while she fired up the samovar. Supper passed noisily, vodka washing away the stress of the day for both drivers and driven. When it was over, Andrei begged a goat skin from the mistress to soften the boards of my bunk and I laid me down with a blissful sigh and slept as soundly as the most inebriate of my companions.

It was freezing cold when we woke up in the morning, and what did I see on stepping outdoors but the drivers warming up their engines by building bonfires under them—yea, verily, bonfires under oil cisterns.

On the third day we emerged from the mountains to see Ulan Bator spread out on the plain below us. The city where Genghis Khan had his beginning lay rimmed by hills, looking like a scattering of cornflakes on a green plate. As we drew nearer we could distinguish the pagoda roofs of a Buddhist monastery rising, but not very high, out of the center of the plate. All the other structures clung to the earth and were made of felt, logs, or adobe. The felt ones were yurts, the log ones were houses such as could be seen in any Siberian village, the adobe ones were clustered together in what Andrei pointed out as the Chinese quarter.

Our truck pulled up in a cloud of dust on the big unpaved central square where a group of lamas were squatting and chatting while from under their saffron robes trickled little streams that were quickly absorbed into the dust.

"Welcome to Mongolia," said Andrei, giving my arm a little squeeze as he guided me around the lamas and into a labyrinth of lanes lined with palisades hiding dwellings on the other side of them. The lanes were jointed like a carpenter's rule, so that you kept turning corners and confronting a haughty camel swaying toward you or one of the shaggy wild dogs that, Andrei explained, were the town's scavengers and devourers of the dead, whose remains were not buried but deposited on a hillside a little distance from the city.

At one point Andrei stopped and opened a gate in the palisade. "Enter," he invited. I entered a yard with a square wooden house at the far end, a one-room log cabin in the foreground, and in between, the flower garden Andrei planted wherever he lived if for but two summer months.

Fenya was the first person I met in Mongolia. There she stood in the doorway of the larger house to greet us, her hands locked underneath her apron, a tense smile on her seamy brown face, a timid look in her black oriental eyes. What would life become now that this strange woman, this *Amerikanka*, had come to live in a house which for the past four years she alone had run for Andrei, his brother Dmitri, and Dmitri's nine-year-old daughter Vyeta?

"Here she is, Fenya," said Andrei as to one familiar with his private life, adding the Russian saying, "*Proshu lyubit' i uvazhat',*" which is to say, "Please to love and respect her."

Fenya said nothing, just stood there smiling and bobbing and clutching her hands under her apron, and as soon as she decently could she returned to the kitchen where wood was blazing in the big stove to supply us with the comfort of hot water and the sustenance of hot food such as we had not enjoyed since we left the train at Ulan-Ude.

"Yes, here you are," said Andrei triumphantly when we were alone in the room. I resented the triumph. He did not know how deep a sense of injury I had nurtured the past year. The doubts, the sleepless nights. It all came back to me when I stepped into this room—the room he must have shared with Alla.

"Why wasn't it last year?" I asked, challenging him with a bold look that disguised the dread in my heart. He was taken aback by the tone and the look. He waited before answering.

"I couldn't bring you here last year. Neither the Mongolian nor the Soviet government would allow me to."

The simplicity with which he said it made my apprehensions seem foolish.

"Mongolia has never been such a closed country as now," he went on. "The Japanese are after it. No foreigners are admitted."

"Oh," I said.

He caught the note of relief in my voice. His own voice became mildly apologetic. "What did you think?" he asked with his crooked smile.

"Oh, nothing, I just . . ." The color that crept up to my hair roots gave me away.

"Margarita," he said reproachfully.

I was chastened. "I'm sorry."

His eyes burned into mine for a moment as if to cauterize wounds that might fester in my brain. No need; I was at ease now.

"The Japanese," I said, picking up the conversation, "I thought that matter was settled in 1921."

"Far from it. They're on the rampage. They've taken Manchuria and now they're determined to get Mongolia. The tussle between Russia and Japan to get it has been going on for years. Long before Outer Mongolia became the Mongolian People's Republic it was under Chinese suzerainty; even then Japan and Russia were fighting for it. It's strategically located, you know. You can bet they didn't want a third country joining in the tussle. So they kept all foreigners out."

"They let in the Americans in the twenties."

"The dinosaur expedition?"

"Yes. I looked it up after Robert reminded me of it."

"That was after the Russians had taken over—the Soviet Russians."

"And they too have clamped down on foreigners?"

"More than anybody else ever did. The country is positively air-tight now."

"Oh, Andrei, why couldn't you have explained all this to me in Moscow? I would have understood."

"I don't doubt that you would, but . . ."

"But what?"

He took a little turn about the room, chin up, hands clasped behind his back, before he came to a halt directly in front of me. "Everything about Mongolia is top secret," he said with such quiet emphasis that I let the weight of it sink in before answering.

"And you were afraid I might let secrets out?"

"Not intentionally. Inadvertently, perhaps."

So he had had doubts about me, too. Seeing me cringe, he added, "It could have been fatal for us both, Margarita."

"It caused me a lot of pain," I said.

"It caused me even more." He put his hands on my shoulders. "I fought hard to get you here. In the end I said, 'Either she comes or I go.' And here you are."

MY ARRIVAL WAS NOT CELEBRATED by either Vyeta or Dmitri. Vyeta came home late from school, and after giving me a mildly amused look and a perfunctory greeting, joined Fenya in the kitchen.

Vyeta was not an ordinary child. She could hardly be expected to be ordinary, raised as she was in no ordinary family and transplanted to no ordinary country. Nor was she endowed with an ordinary character. She was by nature peculiarly suited to the Mongolian scene, its freedom, its spaces, its wild life. Vyeta herself looked like a wild creature. Her body was lean, almost scrawny, as if she hunted her food. Her hair was unkempt. Her covering was unshapely, a loose cotton shift. When she wasn't at school she was wandering over the steppe or through the jointed lanes with a string of wild dogs behind her that she charmed as the Pied Piper charmed the rats. Most residents filled their pockets with stones against the dogs; Vyeta made friends of them. She had inherited her mother Sonya's long gray eyes. Perhaps it was the drawing power of those eyes that made it impossible for Dmitri to part with Vyeta as he had had to part with Sonya. He had brought his daughter here against Sonya's wishes, and her objections had not been groundless: Dmitri's responsibilities as supervisor of the construction of Mongolia's first power plant left him no time to supervise his daughter's upbringing. Luckily for Vyeta this was left to Fenya.

As it turned out, there was a more important reason why Vyeta's being in Mongolia was lucky for her. Just before Andrei and I left Moscow Georgi, Sonya's present husband, had been arrested. The only crime that could be laid to his door was that he held an idealistic world view inimical to Marxist materialism, a view shared by a group of friends including Andrei and Dmitri.

Andrei and I went to see Sonya before we left Moscow to give her the money Dmitri had sent to tide her over this difficult period. We found her in one of Moscow's old apartment houses. She was sitting in an armchair holding her newborn son, Arseni. In a far corner sat Yuri, her thirteen-year-old son by a first marriage. The eye was caught by the elegance of the room, its high ceiling, long windows, elaborate cornice and parquet floor. The only prominent piece of furniture was a grand piano. Everything was clean and quiet. Most quiet was Sonya. Her gray eyes lost none of their tranquility as she told us how "they" had come in the night and taken Georgi away and how, already in prison, he had tried to take his own life. No, she did not know how long he would be kept in prison before being sent to a labor camp. What would she do? She would gladly give music lessons (she was a pianist by profession) but it was doubtful any parent would entrust a child to her, wife of an Enemy of the People. In time she found that no parent would. When all other efforts to get work failed she became a postwoman, carrying heavy sacks of mail on her frail shoulders.

On the day of our arrival in Ulan Bator Dmitri came home from the construction site as late as usual. We all had tea together and he tried to make me feel at home by pressing Fenya's *pirog* on me. I don't know whether he approved of me or not, but he certainly did not feel at ease in my company. Not then or ever, really.

Fenya soon relaxed. Her initial fears proved groundless; nothing changed in the running of the house after I got there, I had not the slightest wish to run it, I was going to write a book about Mongolia. (I did write it and it was not passed by the Soviet censor. I kept the manuscript on a Moscow shelf for years in the hope that changing times would change censorship, but when we returned home after being in evacuation for the first two years of World War II, the manuscript was gone. Probably it had been used to fuel one of those little tin stoves, which were the only source of domestic heat during those years. The few people who remained in Moscow after September 1941 were urged by the government to concentrate in vacated homes to simplify servicing. I knew the neighbors who moved into our apartment but I never mentioned to them the missing manuscript or other missing papers and books. It was a fearful war, as the reader will see when we get to it. Everyone survived as best he could.) Fenya and I became friends. Vyeta and I did not. Vyeta rejected me. I was more than a foreigner, I was a foreign body in her world. She shrank from being associated with the gossip about me that had spread through the small Russian colony in anticipation of my coming. I wanted to be her friend but one of my first overtures: "Let's go to market together," filled her with dismay. After a pause in which her unwillingness to hurt my feelings battled with her disinclination to be seen with me, she came up with an ingenious solution: "Let's, but you go this way and I'll go that and we'll see who gets there first."

Fenya and I were alone most of the day because Andrei was busy staging a pageant for the summer festival of Nadom. I had plenty of time to explore my new environment, to wander about peering and sniffing and pricking up my ears.

Early in the morning a furry brown booming came from the monastery at the far side of the central square and hung vibrating in the air, muted by the immenseness of these spaces as colors were tempered by the blueness of these skies. I wondered what could make such a sound, for no instrument I was acquainted with could produce such depth and volume. I went to the monastery in the hope of finding out, but the sound was not repeated while I was there. I heard only the tinkling of temple bells and the whirring of prayer wheels set in motion by pious old women crawling on hands and knees around all four walls of the monastery to move the Ineffable One by the staggering sum of the prayers spun out by the wheels encircling the site.

I never missed an opportunity to go to market with Fenya. We didn't walk, we ran. Fenya's feet flashed under her voluminous skirts as if trying to catch up with her head, which always led the way. When we got there I would leave her to the Mongolian vendors of mutton and the Chinese vendors of vegetables while I went to browse in the little lane called *zakhadir* where Chinese merchants sat in the shadowy depths of tiny stalls exhibiting a jumble of wares: hammers hobnobbed with little brass Buddhas, an unaccountable pack of Lucky Strikes glanced out from under a bolt of Chinese silk cushioning a string of semiprecious beads and a paper of sewing machine needles.

Often I found almond-eyed neighbors staring at my loafers as at something as exotic for them as their robes, called *dels*, were for me. Very beautiful they were, these bright-colored *dels* with long kimono sleeves reaching below the hands and with ample folds held in at the waist by yards of gauzy Chinese silk wound tightly round and round, the girdles as bright as the robes but invariably of contrasting color. It was as if an artist had decreed what the Mongols should wear, for Mongolian horsemen against the background of the gray-green steppe and tawny hills supplied just the splashes of color an artist would seek. Once when I was engrossed in the examination of a jade pendant, I felt someone breathing on the back of my neck. I turned around to find myself looking into a camel's hooded eyes shadowed by whisk-broom lashes. Through the loop of its neck I caught sight of Fenya staring at me. She gave the beast a whack on the rump that made it turn majestically and meander down the lane. Then she pointed to the bulging sack on her back to let me know it was time to go home. She never bought anything for herself but the mordant weed called *makhorka* that Russian peasants smoke.

Although Fenya and I spent a lot of time together we didn't talk much. This was not because of the language barrier; my Russian was pretty good by this time and Russian was her native tongue. She came from Buryat Mongolia (the land north of Outer Mongolia where we had left the train to continue to Outer Mongolia), which has belonged to Russia for centuries. Even Fenya's name was Russian, as were all her habits. The thing that kept us from communicating was, I think, a native taciturnity. But taciturnity suggests sullenness, and Fenya was never sullen. Rather it was an inordinate modesty that made her shrink from sharing confidences and talking about matters that concerned her alone.

I, on the other hand, was inordinately inquisitive. How could you live so close to a person and know so little about her? She was with us twenty-four hours a day, washing clothes, scrubbing floors, chopping wood, making fires, an incessant round that put knots in her fingers, and muscles in arms that looked as if carved out of mahogany.

Often of a morning she and I would take time out to sit on the doorstep and watch Andrei's flowers grow. Thank goodness Andrei had flowers as a hobby; in the troubles of later years his wildflower garden in a Moscow suburb was a saving preoccupation. As Fenya and I sat there on the step I tried to satisfy my curiosity about her.

"Don't you ever get homesick, Fenya?"

"Homesick for what?"

"Well, you do come from Ulan-Ude, don't you?"

"I do." She reached in her apron pocket for a scrap of newspaper from which she made a "goat's leg," the same sort of "goat's leg" the *muzhiks* were smoking in the local train that took us to our Ukrainian honeymoon. When she was happily drawing on her paper pipe, I began again.

"You must have relatives back there, don't you?"

"I do."

"A husband?"

"No husband."

"Never had one?"

"I had one."

She turned with such concentration to the repairing of her pipe, which was coming uncoiled at the mouthpiece, that I knew I was treading on forbidden ground. So we just sat there watching the flowers until her pipe was smoked out, when she threw the remains down on the hard ground beside the step, spat on it to extinguish the sparks, and ground her spittle into the dust with her heel.

Another time I had the temerity to ask if she had children, to which she replied "No children." And that was as much as I ever learned about Fenya's private life.

It was a pity she had never had children. I admired her way with Vyeta. She neither coddled nor bossed her, just took care of her as naturally as a tree with a bush growing beside it shelters the bush from the sun with its shade and from the rain with its boughs. There were none of the statutory oughts and ought-nots usually laid down by guardians. I, whose upbringing had left me riddled with rules, admired her freedom from them. This was a woman I would choose to help bring up the children Andrei and I were sure to have. If only she would go back to Moscow with us in the spring!

"Would you go?" I asked on a Saturday morning while we were sorting out the things we had brought from market. Before answering she characteristically pushed her kerchief back over her left ear (she wore the kerchief like a cap, the ends crossed in back and knotted above her forehead).

"Vyeta?" she asked. "Will she go, too?"

That was fair and so like her. "Not in the spring, Dmitri's contract runs for another two years. You could come with them in two years. Would you do that?" Instead of answering she began ladling hot water out of the tank at the end of the stove into a big soup pot. When she set to work on the mutton, wiping it and cutting off the fat, I gave up.

AUGUST CAME, the month in which the Mongols have held the festival of Nadom from time immemorial. Now that their flocks were fat from summer grazing and the young were old enough to take care of themselves, the herdsmen were free to come from far and near for five days of games on the plain outside of Ulan Bator where the Tola River flows. I was astounded when, on the day before the festivities began, I surveyed the scene. Another city had sprung up. Yurts and tents extended as far as the eye could see, fields had been marked off for wrestling and archery contests, grandstands were provided for important personages and as judges' stands, barrels of free *kumiss* (mare's milk) placed everywhere to quench the thirst of onlookers, fireplaces built for the roasting of mutton, and for the first time an outdoor stage had been put up.

Andrei and Vyeta and I moved out to the grounds and lived in a yurt. Every day we attended the games. I found the wrestling matches—hundreds of them—the most picturesque. The wrestlers were naked but for a loincloth, tooled boots, and embroidered sleeves held on by a band across the back of the neck. They leaped in pairs onto the field with hoarse cries, with outstretched arms and flapping hands in imitation of the eagle's flight. Having thrown their opponents, the winners resumed their role of eagles and "flew" to the judges' stand to receive their reward of a handful of cakes, some of which they threw on the ground as an oblation to the earth from which came their strength; the rest they tossed to the crowd.

The horse races were less picturesque but also unique. Where else could you find hundreds of horses with little children as jockeys, some so small they had to be tied on, setting out in clouds of dust on a cross-country race covering many miles of rough terrain? This could only take place in a land where a baby leaves the cradle for the saddle, where the people walk clumsily on their legs but are centaurs on horseback, and where the women gallop away in heavy horned head-dresses branching far out over their shoulders.

The archery contests were made colorful by the costumes of the archers and their richly ornamented bows. Each archer was allowed a certain amount of shots, the last one being without considered aim, the archer swinging around from a back-to-target position and shooting instantaneously. Songs instead of cheers greeted a bull's-eye hit, or what would have been a bull's-eye on our targets instead of the honeycomb of little leather cylinders shot at by Mongolian archers.

The theater was a novelty at Nadom. The pageant it presented this year was geared to the scale of the steppe. The scenery was natural scenery and the actors rode their horses through the audience up onto the stage. The first tier of viewers sat on the ground, the second stood behind them, the third were on horseback. With the trepidation of American teenagers watching a western, they followed the melodramatic story of the abduction of the heroine by a nobleman and her rescue in the nick of time by a revolutionary lover.

Nadom came to an end without mishap except for a fire in our yurt which left no serious damage, only singed the edges of my journals. The herdsmen packed up their yurts and tents and rode away and we went back to live in a house.

SUMMER WAS FAST WANING and still no opportunity had arisen to do what I had most wanted to do on coming to Mongolia: visit the Gobi Desert. And then one day Andrei announced that that was precisely what we were going to do. We had been invited to join two Leningrad filmmakers who had come to Mongolia to make a documentary about the Gobi. In addition to these two, the party was to consist of Andrei's best friend in Mongolia, a professor from Leningrad's Oriental Institute who with his wife Nina had been living in Ulan Bator for several years. His name was Mikhail Israelovich Tubiansky, and he was taking with him not only Nina but two lamas of his acquaintance. In addition, there were Boris, who was to drive the truck, and Vasya, handyman and guide.

The morning of our departure dawned fiercely bright, as do most Mongolian mornings. But Dmitri took leave of us before the break of day.

"Have a good time," he called out as he climbed in beside the Mongol driver of a decrepit car that regularly took him out to the building site at this unearthly hour.

Later, Fenya and Vyeta stood on the doorstep seeing Andrei and me through the yard to the waiting truck whose passengers rearranged themselves on duffles, packing cases, and folded tents to make room for us.

Gaily we sailed away as in a tossing galleon on an emerald sea dappled with the whitecaps of grazing sheep and the little brown boats of darting horses under the colorful sails of their riders' *dels*.

We headed in a westerly direction, for our first big stop was to be Erdeni-Dzu, Mongolia's oldest and biggest lamasery. On the way we camped for the night wherever the setting recommended itself. The first night it was on the banks of the Tola River, with mountains sheltering our backs and the steppe rolling away like the ocean in front of us. The men fished for our supper and Nina and I made their catch into chowder. Mongolian rivers teem with delicious fish that live out their lives undisturbed unless by intruders like us, for fish is to the Mongol what pork is to the Hebrew. So the lamas ate their bread and cheese while we—especially Andrei, who always chose fish—feasted on Nina's and my incomparable chowder. After supper we sat around the fire until the cold drove us into our tents.

We set out again early the next morning and kept going until afternoon, when we stopped at a little settlement of yurts. Children ran excitedly to surround and examine our truck, their elders came out of the yurts to greet us.

"*Sain bainu*," was their salutation.

"*Sain bainu*," we returned.

We treated the children to candy, their elders treated us to *kumiss* from the skin that hangs on the inside doorpost of every yurt. In this skin, constantly replenished, the mare's milk ferments slightly, acquiring the tang that makes it so delicious.

Refreshed by the *kumiss* and glad to be on our feet after so much cramped riding, we wandered about the steppe, saw cheese and thick cream set out in slabs on the roofs of the yurts to dry, saw camels browsing, saw a man on horseback wielding a long pole with a noose at one end as a lasso to round up horses, saw an old woman with a basket on her back scooping up fresh *argal* (dung) with a long wooden fork and tossing it deftly into the basket to be taken home and dried for fuel. And these little boys and girls in miniature *dels* and with amulets hanging around their necks, chasing dogs across the plain or throwing fluffs of camels' hair into the wind to see how far it would fly—did they look upon such shriveled hags as witches or as beloved grannies?

Later we were invited into one of the yurts and seated around a cold hearth for the evening meal, which consisted of cold mutton from which we all hacked off a chunk, then set our molars the hard task of grinding it up—the sheep's meat was of the same consistency as its hide. The mutton was followed by tea.

A nudge from Andrei reminded me of the rule never to drink out of any vessel but the little bowl I always carried with me. Later, when I was deathly ill, Andrei insisted that at some point I had broken the rule. I doubt it. I never drank Mongolian tea after the first time. It was the most abominable potion I ever had the imprudence to take into my mouth. It was tea, certainly—green brick tea—with salt and mutton fat added and flavored with dung smoke.

Toward the end of the meal we heard a horse gallop up and a voice call out, "*Sain bainu*!" Our hostess went out (and we in her wake) to greet a most rare and engaging visitor. He was a smiling old man with a scraggly beard and wearing a pointed hat perched jauntily over one ear. On his back he carried a *moren-hur* (Mongolian equivalent of a cello), which he handed to our hostess before he dismounted. People from other yurts had heard or seen him arrive and they came flocking around. This was precisely what he wanted—an audience, for he was a bard, a troubadour, stepping graciously out of the Middle Ages for our entertainment. He chuckled and gurgled as the nomads made much of him, brought him *kumiss* and meat, laughed at his jokes, petted him affectionately.

In due time he took up his *moren-hur*, squatted down on one knee, and sang a song. It was, said Tubiansky, about the beautiful wife of a Mongolian prince whom Genghis Khan abducted. So bitterly did she pine for her spouse that she ran away and made a hill for herself to hide behind on the banks of the Yellow River. When she was discovered she threw herself into its waters. The Mongols have called this river Hatun-Gol, or Lady River, ever since.

He sang many other songs, and when he finished he was led away to one of the yurts for the night. So fine was the weather that we made our beds under the stars without bothering to pitch tents.

The next day we arrived at Erdeni-Dzu. That is, we reached that spot on the Orkhon River where, on the opposite bank, the temples and innumerable yurts of the lamasery were spread. Here it was that an incarnate Buddha, a *hutuktu*, second in rank only to the Bogdo Gegen of Urga, had his seat. Thanks to Tubiansky's friendship with the lamas we were to be given an audience with the *hutuktu*.

We fell asleep that night with the cries of jackals in our ears. It was not they, however, that woke me up in the morning; it was the furry brown booming I had heard in Ulan Bator and been unable to identify. I quickly sprang up and ran to the river, from which direction the sound was coming, and there, on the high opposite bank, I saw a picture that will remain with me as long as mind remains. It was an aquarelle, with great swaths of green, blue, and beige as a background against which moved a procession of lamas in yellow robes and red togas, the whole washed in the golden light of early morning. At the head of the procession went enormous horns, perhaps ten feet long, each borne by two monks, one at either end, and from these horns issued the deep sound that had puzzled me: *ommm, ommm, ommm*. There were bells, too, flashing about the horns like satellite fish about whales. Slowly the procession approached the riverbank, then turned and went back, still ommming, still tinkling, vanishing at last behind temple walls. As I watched, entranced, I was aware that Andrei had joined me. I looked into his face. It showed possessive pride, as if he had conjured up this vision and was offering it to me as his gift, his surprise. Gradually the golden light pouring out of the sky spread and intensified and seemed to draw everything up into it. The gleaming riverwater became one with the gleaming light, the yurts and temples of the lamasery rose in shimmering waves to join it, the green of the steppe turned to gold and the burnished hills dissolved in the blaze. All things melted and merged, leaving nothing but this all-embracing, all-effacing, singleness of light. Ommm.

WHEN THE MOOD PASSED, Andrei and I turned back and woke up our companions. Tea was our main concern; we must be drinking our own before our Mongolian neighbors invited us to drink theirs. During breakfast a messenger came from the lamasery to say that horses were being sent to take us over the river, there being no bridge. This was alarming news. How was I, with no equestrian skills, to cross a good-sized river on a spirited charger fitted with a narrow wooden saddle turned up sharply behind and before? Somehow I mounted and off we went—plop! plop! Surprisingly, I did not fall off until we reached the opposite shore, when my little horse shook me off along with the wet.

We were met by a delegation of lamas who took us to the large yurt reserved for our use. We had to bend to enter, but the domed roof enabled us to walk about inside at full height. Indeed it was very roomy, and now, when the days were still scorching and the nights freezing, we learned what excellent protection a yurt offers from both heat and cold.

While Tubiansky spent his days in consultation with the leading lights of this lamasery (who, he assured us, were accomplished scholars engaged in the exegesis of Buddhist writings), Andrei, Nina, and I joined the filmmakers on excursions into the countryside. The most notable one was to Karakorum.

If any credence can be attributed to Coleridge's fantasies unleashed by opium from the unconscious, the Xanadu of his poem can be interpreted to be Karakorum, for it was there that Genghis Khan's grandson built his extravagant capital, using carpenters, stone masons, artists, and goldsmiths brought back with him to Mongolia from Persia, Italy, and other countries of the West subdued by the Golden Horde.

It was from Karakorum that most of the civilized world was ruled at the beginning of the thirteenth century, but by the middle of it Kublai Khan abandoned the palace at Karakorum and shifted the capital of the Mongolian Empire to Peking, inaugurating the Yuan Dynasty. A little over a hundred years later, after the Chinese had put an end to Mongolian rule, the Ming Emperor Chu Yuan-chang invaded Mongolia and razed Karakorum to the ground. What Chu Yuan-chang began was carried to perfection by seven centuries of winds and rains and the blazing sun of Mongolia.

Without a guide we should never have found the site. It was betrayed by no protuberance on the face of the steppe except a big stone turtle with a hollow in its back suggesting it was once the pedestal of a stone pillar. Now this handsome turtle stands in eloquent solitude in the silence of the steppe.

OUR JOURNEY became an ordeal for me on the fifth and last day of our visit. On that day we set off, still in a westerly direction, for Tsetserlik, the administrative center of this *aimak* (district). On the way our truck foundered in a bog at the edge of a stream we were about to ford. After some wheelspinning that caused the truck to sink up to the hubs, we all got out to help extricate it. Foresight had provided us with boards to be used in such an emergency, but the boards had to be gotten out from under the mountain of baggage in the back of the car, and stones had to be brought to lay the boards on. The men took off their shoes, rolled up their trousers, and set to work. Four men: Boris, Vasya, and the two filmmakers. Not Tubiansky and Andrei. Tubiansky and Andrei withdrew to a grassy knoll where they paced up and down talking philosophy while the navvies toiled. For an hour. An hour and a half. I brought stones. I kept glancing in Andrei's direction. Tubiansky, poor soul, could be of no use with his great head, flabby muscles, myopic eyes, and protuberant belly. But Andrei? Andrei was a fine specimen. How could he not lend a hand in a situation like this? I despised Andrei.

The truck was extricated, the patricians came down off their knoll, and we proceeded on our way to Tsetserlik. The ride over rough ground nauseated me. I took no pleasure in the scenery. Nina tried to engage me in conversation. I wished she would let me alone.

When we got to Tsetserlik, thoroughly exhausted, we were given hard beds in an administration building. I woke up the next morning aching all over. Andrei wondered at me. Was I well? Yes. We left Tsetserlik and turned south toward Gobi. We had to cross a spur of the Hangai Mountains. The air was bitterly cold and there was very little of it at so high an altitude. As we climbed the vertical face of a cliff, the motor sputtered and threatened to die. There was a split second of suspense. Of suspension. Hanging on the brink. The gears held. We reached the top.

We got out and donned fur coats like the shaggy coats the grazing yaks were wearing. We had a picnic lunch but I could not eat. I felt sick. I dreaded the descent.

"What's the matter with you?" Andrei asked.

"Nothing," I said.

The descent was dreadful. I cowered in a corner and shut my eyes. When we were out of the mountains we drove steadily south over the steppe toward Gobi. The heat was worse than the cold on the mountaintop.

"There *is* something the matter with you," said Andrei. "You don't eat."

"I can't eat," I said.

"Is it . . . ? Could it be . . . ?"

"It could."

We stopped at yurts as usual and Andrei boiled milk over *argal* fires to keep me from starving, but I couldn't drink it. I was so sick that nothing in the world existed but my sickness. Andrei was frightened.

"Do you think we ought to turn back?" he asked me.

"Can we?"

"If we must. But you wanted so badly to see Gobi."

"No longer."

"You feel that bad?"

"Worse."

"Then we must go back."

Nina and Tubiansky agreed with him, but one of the filmmakers said no, they had come all the way from Leningrad for this expedition and we would have to go on. He said it crisply, as if getting back at Andrei for pacing on the knoll when they were sweating in the mire.

We went on until a tire blew out. While Boris and Vasya were changing it, I suffocated under a yak skin to protect myself from clouds of insects that bit my face, crawled into my eyes and nose, and made excursions under my collar. The other filmmaker caught sight of me when Andrei lifted the skin to give me some water. He said nothing to Andrei, but when the tire was changed he told Boris to turn the truck around, we were going back to Ulan Bator.

We got there on an evening in September during one of those immense Mongolian downpours. Fenya opened the door to us. She said nothing, but her face grew tense, her movements swift. She undressed me and put me to bed. For three months.

It was typhoid fever *and* pregnancy.

The morning after we got back I opened my eyes to find an old man with a long white beard bending over me and holding my wrist. He was Dr. Shastin, a legendary figure in Mongolia; his name had become synonymous for a Western doctor as contrasted with a Tibetan *emchi* ("Have you seen a *shastin* about that sore?"). His was the quiet rather than the jovial bedside manner. He made great use of his stethoscope, listening to front and back and right and left, once, and again, and still another time, and he thoughtfully explored my body's hills and valleys, confirming the supposition Andrei had advanced.

"This," he said, turning to a woman standing in the background, "is Maria Petrovna. She's a nurse from our hospital and she's going to help us get you out of this."

As he packed his bag she unpacked hers, taking out an array of formidable-looking instruments. She turned her head to give me a big smile. "If anyone can do it, Dr. Shastin can," she chirped. I didn't like the if-clause.

When the doctor was gone, she came over and put her hand on my forehead. Then she picked up something that looked like big wooden pliers.

"That woman who works for you—what's her name?"

"Fenya."

"That's it, Fenya. I met her earlier this morning. Where could I find her?"

"In the kitchen, I guess. Or out in the yard."

Maria Petrovna went out of the room and came back in five minutes with Fenya carrying a pail of hot water and a sheet of oilcloth. Maria Petrovna opened my womb with the wooden pliers.

This was the beginning of ministrations that went on and on, the worst of them being the puncturing of my flesh with needles as blunt as a pig's snout, squirting camphor into my bloodstream that saturated my body, my nostrils, my tastebuds.

Now that the typhoid bugs had me flat on my back, they indulged in a Bacchanalia, an orgy of pullulation. No typhoid shot had supplied me with cohorts to range against them. They grew and multiplied unopposed, and they drank my blood, and they fed on my flesh, and in the furnace of my womb they killed the child evolving there. I knew they wouldn't win the fight. I was strong, I could stand up to them. Andrei knew it too, at least he gave me no reason to think otherwise. He never showed a long face, he was even jocular on occasion. "What? Lost your hankie again? The only item in your inventory and you can't hang onto it!"

Now Fenya had two households to take care of, for my room was a world apart, with special demands of laundering, scrubbing, fetching, and disinfecting. All day long I could hear her pattering about on little mice feet, as quick and silent as a mouse with eyes as black and shiny as a mouse's. She took pains to muffle the clash of pots and pans, the banging of doors. This annoyed me, as did the frightened look in her eyes whenever she glanced in my direction.

I felt the natural antipathy of the robust to sickrooms and everything associated with them: bedpans, feeding cups, tiptoeing, darkened windows. "Oh, come on, Fenya, I'll be all right. Just give me time." She'd just smile in her timid way and push her kerchief behind her left ear. All means available in Ulan Bator were mustered to help me, and

Moscow friends pitched in, too. An American correspondent of my acquaintance sent me a Simmons bed to replace the hard wooden slats I was lying on, and a Frigidaire to supply me with ice. But most important was Dr. Chalatov, the physician who had cured me of a rash the previous winter when I was in Moscow and Andrei in Mongolia. As soon as I realized how ill I was I wired him for help. His response was immediate. Fenya signed for his return wire and brought it to me. It read, "Ferrus 0.02 three times a day."

"Give it to Andrei the minute he comes home," I said.

When Andrei entered the room, I remarked no momentous change of expression on his face.

"Did Fenya give you the telegram?" I asked.

"What telegram?"

"From Dr. Chalatov."

"Chalatov?" he repeated with a frown.

Andrei didn't like Dr. Chalatov, who had been my friend as well as my physician that winter. He had taken me to the Bolshoi to hear *Khovanshina* and to a Georgian restaurant to taste that country's spicy cooking. I had wanted Andrei to meet him when he got back to Moscow, but he refused to do so.

"But he's an old man," I had expostulated, flattering myself by thinking Andrei was jealous. "At least sixty. And he took me to his home to meet his wife. She gave me and some other foreigners a wonderful Russian meal."

"Some other foreigners?"

"Four of us."

Andrei had liked this least of all. Later, years later, I was to understand that Andrei's dislike of Chalatov sprang from a cause more dread than jealousy.

At the present moment I was too intent on getting well to care about Andrei's opinion of Dr. Chalatov.

"Fenya has it," I insisted.

"Has what?"

"The telegram. With a prescription that will cure me." Andrei looked nonplussed.

I was impatient. "Ask Fenya for it. Don't lose any time. Have it filled at once."

"Fenya said nothing to me about a telegram."

"You've seen her?"

"Yes."

"And she didn't . . . ?" Oh, this was too cruel. "Call her," I said sharply.

It was a little time before he came back with Fenya looking like a cornered mouse.

"Where's the telegram?" I demanded.

"What telegram, dear?"

"The one from Moscow."

"No telegram from Moscow, dear."

"You brought it to me. I gave it back to you."

"No telegram, dear."

I was speechless. How could she deny it? She was lying. Looking me straight in the eye and lying. I had been most bitterly deceived in Fenya. Now as she cowered at the foot of my bed, clutching her hands under her apron, I saw the malice in her slanting eyes and noticed for the first time how ugly her left ear looked sticking out from under her kerchief.

"You'd better go, Fenya," said Andrei. The gentleness of his tone wounded me more than her lying.

"You believe her?" I asked when she had left. "Her and not me?"

He came over to the bed and leaned down to put his lips on my forehead the way mothers do to test their children's temperature. I brushed him away and turned my face to the wall.

I kept my head turned to the wall, or rather to the window in the wall, most of those long autumn months. The little square framed a picture of weeds growing out of the cracks in the roof of the adobe house next door. If offered me my only view of the change of seasons. In September the weeds were strong and supple, they bowed gracefully under the wind's cuffings, holding tight to their seed and easily regaining their stance. Under the winds of October they turned brown and stiff and scattered their seed. By early November they were rigid with age and hoary with frost. As they lost vigor I gained it. Quietly I lay, feeling the buoyance of the incoming tide, waiting for it to deliver me on to solid ground.

Solid ground? Was there any? That was the matter that occupied my mind throughout those days of waiting. I had plenty of time to ruminate on what had happened to me, and a most uncanny thing had happened. I had crossed over and back between two worlds, the real world and the dream world. But why was *that* world dream and *this* one real? The telegram I had held in my hand was as real to me then as the cup I held now. The Simmons bed and the Frigidaire had shared space on this floor with that chair and the stove. Why had *they* vanished and *these* remained? And the pain of Fenya's perfidy (I had accepted it as nothing less) was as acute as the pain of my questioning Andrei's worthiness as he and Tubiansky talked on the knoll while the rest of us worked. There had been no perceptible transition from one world to the other. No lights flashed signaling a crossing. I had moved in one continuous line, one uninterrupted state of being. And all that I had experienced was fabricated by the same brain in different circumstances. What, then, was real? The brain? The circumstances? Nothing? All a dream? Or rather dreams within The Dream? Ah, but that early morning on the banks of the Orkhon River—did not the light transcend the dream?

So I lay watching the weeds and thinking about the nature of reality. Thinking too about Andrei and me.

Twice I had been tormented by doubts of his love and his goodness. My illness dispelled these doubts. If, at the river-crossing, Andrei had displayed a flaw in character, this flaw was like a knot in fine wood, was like those imperfections, those cracks and crinkles in the crust of fresh-baked bread which Marcus Aurelius pointed out as only making the bread more delectable by adding crispness to flavor.

As for Andrei's devotion, I could not doubt it. He spent every hour free from professional duties at my bedside. His steady gaze at the height of the battle assured me I would win it.

"Did you think I would die?" I asked him when it was over.

"Not once," he said with the assurance I found so disarming.

"Dr. Shastin did and the nurse did. They told me so when the danger was over," I said.

"They told me so before it was over, but I didn't believe them."

"Why not?"

"After you had traveled all those miles and I had traveled all those miles to meet each other?"

Came the November day when I heard the front door open and shut and then Andrei was standing in the doorway of my room in coat and cap. "Some cold!" he said.

"I wouldn't know. Fenya stokes this stove like a ship's furnace."

"Shastin says you can sit up in three days if your temperature stays normal."

I made a joyful noise.

"So don't get another relapse," he called from the coatrack.

I was embedded in the thin mattress like a fossil in stone. The only time I had been separated from it was when Maria Petrovna and Fenya had propped me up to crop my hair.

Some weeks later, after Andrei had taken me for my first walk around the table, he told me a grave piece of news. "Kirov has been assassinated."

My reaction was not a fitting one. I did not take in all the awful implications (even though Andrei had prefaced the announcement with the way he had of prefacing bad news by taking a turn about the room, hands clasped behind his back, chin up, lips tight). I knew little about Kirov except that he was head of the Communist Party in Leningrad. "He's the man Stalin is said to have chosen as his successor," Andrei explained.

"Who could have done it?" I asked.

"Trotsky's followers. Zinoviev's name is mentioned."

"But why Kirov?"

"Because his popularity is second only to Stalin's. A great orator. A man of the people."

"How did they do it?"

"Shot him at his desk, they say. That's the most ominous aspect. It means there are enemies on the inside, in high places. It means there is an effective underground organization. It isn't easy to assassinate leaders in our country—not after the attempt on Lenin's life."

An effective underground organization. Sinister words. My American mind associated underground organizations with gangs and gunmen, not with politics. Of course I knew about the underground movement in Czarist Russia, but it was a refined underground led by members of the intelligentsia fighting against tyranny and serfdom. Why would anyone want to overthrow this young state dedicated to the proposition that all men are created equal, with no advantages of wealth to modify the proposition?

Nothing in the Soviet Union had impressed me more than the new attitude toward money. There was not enough of it after the bleeding of the country by war and revolution. Not enough for anybody, so when your money ran out, you asked a friend or neighbor for a loan, and if this person's wages were not yet spent, he or she would give it to you as simply as a housewife lends her neighbor a cup of salt or flour. Because money, like salt and flour, was an essential commodity, nothing more. No one hoarded it; there was no reason to, you knew your wages would be paid every two weeks, that if you were sick there would be no doctor or hospital bills, and that when you were old you would get a pension.

There was, however, no contempt for money, only indifference to it. Psychologically, money had been put in its place. Economically, it had been taken under control. The little that was left to the young republic was circulated regularly and divided equitably. It did not disfigure the body politic by accumulating in big blobs. Was not that the crowning achievement of the twentieth century?

I thought so.

As winter waned I gained strength and Andrei lost it. He slept so much I was alarmed. One afternoon when I found him taking a nap on the couch, I observed in fright the unevenness of his breathing. I felt his pulse. Tick, tick, tick . . . tick, tick . . . tick . . . , tick, tick, tick. Oh, this would not do. This would never do. Ulan Bator's altitude was playing havoc with Andrei's heart; five years of it was an overdose for him.

I began counting the days until we should leave this high plateau. Not only did I want to get Andrei away, but I wanted to get away myself. I was homesick. I wanted to be back in Moscow where only an ocean would separate me from America, where I could get word of family and friends, from whom I had heard nothing since I arrived in Mongolia, and to whom I had sent nothing but two telegrams saying I was alive and well. I intended, moreover, to go home that summer, to visit the States before I resumed my teaching duties at the Foreign Language Institute. Wouldn't I have a lot to tell everybody!

By the end of April I knew I would not go home that summer.

"But are you sure?" Andrei asked when I made the disclosure.

"Dr. Shastin is sure. And I don't want anything to spoil it this time."

So I made a habit of going into the garden early in the morning to get the benefit of ultraviolet rays for myself and the child within me who had come to take the place of the one lost to typhoid. If not yet as fit as ever, I was well on the way to being so. Nothing could further this better than spring sunshine if taken in prudent doses.

On such a morning I was sitting on the doorstep when Fenya came out carrying empty pails to be filled at the water boy's cart outside the gate. The splashing and clanking over, she came back with full pails, set them down, and took her place on the step beside me to enjoy the freshness of the morning.

"Only a month left," I said.

"Only a month," she repeated as she pulled a scrap of newspaper out of her pocket. She screwed up the paper and shook *makhorka* into the "bowl." When the weed was aglow we just sat and "enjoyed" for a while.

"Look, Fenya," I said at last, "remember my asking you last summer if you'd go to Moscow with us in the spring?" She threw me a frightened glance. "No, no," I hastened to add, "Not this spring, in two years when Dmitri and Vyeta go. Will you come to us then?"

She didn't answer. I followed her disconcerted gaze to where an ant was struggling with a twig twice its size. The twig kept catching on little protuberances in the soil. The jolts seemed to cause twinges of pain because the ant would stop and shift its burden every time. I counted five stops-and-starts before it disappeared in a patch of grass. "You won't," I concluded unhappily. Her silence was confirmation.

"Here," I said on a moment's impulse, unfastening the brooch at my collar. "This is yours. It's nothing, of course, except that I love it." It would mean nothing to Fenya to tell her how I had made it myself at a camp where I was counselor for three summers before leaving for Russia. The jewelry counselor had taught me. It was flat silver in the American Indian tradition set with a large turquoise surrounded by little silver balls (amazing how those segments of silver wire squirmed under the blowtorch and whirled themselves into perfect little balls!). Below the turquoise I had innocently etched a swastika, ancient symbol of good luck. When Hitler came to power, I destroyed the symbol by having a Moscow jeweler etch lines connecting the swastika's legs, turning them into four meaningless squares. I pinned it to Fenya's cotton blouse. "You can lose it, sell it, give it away, or just throw it in a drawer and forget it." She smiled and put up her free hand to feel the brooch.

Just then the deep dark early-morning sound filled the air above Ulan Bator's lanes, the dark booming that had so puzzled me when first I heard it. It hovered in still air, waxed and waned when the wind blew. I looked at Fenya.

"Do you know what it is?" I asked.

"I know," she said. Her face was lifted and wore a listening look.

"*Ommm*," said the sound. "*Ommm.*"

ANDREI AND I LEFT Ulan Bator in May 1935, never to return. In the sixties the Mongolian government invited Andrei back on a visit, but the Moscow doctors wouldn't let him go. The irregular ticking of his heart that I had noted with alarm in the thirties had by this time developed into an advanced case of *angina pectoris*. He could not have withstood the high altitude.

Perhaps it is better that we never returned. We would have seen "civilization" making inroads we could not but regret. Our regrets would have been the study in futility undertaken by all who cherish the exotic even though the exotic exists in the modern world at the expense of "progress."

Who is to say which is better, the Mongolia of the thirties or the Mongolia of the nineties? Certainly the elimination of the lamas as a parasite class (40 percent of the population) cannot be lamented. Nor can the introduction of modern medicine, for without it the steady depletion of the population by syphilis would have left no Mongolia at all. Nor can it be a cause of regret that a population basically illiterate has become one basically literate, serviced by its own doctors, lawyers, teachers, diplomats. But it is hard to imagine Ulan Bator reconstructed in the image of a Moscow suburb of cheap prefabricated apartment houses. An article in *The National Geographic Magazine* for February 1984 stated that agriculture has been introduced in this land of flocks and herds, that grain fields stretch mile after mile in an *aimak* near the Soviet border, and that "Soviet-bloc capital and Mongolian labor have built Darhan, a city where the harvests come from mines and factories." It speaks of the "smoke-daubed skyline of Darhan." Those lustrous Mongolian skies smoke-daubed! Further: "If the past lives on the steppe and the future in the city, Mongolians are almost perfectly poised between eras. By official figures half of all Mongolians now live in a town or city."

The picture I carry in my mind of the Mongol flying freely over the steppe, as much a part of his swift little mount as of the vast spaces that have been his habitat since before the days of Genghis Khan, makes it hard for me to envision him as a farmer on the land or a factory worker in the city.

But the greatest shock of all was to learn that ". . . the Gobi has become a tourist attraction. Planes full of tourists fly from Ulan Bator to . . . an international yurt camp in the southern Gobi." The camp supplies the tourists with food and shelter, even plumbing of a sort I presume, and guarantees each sportsman an ibex and a wild sheep as his kill. I have also been told that a sawmill has been built within half a mile of the great stone turtle marking the site of Karakorum.

Last but not least: the closing of the monasteries silenced the great horns saying *ommm, ommm.*

I guess it is just as well that Andrei and I did not revisit Mongolia.

seven

Back to Moscow

Life admits not of delays; when pleasure can be had, it is fit to catch it.

—Dr. Samuel Johnson,
in a letter to Boswell, Sept. 1, 1777

ON RETURNING TO MOSCOW that spring of 1935 Andrei enjoyed a rise in spirits in direct ratio to the drop in altitude. He frequently woke me up in the morning by pacing the floor with his hands clasped behind his back singing scraps of song sadly out of tune, or intoning Virgil's first line, which had served as a voice-training exercise at the Griboyedov Studio: *Arma virumque cano, Troiae qui primus ab oris* . . . (on middle C); *Arma virumque cano* . . . (on E); *Arma virumque cano* . . . (on G). He would hurry me through breakfast to take me for nostalgic strolls along the streets and lanes of Moscow's Arbat quarter (Dog Square, Tablecloth Lane, Bread Lane) where his youth had been spent: "See that building over there? Our studio was on the second floor. And that house with the wrought-iron balcony? That's where we students talked the nights away with nothing in our bellies but weak tea sweetened by the sight of a lump of sugar swinging from the chandelier. . . . And that house next door to it? . . ."

The light in his eyes told me what the studio still meant to Andrei. The years spent there were the most glamorous of his life. He became "First Student"—that is, the one chosen to represent all the others. Among the privileges attending this office was that of calling for Stanislavsky and taking him in a droshky to the classes he taught. Because of these private encounters Andrei enjoyed a more personal relationship with the great director than most of his classmates.

From his glowing account I learned that revolutionary zeal animated all of the students' activities. With their art they defended a cause which their contemporaries were defending on the battlefield, for the revolution soon turned into a civil war that ended only in 1921. The deprivations that came in revolution's wake meant nothing to these young people. They associated comfort and satiety with the bourgeois values they eschewed and were uprooting. Sacrifice was a badge of honor worn proudly. Life at the studio was lived in common. When the young actors found their strength ebbing from undernourishment, one of them would pick up a sack and go off into the countryside on a foraging expedition. Whatever was brought back belonged to all. In the summer they went south together, to the Black Sea, to store up the energy dispensed by sun, sea, and mountain air, for another strenuous winter of training and production.

As representatives of the new society they were dedicated to the highest ideals of service in general and service to the theater as taught by Stanislavsky in particular. The actor's art, according to Stanislavsky, was not one of mimicry but of revelation, and its purpose was to stir men's hearts. The theater was a temple, the actor a celebrant. Such a conception of art imposed stringent ethical demands on those who practiced it, and while the students embraced all the freedoms won by revolution, they did not take advantage of them. If they fell in love they lived together openly, with no need of public vows to impress their responsibilities upon them. But they could have a ceremony of marriage if they wished, even a church ceremony, as Andrei had had when he married Alla.

Horse-drawn carts and carriages passed us on our walks, rarely an automobile. But Moscow was preparing for the automobile age. Its cobblestone streets, which were filing off the soles and nibbling into the uppers of my American shoes (I could replace them with nothing but flimsy sneakers) were being asphalted, and the steep Tverskaya (later Gorky Street) was being graded. The only big buildings on Tverskaya were the Central Telegraph and the National Hotel, which reared like mother hens surrounded by broods of one- and two-story chicks; but a yawning excavation obliquely opposite the National proclaimed that a modern skyscraper of at least fifteen stories was under construction.

There were other changes, too. Food rationing had been abolished and new commodities such as woolen goods were appearing in the stores. (I made myself a suit of fine beige wool to show off when I went to America.) There were even signs of frivolity: a café had been opened on Pushkin Square near our house. A café, mind, with music and dancing! After all these years of austerity! Andrei and I went there almost every evening in the flush of return. In other words, the tide had turned; its ebbing, which had left Russia a bone-bare beach, was over, and the waters were creeping back, bringing with them all sorts of lovely gifts.

Andrei and I had nowhere to live. We were staying with his father, Andrei Nikolayevich, but this could not go on. Residence registration buttoned every Moscow citizen onto a square of living space. Andrei's square had been Alla's apartment, and when he left her he came unbuttoned—not a dire state in those early days, but a fatal one later on, when a person could be expelled from the city in twenty-four hours if it was discovered he had no place to call his own. Andrei and I had none. True, I had joined the cooperative that winter when Andrei had left me with his father, but there were no available apartments. But for Andrei Nikolayevich's sufferance we would be on the street. So it was a great piece of good news when we found out that a stage director and his actress wife who lived in a two-room apartment (not counting the kitchen—kitchens don't count in Russia) on the second floor of our cooperative were leaving for Novosibirsk on a one-year contract, and they would let us live in one of their rooms, locking up their belongings in the other one. What luck! An apartment all to ourselves!—well, not exactly all to ourselves; with our prospective son and fat Sasha, the maid who volunteered to work for us when she quarreled with her mistress across the hall. Sasha would sleep in the kitchen as most maids did in Moscow. An apartment in this house enjoyed the rare advantage of having gas—a gas stove in the kitchen and a gas water heater in the bathroom. Most Muscovites depended on public baths to keep them clean, and oil stoves to cook their food; the kerosene man came around with his cart once a week, stopped his horse on the corner, and blew a horn like Little Boy Blue's to announce his arrival, at which the housewives flew out of their doors with bottles and buckets to line up for refueling.

So a one-year solution of our housing problem had been found. The problem of work was simple. Andrei was invited to join the faculty of the Moscow Theater Institute where he was to create a theater for the Kabardinian Republic in the North Caucasus. He would bring young people of his own selection from this republic to Moscow where they would form a studio and study for five years, then return and open a national theater in Nalchik, capital of the Kabardinian Republic.

As soon as we reached Moscow Andrei renewed his contact with Stanislavsky. At this time the famous director had lost interest in the

Moscow Art Theater, detecting in its activities a reactionary tendency to live on past achievements. He himself, though confined to the house by ill health, worked ceaselessly on his method of preparing actors and stage directors. As his fame grew and his Method exerted ever greater influence on the world stage, he was frightened by the tendency to make hidebound rules out of a body of generalizations he had drawn from life itself and which ought, therefore, to remain as flexible, as subject to change and adaptation as life itself, and to be accepted by practitioners in the exploratory spirit he himself brought to his art.

He had formed a new studio whose members were selected by examining hundreds of applicants, for above all else he deplored the idea that any system could make actors out of clods as some people seemed to imagine. Talent! It was from the most talented—from Duse, from the great Russian actress Yermoleva—that he had gleaned his ideas, and it was to serve the most talented that he had organized them into a system whose sole purpose was to achieve the fullest flowering of talent, to prevent the waste of it, and to induce inspiration, which alone could make a performance great.

From 1935 until Stanislavsky's death in 1938 Andrei was his "telephone pupil," as he is referred to in one of the books on Stanislavsky. The master entrusted to him the leadership of a small group of stage directors with whom he wished to verify his latest ideas. This group met several evenings a week to discuss and work out in practice the suggestions and advice conveyed to Andrei by telephone almost daily and in less frequent consultations at Stanislavsky's house in Leontievsky Lane, now named Stanislavsky Street.

One day after Andrei and I had seen Gorki's *Mother* staged at the Realistic Theater, Tsetnerovich, who directed it, came to see us. He enthusiastically endorsed the innovations of Okhlopkov, founder of this first professional theater-in-the-round.

"You felt it?" Tsetnerovich asked us. "The excitement of the audience? Here were the actors right next to them, walking beside them for their entrances. You could put out a hand and touch them. It helped make the audience feel part of the play. That's one advantage of theater-in-the-round: audience participation. And then there's the new look of it. I noticed this especially at a recent rehearsal. I saw the figures bathed in light on all sides, moving in space, surrounded by air as people are in life, as full statues in contrast to bas reliefs. This is the theater of the future—no doubt about it. Meyerhold thinks so too.

You've seen the plans for his new theater? The stage juts right out into the audience."

When he left I asked Andrei if he agreed with him.

"I agree that anything that adds to the impact of a play is good and is likely to survive, and theater-in-the-round is probably one of these things. But it's a technical innovation like . . . well, no curtain, or ramps and cubes in place of realistic scenery. The actor's the thing for me. The actor's the lord of the stage and anything that helps him is good, and anything that hinders or overshadows him is bad. It's only the actor that can 'sear men's hearts,' as Pushkin said of the poet. And that's what the theater's for as I see it: to sear men's hearts. The theater's a kind of holy trinity, the trinity of playwright, actor, and director. This trinity can work miracles. It can leave the audience speechless, as the Moscow audience was left speechless after the Art Theater's first performance of Chekhov's *Sea Gull*. The actors thought they had failed, so profound was the silence when the curtain fell at the end. Only when the audience woke up to their surroundings did the applause come, and then it rocked the house. Peaks in art like that aren't scaled very often. Sprinting records aren't set very often either, yet that's what runners aim for, what they train for. Who wants to see the theater debased to a mere spectacle? Circuses are spectacles. I love the circus—especially circus performers. If all actors trained as hard as the man on the trapeze, we'd have better performances. But circus and theater are as far apart as beans and caviar. That's why I can't get overexcited about technical innovations. They're not the main thing."

"Perhaps not, but it's only natural that the new theater should want to wear new clothes. You wouldn't want her to look dowdy, would you?"

"No, nor flashy, either. Fact is, I don't suppose I'd notice her clothes if she had something to say."

We didn't have many discussions like this because Andrei was not one to argue. He just went his way and let others go theirs.

His teaching at the Theater Institute began in September, and so did mine at the Foreign Language Institute. I was glad to be back among my colleagues—the phoneticians, the grammarians, the teachers of oral practice. I had no end of admiration for these Russian scholars who, never having heard English spoken in its natural environment since they had no opportunity to go abroad, made research studies of its structure and literature, spoke it impeccably, and taught students to do the same. There was an eminent Leningrad phonetician, Professor Boyanus, whose school trained tongues to just the right position for producing an Oxford accent (an American one was taboo). It was this impeccability and a certain rigidity that branded their speech as non-native. They knew it, and when they held conversation with an Englishman they looked at him with eyes at once apologetic (were they being very inept?) and ravening (for a new word, phrase, intonation).

I discovered a newcomer on our faculty. Shura, who had been commandant of the American Village at Autozavod, had moved to Moscow with her husband and Vova (when I met her husband, I saw where Vova got his splash of eyelashes), and had taken to teaching. Evelyn Rogers, the reserved young lady from New Zealand whose acquaintance I had made in the hotel that first Moscow autumn, had been teaching at the Institute ever since then. With her British accent and her skill as a trained teacher, she had won for herself a position of authority. The few other teachers whose native tongue was English were Americans and, like me, they had to adapt their teaching to the Oxford standard demanded by the English Department. We had to learn the signs for transcribing words according to their sound elements and learn the notation used for recording speech intonation. And we had to learn English grammar in its most recondite form. (Did you know, for instance, that English nouns have five or six cases? Their endings, fortunately, have been worn away by the centuries. That was the trouble [for me] with Russian—none of its case endings have been worn away, one might as well be speaking Latin or ancient Greek.)

Our students were not at all like American college students. They came mostly from the families of peasants and workers, since entrance applications from young people with such backgrounds were given preference. If a young person's antecedents were from the aristocracy or merchant class he had practically no chance at all to receive a higher education. All of my students were Komsomols (Young Communist League members) and most of them were activists who had already made a contribution to the country's needs as members of Literacy Brigades sent to factories and villages to teach older people how to read and write, or of Propaganda Brigades sent to the countryside to urge the peasants to join collective farms. I worked with senior groups. It was my task to develop fluency of speech by making them speak, and in this way I heard many interesting stories about their experiences. I heard about violent opposition to collectivization ending not only in the killing off of cattle (those carcasses I had seen strewn along the

Nizhni Novgorod road?), but in the murdering of people trying to convert the peasants to a new outlook.

My students recalled childhoods spent in villages trampled under the horses' hoofs of opposing bands—today the Whites, tomorrow the Greens, the next day the Reds—each band bringing hope to some, horror to others, hunger to all. Some of the young people in my classes were older than I was, all of them had rich and grim biographies, and all were convinced that their country was building a new civilization in which men would never again know war and poverty. They believed this implicitly, and that is why, for all their deprivations, they were gay and full of cheer. They laughed a lot, laughed at their own ignorance, for the Soviet school system, which had so fascinated Dr. Lucy Wilson, and which I had thought to be the crowning achievement of progressive education, proved to be a dismal failure. And this was only natural. Ravaged, impoverished Russia lacked every element for implementing on a country-wide scale a system like the one I had used at Media High School requiring that students work independently. Where were the armies of highly trained teachers capable of planning and directing such study? Where were the school libraries? Where the textbooks? Where the paper for printing individual plans? Where the mimeographs? Nothing. Nothing but bare rooms, teachers whose main (sometimes only) qualification was that they could read and write, and children who were delighted to be able to do as they pleased. That is exactly what they did do, merrily sailing past anything that looked like organized study.

Now they rued it, and the government rued it even more; had, in fact, put a stop to it in a series of government decrees that reinstated the old-fashioned teacher-pupil relationship with its *be-so-kind-as-to-learn-what-is-required-of-you*. My students were of the earlier vintage, and so they thought that Texas was in South America and Constantinople in the Far East. The discomfort they experienced when exposed pricked them to vigorous effort, for they were a proud lot (were they not citizens of the most progressive country in the world?) and extraordinarily eager to learn (had not Lenin adjured them to "Study, study, and again study"?). The quality, however, that most distinguished them from the American students of my day was their lack of sophistication. They were simple and unaffected in everything, almost childlike in their gratitude for any service rendered, always ready to help one another, always sharing, always seeing that justice was done.

Our students made a positive effort to combat any antisemitism that might have been handed down from prerevolutionary times. One day the following article appeared in the Institute's wall newspaper (a pinned-up sheet that took the place of a college publication):

> A SHAMEFUL OCCURRENCE
>
> What does it mean to be a Komsomol? It means a young person endorses all the principles of the Communist Party, among them the principle that all men are equal regardless of race, religion, nationality, sex. It is impossible for a Komsomol to consider a person inferior because he belongs to a minority group. Such an attitude is a bourgeois hang-over. In czarist times there was the pale, and there were pogroms. And there were despicable individuals who allowed themselves to call Jews by an insulting name. That is what one of our own students has done. She has disgraced herself and the Institute's entire Komsomol organization. We take this opportunity to make whatever amends are possible by publicly acknowledging the offense, reprimanding the offender, and offering our sincere apologies to the one offended.
>
> Komsomol Organization of the
> Moscow Institute of Foreign Languages

I could imagine Annushka's son Jhenya, as Komsomol secretary, writing just such an article for the wall newspaper of his institute. This young prodigy was now in his senior year at an engineering institute, head of his class, head of the institute's Young Communist League, and the youngest of his friends to take unto himself a wife.

The wedding was just a gathering of good friends, mostly classmates, in Jhenya's room, where most of the floor space was taken up by an extended table laden with the food Annushka and Grusha, the old nurse, had baked and boiled for days, out of products set aside by stinting for months. Anatoli was there, sitting darkly uneasy for an hour or two, but as pleased with his son as his son was ecstatic to have him there.

The feast was introduced by a toast to Stalin, a ritual as common in the Soviet Union of those days as the saying of grace before meat in pious American homes. Annushka hovered above the scene, pressing the guests to partake of her famous *pirog* ("This has cabbage filling, this meat") and vinaigrette, and calves'-foot jelly. Toast after toast was drunk, interrupted whenever Jhenya's burly friend Sergei called out the village wedding cry: "Gorky! Gorky!"—which is to say "Bitter! Bitter!"—demanding that the wine be sweetened by having the couple stand up and kiss each other. After one such boisterous ceremony had been gotten through with, a discussion arose as to why Mayakovsky, the foremost poet of the revolution, had committed suicide.

"*Cherchez la femme,*" said one.

"Rubbish, Mayakovsky wouldn't kill himself for a woman," said another.

"Pushkin did."

"A duel isn't exactly suicide."

"Lilly would have saved Mayakovsky if she had been here."

"Why wasn't she here? She shouldn't have gone away just then."

"Oh, shouldn't she? You men still think women ought to flutter around you like nannies. Lilly had her own life to live."

The conversation broadened into a general discussion of the relationship between men and women, men versus women. They turned to me:

"How is it in your country, Margarita? How far have your women come in their fight for equal rights?"

"Not very far I'm afraid. Most Americans still think a woman's place is in the home. I don't think I'd have much chance of keeping my job in the conservative town where I taught if I got married. The chances would be less if I had children, and absolutely nil if I had a child out of wedlock."

These young people, the first generation raised by the revolution, found this last circumstance amusing.

Anatoli had to leave early to catch the night train back to Autozavod. Jhenya and Anna went out into the corridor to see him off while the assembled company shook their heads and clicked their tongues in wonder that a man couldn't even spend a whole evening at his son's wedding. The little dent this made in the festivities straightened itself out as soon as Anna and Jhenya came back. Another round of toasts set off another round of topics for discussions that grew in heat as they were fired by vodka. This in time brought on the lassitude of exhaustion and inebriety and converted talk into the more relaxing diversion of song—mostly Russian folk songs, the jolly ones accompanied by a tapping of feet that would gladly have danced had there been room in this room. A few couples ventured into the corridor, but Annushka was so worried that it might disturb the neighbors that they didn't dance there long.

A pale green morning sky set off the silhouette of Moscow's roofs and onion domes when the party broke up and the young people straggled out into the empty streets of Moscow's Arbat quarter.

IN AUGUST OF THAT YEAR I saw with great joy how simply the Soviet way of life recognized a woman's right to have a child on her own if that was what she wanted. By that time I myself was unmistakably a woman with child. Indeed, the time for me to go on my four months' leave was calculated to begin in the middle of September. I taught for half a month and I attended meetings of the English Department. At the first one, held at the end of August, we were sitting in the dean's office waiting for the meeting to begin, talking of this and that, when in the doorway appeared Evelyn Rogers with an infant in her arms. She stood there smiling, a little embarrassed.

"I had no one to leave her with."

"Oh, Evelyn!"

The men sprang to their feet, the ladies rushed to her; they craned, they cooed, they clucked—She's got your nose, Evelyn; Oh, what a darling! Three months already! A bottle baby? Her name? Irene?—as good in Russian as in English! Smile for us, Irochka! See?—she's smiling.

We were all smiling. Presently Ina Galperin, Head of the Department, came in and warmed her big dark eyes at the baby's face before she seated Evelyn Rogers, who had no husband nor even a nursemaid to leave the baby with, in an armchair in front of her and opened the meeting with greetings to the newborn babe. "Welcome, Irene Rogers. You shall be a member of our Department some day—if your mother has the sense to speak nothing but English to you."

"Not much chance of my speaking anything else, with my Russian," laughed Evelyn. And the meeting went on with everyone in a particularly benign mood.

Now it was my turn to have a baby, which I did very nicely for the first time, without causing anybody undue trouble. It was about seven o'clock of a November evening when I said to Andrei, "I think we'd better be going." So we went, walking down Tverskaya to Leontievsky Lane, up Leontievsky almost to Nikitsky Gates where we rang the doorbell of an unprepossessing brick building with a sign over the door: *In Patients*. The door was opened to us by an attendant in a white smock with her head tied up in a white kerchief, who told Andrei to wait in the hall and led me into an inner chamber where my clothes were exchanged for a coarse nightgown and delivered to Andrei to be taken home and brought back when he called for us—me and our son.

There was no nonsense about having a baby in Moscow in 1935. They just slapped you down on a table with five other expectant mothers on five other tables, the ladies groaning and screaming, nurses and doctors going from one to another to peer, to scold: "Stop it! Shrieking won't help, only waste your strength"; to soothe: "Coming along fine, dear, it'll soon be over, hang on"; to rush to your aid: "This mother needs help, she'll never bring it off alone."

There were no painkillers, you had to go through it as nature has decreed: not a whiff of ether, not a shot in the arm, no, not even when they sewed up your rents. They said it was better for you like that, *au naturel*; I suspect it was just lack of anesthetics.

Mine was a boy, of course. That was what Andrei had wanted and what he was sure we would get. I named him Andrei and we called him Adya to distinguish between father and son. In ten days' time Andrei brought me back my clothes and met me at the unprepossessing door and took the baby out of my arms and now we were three. In another month or so we went to our district ZAGS to register our son's birth and we decided, once we were there, we might as well register our marriage.

Now that Adya had made his entrance into the world, I could again nurture the hope of visiting America. I nurtured it assiduously, night and day, by making arrangements, saving money, tuning my mind to it. I was determined that a hope frustrated first by Mongolia and then by pregnancy should not be frustrated a third time; I would go that very summer of 1936, as soon as my work at the Institute was over, with my eight-month-old baby on my hip.

If only Andrei could go with us! This was my constant thought, and not once did I speak it, and not once did he speak it. This was how it had to be for reasons we accepted, and so neither of us gave vent to useless regrets.

AT THE END OF JUNE Adya and I made a turbulent crossing on the *Ile de France*. The voyage was a six-day ride on a roller coaster. I was deathly sick, but Adya seemed to enjoy it. I decidedly did not. He could have died of starvation for all I cared, and well he might have but for the ministrations of a nursemaid provided by the French Line.

In New York we were met by my father and brother, Dan. How was Mother? Not too well, she hadn't really been herself since that operation in 1932; she was up and about but very weak. My sister, Helen, was running the house. I was also met by some college friends who broke the good news that, knowing I had no money, they had arranged a series of lectures for me—for me, who had looked upon my visit as a longed-for rest! I think they did not notice my chagrin and later I was to be very glad they had done this for me.

We rode from New York to Philadelphia over the new highway that vaults over the heads of towns and cities; we looped off of it from time to time to stop for coffee and hot dogs, and we put nickels in slots for this and that, and I knew, oh so poignantly, that I was back in America. My heart slipped into it like a bolt into its socket. I kept drawing Adya's attention to all sorts of things that must have seemed strange to a Russian, but he went on sucking his thumb complacently, pretending to be unimpressed.

But what were *my* flushes and flutterings about? About being home again? About sitting here with Father at the wheel of his first car and having Esther and Joyce following closely behind us? About being back in my own, my native land? Flushes of patriotism, were they, when I was so sure I gave Dr. Johnson no grounds to call me a scoundrel? I looked upon myself as a citizen of the world capable of living anywhere on earth. I could do that all right. That was one test I had passed with a fairly high mark. What I felt was something different, was what Andrei had felt when he took me through Moscow's Arbat quarter. I was back in the groove I was born into, the groove I had worn deep and had lined with all sorts of colorful patchwork by living in it for twenty-five years. Here was the Delaware River we had crossed to escape the sheriff's sale, and which I had ferried across daily when commuting from Haddonfield to Philadelphia in my first year of college—the Delaware with its thin skin of tomato refuse disgorged by Campbell's Soup Factory on the Camden bank; now we crossed the river by the new bridge that had been opened not long before I left the country. During my freshman year I had, when my classes began late enough, walked up from the river to Thirty-fourth Street instead of taking the El so as to give myself the pleasure, renewed and deepened each time, of crossing Independence Square and seeing Independence Hall sitting so lightly, so unpretentiously, on its brick pavement. The colonial style of architecture does not think of competing with its grand brothers, but its very modesty confers upon it a warmth and intimacy they might well envy. Greek temples do not invite you inside; Gothic cathedrals do, but they overawe; they were made for communion with God, not man; baroque public buildings can be handsome but too heavy for my taste. Modern architecture is a marvel of technique and design, serving but a single purpose: function. Turn from these imposing edifices to the colonial public building. Does not your heart warm to it? Its inviting entrance, the steps not too high, not too wide, leading not to a massive portal but to a paneled door that even an aged hand can open. And the staircase inside, whose curve is like the sweep of an arm waving you up, and the cool rooms to left and right with light falling abundantly on polished floors through windows decoratively broken up into little panes of glass, and the walls, chastely white, unornamented, the better to set off the elegance of line, the richness of material, of a Chippendale chair or a Sheraton sofa.

My walk would take me past the Walnut Street Theater where I had seen Walter Hampden as Cyrano de Bergerac, and George Arliss as Disraeli, and John Barrymore as Hamlet; past the Academy of Music in front of which I had stood in line with fellow students every Saturday night for four years to be admitted to the best seats in the house—top gallery seats—so that Stokowski could teach us the highest standard of performing Bach, Beethoven, Mozart, and at the same time, with patient persistence, train our ear and our taste to an appreciation of Prokofiev, Bartok, Schönberg, Webern; past Rittenhouse Square that boasted a *Maison de Somebody*, displaying in its window a gorgeous gown at a fantastic price for the gorgeous daughter of a fantastically rich denizen of one of the tall apartment houses encircling the square.

This walk from Philadelphia's riverfront to Thirty-fourth Street is where the roots of my youth were planted as Andrei's were planted in Moscow's Arbat quarter, and the feelings evoked by these separate environments may be called patriotism or love of country, if by that is meant an acute sense of belonging, and the joy of belonging. Not at all a sense of "mine" being superior to "yours." My life in Russia had shown me how badly that country was in need of some of the things America had produced and how seriously she was handicapped by not having these things. And I also knew that Russia had achieved things I believed America must adopt if she was to be in actual fact the land of the free. I was eager to do any small thing that would facilitate this exchange, and so of course I lectured that summer of 1936. I left Adya with Mother and Father, who were only too happy to have the first grandchild with them, and I went about telling what I knew, and oh, how people listened, and how they talked back, and asked questions, and wanted to know, and wondered if after all . . . but still you couldn't . . . and perhaps, but then . . ."

My first lectures, all of them in and around Philadelphia, led to invitations to give others, and in the end to an invitation to come back the following summer on a lecture tour of the country. I gladly accepted it. My life, it seemed, was taking purposeful shape. I was in the unique position of being an integral part of two entirely different worlds, worlds that not only had no understanding of each other but had the most distorted conceptions, Americans seeing Russians as bearded Bolsheviks bristling with bombs, and Russians seeing Americans as bloated capitalists sucking the workers' blood. Narrow political prejudices blinded people to the fact that here were two nations similar in that at different times each had been the pioneer of a new way of life; and here were two peoples similar in that both were born and bred in lands of vast expanses and untold resources. The feeling of having space all around, of always being able to move over, move out, move on, is inimical to pinching and finicking; I find that Russians, like Americans, are not petty, and, like most Americans, are not snobs, because they, too, have torn down the fences putting people in their places; and they laughed at themselves as Americans do, sometimes with Rabelaisian ribaldry, sometimes with *New Yorker* subtlety—how else could they have survived what they have survived?

Could I, if only in a small way, help Americans and Russians to understand and help each other? It looked as if I was being given the opportunity to do so. It looked as if, as Andrei felt, the circumstances of our two lives were not mere chance, but were arranging themselves into a meaningful pattern. I wanted this with all my heart. I went to New York and signed a contract. My future was full of promise. Mother, I knew, had been dreading my leaving, certain she would never see me again. Now I could cheer her with the assurance of my coming back in the spring—yes, yes, with Adya, I would surely bring Adya with me. In my mind I was already speeding to Andrei to tell him the good news.

Then, suddenly, my chances of speeding to Andrei were threatened. Civil war broke out in Spain. Here it was, the first confrontation with fascism. Forecasts were disturbing. Who could say this would not turn into a world conflagration? Who could say communications would remain open? Who could say crossing the ocean would not become perilous? I must go as quickly as possible! I curtailed my visit. I exchanged my ticket. I said good-bye to Mother, Father, brother Dan and sister Helen, Joyce and Eddie, Esther and Leonard, Althea, Patty, Marian. I said good-bye to America. Till spring.

PEOPLE TRAVELED MORE ROMANTICALLY before the jet age. The steamer that took us from London up the Baltic Sea to Leningrad allowed Adya to crawl about on the floor of the dining room at mealtime, and me, when the baby was taking his nap, to stand at the railing gazing through the gray haze above the gray billows, waiting for the gray masses of the Kronstadt Fortress to emerge at journey's end. When they did, I had a thrill comparable to the one experienced on that hot July fourth when the *Ile de France* steamed into New York harbor and I caught sight of the Statue of Liberty dwarfed by Manhattan's towers, precisely as seen on all those glossy postcards. How superior is the thrill of these visions to the thrill of feeling jet wheels touch the landing strip, saying only that one has arrived safely, thank God!

When we got to Leningrad there was Andrei waiting for us on the wharf, as brown as a Moor from a month of mountain-climbing in the Caucasus. How I envied him a complexion that the sun turned to golden brown instead of freckled red, like mine. Here was the face I had carried with me to America and back—intact and made even finer by the sun of the Caucasus. But its brownness created difficulties in restoring rapport with his son: a first moment of withdrawal from the outstretched arms, a flinging back upon the maternal bosom, then the slow recognition of familiar accents in the masculine voice and reassuring beams in the paternal eyes. By the time we reached the Hotel Europa we were a reunited family, which Adya celebrated by falling into a deep sleep and his parents by ordering broiled sturgeon and a bottle of Georgian wine brought to the room.

No doubt Andrei would take advantage of our being in Leningrad to try to reverse my first impression of the city. He could not bear to have me think ill of it, for to Russians it is not only the city from which the Russian Empire was ruled in all the grandeur of a great European court, with parks and palaces rivaling Versailles and Potsdam; it was also, and above all, the home of Pushkin, the poet whom Russians revere as Englishmen revere Shakespeare, but with whom they are on much more intimate terms. Shakespeare is too far removed in time for us to preserve the remembrance of him as a man. Pushkin died only a hundred and fifty years ago, and down all those years the story of his romantic and tragic life has been vividly preserved: his youthful escapades in the lycée; his devoted friends, the Decembrists; his surpassingly beautiful wife Natalia Goncharova, too greatly admired by Alexander I; his involvement in court intrigues; his banishment; his untimely death in a duel fought to defend his good name from evil gossip.

The names not only of Pushkin, but of Gogol, Dostoyevsky, and many other great Russian writers are associated with St. Petersburg-Petrograd-Leningrad, the seat of Russian culture and also of the Russian state until this distinction was returned to Moscow soon after the revolution.

But this visit was not to be devoted to my reassessment of Leningrad. As we talked about our summer experiences, about our plans, about the war in Spain, I noticed that Andrei, a chain smoker, seemed preoccupied. I also noticed that he did not take a cigarette.

"How's that?"

"I've given it up. Haven't smoked since the first day I went into the mountains." This, then, accounted for a nervousness I had taken for preoccupation.

"Has it been very hard?"

"I have a magic formula: I say to myself when tempted, 'Haven't you got the willpower to resist just one cigarette? Just one miserable weed?' "

A little later, reassured that there was little likelihood of our son's waking up and none at all of his falling out of bed (we put him on the floor bolstered by pillows and blankets), we went for a walk around the block.

Once we were outside Andrei said bluntly, "Anatoli's been arrested."

"What?"

"Anatoli has been arrested."

It took a little time for this to register with me.

"You mean—Anatoli, Annushka's husband?"

"Yes, Annushka's husband."

We walked on, he holding my arm very tightly and looking straight ahead, neither of us able to speak for a while. Andrei broke the silence: "Things look bad," he said.

"What things?"

"Violence. Sabotage."

"At Autozavod? There was none of that when I was there."

"Not only at Autozavod. It looks like a big underground organization."

There it was again, talk of an underground organization, as at the time of Kirov's assassination. No one in the Soviet Union had been allowed to forget the danger. Calls for vigilance, reminders of the enemy within, of capitalist encirclement, were the daily fare offered by the media. There certainly were enemies, but . . .

"But Anatoli? He's a Bolshevik."

"He's not alone. All the top men at Autozavod—the executives, the chief engineers—all of them have been arrested."

I was overwhelmed. I thought of Martha's Boris. Of Vera Abramovna's husband. Of Rosalie's. I thought of other young engineers I had met in the American Village, all of them Communists who had been sent to be educated at American universities.

"This is crazy. Didn't I see with my own eyes how these men gave their lives to the plant? Sacrificed their wives to it? Their families? There must be some mistake."

"That's what we hope."

"Where's Annushka?"

"I don't know."

My blood froze. "Could she, too . . . ?"

"No, she's all right."

"How do you know?"

"Jhenya knows. He told me so. But that's all he told me. He's sick."

"The shock?"

"He worshiped his father."

This was a far cry from the homecoming I had looked forward to. Apparently I had not overestimated the significance of the war in Spain for all of us. The violence here was a reflection of the violence there. It was a battle to the death, and battlefields are strewn with the bodies of the innocent.

On entering the hotel room we were greeted by a startling sight. Adya had awakened, crawled out of pillows and blankets, and was sitting on the bare floor, his face smeared with excrement. Thank God for comic relief! We rushed to the clean-up—I of my baby, Andrei of the floor.

"Have we got a place to live in when we get to Moscow?" I called from the bathroom.

"There's always the street."

"No, seriously. I don't want Andrei Nikolayevich to bear the burden of us again."

"He won't. We're to live on a grander scale than ever before. Two rooms this time."

"No-o! Where?"

"In the cooperative."

"Some more actors going away?"

"Yes, but again for only a year."

"Which apartment?"

"On the second floor of one of those cottages in front of the big house Father lives in. The second cottage from our old front door."

"Oh, good. We'll have a little garden under our window."

"You thinking of gardening?"

"I'm thinking of you."

"I've already planted a walnut I brought from Nalchik. I also brought back some lemon slips. They're in pots on the windowsill."

"Of our new apartment?"

"We're installed. Sasha saw to that."

"Bless her heart."

Andrei could not keep his fingers out of the soil. And everything he planted thrived. But he could not so much as hang a picture in the house and was so dependent upon a woman to do every little chore, like sewing on a button or putting on the tea kettle, that at the very outset of our life together I determined I would always have a maid. If he expected me to do all these things I would resent it; it would be a smoldering coal inside of me that would one day burst forth into flames of dissension. I did not want my love to be incinerated on such a paltry pyre.

It was a great relief to know a new apartment was waiting for us. I knew Sasha would have it ready, would have it spick and span for her precious Adya, who had been entirely in her charge the first six months of his life while I had been teaching English not only in the Institute but in night school as well to make extra money for our trip to America.

Two days later Sasha opened the door and met us with a flash of gold teeth and a delighted chortle muted by the fat that padded every part of her. Adya recognized her at once and went right to her, and she led the way upstairs where everything was scrubbed and rubbed and stripped of the least vestige of personality by having chairs pushed into corners, tables and desks without so much as a thread or a pin to impede the vapid stare of their polished surfaces. This would soon be remedied now that we were home. I had brought with me the materials for making a lot of litter—notebooks, writing paper, pencils, a pencil sharpener, photographs, books, mats; I had also brought a pretty lamp to throw a white light on the red-lacquered chest we had brought from Mongolia. I would hang curtains, I would move the furniture around, and before we knew it the apartment would be unmistakably ours.

Now that the period of rationing food and clothing was over and more and more commodities were appearing in the stores, more and more money was needed to buy them. Andrei supplemented his salary at the Theater Institute by teaching a two-year course for raising the qualifications of directors of amateur dramatic groups. I supplemented mine by teaching part time in another institute. I disliked giving private lessons and made it a rule to refuse them.

I could not refuse Tolya. Tolya lived on the fourth floor of the big house, and when Andrei had left me alone in Moscow that winter three years earlier, I had made friends with this charming little boy and had taken him to the circus once or twice. Now Tolya was twelve and I saw less of him, but we were still friends.

One day when I was unexpectedly given a pass to a performance of the Children's Theater, I climbed the stairs to invite Tolya to go with me. I found Tamara Vasilyevna, Tolya's mother, rolling out dough for *piroshki*. The kitchen being small and she being large, she had taken her baking board into the dining-living-Tolya's room for elbow space. She was very fair, as was Tolya, and almost as shy. Poor Tolya could hardly make himself squeeze out a word; Tamara Vasilyevna got them out, but not without the lubrication of blushes. The blushes emphasized her whiteness of skin, blueness of eye, and modesty of nature. In two minutes one knew exactly what she was: a devoted wife and an adoring mother. In the radiance of her blushes I was given the best chair and the *piroshki* brought hot from the kitchen. She was repaying me for appreciating Tolya: he was such a good boy, had never given her a moment's trouble from the day of his birth; he had his father's brains and would no doubt become an engineer like his father (I felt no sympathy for his father—a dour black-haired man inclined to pass you on the stairs with the merest grunt); she wanted so terribly for Tolya to have advantages that were hard to get in these times (she shot me a significant look that I thought very bold of her and gave me a glimpse of subliminal fields sown with bitter weeds by that dour husband of hers); an engineer ought to have a broad education, ought to know languages; his father knew German perfectly, was educated in

Germany—oh dear, she hoped I wouldn't mention that, one didn't mention such things these days, it just slipped out; but wouldn't I help Tolya?—she had heard I didn't give private lessons, but Tolya would come at whatever time was convenient for me—half an hour here, half an hour there.

So that was how we arranged it. Tolya began dropping into the cottage at odd times and we enjoyed each other immensely. I found him an unusually intelligent boy with emotions the stronger for being painfully suppressed. I thought I could render him a greater service by helping him overcome his inhibitions than by teaching him English, the one being the means of accomplishing the other.

Andrei and I were so busy, each in his own way, that we had little time to be together—only at mealtimes, or on the nights I went with him to the group trying out Stanislavsky's latest ideas, or at bedtime when the day's events took shape in our minds and we talked about what pleased or worried or amused us. We both came home to Adya whenever we were able. He was the pivot around which our little household revolved. Sasha not only provided for his every material need, but she also lavished upon him all the love which her simple heart had stored up for the child of her own that never came. Hers was a warm and cushiony bosom to be clasped to, and I had all I could do to tear him away from it. Neither he nor Sasha could understand that this was not the best pad for taking off into the world.

The country at this time was marking the end of one phase of its development by adopting a new constitution, the Stalin Constitution, advertised in the press and by public speakers as epoch-making. It bore witness to the achievements of almost twenty years of Soviet power, in which time the exploitation of man by man had been completely done away with. Not only were there no longer any private owners of factories, plants, and public services, but with collectivization completed in the countryside and *kulaks* eliminated as a class, there were no longer any private owners of farms. The peasants as well as the workers were emancipated. Only two classes remained: workers and peasants—plus a "stratum" of intellectuals. This meant that former restrictions on the franchise could be removed; there would from now on be universal elective rights and direct election by secret ballot. That there would be but one candidate for every office was not mentioned.

This did not matter to me. What mattered was that every person was guaranteed the right to work, to have a vacation, and to be cared for when sick or old. These, for me, were the basic democratic rights. What if a Soviet citizen was not allowed to travel abroad for the time being? What if he was not allowed to shout "Down with the Soviets!" in the streets? What if he was not allowed to organize an opposition party? The new state was too shaky on its legs to allow such luxuries. As it strengthened, democratic restrictions would be discarded.

We were constantly made aware of menace. Even in the exuberant speeches hailing the new constitution, there were invariably grim reminders of capitalist encirclement and fascist aggression. At the present moment fascism was fighting to get Spain, and the fifth column there told us how treacherous were the ways of the enemy within. In Russia the word *Trotskyite* had become synonymous with treachery. But we were vigilant. We would ferret out the hidden enemy and repulse the open one. We were armed, were arming, were building tanks and airplanes, training modern soldiers. All the young boys and many of the young girls wanted to become pilots; military sports such as parachute-jumping and sharpshooting were the fad. Stalin's slogan was on everyone's lips: "Not an inch of other people's land do we covet, not an inch of our own will we give up." Oh yes, anyone who attempted to attack the Soviet Union would get what was coming to him!

This was the atmosphere within the country when, as a foreigner, I went to have my residence permit renewed, as I had been going at regular intervals for four years. This time I was told without the slightest warning that according to a new government decree all foreigners except accredited newspaper correspondents and those in the diplomatic service would have to take out Soviet citizenship or leave the country.

I was taken so completely off guard that it took me some time to ask the obvious question:

"If I leave, can I take my husband with me?"

"Is he a Soviet citizen?"

"Yes."

"Soviet citizens can leave only on government assignments."

It is significant that I remember the fact of my taking out Soviet citizenship and none of the dressings of the fact. Hard as I have tried, I cannot recall how it was accomplished; where, in what room, with what people, at what time of day. Nor can I recall discussing it with Andrei. I am quite sure we did not discuss it, just as we did not discuss his being unable to go to America with me. There was nothing to discuss. I was not averse to adopting this country as my own. All my sympathies were with it. I believed in the principles on which it stood and was filled with admiration for the people who were giving practical application to these principles against such odds. I clearly saw that some people, resenting deprivations not of their own choosing, lived the life of victims rather than of heroes, but I discounted them. I held them in contempt, as I held in contempt the middle-aged lady who, the minute we were outside of the friend's house where we had met, whisked up her skirt to show me cotton stockings held up by string tied above the knee. "See what they've brought us to!" she spat out viciously.

No, I was not averse to becoming part of this courageous country and living in it on an equal footing with everyone else, on an equal footing with Andrei, with Annushka who was now in such trouble, with the lady who had shown me her stockings, with my students who had taught me so much. But doing so meant I must give up all thought of continuing the activities I had begun in the summer and had thought so fitting. Where was the "meaningful pattern" my life had assumed? I had believed that individual lives were shaped less by chance than by determinative decisions, toward which one was propelled by one's aims and aspirations.

And now in a single blow the myth was blasted. An extraneous force had spun me around like a weathercock. It stunned me out of my belief that I was master of my fate and that mysterious forces were furthering the end I wanted. It showed me the childishness and arrogance of such an outlook. There might be a pattern to life itself, but the individual within the pattern could only adjust to it, and the more graciously he did so, the less painful it would be. I would adjust. I would accept. I would not make a tragedy of it.

But one night when Andrei was late coming home from a rehearsal and I was lying in bed reading Pearl Buck's account of her mother's homesickness in China, I found myself heaving great heaves. I found myself crying for people I would never see again, for Walnut and Chestnut Streets where I would never walk again, for Thanksgivings and Christmases I would never celebrate again, for chocolate sodas and pumpkin pies I would never taste again. Down upon me like a smothering canopy came all the things, big and little, that meant America to me—America which, in 1932 I had left for only a year, and which now I was sure I would never see again.

Andrei came home and found me like this. He did not try to distract me by telling me about the rehearsal or asking about Adya, he just sat down on the side of the bed as he had done when I was sick, and waited. It passed.

MUSCOVITES, LIKE PARISIANS, try to get out of the city for the summer. Andrei and I were no exception. Now that we had Adya, what had been choice became necessity: keeping children in the city in summer was looked upon as a form of child abuse. In the summer of 1937 we went to Polyenovo, once the Polyenov estate. Andrei had made the acquaintance of my old friend Olga Polyenova, not through me but as his pupil; she was one of those attending his two-year course for stage directors. I had seen little of her since my early days in Moscow when we had gone to the theater together. Now she made a permanent reentry into my life through Andrei. Olga invited us to go with her to Polyenovo, which is a day's journey from Moscow on the Oka River, the same river I had met in Autozavod. I would not have recognized it. After trickling in the shallow way rivers begin, it picked up enough water by the time it reached Serpukhov to float a little steamer through the soft dreamy countryside of central Russia, now with farmland rolling away to limpid horizons, now with mixed woods whose firs, birches, maples, and ashes grew spaciously, making it easy to wander among them in search of wild strawberries at the beginning of summer, of mushrooms later on. I can still hear the hoot of the steamer at five o'clock in the evening as it swung around in a great half-circle to stop at the Polyenovo landing to discharge passengers. If we were in the neighborhood we would rush down to see whom it had brought this time, for the Bolshoi Theater had chosen this bucolic spot for its dancers and singers to rest in after the season's exertions. They lived in cottages in the woods surrounding the big house, now a state museum preserved much as it had been in Polyenov's lifetime: the dining room with its oaken staircase and fireplace, refectory table and chairs, great window hung with linen curtains hand-blocked in a pattern designed by Olga's sister, Natasha, also an artist; the little sitting room off the dining room holding the collection of art objects Polyenov had brought back from his travels in the Holy Land; pictures on all the walls, not only by Polyenov but by his friends Serov, Korovin, Levitan, and others of the Peredvizhniki.*

*Peredvizhniki: "The Travelers." A group of the foremost Russian artists of the end of the nineteenth and beginning of the twentieth centuries who called themselves by this name because they were dedicated to bringing art to the people by holding traveling exhibitions of their works.

The top floor of the big house was reserved for the family, and so were two small houses that had once been servants' quarters; one of them was now occupied by Olga's brother, curator of the museum. Another building of the family cluster was a gray stone studio in Gothic style called The Abby. Polyenov's easel still stood in it, as did a grand piano, and there on summer evenings we often enjoyed concerts by members of the Bolshoi Theater, or amateur theatricals acted in by village people, staged by Olga, with settings by Natasha, for both daughters continued their father's tradition of helping the villagers produce plays and paint pictures.

Olga had arranged for us to live in the village school for the summer. It was a square wooden house so close to the ground that you could go in and out by just swinging a leg over a window ledge. It stood on a hilltop along with the schoolteacher's house and an abandoned church. In the twenty years since the revolution the church had crumbled, lost the cross on top of its cupola, and was, inside, ankle-deep in the debris left by tramps, icon hunters, and escapading schoolboys.

It was a languid golden summer. We swam in the river and basked in the sun, and when the heat of the day subsided Olga would come striding up our hillside with a stick in one hand and an empty basket in the other. Adya would toddle toward her, perhaps across the laundered bedsheets spread out on the grass to bleach, which brought a cry of dismay from Sasha and a snatching up of sheets from under his feet. Olga didn't baby babies, she just bent down and showed Adya an oddly streaked stone or a spiked seedpod she had picked up on the way, never doubting his ability to appreciate them. If Andrei was not in town teaching at summer school, he and Olga and I would go to the woods where, to my annoyance, he turned the brisk walking I enjoyed into a meandering botanical expedition. He was hot on the trail of vanishing orchids, Olga having assured him she had seen a certain variety blooming in ferny glens. And so his slow-roving eye eagerly sought out the plant's long, pointed leaves. From time to time he would turn stones over with his toe to see what grubs or other horrors were aestivating under them, or he would delightedly hold to our noses a flowerlet whose perfume only his extraordinary olfactory powers could detect. When my muscles began twitching for exercise I would strike out alone for the road skirting the fields, drawn there by my love of open spaces and vigorous motion. I would suit the motion to my state, for I was making a daughter then, and I kept strictly to the road, because if Andrei could advance for hours into the densest wood and always know how to come out, I would get lost "in three pine trees," as the Russians say. When we all got home I brought with me nothing but the exhilaration of a brisk walk; Andrei brought pockets full of roots and seeds, Olga a basketful of berries or mushrooms.

The peace and beauty of these months at Polyenovo made of them a kind of Indian summer, a benign interval preceding the sterner, darker season to come.

eight

Enemies of the People

> Perhaps this is the hardest, most expensive lesson the layers of the fungus brain have yet to learn: that man is not as other creatures and without a sense of the holy, without compassion, his brain can become a gray stalking horror—the deviser of Belsen.
>
> —Loren Eiseley,
> *The Star Thrower*

WAS IT IN 1936 that the ban on Christmas trees, no less effective for being unofficial, was lifted? A newspaper article championed their cause. Why, it ably argued, should children in capitalist countries enjoy the delights of a Christmas tree and our socialist children be denied them? The trimming of fir trees was, after all, a pagan custom taken over by the Christians but having nothing to do with Christianity, having to do rather with the ushering in of the New Year. New Year's trees, that was what they were, and that was what our children should have with all the trimmings—balls, tinsel, a Red Star on top and, at the foot, a Grandfather Frost (who was every inch a Santa Claus).

From out of some trunk Andrei Nikolayevich produced ornaments dating back to his sons' childhood, and we had a party for Adya in his grandfather's house, our room being too small to hold a tree. We were no longer renting rooms in our cooperative; the only living space we had been able to find this time was one room in a communal apartment occupied by five families in a house in Degtyarny Lane a block away from the cooperative. The room was hardly big enough to hold the dining table (that served as a desk and washstand between meals) and beds for all of us including a termagant of a redheaded maid named Veronica, at whose mercy Sasha had left us when she decided that even her love for Adya could not make her live in such conditions (why, she could not even turn around in that tiny kitchen with all those tables and kerosene stoves in it and where would she do the washing?—in that slimy bathtub everybody spat in because there was no washbasin to brush your teeth at?—no, Margarita Danilovna, she said to me, her former mistress had asked her to come back, and she was afraid she'd have to go). And so here we were, Veronica and I, two hot-tempered redheads cooped up within four short walls, with every domestic circumstance designed to inflame our tempers.

Fortunately Andrei was away most of that fall. I gladly saw him off to Saratov, a university city on the Volga where he was staging *Anna Karenina.* His presence could not have eased our life in Degtyarny Lane, especially with me about to give birth. By December I had grown to battleship dimensions, and still my time did not come. Every neighbor I met on the street exclaimed, "What? You haven't had your baby yet?" I was supersensitive when pregnant; I didn't want my man around. And today I cannot understand wives wanting to have their husbands present when they give birth.

At the end of October I went on confinement leave but I had lots to do for the Institute at home. At a meeting in September we had been solemnly informed that Ina Galperin, head of the English Department, had been arrested as an Enemy of the People. The damage she had done at work was not irreparable, was in fact inconsequential because she, like others of her ilk, wormed herself into the confidence of her associates by putting up a front of loyalty and conscientious effort. The times demanded, however, that we be more vigilant than ever before. And so we spent the first semester going through textbooks to make sure that no passage threw a favorable light on capitalist society and an unfavorable one on socialist society. Exercises and drills had to be changed in accordance with changes in the texts.

Enemies of the People, it seemed, were all around us. At the time of the Kirov assassination Andrei had said it must be a big underground organization. Only now, three years later, did we realize how big. While we had been enjoying ourselves in Polyenovo, Moscow had been rooting out these enemies. Some of our neighbors in the cooperative had been arrested. Bogdanovich's son-in-law was one (Bogdanovich and his wife were opera singers at the Bolshoi). Yuri Golovin, a young engineer, was another. Tolya's father was still another.

There had never been any doubt in my mind as to which side of the fence Tolya's father was on; I readily believed he could have allied himself with those seeking to undermine Soviet power. If he had done so it was only natural that he should answer for it. But I was shocked to hear that Tolya's mother had been arrested a month after his father. Here was a woman innocent for sure. That fair head certainly held no chambers devoted to anything but her beloved Tolya and her housewifely duties. Such, however, was the rule of the day: the wife must answer for the sins of the husband. Thirteen-year-old Tolya was left alone in the kitchen of their fourth-floor apartment, the other two rooms were locked and sealed by security officers. Tolya was expected to go and live with relatives or to enter a children's home. He did neither. He went on living in the kitchen. I could imagine him standing with lowered eyes and flushed cheeks in front of a desperate aunt, "But you've *got* to come and live with us, Tolya!" No answer, only an obdurate shake of his head. I met him on the stairs one day when I had dropped in to see Andrei Nikolayevich. Tolya slipped past without looking at me. I stopped him. "Tolya," I said timidly, "you might come and have dinners with us." His face turned fiery red, he mumbled something unintelligible and plunged on. I could have bitten my tongue out for having said it. I did not fully appreciate what he was going through and I ought to have, knowing him as I did. I ought to have known he would not allow anyone to come within a mile of his wound, no, not his own mother's sister, to say nothing of his English teacher. He would live alone in that kitchen under the stare of those two sealed doors, eating heaven only knows what, sleeping—where? on the floor?—rather than expose himself to the sting of curious or, worse, pitying eyes. He was not only sensitive, he was proud and strong-willed, was Tolya. He could stand up to those who told him to do this when he chose to do that. I had thrown him a rope as if he were drowning, whereas he had deliberately swum out to the deepest possible depths and would stay there until he chose to come back.

There were the Zhurevlovs, too, who had a handsome apartment on the third floor of the first entrance. It was their doorbell I rang when, on Andrei Nikolayevich's advice, I had applied for membership in the cooperative, of which Zhurevlov was president at the time. I was admitted through a steel door suggesting that there were treasures inside to tempt thieves. And so there were. Fine paintings hung on the walls of the study in which Zhurevlov received me, and Saxe and Sevres china was much displayed in the dining room where his wife gave me tea. He was an engineer who had been sent on government missions abroad. His wife, Antonina, was much younger. She had a cameo profile which she made the most of by knotting her thick wavy hair loosely in her neck. Her figure had a richness of curves, her voice a richness of overtones that made her an altogether seductive female. Often that fall while waiting for my daughter to be born, I would escape Veronica by taking Adya to walk in the yard of the cooperative, where I might find

Antonina with her three-year-old Tanya in a brown plush bonnet with red cherries dangling at the ears. Antonina knew there was something wrong with this confection, the best to be found in Moscow Department Store's *Children's Wear*, and she implored me to get the child some American clothes—a woolen cap, a sweater, a pair of shoes—anything, money was no consideration.

Soon all such trivia was knocked out of Antonina's head. Zhurevlov was arrested before the New Year and there began that surreal period between his arrest and hers. She was immediately dismissed from her job teaching Russian literature, which left her more time to spend in the yard with Tanya. She spent scarcely any. We never saw her. Quite naturally she avoided meeting neighbors who were sure to snub her—not overtly, perhaps, but in the evasive way of hurrying past intent on some pressing business, seeing her only out of the corner of an eye and bestowing the barest shadow of a smile. One reason for this was the instinct for self-preservation that made people anxious to disclaim all connection with families contaminated by arrest. It was not, however, the only reason. Another was the natural impulse to turn away from the sight of suffering you could in no way alleviate. Words must be spoken, and what words could be found? That is how we felt at the New Year's party held for the children of our cooperative. Antonina brought Tanya. Like the rest of us she came in her best dress; she smiled; she pointed out the toys on the tree to Tanya; she joined the other mothers in clapping time when the children danced around the tree; she laughed with us when a two-year-old lisped a verse for the occasion; she helped hand out the presents. All of this she did while we stole frightened looks at her and tried to make our voices sound offhand when we asked her to move that chair, or to count the bags of candy to be given to the kids. And all the while the words screaming in our hearts were that tomorrow or the next day she would be torn away from Tanya and, oh God, what would become of her, and of Tanya?

Antonina was arrested in January and Zhurevlov's aged mother left her home in Kiev to come and raise Tanya.

Did I say the arresting of wives was the rule of the day? Annushka was not arrested. Neither was Bogdanovich's daughter. Was it because these wives were not involved in their husbands' activities? That was the implication. And Tolya's mother *was* involved? Absurd. But perhaps she had been used without her knowing it—had delivered messages, had unsuspectingly given sanctuary to conspirators. Or perhaps her arrest was a mistake that investigation would discover and correct. We knew by this time that arrests were being made all over the country, appalling evidence to the size of the counterrevolutionary web whose every filament must have been laid bare in the two years since Kirov's assassination. In an operation on this scale there were bound to be innocent victims. As the Russians say: *Kogda lyes rubyat, shchepki letyat* (When trees are chopped down, chips will fly). Well, nobody wanted to be a chip, and so caution outweighed compassion.

Annushka was not arrested thanks to her friend Katya. Katya and her husband had been close to Anna and Anatoli for years. Now Katya's husband was dead. He had been a Communist enlisted to work for the secret police as soon as the Civil War, in which he and Anatoli fought long and hard, was over. Katya had learned a thing or two from him about the workings of the secret police, one of these things being the rule that when husbands were arrested for political reasons wives were arrested too, sometimes weeks, sometimes months later. She also learned that if people marked for arrest disappeared in time they were rarely tracked down. And so as soon as Katya heard of Anatoli's arrest she set out for Anna's house in the Arbat and brought her home with her. Secretly. To be held in secret for as long as necessary. In one of the three rooms of Katya's apartment in Krivoi Lane, only a few blocks from our cooperative. For over a year Annushka lived under Katya's wing, never going back to her apartment in the Arbat and rarely going out at all.

Katya saved Annushka, but Ossip helped. Ossip knew Anna when she was Anatoli's wife, knew and loved her, and it would be hard to imagine that this warmly affectionate woman, bound in wedlock to a man she rarely saw and with whom she had little in common but their son, should have failed to respond to Ossip's gentle presence. He made no advances when advances were hopeless, merely kept his great dark eyes on her, and when the time came when she needed his help, he was there. He ferreted her out, and as soon as it became known that Anatoli was dead, that Anatoli had been shot, he persuaded her to marry him. It took time and persistence, but she did marry him in the end. When this was done she was a woman with an entirely different identity. Ossip moved into Katya's third room with Annushka and tried, through daily solicitude, to relieve her of the shock and horror of Anatoli's murder.

For the first time in her life, Anna was cared for instead of caring for. From a bus window I once caught sight of her and Ossip walking along Gorky Street arm in arm. Plain as ever in her brown coat and brown beret, she had tilted her face up to that of her tall companion, and both of them were laughing at some absurdity the street presented. This passing glimpse was enough to assure me that here were two people well matched, two who took pleasure in going shopping together, going to the play together, eating a meal together, and who sorely missed each other whenever they were separated, as when business took Ossip away for a few days or when Anna went to Tula to see her deaf-mute brother and his deaf-mute wife.

In this period Anna came as near to happiness as her grudging destiny allowed her to get.

Andrei arrived for the New Year full of talk about his new production and the heroine of it, Valya Sobelyeva, who played Anna Karenina. He showed me her picture. She was beautiful and he went into such raptures over her charms and talent that I suspected he was in love with her. He admitted that he always fell in love with his heroines, but I need have no fear, it was a professional function that did not intrude upon his private life. He had never been untrue to Alla while he was her husband and would never be untrue to me while he was mine, not because he was a prude but because he was a freak, a one-man dog.

I was glad when he went back immediately after the New Year and left me alone to perform a task he could not help me with. I performed it on the seventeenth of January—and very badly this time; I would have bled to death if they had not scraped things out of me. While I lay bleeding, they kindly asked me to tell them when things went black before my eyes, and then they kindly asked me if I consented to be operated on. Well, sure, I said, only give me an anesthetic. They shrugged that off as if it went without saying, and then the operation went—without anything: *au naturel* again. The nurses tied me down and the lady surgeon gutted me as she would have gutted a chicken for broiling, only the chicken would have been dead and I was not quite. So shattered was I by the brutality of it that for twenty-four hours the tears oozed out of the corners of my eyes in ceaseless lamentation for my lost humanity; I was no longer a human being, human beings were not treated like this in the twentieth century; the SPCA saw to it that even dogs were put to sleep for laboratory experiments.

On the third day when I was beginning to take an interest in my ten-pound daughter with the long black hair ("Is your husband an Uzbek?" the astonished doctor had asked when Daria made her appearance in this world)—well, on this third day an attendant came to my bedside and whispered in my ear conspiratorially that I was to follow her. She put me into a bathrobe and, after first glancing furtively up and down the corridor, led me to a little square room where she pushed me through the door and quickly shut it behind me. There in the corner stood Andrei in a white surgeon's smock. "How did you . . . ?" I gasped in amazement.

"Sh-h-h! It's only for a moment. I had to see you. You all right?"

"It's a girl," I said.

"I know. How are you? Father said—"

"Daria is her name, like we agreed. We'll call her Dasha."

"Good. How do you feel?"

"Oh, Andrei!" and I had one of those let-go cries that flood away all the sorriness you feel for yourself. It wasted a lot of precious time but it restored me; I was a human being again.

"I must go," he said when the seizure was over. "There'll be hell to pay if they find me here."

"How in the world did you ever get in?"

"If a person wants a thing badly enough . . ."

"We've had that before," I said with a small smile.

"And we'll have it again." His tone was jocular, but tinged with the overweening self-confidence that had struck me when first we met. It still puzzled me. I didn't really get through to this man. That thought made my knees buckle under me. I put out my hand to touch him.

"Andrei."

He drew me closer with a gentleness that nearly started my tears flowing again. "I've got to go, Margarita; I mustn't get caught here. I'll be back soon, the play's almost ready."

He opened the door a crack and looked up and down the corridor. "Good-bye, see you soon."

When the way was clear I slipped back to the ward. Shortly afterward, safely in bed, I heard feet clumping down the hall and an angry voice shouting, "Who did it? Who let him in? How dared they?" It was the head doctor's voice. No rule of lying-in hospitals is so strictly enforced as the one denying entrance to all outsiders, be they ever so loving husbands or mothers. I ducked under the covers and feigned sleep.

Three weeks later I brought Dasha back to the junkroom to which her little wicker cradle had been added in my absence and from which the fiend Veronica had not been subtracted. It was not difficult to find servants (euphemistically, "houseworkers") in those days when country people were running away from collective farms that were forced to feed themselves last, after cities and industrial centers were supplied, which meant they went unfed, there not being enough to go around. I could easily have dismissed Veronica and found another helper if, when I was up and about again, she had not developed such a bad case of worms that the doctor kept her in bed for treatment.

Adya's aversion to Veronica matched mine and had made a very irritable child of him in the three weeks I was away. With all the things I had to do, I could not possibly pick him up every time he howled. After ten minutes of that, one of the neighbors was sure to knock at my door and, when I opened it, put on a look of surprise: "Oh, you're in! I thought you must be out, your little boy is crying so!" I would smile imperturbably and assure them everything was all right, although I knew it was all wrong to have to endure the crying of other people's babies, just as I knew it was impossible to further handicap movement in that crowded kitchen by hanging up wet diapers in it, yet I was deeply injured when the neighbors vehemently opposed my attempt to do so. "Where am I to hang them? They freeze out in the yard," I appealed in desperation. With little snorts and a jerking of heads they flounced out of the kitchen or turned back to the cutlets sizzling in sunflower-seed oil on their primus stoves. For all their indignation, not one of them had the heart to put the answer into words: "In your room, of course." Hell, what difference did it make? Let the diapers hang in the room. Simplify my work. I had to wash them in the room, didn't I? Had to bring tea kettles full of hot water from the kitchen, had to throw out the suds in that bathtub embossed with unspeakable gobs. Easier just to fling the washed diapers over a line strung above our table and beds with newspapers spread to catch the drippings. Now if I was not getting bruised by table corners, I was being slapped in the face by wet diapers.

By the time Andrei's play was launched and he came back to Moscow, Veronica had gotten rid of her worms and I had gotten rid of her.

Our new maid was Rima, a quiet young woman from the Tula province. Her face bore the scars of smallpox, but the intelligence shining in her gray eyes and the gentleness of her manner made her exceedingly attractive. She and I took to each other at once. I assured her our living conditions were temporary. (I kept assuring *myself* they were. I could not have gone on if I had thought they would last the three years the rightful occupants would be away; surely some family in our cooperative would be leaving Moscow and sublet to us.) The maternal instinct was strong in Rima, and her having made an unhappy marriage and buried a six-month-old son had left no bitterness. She loved Adya and Dasha, especially Dasha, who was put into her charge at an age when those petallike fingers take a lethal hold on the heart.

I hadn't seen or heard from Sonya for a long time. I knew she had traded her Moscow room for a room in a small town a hundred kilometers from Moscow so that Georgi would have a home to come to when he had served his five-year sentence (political prisoners when released were not allowed to live within a hundred kilometers of the big cities). I had heard of the Herculean efforts she had made to procure deficit nails, paints, varnish, to convert a scrubby provincial room into one acceptable to his artistic taste.

Great, then, was my surprise one winter morning when Andrei was at the Institute and Rima had gone with Adya to the grocery store, to answer a knock on the door and find Sonya standing there. She smiled wanly, that smile of the lips without the eyes. The smile persisted as she chose a dripless spot to stand in while she unwound her shawl.

"Tea?" I asked.

"Yes." She sat down on the other side of the table on which my washbasin stood.

"What has brought you to town on such a cold morning?"

"This," she said, holding out a piece of paper folded into a triangle as peasants who have no envelopes fold letters for mailing.

"Who's it from?"

"Yuri."

Yuri, Sonya's eldest child, must have been fifteen years old at this time.

"Where's Yuri?"

"Read it and you'll find out."

"The postal stamp says Karaganda. What's Yuri doing in Karaganda?"

"I told you to read it."

The letter was a cry for help: *I'll die if you don't help me, Mother.*

"Why? Oh, my God! When did this happen?"

"He was arrested eight months ago, he's been in camp for two months."

"He's only a kid."

"They arrested him at school."

"Did he steal something? Has he taken up with bad companions?"

"He's a political prisoner."

"Political!"

"Perhaps he talked too much. Perhaps he said Georgi's arrest wasn't right, wasn't fair."

"But they can't—"

"Oh, yes they can. The thing is, he's been put among criminals and he belongs among politicals. The thugs are stealing his food, what little there is of it. They beat him up if he protests. You know Yuri. He's not the fighting kind. He can't defend himself."

"What can *you* do?"

"I'm going there to see."

"To Karaganda? Do you know where that is?"

"Of course."

"What makes you think they'll let you see him if you ever get there?"

"I've got a permit. Here it is," and she drew another paper out of her bag.

It took a little time for me to fully comprehend the situation. This miniature woman (she couldn't have weighed over a hundred pounds), this delicate creature with the tranquil eyes, born of a French mother and Russian father, this beautiful woman who, when her parents had emigrated to Germany in the twenties, had elected to remain alone in Russia and continue her studies at the Moscow Conservatory of Music, this intrepid mother gazing steadily at me over the washbasin, was setting out in the dead of winter with very little money. . . .

"How much money have you got?"

"I won't need much, I'm taking food with me—for me and Yuri—and I have a round-trip ticket."

This woman of indomitable will was off on what anyone in his right mind would have called a fool's errand—off to a prison camp in the desolate wastes of Central Asia to rescue her son. She had another son, little Arseni. She had a daughter, too, but Vyeta was safe in Mongolia with her father and Fenya.

"What about Arseni? Who's taking care of him?"

"My landlady and her daughter Zina. Zina's a classmate of Yuri's. She'll do anything for him, she's in love with him. Puppy love." A flicker of amusement disturbed the tranquility of her gray eyes. Sonya was mistaken. Years later Yuri married Zina.

We sat talking until the water in my basin was cold and Rima, who had stood in five lines for the food she brought back, entered the room.

Sonya got up and said it was time for her to go.

She came back in a month, mission fulfilled. She had convinced the authorities to transfer Yuri from a criminal to a political barrack. "The political prisoners will take care of him."

WHAT DID I THINK of this? I didn't know what to think. I couldn't possibly think that the terrible things happening all around me were done at the bidding of a government dedicated to the highest good for the greatest number. A person convinced of the rightness of a cause is incapable of passing judgment on it. The deeper a person's commitment, the more closed his mind. Accordingly I concluded that there were monsters among those who, in their zeal to overthrow the young socialist state, had wormed themselves into high places from which they perpetrated such atrocities. How better could they discredit Soviet power?

At about the same time we learned that Fyodor Trusov, the architect who had designed our cooperative and occupied an apartment in it, had been arrested. His ballerina wife, a member of the Bolshoi Theater company, was taken later, and another teacher from our English Department turned out to be an Enemy of the People in league with Ina Galperin.

Naturally I was eager to be out of this wretched room and away from this distressful city infested with Enemies. And so I was delighted to learn that Andrei planned to spend the summer of 1938 in Polyenovo again. This time Andrei's entire group of stage directors experimenting with Stanislavsky's latest ideas went with us. Our family lived in the schoolhouse as before; the others found accommodations with the schoolteacher and in the village. We were a summer colony of theater folk who cooked our meals on the wood stove in the schoolhouse, ate them together on a trestle table under the trees, worked together in the mornings, swam and tramped together in the afternoons, roamed over the moonlit hillside on fine evenings singing the wistful Russian folk songs that gave Tchaikovsky his loveliest themes, and spent a lot of time talking over a bottle of wine at the trestle table. Talk was about theater, of course, because theater folk never talk about anything else. They gossiped:

"Funny Masha should have married Volodia."

"Funny? He's going to stage *A Doll's House*, isn't he?—and she's always thought she was Nora."

"Her Nora? Good God!"

But they didn't talk about the biggest thing that was happening in the art world then and had been happening for some time. They talked around it, because this biggest thing, this new campaign against *avant-garde* art, this wiping out of trends away from realism, this declared war on what was lumped under the single label of "formalism," was enunciated *ex cathedra* and there could be no two opinions about it, any more than there could be two opinions about collectivization or the Five Year Plans.

Andrei's group ought to have rejoiced—they were realists, they were on the side of the angels. But I sensed that they felt aggrieved: here were they, brave warriors in defense of Stanislavsky's principles, and suddenly they found themselves alone in the lists with no one to level their lances at. What sort of warriors could they be? At least I think they must have felt something like this, because they were decent people and could find no satisfaction in their opponents' defeat when they had no hand in it. Their opponents were just picked up and tossed away like figures on a chessboard: Meyerhold, Okhlopkov, Tairov.

Vividly do I remember that day at the beginning of the campaign when, as we were having breakfast with Andrei Nikolayevich and Andrei was glancing through the paper, he exclaimed, "Bah!" with a vengeance that stopped my spoon in midair; then, when he had slid his eyes down the page, "Okhlopkov's theater's been closed."

"What for?"

He glanced at me reprovingly over the top of the page.

"But Okhlopkov's a realist," I protested. "That's even the name of his theater, 'The Realistic Theater.' "

"Was."

"And they put on revolutionary plays—Gorky's *Mother*, for instance."

Andrei read on.

"But you mean closed? Really closed?" I persisted.

"Worse. Merged. With Tairov's Kamerny Theater."

"Okhlopkov can't work with Tairov. Their ideas are entirely different."

"And Tairov can work with Okhlopkov?"

So the Realistic Theater was tossed away. Later the Kamerny was as good as tossed away by virulent criticism of Tairov's productions, even though the theater was not actually closed until a few years later. But the tossing away that made the biggest bang was of Meyerhold's theater. It was closed in the year of our colony at Polyenovo, and the closing was accompanied by an official denunciation of Meyerhold intimating things far worse than formalism in art. In March Stanislavsky held out a helping hand to Meyerhold by offering him work at the opera theater he and Nemerovich-Danchenko had founded. It was not the first time Stanislavsky had been generous with Meyerhold. Years before he had offered him (then an actor of the Moscow Art Theater developing a method of directing and actor-training opposed to Stanislavsky's) a stage on which to experiment with his own ideas. Later, when Meyerhold had broken with Stanislavsky and made a name for himself as an innovator, he was not very kind in his criticism of Stanislavsky. And now Stanislavsky had done this courageous thing, and one must know the atmosphere of those days to appreciate just how courageous it was to offer a helping hand to one who had been denounced by, soon to be murdered by, the powers that be.

My love of theater made me tag along after the others when they went to the woods to work in the mornings. I was even impressed to act as a foil for two of the actors who had chosen Chekhov's short story "Daughter of Albion" to dramatize, perhaps with me in view: it wasn't every day they had a real live daughter of Albion (or as good as one) to spark off their talent. Two well-known comedians from the Vakhtangov Theater crouched naked in the bushes beside the stream and poked ribald fun at me where I stood on the embankment above them, a skinny straitlaced English governess holding a fishing rod stiffly in her hands.

Work and companionship were new pleasures added to the delights Polyenovo had offered us the preceding year. The summer was advancing with a speed we regretted, when one day Andrei returned from a trip to Moscow with the news that Stanislavsky had died. We knew he had been very ill with a heart complaint that had first confined him to the house, then to his bed. Andrei had described to us how he lay ensconced among books and papers with the telephone at hand, with countless phials and pillboxes distributed over the tables, with windows closed and curtained to keep out drafts, and with a perfect frenzy of solicitude shown by family, doctors, nurses, servants. "They starved him to death," Olga Polyenov declared indignantly. "A man his size and they kept him on gruel and grated carrots!" We were told later that the autopsy disclosed a heart worn to a shred and a brain that could have gone on working for years.

Stanislavsky's death did not stop the group's activities, but it saddened our remaining days in Polyenovo. The moment came when we had to say good-bye to all this loveliness and go back to the city—my family to that terrible room in Degtyarny Lane that was sure to suck out all the rich juices Polyenovo's good air and green spaces had injected into Adya and Dasha. Dasha would soon take her first steps. Where would she take them? Where would Adya build castles with his blocks? Rima was a comfort. Not by a single wrinkling of her brow did she show reluctance or dismay; it was as if we really did have a home we were returning to. When we got there the two of us did our best to distribute things in a way that would cause the fewest bruises and make the best appearance. She and I were a good team at that, but our talents hadn't a chance—it was like building a house of sand at the sea's edge. Well, we went on living, even harmoniously with Veronica gone. We were out of the house as much as possible. Andrei spent most of his time at his institute, I at mine. If I came home early I took the children out walking; in the evenings Andrei and I went to sessions of the group or to the theater or to see friends.

One evening when we were at Andrei Nikolayevich's he told us the apartments made vacant by arrests in our cooperative were to be distributed. Did the announcement cause me palpitations of the heart? It did. Did it raise my hopes? Oh, yes! Did I have no qualms about stepping into dead men's shoes? What qualms could there be when the shoes stood empty and my cramped feet were aching so cruelly? Besides, the shoes had belonged to people who had attempted to undermine all that I held most dear. Andrei Nikolayevich said Andrei must go and talk to Raphaelov, the new president, as soon as possible. Andrei went the next day. Raphaelov, who with his daughter occupied one of the two-story cottages belonging to the cooperative, told Andrei rather high-handedly that nothing had been decided, our family was not the only one in need of an apartment and, besides, the children of the arrested had to be provided for (he meant Tolya, still living in the kitchen, and Tanya in one room with her Granny, the other rooms sealed off). We certainly were no rivals of Tanya and Tolya; let their needs be satisfied if it meant our living in Degtyarny Lane for the rest of our lives. But we thought none of the other people on the waiting list were as badly in need as we were. Our faces lengthened, we sensed machinations on Raphaelov's part, but at least there was something to fight for, and fight we would.

A week or so later Raphaelov sent for Andrei and told him "it had been decided" to give one room of the Zhurevlov apartment plus the small maid's room off the kitchen to our family, a second room to a musical comedy couple and their daughter, leaving Tanya and her Granny in the third. Again the four of us in one room, and again a communal apartment! I stamped and raged among the tables and chairs and said how dared the man suggest such a thing, he in his two-storied mansion! Who were these musical comedy people? Since when had they been members of the cooperative? Who had ever heard of them? Where had Raphaelov picked them up? For what price? I was not fair, said Andrei; just because I had never heard of them it didn't mean they were not members of the cooperative in as good standing as ourselves and with as much right to an apartment. I was always flying off like this, he said, without looking into things; what we had to decide now was whether we were to accept the offer or not and he thought we ought to. Once we had our foot inside the cooperative other arrangements might be made.

I deflated as quickly as I blew up. Of course we must move in, we would be one of three instead of five families living together, the room was—how big?—oh, twice the size of the one we were in now and, best of all, there was gas in that house, which meant hot water, and a decent bathroom, and there was a balcony where I could hang up diapers. Yes, yes, we must move in and as quickly as possible. Today. No, impossible. Tomorrow. We moved in tomorrow. The musical comedy couple were in already. They were charming, we quickly became friends and discovered they were as dissatisfied with arrangements as we were; that was fine, we could advance in closed ranks on Raphaelov, which we did, and in a month a new plan was proposed: the Volkonskys—he a director, she an actress of the Maly Theater—had a separate two-room apartment on the first floor; they needed a third room for the wife's old and ailing mother; if they were given the entire Zhurevlov apartment they would cut one of the big rooms in two, give a room to Tolya, remodel the first-floor apartment so that Tanya and her Granny would have one room and kitchenette and our family would have two rooms and kitchenette; the only thing we would share was the bathroom. Under this arrangement the rooms of Tolya's apartment would be unsealed and go to the musical comedy couple. All of us agreed. Hammers, saws, drills. Our apartment was ready. Joy unspeakable! A home of our own! A sunny room for the kids, a smaller darker one for ourselves, but with our books in a permanent place, with our beloved Mongolian chest topped by the white porcelain lamp, with a handsome paisley shawl twelve feet long (a family heirloom given us by Andrei Nikolayevich) serving as a portiere to cut us off from the windowless dinette and kitchenette, and with a passage between rooms that held Rima's couch. Was ever a woman so lucky?

And there was more luck awaiting me. One day I was called to the

Dean's office at the Institute and told that a special three-year language course was being opened to prepare small groups of interpreters in English, French, and German for the use of the Central Committee of the Party. The best possible conditions were to be provided: the students were to be handpicked from among the freshmen of universities and language institutes throughout the country; they were to be given a stipend double that of ordinary students; a special building with classrooms, dormitory, library, and dining room was to be assigned for their exclusive use. I was one of six teachers invited to form the English faculty. I was pleased not so much by the professional as by the political trust this invitation implied. The 1937 spate of arrests had somewhat subsided, but had not stopped by any means. No one felt secure. A baleful black figure appeared on our stairway from time to time, sitting silent, with back turned, gazing out into the yard, watching the movements of nobody knew whom.

Those years at the courses were undoubtedly the happiest and most rewarding of all my teaching years. The students and I were in complete accord; we knew exactly why the job we were doing was important and that lent zest to the doing of it. These students were not to be language teachers. They were to work with Soviet statesmen engaged in international affairs at a time when international affairs were at the boil. Hitler's Germany was on a rampage. The Soviet Union was making itself impregnable. In the east it delivered a blow to Japanese plans of expansion by staring down the Japanese at Lake Khasan in Manchuria and defeating them at Khalkin Gol in Mongolia. In the west it won Baltic shores by absorbing Lithuania, Latvia, and Estonia. It forcibly widened the approaches to Leningrad by taking territory away from the Finns that bitter winter of 1939–1940, and it annexed the western lands of the Ukraine and Belorussia. Obviously these measures were in contradiction to the Stalin slogan about not wanting an inch of other people's territory and not giving up an inch of our own, but Soviet newspapers presented the measures in such a way that no loyal citizen could doubt the necessity of them.

And indeed, nobody the world over was considering niceties in those days. The only thing that knocked the ground out from under our feet was the appearance in *Pravda* one unforgettable day of a photograph of Molotov standing beside von Ribbentrop and beneath it the announcement that the Soviets had signed a nonaggression pack with Nazi Germany. It took a great effort for us to recover our legs, but we did recover them. Not a word was printed about this being a retaliatory measure—retaliation for Chamberlain's Munich Pact—but that was one of the interpretations we gave to it. Later as the Germans swarmed over Europe, we looked at the Russian pact as a means of gaining time. Munich did not save England from the blitz and we deeply sympathized with her. At home, in our classes, at lunch with my students, we talked about the sufferings of the English, we mourned Coventry, we discussed the chances of Hitler's invading Britain. Such a fate could not be Russia's. Russia was no island and no small European state, it was one-sixth of the globe with a monolithic population (what was this purge for if not to eliminate the possibility of a fifth column?), and it was bristling with arms. Hitler would think twice before he attacked Russia.

That was what we thought in 1939 and 1940 when I was teaching my interpreters and Andrei was training his Kabardinian actors. Their training came to an end in 1940 and the actors went back to the city of Nalchik in the Caucasus and opened a theater there. Andrei went with them to supervise the opening. He came back tanned and in high spirits, barged in on us in his unexpected way at six o'clock in the morning with—not a bouquet of flowers but a whole gardenful of violets, anemones, edelweiss, and arbutus, gathered lovingly in the mountains along with native soil and stones, packed painstakingly to withstand transportation in the train compartment, and set out triumphantly on the window ledge of the children's sunny room with me putting down newspapers, Adya fetching water, Dasha watching wonderingly, with spread fingers, and Rima making our breakfast.

nine

Chosen

> Perhaps one day, if we wait long enough, he (the informer) may step forward and write it all down himself. The chances are infinitesimal, but miracles do happen. There is just no telling who may speak up and what they may say.
>
> —Nadezhda Mandelstam,
> *Hope Abandoned*

I WAS ALONE when the phone rang that memorable evening. Rima was putting the children to bed; Andrei had told me not to wait up for him, it would be a long rehearsal. When I picked up the receiver a bright male voice answered to my hello:

"Is this Margarita Danilovna?"

"Yes."

"Good evening. I'm speaking from the security office. Have you any plans for this evening?"

A pause on my part. The security office. The KGB. The secret police.

A hasty reassurance on his part: "Don't worry, Margarita Danilovna, we won't keep you long. We just want to consult you on a certain question. We'll come for you in a car at, say, nine-thirty. Will that suit you?"

Come for me in a car. Nine-thirty is not one or two in the morning when they come for most people in a car—a black van, Black Crow in Russian, Black Maria in English. And certainly they don't call people up and ask them if the time is convenient. But who knows?—maybe they have different ways of doing it. Maybe my being an American calls for different tactics. Nonsense. They know I'm loyal. Didn't they choose me to teach at the Central Committee courses? And Andrei knows, and he promised to fight tooth and nail for me if I were arrested. God! What if he comes home and finds me gone? And the kids? Thank goodness there's Rima. What's Dasha crying about? I won't go in to them, I don't want them to see me like this, I couldn't make myself talk to them naturally. Oh, for goodness sake, Peg! It's nothing. Didn't they say they just wanted to consult you about something? Panic is disloyal, it means you don't trust them. It does not. It means I learned about the coefficient of error in high school mathematics. Who am I that I should escape falling within the percentage of error and others should not? That's why I'm panicking. That's why I'm pacing the floor and smoking one cigarette after another like a ham actor before his entrance, unable to pull my eyes off the clock.

It was something after half-past nine when the doorbell rang. Two gentlemen stood at the door; both of them smiled, the taller one apologized for being late. He helped me on with my coat. They escorted me out to the car. It was not a Black Crow, it was an Emka touring car with a driver waiting for us, and I sat on the back seat with one of my escorts. The other sat with the driver. My mind was gyrating at the rate of fifty revolutions a second and this gyration obliterated impressions. We must have gone to the Lubyanka*—where else? I have a vague remembrance of walking down an endless corridor and being ushered into a sumptuous office where a man rose from behind a desk as we entered and held out his hand to me. "Margarita Danilovna? I'm Sergei Petrovich" (or some other Russian name just as common). I was putting such pressure on myself to disguise the state I was in that I don't think he could have seen it, but apparently he guessed it, for after offering me a cigarette I didn't take because I was afraid the trembling of my hands would give me away, he began rummaging in a drawer of his desk for something he didn't find, as if giving me time to collect my wits. After the pause he began a speech that went something like this: he knew I was an American who had come to the Soviet Union for "ideological" reasons and that I had been reluctant to take out Soviet citizenship, also for "ideological" reasons, thinking it unfair to enjoy the benefits of revolution without having done anything to win them, and that if my beliefs were sincere I ought to go home and put them to the test by joining the American Communist Party. How did he know this? I had expressed these sentiments to others but never to this man I had never seen before. He sympathized with my view but the political situation and my personal circumstances had made it expedient for me to change my citizenship. That, however, did not mean I could do nothing to serve the revolution. I had not participated

*Lubyanka Square in the center of Moscow, where the KGB headquarters are located.

in it, but I could defend it, and it had to be defended every day, every hour, from enemies within and without.

By this time I was sufficiently composed to notice his face. It was a strong face, gashed into lines and hollows under high cheekbones. The expression of the eyes, I thought, was a touch too soft for the general cragginess. Meanwhile he went on talking about things not unfamiliar: about capitalist encirclement, about imperialist aggression, and especially about the enemy within. The enemy within was the most treacherous of all enemies and had to be rooted out at any cost. For this they needed my help.

He must have noticed the tremor pass over me, for a twinkle came into his eyes and the crags crumbled into a reassuring smile as he said it was nothing complicated they were asking of me; I was only to help them understand people whose position was not clear to them, "for their own sakes as well as ours. If they are honest citizens you can help us know it, and in that way do them a service. If they are not honest citizens—well, we've got to know that, too." I said I was afraid I didn't have the necessary qualifications. He said the only qualifications required were loyalty and honesty. They didn't expect me to be cunning, to use tricks and provocations. *Bozhe upasi!* (God forbid!) They only wanted me to give them a true picture. I said this might not be easy. "To the best of your ability, we can ask no more."

There was nothing intimidating about this man and much that was engaging. His simplicity, for instance, and his earnestness. And his cultivated manner. The office we were sitting in and the deference shown him by my escorts indicated that he was near the top. My imagination supplied the personal history that had gotten him there: he had been an officer in the czarist army who had gone Communist and spread pamphlets among his men, or he had been a naval officer who had led an insurrection on a czarist battleship; in either case he had been arrested, sent to Siberia, escaped, taken part in the storming of the Winter Palace, led Red battalions in the civil war. . . .

"Will you help us, Margarita Danilovna?"

People had done harder things to achieve the revolution. This job had to be done, and if I was asked to take part in it, how could I refuse? "I need not mention that it is top secret." Indeed he need not, I felt only too keenly the palpitations of its secrecy. "Not even your husband must know." Not even my husband, who knew everything about me words could tell, emotions convey! Even Andrei must not know. "I will not tell you anything else now. In a few days you can expect a phone call."

I arrived home in a state of daze. And of exhilaration. I felt that I had been chosen, been distinguished, that in this terrible period of trial I was trusted. It was as if I had had a medal pinned to my chest.

The children were asleep, Rima was in bed, and Andrei had not yet come home. That was a break. I could not fix my attention on simple things: cups and saucers were unreal and I did not comprehend the tea kettle. Andrei would immediately see that something was wrong and ask questions. How would I answer them? Lie to him? A strict Methodist upbringing had conditioned out of me any aptitude for lying I may have been born with. Mother had washed my mouth out with soap one day when I had been caught fibbing at the age of ten. Ever since then the most harmless white lie like, "Time to get up, it's half-past eight already," when I knew it was only eight, was betrayed by a pink spray up to my hair roots. I had better be in bed and asleep when Andrei got home. I went to bed and shut my eyes. Fortunately Andrei had had such a long day that when he got home he was off to sleep in a minute.

I spent most of the night trying to fit into my new self. Who was I? A spy? I knew very little about spies, they were not celebrated in paperbacks in those days. A secret agent? A counteragent? The words held about as much meaning for me as *zygodactyl*. But as *zygodactyl* was vaguely associated in my mind with dinosaurs, so *spy* and *secret agent* were associated with duplicity. That, of course, was because up to now they had served tyrants and capitalist states. In this country they served the worthiest of causes, and I would be as worthy as the cause. I would stoop to no artifice, I would be but a flawless mirror giving back the image, and if the image was that of an enemy, I would be proud to have caught it.

The telephone call came two days later. I was given an address to report to. Again I found myself full of trepidation as I set out on this extraordinary rendezvous. The address was of an apartment house in a bystreet about a fifteen-minute walk from where I lived. I stepped into the elevator of the building, got out at the appointed floor, rang the bell of the appointed apartment, had the door opened to me by an aproned housewife who, when I asked for Mikhail Vladimirovich, led me without a word and with averted eyes to the living-dining-room where she closed the door on me and went, I supposed, back to the kitchen sink. I sat stiffly waiting for whatever was to come. Presently the doorbell rang. In my mind's eye I saw the housewife open the door again. I heard a rustle of conversation in the hall, then the door of the room I was in opened and two men came in. Always thereafter, two. One of them was Mikhail Vladimirovich, the younger of the two escorts who had come for me that first night. They greeted me in an easy, friendly way as they seated themselves at the table opposite me. They were both so young, under thirty, and so like my students at the Foreign Language Institute, that I soon relaxed.

They talked about this and that at first—the weather, the unexpected flu epidemic ("You had better take shots, Margarita Danilovna")—and then Mikhail Vladimirovich took out a paper with a list of names on it and pushed it toward me. "Do you know any of these people, Margarita Danilovna?" I knew most of them. All of them were foreigners, some teaching at the Foreign Language Institute. After a little discussion we chose three for me to investigate—two teachers and Herbert Habecht. Herbert was a foreign correspondent and the friend who, in my delirium, I had imagined had sent me a Simmons bed and Frigidaire when I was sick in Mongolia. I had met him through Maurice Hindus, if I am not mistaken, soon after I arrived in Moscow. A great change had taken place in the political atmosphere since then. The warm, outgoing Russians who had welcomed foreigners with open arms in 1932 had become secretive and withdrawn by 1938. The spate of arrests had made all people suspect, but none more so than foreigners. The media made it clear that the web of counterrevolution inside the country had its origin outside the country. Any contact with that "outside" was dangerous. I had adapted by writing fewer and briefer letters to friends and family abroad, and by making no additions to the small circle of foreign acquaintances I had in Moscow. Herbert Habecht was one of these acquaintances. I was convinced of his loyalty to the Soviets. It was rumored that he had given a small fortune to the young republic and he had married a Russian girl who was a Party member and a teacher of Marxism. They had a little son as Teutonically blond and round-faced as Herbert himself. When I first met them they lived in the Arbat quarter, but recently they had moved into an apartment just around the corner from me. This made it convenient to drop in occasionally, which I always did with pleasure. The talk would be good and the coffee welcome. Galya, Herbert's wife, was an example of the most progressive type of Soviet woman: bursting with energy; finding time for husband, child, career; up on all the news; acquainted with the latest in books and magazines, theater and films.

She was of peasant origin, with lively black eyes and curly dark hair set off by cheeks that glowed with febrile intensity. The abruptness of her change in social position was made striking by a visit from her mother, an illiterate country woman who padded about the Moscow apartment in bare feet, her head wrapped up in a white linen kerchief with a woolen shawl on top.

Periodically I wrote all that I knew about Herbert and his family and submitted it to Mikhail Vladimirovich and his various companions at meetings in that same apartment house. Further acquaintance with the Habechts only confirmed my opinion that Herbert and Galya were staunch supporters of the Soviets. Herbert hated the Nazis with all his soul and was greatly perturbed by information he got from foreign broadcasts. (At that time only foreign correspondents and diplomats were allowed access to short-wave radios. Russians received all their news from the Soviet press and radio stations. It was not until much later that transistors brought the BBC and Voice of America into the home of anyone interested in what was going on in the wide world.) From what he heard Herbert was convinced that Hitler meant to invade Russia and soon. This was in direct contradiction to Soviet information. The signing of the Molotov-von Ribbontrop pact had dispelled fear of the immediate, if not of the ultimate, reality of this threat. The media assured Soviet citizens that the country was an invincible fortress whose defenses were being strengthened every day, and every day the slogan about not wanting an inch of foreign soil and not giving up an inch of our own was reiterated. This is what I wanted to think and what most Soviet people wanted to think and what the government wanted us to think. It was not what Herbert thought.

One evening when I dropped in to see my friends I was met by a whitefaced Herbert. He drew me into the dining room and said in a tense voice and with his brown eyes sharpened to gimlets, "Galya's been arrested."

My heart turned over. "When?"

"Today."

"Where?"

"Picked up on the street when she was shopping. They sent for her things."

I was dumbstruck. I sank into a chair and sat staring at his white face. While the clock ticked on and the nanny in the next room coaxed little Herbert to eat his stewed fruit, I searched my mind to discover how this could have happened . . . how? . . . was I responsible in some

Right: *My mother, Lillian Turnbull Wettlin.*

Below: *My father, Daniel Frank Wettlin, and my brother, Dan, who in the 1970s persuaded me to think about coming to America.*

Above: *Andrei, with his father, in 1905.*

Left: *Andrei, in 1925, before I knew him.*

Left: *Andrei, in the early 1930s, shortly after we met. This is the photo I had on my wall in Autozavod.*

Below: *Me, in 1932, shortly after arriving in Moscow. This photo was taken by Nappelbaum, the famous Moscow portrait photographer, who was part of the group that traveled by train from Nalchik to Tbilisi.*

Camping for the night on the way to the Gobi desert in 1934.

Above: *With my children, Andrei, Jr., four years old, and Dasha, two, in 1939.*

Left: *Andrei, in 1950, as he looked when he headed the Russian Theater in Riga, the capital of Latvia.*

Our duck of a house at Leonozovo, outside Moscow, and Andrei showing his wildflower garden to visitors from Moscow.

Andrei in his greenhouse, where he was happiest during his last years.

With Ivy Litvinov, in about 1960.

Back home, in Philadelphia, about 1987. (Photo by Peter A. Zinner)

way for this mistake? . . . but if it was not a mistake? . . . if there were things I didn't know? . . . something connected with Galya's brother who was a Red Army commander? . . . with military secrets? . . . with Herbert's German origin? . . . his connection with the American Embassy? . . . Oh, stop it, Peg! If you allow your mind to wander down such corridors of doubt and suspicion you'll cut yourself off from the testimony of your own senses; it will dissolve as the meaning of a word dissolves when you hold it up to too close scrutiny. And then what will you be left with? Distrust. Distrust of everybody and everything. You've always trusted Galya. Have you met any new facts to make you change your opinion? None. Then it holds. "It's a mistake," I said to Herbert firmly.

"So what?" he answered.

"She'll be released."

"By God she will if I've got anything to do with it!"

I got up to go home, and Herbert went with me into the hall. The bell rang as I was putting on my coat. Herbert made a dash for the door. Four people were standing there. One was a woman, the yard porter; another was a man who, like the porter, looked uncomfortable; the other two had uniforms under their topcoats and one of these men was Mikhail Vladimirovich. The detonation inside my brain was terrific, but even if Herbert had had eyes for me I don't think he would have noticed it. I jammed the brakes down on all my responses.

"Who is she?" demanded the unknown man in uniform, indicating me. Herbert looked up from reading the search warrant.

"A friend," he said. "She was just going home."

The man turned to me. "You may go," and he held the door open. I swept past Mikhail Vladimirovich as past the gatepost.

The next morning I received a phone call. It was Mikhail Vladimirovich. I met him. He congratulated me. "You showed fine control," he said.

"A mistake's been made," I said.

"You can't know," he said.

"Why can't I? I've known these people for years and been meeting them with a special purpose for months. If I can't know, then why am I doing it?"

"You've seen only one side of the picture. There are higher levels where the information obtained through various channels is coordinated."

Various channels? The idea gave me pause. I thought *I* was the authority on the Habecht family. My original conception of being chosen, of being responsible, of participating, suffered severe damage. The "higher levels" and "various channels" made me feel very small. They conjured up a picture of a huge edifice in which I was just a tiny back window. But perhaps I was wrong. Anyway, I had put my protest on record, and some eye "on a higher level" might notice it and give it consideration. Herbert began fighting for Galya "tooth and nail" as Andrei had promised to fight for me. And in a short time (for those days) Galya came back. I was reassured. The mistake had really been a mistake and the mistake had been corrected.

No sooner was Galya back than Herbert took the family to America, and no sooner were they gone than Herbert's warning proved correct: Hitler invaded the Soviet Union.

To most Soviet citizens the excitement of war, whose depredations they could in no way foresee at its onset, came almost as a relief from the purges. Here, at least, was a concrete enemy they could pit themselves against instead of an invisible enemy against whom no weapon could be leveled.

For me the war brought the added relief of severing my connections with the Soviet secret service. Or so I thought.

PART TWO

Bellum

War is such a terrible, such an atrocious thing, that no man, especially no Christian man, has the right to assume the responsibility of beginning it.

—Leo Tolstoy,
Anna Karenina, Part VIII, ch. 15

Nothing could have been more obvious to the people of the early twentieth century than the rapidity with which war was becoming impossible. And as certainly they did not see it. They did not see it until the atomic bombs burst in their fumbling hands.

—H. G. Wells,
The World Set Free

We have learned, and *paid an awful price to learn*, that living and working together can be done in one way only—under law. There is no truer and simpler idea in the world today. Unless it prevails, and unless by common struggle we are capable of *new ways of thinking*, mankind is doomed.

—Albert Einstein
(quoted by Jonathan Schell in *The New Yorker*, Jan. 2, 1984)

ten

Fleeing Moscow

"*WAR!*" announced the radio.

"War!" shouted the neighbors.

"War!" called Andrei.

Adya came running from the sandpile, his eyes popping with the excitement in the air. "What is war, Mother?"

That is the question he asked me on that Sunday of June 22, 1941, when we had just moved out to the country for the summer, "What is war, Mother?"

I didn't know. I had lived through World War I and retained the pleasantest memories of it. I was seven when it began and ten by the time America was in it. I remember Mother and her friends in Newark gathering to "snip"* for the Red Cross, and the kids making lemonade and selling it from a soap box to raise money to buy Liberty Bonds. We also set up a hospital on our front porch for wounded dolls, whom we attended in fetching white headdresses falling down to our shoulders, a Red Cross on our foreheads. And I remember later, when we had moved to Haddonfield, sitting in the baseball bleachers behind the Presbyterian Church for the Community Sing, fairly bursting our lungs with "Johnny Get Your Gun," "Over There," "I Didn't Raise My Boy To Be A Soldier, but . . ."

"War!" came the neighbors' frightened voices at the dacha in 1941.

"Invasion!"

"Four o'clock in the morning!"

*"Snipping" gauze with scissors for use as a substitute for cotton in dressing wounds.

"Kiev and Sevastopol bombed!"

A little noise made me look into the next yard. Our neighbor was standing in the midst of rosebushes, hands clapped to his head, garden shears sprouting out of an ear. His lips moved: "Mother and Father are in Kiev."

Everybody began discussing what we should do. My friend Vera, who shared the dacha with us, decided to take her children and go back to Moscow.

She began to pack. Her husband went to hail a truck on the highway to move their things. "Everyone will be going at once. If we don't move now we may not be able to move at all." Andrei thought we ought to wait. "In case of air raids the children will be safer here than in Moscow." So we waited. The next day he and I went to town. We held a family council and Andrei's father agreed that the children should be kept on the dacha with Rima until the situation became clearer.

Moscow was in the throes of this tremendous event. Steps were quicker, glances more intent. Everywhere you could see the city adjusting. People dug up parks and vacant lots to make slit trenches. They put extra posts in cellars to reinforce ceilings and covered the windows with metal shields against shrapnel and blast. They organized defense squads in every apartment house, in every block of small residences. In the yards behind houses you could see men still in civvies marching back and forth in crowded spaces, holding rifles awkwardly. I was amazed to see how quickly lives shifted into new channels. As soon as men were off to the forces, women took their places in offices and factories.

Then came the announcement that Moscow's children were to be evacuated. Andrei learned that the All-Russian Theater Society was changing its Rest Home on the Volga into a home for evacuated children of theater workers. The home was in beautiful country, had a farm of its own, and buildings equipped for wintering. So that was where Adya and Dasha should go.

Andrei moved them and Rima back into the city and in early July, he, Rima, and I, saw them off to the Volga. We easily found the theater group in the square in front of the railroad station. There were several pleasant chaperones for the children who did not seem in the least disturbed at the prospect of taking them away from their parents. I must have looked unhappy, for they began to cheer me with bright stories from their professional experiences with children. All of a sudden the crowd began to move out to the station platform, drawing us along with it, and there the chaperones disappeared in a welter of parents and children and brusque train officials who kept urging us to make our farewells brief. There was no one we knew in sight. We could not separate like this, just put Dasha, three, and Adya, five, into compartment 10, wave good-bye, and wish them a nice vacation until the end of the war. I turned to Rima.

"Would you be willing to go with them?" I asked.

"Of course," she replied at once, though she was in a sleeveless dress and without so much as a spare handkerchief.

We pushed some money into her hand and when the train pulled out we saw her smiling face framed by two sober little ones.

After that there was no time for moping. I was transferred from teaching to radio work, which kept me busy almost without respite. My days were occupied by getting and writing up news, my nights by broadcasting it to America (because of the time difference we went on the air at one o'clock in the morning). Andrei's new studio at the Moscow Theater Institute was to prepare a national theater for the Chuvash Republic on the Volga. Andrei, like most of his colleagues, volunteered for the "People's Guard"* but was rejected because of his heart (that tick, tick . . . tick, tick, tick . . . tick . . . I had heard in Mongolia). He was, however, a member of the defense squad, learning to do roof duty during air raids. Until the twenty-second of July his learning was purely theoretical; on that night it became practical. The twenty-second of July was my night off. Andrei and I were having a cup of tea when the siren wailed. "Go to bed," he said over his shoulder as he went out. I intended to, but the neighbors' voices and the shuffling of feet as they descended the stairs into the shelter made me want to go with them.

Most of the people sitting on benches under the reinforced ceiling were actors, for our apartment house was a cooperative of theater people. One of them was comedian Vladimir Chenkin, Russia's Bob Hope. "I need some new stuff," he was complaining. "You can't go on cracking jokes about Moscow's bus service with the war on."

The gossip would have gone on until the "All-Clear" sent us to bed, but not that night. Suddenly the air was rent by terrific explosions. This was, without question, what we had been drilling for, what we had made such futile efforts to imagine when reading accounts of the

*A volunteer defense organization of civilians that originated at the time of Napoleon's invasion of Russia in 1812.

London blitz. We waited. The din began again and kept up. It was unpleasant to be shut up in that cellar. When a man came and called for Dr. Feldman, people whispered "Someone's been hurt." Andrei was out there. We could smell smoke. A fire warden who passed through relieved the tension with noisy bravado: "Nothing like as bad as it sounds," he said. No one was allowed to leave the shelter. When Andrei came off the roof a few hours later he was besieged with questions: "Many planes?" "Much damage?" "Anyone hurt?" "Fires?" At last he bent down and whispered in my ear: "I'll sneak you back up with me."

The doorway at the top of the cellar steps, open in case of blast, was a proscenium arch framing Moscow's blazing sky. Flares hovered and went out, multicolored tracers stitched through the blackness, searchlights wove their beams into webs to catch swastika-flies. I saw one caught and writhe, dipping and twisting, wrenching itself free at last. The fitful light showed the buildings in changing aspects, now blacking out the men darting about on roofs, now silhouetting them against a fiery sky.

When dawn brought the "All-Clear," people crawled exhausted into the coolness of the yards, where they collected flak, examined the pieces, compared them, marveled over them, then went home for a few hours' rest before the day's work. I was glad we had sent the children away. Rima wrote that they were well, well fed, well taken care of.

But toward the end of August we received other news from the Volga. We were told German scouting planes were seen there, and a little later we were officially informed that if we did not take our children before the river froze we would not be able to take them until spring. The implication was that we ought to take them.

"That settles it," said Andrei. "I'll go and get them and we'll all leave for Nalchik."

I knew he had received several wires asking him to come to Nalchik and take over the theater—his theater. That was probably the best thing for him to do now that his Moscow studio had been practically disbanded by the war: take Rima and the children and go to Nalchik. But without me. My job at the radio was a war job; I had no right to leave it. So when Andrei left to bring the children and Rima back from the Rest Home on the Volga, I packed his bag and the children's and Rima's, but I packed no bag for myself.

Radio Moscow was so important a war project that it had become a target for the Luftwaffe, and a target they actually hit one unforgettable night. Ever since that first raid, German bombers had been appearing over Moscow with mechanical regularity every night at ten or ten-thirty. We reported for work at six in the evening and worked steadily until the zero hour preceding the alert, when we began to gossip and tell jokes to keep up our spirits. The wail of the siren sent us down into the basement, whose Roman arches suggested the catacombs and, accordingly, that it would make a fitting place to be entombed in. But announcers had to come upstairs to the studios for broadcasts, raid or no raid. On the night in question I was upstairs waiting outside the studio for Pat, my partner on the broadcast, when there came a gigantic crash that almost knocked me down. When I recovered balance I saw Pat rushing toward me through a thick haze of powdered plaster, and behind him ran the fire wardens shouting us out of the way of their hoses. We had been hit. Yes, the Germans were right when they boasted that they had hit Radio Moscow, but they did not know then that their bomb had miraculously fallen smack into a deep and ancient well whose existence nobody even suspected, paved over as it had been for many years; the well was in the middle of the courtyard around which the radio building on Pushkin Square was built. The well saved us.

No, I could not leave my job. Andrei thought I could and should. I, like most people in those first days, had imagined we were doing the country a service by totally expending ourselves. As soon as Andrei had left for the Volga I collapsed. He came back to this besieged city with Rima and the children to find me in bed with a high fever, a sore throat, and an execrable rash. He rushed out for the first doctor he could find, a surgeon with the Defense Corps quartered across the street.

"Ever had scarlet fever?" the surgeon asked me.

"No."

"Looks like you've got it now. Forty days' quarantine if it's scarlet fever."

Andrei ran for another doctor, an eye specialist living in our house.

"Ever had scarlet fever?"

"No."

"It may be scarlet fever . . . temperature, throat, rash. Rotten time to get sick."

"But we're leaving for the Caucasus tomorrow," protested Andrei.

"I'm afraid she isn't," said the eye specialist.

Andrei's jaw stiffened. He went out again and was gone quite a while this time. When he came back he brought an epidemiologist.

"It's not scarlet fever," said the epidemiologist. "It's nervous exhaustion. There's no reason why she shouldn't go to Nalchik."

"Ah, but there is, and the reason is not my health," I said to Andrei when the doctor had gone. He looked at me very hard and, as I thought, reproachfully, as at an exasperating pupil who cannot understand one of the simpler geometry theorems. What was it I didn't understand? The issue of this war was clear.

Was I to abandon the principles at stake after having made such sacrifices for them?—after having given up my native land for them? Oh, come, Peg, you gave up your native land for Andrei. Very well, for Andrei; but my meeting Andrei was a link in a long chain leading me not to the Solomon Islands but to Soviet Russia. To Andrei and the ideas he stood for.

I knew why Andrei was so set on going to Nalchik. It was because Russia's "Gold Fund," as they called the most outstanding representatives of the art world, had been evacuated to Nalchik, and among them was Nemirovich-Danchenko, cofounder with Stanislavsky of the Moscow Art Theater. Nemirovich did not share all of Stanislavsky's views on stage directing, and when Andrei learned that Nemirovich was in Nalchik he said wistfully, "What a chance to discover their differences at first hand!" But surely this was no time to study art; it was a time to fight for art. Andrei had volunteered to do this and been rejected. That gave him the right to go to Nalchik. But not me. How could he expect it of me? I turned to him. His eyes were still on me—reproachful, compelling. They were not pleading with me. They were exerting a force I could not define but one that had been guiding me all the days of my life with him. His were lustrous eyes, like Princess Mary's in *War and Peace*, and never since those long evenings of conversation in Andrei Nikolayevich's house, never since that ride in the smelly Ukrainian train when we had sat facing each other, I clinging to his eyes like a bird to a bough, had I read anything but goodness in them, not even at that moment of doubt in Mongolia when the goodness was made human by human failing. Now they looked at me steadily, compellingly. I felt my resistance collapsing but I did not give in; I kept my gaze as steady as his. Suddenly he cut the rope of this tug-of-war between us by turning on his heel and going out the front door.

Andrei Nikolayevich had already left Moscow. Dmitri had seen to this. He and Vyeta had been living in his father's apartment ever since they had come back from Mongolia, and in that time Dmitri had added to their family a wife named Tonya, a young widow very different from Sonya. More earthy. Lacking Sonya's elusive charm. On the very eve of the German invasion Tonya had given birth to a son. It was these four—his daughter, his wife, his infant son, and his elderly father—that Dmitri had escorted to safety in a village far from Moscow before he left to blow up power plants in German-occupied territory and to rebuild them after the Germans were driven out.

Andrei was gone for a long time. When he came back he said: "I have spoken to the head of the Radio Committee. He said mothers are expected to evacuate with their children. He said it was not in the interest of the state to have war orphans, there are too many of them already." I gave in.

We went to the Moscow railroad station an hour before train time the following evening. The compartment we entered was empty, spacious, with an air of comfort lent by a little green table lamp. Contrary to rumor, it seemed that traveling would not be so difficult. Since we expected to stay in Nalchik for the duration, we had brought as many of our things as we could carry, including our most precious books. Other passengers had done the same. As they came and came, endlessly, my first hope of an easy trip faded. Soon there were ten people in a compartment designed for four, and baggage to fill a moving van. There was not only no place to sit, there was not even floor space for our feet. A corner was measured off for the children to curl up in and adults took turns standing out in the corridor. Departure time came and went and still the train stood still. It stood still until daylight waned and the dread of an air raid grew in everyone's eyes. To our infinite relief the engine signaled its leave-taking at last and puffed slowly out of the station.

All unsuspecting, we were off on an Odyssey.

Fellow passengers were bound for various destinations: the Caucasus, Central Asia, the Donbas. Every waking hour was spent in discussing the course of the war. The surrender of Belaya Tserkov, Nikolayev, Krivoi Rog, was alarming. It meant the Germans were getting what they had long advertised as their first necessity: Ukrainian wheat, coal, iron, and manganese.

Soon the armies would be lined up along the Dnieper River. Most people assumed that this natural barrier would mark the end of Soviet retreat.

It was said that the Russians had destroyed the dam at Dniepropetrovsk which was their pride and the bulwark of Ukrainian industry. But nobody regretted it so long as it meant keeping power out of the hands of the Nazis. During the morning of the second day on the train I crawled out to stretch my legs on a rural station platform while our locomotive was being overhauled. Suddenly I became aware of a crowd of peasant women milling about our train. I heard them wailing, and as I came near I saw the rugged features of their men standing on the steps and platforms of the cars. One woman hung prostrate to the breast of her husband while a little boy tugged at her skirts and the dim-eyed man stroked her heaving shoulders. This was no simple farewell.

Such scenes became common as we moved from station to station. We traveled by the eastern route to avoid air raids. By the time we reached the Donbas many of our passengers had left the train, and as we approached Rostov-on-the-Don we were traveling almost spaciously.

At about this time I saw my first *bezprizorni* (homeless child) created by this war. I had not noticed him before, but was distracted from my book by the sound of a child's high-pitched, nervous voice. I looked up to see a boy of about twelve standing in the aisle addressing the passengers in the next compartment. He was wearing a cotton shirt and pants, barefoot, with unkempt black hair and black eyes that kept roving. He spoke quickly. He said he had run away from a village near Krivoi Rog after the Germans got there. Shooting began while he was out in the fields and he had saved himself by hiding in a haystack. When the shooting stopped there was nobody around. He ran to the railroad station and hopped trains until he finally boarded this one for Rostov. People had told him he might be able to find someone from his village there. The passengers fed him and tried to comfort him. He did not cry. He kept talking quickly and looking about him with dilated eyes.

We arrived in Rostov at five o'clock in the evening. We were told we would have to wait until two in the morning for the train to Prokhladny, a town thirty miles north of Nalchik, where we had to transfer.

The Rostov station was a joy after our canned existence in the train. Dasha and Adya made off at top speed for furthest corners, thereby calling down a thunderous lecture from their father, for nothing could be more terrifying than the thought of losing one another.

That evening we put the children to bed on waiting-room benches in the gloom of the blackout. The faintest of blue lights facilitated movement inside, but the night beyond the windows was impenetrable. Shadows of people hovered nervously about bulky baggage. When the midnight train from Moscow was announced, hundreds of people streamed to the exit. They knew the train would not accommodate all of them, and each was intent on getting through the door first. A woman's cry rose out of the darkness:

"Vanya! Vanichka!"

The locomotive signaled departure.

"Vanya! Vanya!"

Slowly the train began to pull out of the station.

"Vanya-a-a!"

The voice and the train moved off in the night.

Soon I fell into a doze. I saw towering ice mountains smothered in smoke. My feet climbing their unscalable slopes kept sliding back, sliding back. Smoke covered my nostrils like a furry paw, and through the smoke, dimly, gleamed roving eyes. A voice was calling insistently, raucously. Not calling. Laboring. The retching of a beast. Here. Beyond the arched windows. The engine.

I was awake and struggling to my feet. Locomotives were signaling an alert. The radio crackled with static. *"Citizens, an air alarm. Keep your seats. See that your baggage is collected in one place. Do not leave the building. Citizens, an alert."*

Andrei was already standing by the children. Their breathing was soft with sleep, their arms curled over their heads.

"Citizens, an alert. Keep your seats."

So the Germans were coming back to have another go at this most important railroad junction connecting roads from the north, the Donbas, the Ukraine, the Caucasus. They had fumbled a raid five days before.

We sat down to wait. Guards walked through the gloom to see that order was preserved, but it was unnecessary. People were utterly quiet. At one-thirty shooting was heard in the west. It grew in intensity. Then it diminished. Then it stopped. At two o'clock we made inquiries about our train and were told it would be late. We noticed people walking about freely, some of them entering and leaving the main entrance.

"Is the alert over?" I asked.

It was. The Germans had been sent back again.

Our train came at three. Now it was our turn to enter the dark and battle to board the train. Andrei planned our tactics.

"Rima and I will handle the baggage," he said. "You take nothing but the children. Skirt the crowd. Under no conditions let go of the children's hands or lose track of me. Once I have boarded the train, hand the youngsters up over the heads of the crowd."

How we managed was a miracle. The car in which we finally found ourselves was jammed with people who defended every inch of space they held by right of priority. We were able to push through only because of the pressure of the mob behind us. Finally we landed, white and trembling, in the last compartment, and into the lap of fortune. For the holders of this final bastion proved to be kindred theater folk, a group of Moscow actors on their way to serve the Black Sea Fleet in Batumi. They further cramped themselves to give us place, and cheered the rest of the journey with stage gossip.

Later on we became aware of other passengers. Next to us was a haggard young woman with three children. The oldest was five and the youngest not yet three months. They had been traveling for over a month, at first on foot, sometimes in peasant carts. Often they had hidden in woods and rye fields to escape the German aircraft which strafed columns of refugees. Somewhere in our car, out of sight but within call, was this woman's old father. Her husband had been serving in the army when the war broke out, so she knew no more about his whereabouts than he did about theirs. The children were petulant, whining, transparently pale. From the wrappings of the infant came the sour odor of unwashed linen. It should have been a fine baby. The fact that it was alive at all proved its sturdy inheritance. Enormous eyes looked wonderingly from its pinched face. The hand-crocheted borders of the now grimy and odoriferous rags were evidence that its mother had planned a different existence for her child. But now she regarded it coldly, or with outbursts of irritation when it cried. She had become apathetic, worn to indifference to everything about her, and sat listlessly in the corner letting this train take her and her incumbents somewhere.

At three o'clock the next morning Andrei called me to wake up the children, for we were approaching Prokhladny, where we would change trains for Nalchik.

We emerged in the cool beauty of the mountain dawn. The contrast was incredible. I looked at my children and was shocked by the change these four days had caused. Their faces were blotched and livid in the pale light, and they tottered behind us as we dragged our bags to a secluded corner of the station platform. But it would be all right now.

Here was air and sun and the fruits of this fertile Caucasus. I made a bed for them on piles of baggage and saw them fall off into a bottomless sleep that would be the beginning of transformation.

The station was filled with troops and evacuees. While Andrei went to inquire about our train and Rima went for milk, I stood guard over the children. Presently a woman approached me.

"Have you by any chance come from Odessa?" she asked.

"No. From Moscow."

"I beg your pardon. I ask everybody who arrives in the hope of getting news of my family."

After that, other people asked the same thing about Dniepropetrovsk, Taraspol, Nikolayev.

At ten o'clock we boarded the train for Nalchik.

Most of the day we traveled through the plains of the North Caucasus, with waving fields of corn bringing reminiscences of America.

As the train swerved eastward and upward in its approach to Nalchik, we got our first glimpse of the Caucasus Mountains. The nearer, lower range merged with the blue haze of the horizon, while the snow peaks of the central ridge hung in the atmosphere like additional clouds. Later they assumed form and solidity, dominating the landscape with their imposing mass.

We were met at Nalchik by representatives of the Kabardinian Committee of Art. A band was playing, but it was not for us. The town was seeing off its latest detachment of recruits.

We had a swift ride through open country leading to the town, past the market, through the narrow streets lined with small wooden houses of the old section. The streets of the new section were bordered with flowers and white stucco buildings in the style of a southern summer resort. The conveyance turned into a circular driveway before the modern Hotel Nalchik, and we were ushered into a corner suite on the second floor.

As we crossed the hall I caught a glimpse of a tall, lean, bald, bespectacled man in linen suit and straw sandals who was the composer Sergei Prokofiev. He was one of the group of famous people from the art world whom the Soviet Government had evacuated to Nalchik. I wondered if I should meet any of them.

eleven

Nalchik

NALCHIK WAS NO LONGER a summer resort full of dance music, hikers, and mountain climbers in spiked shoes and feather-trimmed hats. Its beautiful park, whose acres of flowerbeds and avenues of trees follow the swift Nalchik river, was still full of people, but mostly people in wheelchairs, on crutches, with bandaged heads, and arms supported by the bulky frames used for fractured shoulders and elbows. Nalchik had become a center of army hospitals, and neither the tang of mountain air nor the brilliance of autumn foliage nor the glitter of snowy peaks could dispel the gloom this threw over everything. The wounded were not reminders of the war, they were shards of the war in our midst.

Soon we were given an apartment in a rambling two-story building which was the headquarters of the Art Committee. All day long we could hear pianists, singers, song and dance ensembles practicing for performances at hospitals or at the front. Andrei's work at the theater did not look promising. "Can I count on keeping a full staff of actors?" he asked Temirkanov,* the young man who headed the Art Committee. "That depends on the War Commissariat, whether they continue to exempt actors or not. And that depends on the Germans, whether they reach the Caucasus or not."

Actually, so many actors volunteered or were recruited for the mili-

*Temirkanov was the father of the Russian (actually Kabardinian) conductor who is frequently guest conductor with world symphony orchestras, including the Philadelphia Orchestra.

tary that the work of the theater was paralyzed. This did not mean the cessation of Andrei's artistic activities. The life of the artist goes on in any conditions, even war. If he is at the front, the battery of impressions to which the artist is exposed sink into the subconscious, which invests them with forms sure to surface in future works of art. If he is spared battle duty, he pursues his calling as unremittingly as in times of peace. So it was with Andrei. Almost as soon as we got to Nalchik he began reviving the Moscow production of Beaumarchais's *Marriage of Figaro* so that he could show it to Nemirovich-Danchenko, the director whose opinion he valued above all others now that Stanislavsky was dead.

I met Nemirovich in the intermission of a concert given by Moscow actors and musicians very soon after we arrived in Nalchik.

"Come on back stage and I'll introduce you to him," Andrei said to me. We found him talking to Olga Knipper-Chekhov, widow of Anton Chekhov and the actress who had played the lead in Stanislavsky's production of *The Sea Gull* that brought renown to Chekhov as a playwright, Stanislavsky as a director, and the Moscow Art Theater as a company. She was standing at the door of the room where Nemirovich was sitting. Somebody called her away just as we got there.

When Nemirovich stood up I was surprised to see how small he was. But the impression of smallness was erased by the stamp of his inner stature on every other outward feature—his handsome face, his noble bearing, his white hair brushed back from his temples, and his white beard worn parted in the middle like Tchaikovsky's.

"This is my American wife," said Andrei.

Deep penetrating eyes took me in. "I forget my English," he said, a twinkle in his gray eyes. "So many years I have no practice. I do not forget America. You are homesick now, with the war? It is difficult. I forget my English but I can still speak—a little. To read is more difficult. To write is still more difficult. In America I did not write. My secretary wrote. I only signed contracts. But sit down, please." He drew up a chair for me and resumed his own seat. "I could not understand America. I come to Hollywood. They meet me—beautiful cars, many people, flowers. They give me much money and a big office. In newspapers and magazines: 'Nemirovich-Danchenko joins our studio.' I want to work. Big men come to speak to me. 'That's all right, Mr. Nemirovich. Soon you will work.' I wait in my big office. I do nothing, only big men come to see me. We have big dinners. Newspapers say 'Nemirovich-Danchenko joins our studio.' At last I begin to write a scenario about Civil War in Russia. I write it for John Barrymore but nobody makes the picture. In my picture the hero is in the Red Army. Nobody makes it. A long time later I see a picture like my scenario, only the hero fights on the other side."

This reminded me of an interview I had had with Sergei Eisenstein when I first arrived in Moscow. At that time he was hailed as the most innovative director in the film world. He and his crew had been invited to the United States to film Theodor Dreiser's *American Tragedy*. After months of intense labor writing the scenario and planning the shooting, they were prevented from going into production by the rejection of his interpretation of Dreiser's story. The film was never made. An even greater disaster for him was the suppression of his magnificent film about Mexican peons. "But worst of all," he concluded with a despairing glance at a Mayan mask which was one of the many Mayan and Aztec works of art decorating his room, "was the later release of my *Mexico* in a Hollywood version that violated all of my principles."

A few weeks after I first met Nemirovich, Andrei's actors gave a private showing of Figaro for him. The play had been well received in Moscow, but even so the actors feared the master's cool eye that for forty years had been appraising performances of one of the greatest theaters in the world—the greatest in its heyday.

The day dawned fair, the valleys sparkled with gold, autumn stung the air. Before the performance Nemirovich spoke to the actors. "Do not be nervous," he said, but the first movements of Susanna and Figaro showed they were nervous. This soon wore off as they swung into the rhythm of the comedy. At first Nemirovich made critical notes. Then he forgot his pencil and began to smile at clever mise-en-scenes and lose himself in the simplicity and grace of the acting. When it was over he said, "Is that all? What a pity!" And though he added many other nice things, the actors found this spontaneous exclamation the best praise.

When we got home Rima had hung blankets over windows for the blackout and the room looked cozy in lamplight. We found just the company we wanted waiting for us—the enormous Moscow artist Radakov and his wife, Yevgenia Lvovna.

No one could mistake Radakov for anything but a painter. His gestures were as expansive as the bow under his double chin, his grease-spotted waistcoat hardly spanned his pouch, sensual lips were mated to an intellectual brow, disheveled locks curled up over his ears. His was a personality powerful and uninhibited. A luscious personality. Saliva bubbled at the corners of his mouth when he spoke and his voice was rich in purple and sepia overtones. In prerevolutionary Russia, Radakov had been one of the founders of the leading humorous magazine, the *Satiricon*, a man of means and position, both considerably diminished by social upheaval. But his huge bulk plowed imperturbably through life's rough waters. He did not take the changing course of history too seriously. This he left to his wife, Yevgenia Lvovna, whose extensive knowledge of current affairs came from a ravenous reading of political publications.

"Well," rumbled Radakov as we entered. "We've come to hear. What said the maestro?"

A discussion of Figaro led the talk naturally to France, to that Paris where Radakov had spent his student days. We talked on and on until we almost overtalked the wartime curfew.

Next morning a buoyant breeze coming through the open window woke us up. Unable to sleep with so much sparkle and color outside, Andrei and I got up and went to the park for the seven o'clock news broadcast.

"After fierce fighting, Soviet troops retreated from Kiev."

This was very bad. Kiev, the leading city of the Ukraine. The people listening to the loudspeaker looked at one another in silence. Andrei and I walked off along a path leading to a greenhouse down in the valley where he had assumed patronage over some rose trees. The head gardener was rotting away with tuberculosis contracted as a prisoner in World War I. Perhaps it was proximity to death that made him so cool in the face of events.

"This retreating isn't important," he said. "We've had the breath knocked out of us; but we'll get it back." I couldn't share his optimism. Neither Andrei nor I doubted that Russia would come out of this war the victor, but with every day we saw more clearly what the cost would be.

I wondered if we had done the right thing in coming to Nalchik. Andrei assured me we had, and I knew his reason was that Nemirovich had not only seen and approved of his work but had invited him to play the part of Gloomov in Ostrovsky's comedy *There's Many a Slip Between the Cup and the Lip*. Nemirovich was preparing a revival of this play with Art Theater actors to take on a tour of the Caucasus. Now Andrei would discover directly rather than from hearsay what the difference between Stanislavsky's and Nemirovich's method was.

But it was not about the theater my mind was occupied on our walk back from the greenhouse.

"It's going to be a long war," I said.

"I believe it is."

"And everything will be different when it's over, don't you think?"

He gave a little laugh. "If a man's house falls down on him everything's surc to be different afterward."

"I wasn't thinking of beams and ceilings, I was thinking of atmosphere. Distrust. Suspicion. That can't go on when the war's over. People have proved their loyalty. If the war does nothing else, it will clear the air. Don't you think so?"

"I'd like to think so. It's not one of the things I know much about."

But he knew a lot more about everything than I did, about history and politics, to say nothing of art. Art, however, eclipsed everything else for him.

Three more of his actors had been called up, leaving Andrei with the single task of training small groups to perform at hospitals and at the front. He arranged his time for this so that he could rehearse with Nemirovich. For three weeks I attended these rehearsals.

Stanislavsky's and Nemirovich's principles produced similar results. The difference lay in how they achieved them. Stanislavsky began with the actor's own personality, gradually building up a role through the long and complicated psychological process of assuming one conditioning of behavior after another (the magical "if's"). Nemirovich demanded that the actor bring to his first rehearsal a total grasp of the essence (the *zerno*, or "kernel") of the role. When Andrei strove to find within himself isolated elements of Gloomov, his boldness, his unscrupulousness, Nemirovich said, "No, no. Too slow. That is not Gloomov's rhythm."

"But I cannot get everything all at once," said Andrei.

"Yes, everything. Everything that is essential must be grasped at once. Both external and internal essence. Roughly. Approximately. But the essence must be there. You must build from that."

Andrei began again.

"You're giving a pulse of thirty, and the play calls for seventy," interrupted Nemirovich. "But do not think you can correct this by a simple speeding up, for you cannot put into seventy-beat intervals what goes into thirty. Alla Nazimova once said of me, 'He takes my heart and sets its pulse. Everything else is easy.' Without this pulse beat, without feeling the essential rhythm of the character and the play, you will always shoot wide of the mark."

As Andrei prepared to repeat the scene, Nemirovich coached him in the familiar manner of Stanislavsky:

"Are you sure your 'apparatus' is set? Remember that your smile is your cliché. It reveals lack of complete relaxation. First you must set your physical apparatus, achieving simplicity and seriousness. Then concentrate on the essence of the role."

Nemirovich smiled at an amusing bit of stage business. "Even if I didn't like it I wouldn't take it away from you. You must not deprive an actor of his 'gadgets.' They are like his toys. They tickle his fancy and warm him up. And that's most important. Everything on the stage must be warm, impassioned. The theater abhors mediocrity as nature abhors a vacuum. Everything must be maximum."

Thus two hours of art.

When the rehearsal was over, we went out into a cold evening. Turning up coat collars and digging our hands deep into pockets, we struck out for a walk in the park before returning home to dinner.

As we hurried along the path we saw three figures huddled together on a park bench. They were refugees. A knapsack and tea kettle stood on the ground beside them. All three of the figures stirred and dropped their eyes as we passed, and one of them, a young man, pulled his foreign-looking jacket tighter across his chest. Perhaps they were Poles.

Every day brought more refugees streaming southward. At the small port of Hatch Mas on the Caspian Sea, a point of departure for Central Asia, more than twenty thousand people were waiting for boat transportation. A Nalchik actor who had set out with his family for Tashkent sent an SOS from Hatch Mas. He said he had been camping on the streets for three weeks, had exhausted his money, and still had no boat tickets.

And every day brought word of new disaster. After the Soviet surrender of Orel came Bryansk, Vyazma, Mariupol, and the Germans were at the gates of Moscow.

News of the capital was gathered from latest arrivals. One young girl who had left at the beginning of October said that Moscow was a city under siege, with most of the population evacuated and all remaining inhabitants serving the defense. Men and women flocked to dig tank ditches and build fortifications along the highways leading to the city. Air raids were so frequent that they came unannounced.

Reports said that even Stalingrad on the Volga had been bombed. On a morning in late October, residents of Nalchik were roused from their beds by an alert which no one knew whether to take seriously. Andrei had gone to the park for the news. I lay drowsing and listening to the drone of a plane. It passed over our building in the direction of the mountains and immediately afterward we heard two explosions. Andrei ran back saying, "Sounds like trouble." In a minute we heard another plane approaching. When it passed I got up and woke Rima. We began to dress the children. From a distance came the intermittent screeching of a locomotive, reminding me of a similar signal in the Rostov station. Andrei went downstairs to find out whether it was necessary to leave the house. Rima hunted for winter coats. I tried to convince Adya that he must leave his warm covers; Dasha was immediately awake and eager.

Andrei returned telling us to get the children out as quickly as possible. We did, and from the park we saw nine planes flying in formation, slowly and low. Andrei said they were Soviet aircraft and the whole thing, including the shooting, was a drill, but an officer who passed told us to hide in the bushes. We did. Nothing else happened.

On the following day we learned that the railroad junction of Mineralyne Vodi, fifty miles north of Nalchik, had been bombed.

That afternoon Adya and I visited the Radakovs, who were living up an alley. We outflanked a pig and climbed rickety steps to a room which heaved out cigarette smoke and the smell of turpentine when the door was opened. Yevgenia Lvovna dropped the *Memoirs of Lloyd George* and swept papers off of chairs for us to sit on. Massive Radakov was squeezed between a wall and the kitchen-dining-drawing table littered with everything from cigarette butts to pencil sketches. "Welcome, Americanochka and son," he said, rumpling Adya's locks.

"Did you know," I said, "that a wire from Moscow advises Art Theater actors to leave for Tbilisi?"

"Everybody knew the Germans would go for the Caucasus," exclaimed Yevgenia Lvovna. "Only artists would choose such a spot for evacuation."

"How's that for a leg?" asked Radakov, squinting at a drawing he had just made.

"As though artists were capable of taking care of themselves!" said Yevgenia Lvovna testily. "Most of them are sick; Radakov is, Pavlov's wife is a paralytic, Yakovlev has had his stomach cut out and has to be fed every two hours through a tube in his side."

"Fancy that," said Radakov.

"The actors are more clever," went on Yevgenia Lvovna. "They are sending Nemirovich ahead to get things ready for them in Tbilisi. The artists can't even make up their minds to leave, let alone where to go and how to get there."

"Let's not go anywhere," said Radakov. "Let's go and see if there's any tobacco in that store on the corner."

But everybody was talking about going. The Russians always did when there was threat of invasion. This was characteristic. Tolstoy wrote about it in *War and Peace* when he described how the inhabitants of Moscow left an empty city for Napoleon to conquer. If their armies could not stem invasion, at least they would not live under the invaders.

Nemirovich left Nalchik at the end of October. I went to the hotel to say good-bye to him the day before he left and found him as usual, with doors and windows wide open, sitting in cap and topcoat as though on shipboard. He gestured toward a bowl of roses.

"Today is an anniversary of our theater," he said in English. "I wish very much to be in Moscow. So much of my life I have been lonely. Not for people. For the theater. In Geneva, Carlsbad, Hollywood, Paris. Only with the theater I am not lonely. Never I missed my wife. Not even my sweetheart, unless I was jealous. But the theater—always.

"Too bad we speak English very little. Perhaps in Tbilisi. I urge Andrei Andreyevich to come to Tbilisi. Maybe we shall there do Gloomov. But maybe it is too late. In general, too late."

Everything was very depressing. When I came home I stood at the window watching the gray wind-driven clouds that marked the approach of winter. Patients from the adjoining hospital were walking in the garden below. Behind some shrubs where he thought no one could see him sat a boy with his head capped in the contraption used to support broken jawbones. Nothing remained of his nose. Bandages parted over two hideous holes for nostrils and one eye. As I watched, he sneaked out a hand mirror and stole glances at the ruin.

The following day brought the news that the Soviets had surrendered Stalino in the Donbas. That meant they had surrendered coal.

EVERYTHING CHANGED in our lives all at once because of what happened on a night in November.

It was ten o'clock. The children were asleep. Andrei was reading. I was knitting the socks necessity had taught me how to. Suddenly the telephone rang in the next room and Andrei went to answer it. I did not look up when he returned, only said, "You had better close the window. A high wind has risen and Adya has a cold."

He said nothing as he closed it. Then, "Military headquarters. I am to report at eight o'clock in the morning."

I felt the flush come and go on my face.

"Called up?"

"Yes."

Of course. I had been sure, after his rejection in July, that headquarters would not be so lenient as the war went on and casualties grew. I had secretly anticipated this moment, but I had kept shoving it back.

"It's all right, Margarita," Andrei said. "You see what's happened to the theater. I'm not needed here anymore. And I can count on you. I know that."

We said nothing else about it. This was our last night together, and we said nothing. We just lay tossing the whole night through, the wind screaming and Adya moaning with cold and fever. I felt the hard muscle of Andrei's forearm thrown across my shoulder, and the strength of his palm gripping it. His hands were broad and solid. They were not artistic hands. They could fight, though they had always shunned it. Their massive restraint had always stopped my own thin nervous hands when they wanted to strike out at naughty children. His hands should have been able to do things like carpentering and wood-chopping. Actually they were ineffectual at practical things. They made apt gestures. They had a habit of opening and clenching in quick repetition to emphasize forceful words. For eight years they had been right here. They had nursed me through typhoid in Mongolia. They had leafed the pages of Pushkin, Lermontov, Blok, helping me, an American, to understand the depth and richness of the Russian mind. All these eight years they had been puttering in the earth making little things grow. I knew how they grasped a glass of tea and a pencil and the old-fashioned razor he always used. They were never cold, not even in the bitterest weather. And now I felt them, warm. Very strong and solid. Tomorrow they would not be here. God!

I turned over, and my thoughts began from the beginning. All night I kept turning over and beginning from the beginning. At half-past six Andrei said, "Let's get up, Margarita. I want to speak to Temirkanov about you and the children before I report."

I would have gone with him, but Adya required washing, gargling, and feeding. I sent Rima to market for eggs and butter, and a chicken to prepare for Andrei, since new recruits were asked to take food along for the first day or so.

At twelve o'clock he returned, had lunch, reminded me to put a bar of soap in his kit. Then he left to settle his salary account.

I wrapped up the soap in a towel and thought: I didn't know it was like this. I suppose the woman downstairs felt like this when her Mikhail went off. And so did the woman next door when her Alexei went off. And the eight thousand wives in Nalchik. And the ten million wives in Russia. And the millions of others outside of Russia. Each of them feeling as I do now. Each of us a digit with an exponent of many millions. That makes an emotional force raised to astronomical figures. I should think it would be enough to stop the war.

Adya coughed and I gave him some medicine.

I thought: I hang on to Andrei because I love him, and because it seems awful that he should go out there and some inanimate chunk of steel should rip up his skills and dreams and purposes. But at the last minute I let go because that is what the fight is about, those very dreams and purposes.

"It wasn't so bad, was it?" I said to Adya.

Andrei stopped in again before leaving for his medical examination. We looked at each other, and it was all right between us. He sat down on the edge of the bed to tie his shoelace.

"Margarita," he said, "if anything should happen to me, I would want you to marry again. I wouldn't want to think of you being alone."

He should not have said that. Everything had been all right between us, and now it was not. He had torn down my barriers. We had done so well, keeping silent. We had forced simplicity into this moment, he tying his shoelace, I packing his kit, both of us concentrating on these trifles. Now the hinterland had become articulate, and the weight of it came roaring down on me and engulfing me, while I held on with both hands and both feet. Andrei saw and came over and the tumult rushed over us and washed past and we were quiet again. Everything was all right again.

Andrei left for the medical examination and Radakov dropped in. He swore that no medical commission would pass Andrei. So did Temirkanov. But I didn't believe them.

Not until two o'clock, when Andrei came back and said the doctors had given him an extension.

But an extension was not exemption. Twice Andrei had been rejected. He might not be rejected a third time. If he was to enter the service, then it would be up to me to look after the children. "I can count on you," he had said. But not here in Nalchik. There could no longer be any doubt that the Germans were planning a drive on the Caucasus. Nalchik was jammed up against the mountains with only a little branch railroad connecting it with the main line. Already this main line was overburdened with troops and refugees. With Andrei gone and the Moscow actors and artists evacuated, my situation might become desperate.

"We must go to Tbilisi," I said.

This decision returned the initiative I had resigned since leaving Moscow. Perhaps my relaxation had been natural after the strain of those first months of the war. But that moment of expected parting had revealed to me the extent of my softening and surrender. Nothing could have been less in keeping with the times. The seventh of November, Soviet Fourth of July, was met this year with stern resolution. Vigilance was the watchword. Martial vigilance and strict discipline. As we passed through the gates of our premises the guard asked us to show our passes.

"But you know us," said Andrei.

"Doesn't matter," came the crisp reply. "How do I know you haven't given your passes to someone else?"

The radio brought the amazing news that Moscow had had its parade through Red Square as usual, and we listened to Stalin's speech, which put to shame any who might have become fainthearted. Russia's fighting was ahead of her, demanding reserves of strength and willpower.

The following days were devoted to realizing our decision to go to Tbilisi. Too little money and too much baggage sent us to join the endless lines of people in the *tolkuchka* ("jostling ground"), Nalchik's flea market, held every Sunday on the plain at the edge of town. Every type of person was to be found standing in these lines: old men of the mountains selling bits of fur and leather; dignified professional people, refugees from Dniepropetrovsk, Kiev, Odessa, selling anything they could live without, in order to buy food they could not live without. All day long they stood silently with their wares hung over their arms or spread out on the ground. Here one could buy anything from fur coats and oriental rugs to empty bottles and chipped dishes.

From early dawn on Sundays, Nalchik streamed out to this plain. Mountaineers in square-shouldered capes called *burkas*, and with karakul hats perched on one ear, rushed past on horseback. The shouting of Kabardinian farmers frightened pedestrians out of the way of their donkey carts bearing flour, grain, meat, for market. A mountain woman clung desperately to the horns of a protesting ram which instinctively felt that its well-being lay in the other direction.

At the trading ground one saw picturesque groups of peasants with unhitched oxen lying in biblical repose by handmade wooden carts. The master sold oats while his wife nursed the baby and cried warnings to older children throwing cornhusks at sniffing mongrels. The market was lavish with the fruits of this good Caucasian earth.

I bargained with a peasant for a quarter of a pood* of flour. His face and beard and ragged clothes were dusted with it, and he had the corpulence of the traditional miller. He asked one hundred and thirty rubles a pood. I got it for ninety. A quarter of a pood of cornmeal and about five pounds of butter made a little store to help us through the uncertain months ahead.

The main problem connected with our journey was obtaining transportation. All automobiles were mobilized for defense, and train tickets were issued only by special permit. With much effort a group of fifteen people, including ourselves, received permits and documents authorizing a journey to Tbilisi.

Among the members of the group were Malyavin, stage director, and his wife, Maria Inokentiyevna, actress. They had begun stage careers in St. Petersburg before the revolution. Later they had moved to Kharkov, in the Ukraine. The taking of Kharkov by the Germans meant the loss of their home and all they had accumulated over the years—books and china and the easy chairs that were to bring comfort to old age.

"I'm right where I was in 1915, only without my youth," said Malyavin.

Another member of our group was the famous Moscow portrait photographer Nappelbaum. He was tall, erect, with a long beard and the fine features of a Jewish intellectual. Now his eyes were dark with trouble, for his was the sad task of caring for a beloved wife stricken with paralysis and bloated with dropsy. A daughter and a nurse helped him fight for her life against the terrific odds presented by circumstances. Two Moscow lawyers and their families, one of their wives nursing six-month-old twins, made up the rest of the party.

So we were leaving Nalchik. We were taking to the road again, to go down to the sea, the Caspian Sea, around those impassable peaks to the ancient Georgian city of Tbilisi (formerly Tiflis).

*One pood is about thirty-six pounds of avoirdupois.

The month was November when, on a cold gray afternoon we clambered over bags and bundles to precarious seats on a peasant cart. Instead of taking a poetic farewell of this lovely Nalchik, all my thoughts were occupied by the bottle of boiled water which kept falling out, and with seeing that Adya's felt boot did not slip off the foot dangling over the front wheel. The horse skidded over the icy road leading past the small houses, the shopping center, the market, and out to the station highway.

On reaching the station we found more people waiting there than any train could hold. Officials were ruthless regarding baggage. They spied us and pursued us, but we split up into three: the children and I entered one car, Rima another, and Andrei a third, with baggage distributed accordingly. The loading cost Andrei ten pounds of flesh, but everything was on board when the wheels went round.

It was pitch dark when we arrived in Prokhladny, where we were to change to the Tbilisi train coming from Rostov. We spent two days waiting for this train. Hopes waxed and waned. On the morning of the second day rumors reached us that the Germans had taken Rostov. If this were true there might not be any more trains coming through, and any that did would be so crowded there was slight chance of our being able to get on. Certainly not with our mountains of baggage. General assembly ruled that we would have to pare down our possessions, so we spent the rest of the morning unpacking, throwing away, repacking, and sewing up suitcases in sheets or any other cloth to protect them from theft.

Station officials warned us to be ready to leave at two o'clock in the afternoon. This two o'clock stretched out to seven in the evening, which meant we would have to board the train in the dark. By six o'clock all the babies and bundles and the sick wife of Nappelbaum were gathered around a little stove in the waiting room. Our ears were strained to catch the first sound of an approaching train and our hearts were pounding in anticipation of the coming ordeal.

When the train arrived a station official helped us push our way to a front car.

"As quick as possible," he urged, boosting up the invalid. I clutched Dasha but lost Adya somewhere up front. When I called, his high little voice assured me he was there, so everything was all right.

We were in a third-class car whose wooden bunks were filled with men, many of them soldiers who had been wounded. The rest of the passengers were workmen. They lay sleeping on the highest of three tiers of bunks, the lower ones too crowded to stretch out on. They had believed this car was reserved for them and they would not be disturbed. After the first shock of our entrance, the protests began.

"What's the idea?" roared a burly fellow from a top bunk. "Can't you see the car's full? Why don't you stay where you belong?"

"Didn't like the *kolkhoz* where the government sent you, I guess, and decided to move on," growled another.

"What are you griping about?" put in a Red Armyman with a bandaged neck. "If they're traveling they've got a right to travel. Or do you think you've got a monopoly on the railroads?"

Maybe this struck home, or maybe the grumblers caught a glimpse of Dasha's startled eyes when somebody struck a match. In a minute the first workman muttered, "The little dame can squeeze in here with me if she wants." The fellow up under the ceiling made a similar offer to Adya. There was plenty of reason for a mother to shudder at the thought of such a bed for her children, but I was only grateful.

Gradually bags and I got wedged down on the floor beside the wounded Red Armyman who had come to our defense.

It was a ghoulish moment when Nappelbaum's wife had a heart attack and the nurse administered camphor injections by matchlight. Later the invalid slipped down on to the floor and her distracted husband, daughter, and nurse made futile efforts to restore her. It took two of the workmen to do it. Otherwise the night passed calmly. The Red Armyman was friendly and talkative. He had been so badly wounded in fighting near Orel that he was invalided from the forces. Now he was going to join his brother in Siberia because his native Ukrainian village was occupied. He had left a wife and baby there.

"They'll be all right," he said. "My wife's a school teacher. She's probably been evacuated. My brother will know where she is."

At dawn the workmen began looking anxiously out of the window to see that they didn't miss their stations. Gradually they, too, became friendly. They kidded Dasha's benefactor: "Trust Vanya to find himself a girl wherever he goes," they said.

It turned out they had been building reinforcements around Rostov for the past month, and they confirmed reports of the fall of the city.

"Fighting in the very center," they said. "The Germans have taken the station and the railroad bridge." The very station where we had spent such a terrifying night! This was a worse blow than the fall of Kiev. Kiev was a climax to the occupation of the Ukraine. It was the end of something. Rostov was the beginning of the descent into the

Caucasus. The Nazis were driving for Baku oil, and as I looked out of the window at the empty expanse, I thought what an easy route it would make for tanks and motorized divisions.

Early in the morning the workmen left the train and we enjoyed the luxury of sitting space. As we gathered about an open suitcase for breakfast, we heard our neighbors talking excitedly.

"What has happened?" we asked.

"They say we've driven the Germans out of Rostov."

"Sixty miles west," said a soldier with a wounded foot.

"I heard ninety," put in a lieutenant across the aisle.

"Nobody knows anything except that it's a big victory. Probably letting them into the city was just a trap," added the fellow with the wounded foot.

"Chort!" burst out a quiet youth whom no one had noticed. "Why couldn't it have been Kiev?"

"Hometown, brother?" smiled the fellow I had been talking to all night.

"Yes."

"Want to go back?"

"Sure."

"Why are you shipping to the rear?"

"Got a shell splinter in my chest."

Everyone seemed to have heard the rumors about Rostov. There was no official statement, but everyone believed it was the truth.

"Why not?" laughed the lieutenant across the aisle. "We've got to start going in the other direction some time."

During the night and all that day we were constantly having our documents verified. Our papers were always found to be in order, so we were totally unprepared for the surprise that came about ten o'clock of the second night.

The nurse had just moved Nappelbaum's wife into a compartment whose occupants had left the train at Mahach Kala, when another inspection was announced. We got out our documents as we saw the darkness pierced by candlelight. To the best of our knowledge, every letter of the law sponsored our journey to Tbilisi. But the abrupt, pockmarked official who nosed our seals had an *a priori* conviction that nine-tenths of the passengers were evading the law. The officialdom he flaunted put him in a category above humanity, beyond reason.

"Your documents give you no right to go to Tbilisi. You must leave the train at Hatch Mas," he said brusquely.

"How can that be?" asked Andrei. "Here you are: passports, a commission from the Kabardinian Government to Tbilisi, a permit signed by the People's Commissariat of Internal Affairs."

"By the Kabardinian Commissariat. It should be signed by Baku or Tbilisi," said the pock, continuing his inspection.

"Nobody told us that."

"I'm telling you. You will leave the train at Hatch Mas."

"But there's no sense in it!" I exploded. Then I caught Andrei's look and shut up. The inflamed eye of the pock glared at me.

"Isn't there someone we can appeal to?" Andrei asked him quietly.

"The captain at Hatch Mas," was the frigid answer as he confiscated our passports.

We were stunned.

"What shall we do?" asked Maria Inokentiyevna.

"Nothing," said Andrei, "until we speak to the captain."

In an hour we arrived at Hatch Mas.

"How long will the train stop here?" we asked the porter.

"About forty-five minutes."

After the men had left to speak to the captain, two uniformed officials entered the car and called out, "All those whose passports have been confiscated must leave the train. Anyone who defies this order and continues on to Baku will be held to account. You can get back your passports at KGB headquarters in the Hatch Mas station."

We women stood looking at one another. I could not make up my mind to wake up the children because I was sure Andrei would come back and say everything was all right.

Suddenly there was a whistle, a grinding of wheels, and the train started. For a frozen moment we stood verifying the fact on each other's faces, then we turned to the door.

Malyavin was the first of the men to appear panting in the doorway. Then the two lawyers came. Only Andrei was missing.

"He'll come," I said, on the basis of eight years of traveling with Andrei.

But he did not come, and after half an hour it became clear that he had been left behind at Hatch Mas. He, and all our documents with him. There we were, defiers of the law, proceeding to a district under martial law. Obviously as soon as we reached Baku we would be arrested. A telegram would be sent ahead warning of our offense and we would be taken off the train and "held to account."

The rest of the trip was a torment of suspense. At every stop we paled and feigned nonchalance until the train pulled out of the station. Just before reaching Baku we received a telegram from Hatch Mas.

> PERMISSION TO PROCEED CATEGORICALLY REFUSED STOP WAIT FOR YOU HATCH MAS ANDREI.

We held a council at which I was for turning back. But the men decided to continue as long as possible.

"We have done nothing wrong," said one of the lawyers, "and the best place to clear up the misunderstanding is in a big city like Tbilisi, not in a dump like Hatch Mas."

So we went on.

For forty-five ghastly minutes the train stood in the station at Baku. No one approached us.

Thereafter the Caspian scenery went past, flat and dull. Most of the passengers had left the train at Baku, leaving us without our main source of heat, body heat. We shivered through two uncomfortable nights after rounding to the southern side of the Caucasus. During the first night, Nappelbaum's wife almost died. Another heart attack left her unconscious with a pulse that all the frantic camphor injections of the nurse failed to revive. A doctor was found in another car who gave us faint hope of getting her to Tbilisi alive. Her husband and daughter, stricken with grief, sat tensely in the dark, listening for any sign of life.

Just after we left Baku I took out a map to show Adya our route. He was six years old now and could understand. Scarcely had I unfolded the map when a military man was at my elbow.

"Let me see that map," he said.

My heart turned over. This was very stupid. Only now did I notice that the map, one I had hastily torn out of an old Intourist Guide Book, had been printed in Leipzig. All the names were in German. No further incrimination was needed: a woman speaking broken Russian, without documents of identification, traveling in defiance of the law through a military zone, and examining a German map.

I hastened to explain and to speak English to him, as though that would prove my innocence. He seemed uninterested and I was sure I caught a significant look to his companion as he returned to his seat. But he took no measures for the moment.

I had no sleep that night. I reproached myself with carelessness that might cause trouble not only for me, but for all these people whose journey had already become unpleasantly complicated.

We reached Tbilisi at ten o'clock the next morning. No uniformed officials entered the car and called out our names. We unloaded our baggage onto the station platform and waited for porters (secretly, for the militia). Nothing happened. We watched a doctor and nurses take Nappelbaum's wife on a stretcher to the ambulance which had met the train. When the porters came, we followed them out through the gates of the station to the streets of Tbilisi—followed them unaccosted, unassailed. We were at our journey's end standing in a drab square where the trollies rounded back to the center of the city.

But Andrei was in Hatch Mas, and so were our documents.

twelve

Tbilisi

HERE WE WERE in Tbilisi, some fourteen of us, mostly women and children, with no place to live and little prospect of finding any because we had no passports. Internal passports were the ID that even in peacetime had to be registered with local authorities whenever a Soviet citizen changed residence if but for a month, and whether for business or pleasure. Without passports no hotel or householder would consider taking anybody in. And this was wartime.

For a while we stood bedazed in the station square with our babies and baggage. We soon rid ourselves of the latter by checking the big bags. Then our little group broke up. The Nappelbaums went to the hospital where their dying mother had been taken. The lawyers set out to contact municipal officials. The Malyavins, after arranging to meet me in two hours, went to look up friends who were evacuees here. That left Maria Petrovna, the wife of one of the lawyers, with her twins and a nanny, and me with Rima and our kids, Adya, now six, and Dasha, four. We wandered through the streets trying to look inconspicuous. As we stood in consultation on a street corner we became aware of a woman in black hovering about us. She finally approached and said:

"Strangers in Tbilisi?"

We cautiously admitted it.

"Poor things. And I suppose you have no place to go? So many refugees."

Her obvious approach told us what she wanted. We jumped at the chance.

"You have a room to let?"

"It's so small. You wouldn't find it suitable."

"We'll have a look," said Maria Petrovna, shifting the twins on her hip and starting off.

The room was indeed small, but it was a haven, and the woman did not ask for passports.

When Rima and I had given the children a wash and a feed and put them to bed for a nap, I went to meet the Malyavins. They took me to the hotel where the Moscow Art Theater actors were staying. Our purpose was to ask their highly efficient manager if he could do anything to help us out of our critical situation.

Some years earlier the Malyavins had spent a season acting in a Tbilisi theater, so they remembered something of the town. They led me down a wide thoroughfare whose shops and trolleys gave the impression of a metropolis to people who had just come from Nalchik. We turned into a side street leading onto a bridge over the Kura River. Above it the city reared against the sky like a backdrop, with houses and buildings piled in the colorful disarray of modernist paintings. The road over the bridge flourished up to the Rustaveli Prospekt, Tbilisi's main street. As we climbed, we glanced dizzily down into backyards on the bank of the river or craned up at apartment houses balanced on the cliffs above. At the top we turned back to see the city spreading vastly beyond the left bank of the Kura. Bare fissured mountains blocked the horizon. Far to the east rose snowy peaks, the highest of which was Mount Kazbek.

Even at the end of November, Rustaveli Prospekt preserved the mellowness of a southern street. Its wide asphalt was bordered with grass and trees from which the green had not yet disappeared. Dry ivy rustled against statues in the garden around the opera house. There were no signs of war. Stores and markets were teeming with food and we were told there was no blackout.

At the hotel, Maria Inokentiyevna and I waited in the tearoom while Malyavin went to speak to the manager.

In half an hour he came back looking annoyed.

"Says he can do nothing."

"Why not?" I asked.

"Because he's that type," said Malyavin impatiently. "Doesn't concern him, so why should he bother?"

Seeing no other option, I accepted the responsibility of getting Andrei here. I set out bravely for the headquarters of the Tbilisi Commissariat of Internal Affairs. But hardly had I reached the building when I realized I could not even enter without showing my passport.

I turned away, wondering to whom I could appeal. I remembered Victor Vesnin, a Soviet architect who was a member of the Academy of Sciences and a deputy to the Supreme Soviet. He was in charge of the "Gold Fund." Everyone knew this great, grave, white-haired academician as a person for whom nothing was too much trouble to do for others. Just for that reason I hesitated to address him. But there was Andrei at Hatch Mas.

I found out his address and set out on foot for a destination that turned out to be several miles from the center. His wife opened the door and immediately recognized me.

"How do you do," she said cordially. "When did you arrive?"

"Only today."

Something in my tone must have suggested trouble, for a subtle change took place in her expression.

"Is everything all right?" she asked.

"Not quite. I wanted to speak to your husband."

The change in her attitude was complete.

"He is sleeping."

"Then of course . . ."

"I couldn't wake him up. He is exhausted from seeing so many people. All kinds of petitions, applications for help . . ."

"Naturally. I'm sorry to have troubled you."

"Not at all. How are your children?"

I did not blame her. In fact I admired her. Vesnin needed such a wife to protect him from his own generosity.

But the door was behind me and the long walk to town before me, unlighted by any hope of a solution.

On my way I passed the Tbilisi University. If I could make connections here, I thought, I might be able to help Andrei. I entered the building and asked the man on duty where to find the office of the Dean of the Foreign Language Department.

"What is your business?"

"I'm a teacher from the Moscow Institute of Foreign Languages."

"Just step over to that window and they will issue you a pass."

I stepped past the window and out the door, for I knew the issuing of a pass meant the registering of my passport.

Maria Inokentiyevna had given me the address of her friends from the Moscow Theater of Satire, Kurikhin and his wife Elena. They had arrived in Tbilisi a week earlier and had already taken a room in a private home. We had agreed that I should meet them there and report the results of my day's efforts.

It was a bedraggled creature that Maria Inokentiyevna spied through the window and called off the street. But my depression was short-lived in this atmosphere. Elena was solicitous with soap and water and face powder. Maria was already smelling of lavender and lounging in her friend's kimono. Kurikhin's irrepressible spirits made him as popular in intimate circles as among the audiences of Leningrad and Moscow. A Georgian host named Tito and hostess named Tamara dined us and wined us and treated our arrival in Tbilisi as something triumphant rather than the ignominious thing I had been feeling all afternoon.

The unexpected pleasure of this evening almost made me forget my troubles. The nicest thing about the walk back to the children was the streetlight. So much groping around in the dark had convinced me that the greatest blessing of civilization was artificial light, and the meanest aspect of war, the blackout. Surely peace would be celebrated first of all by a blaze of night light.

I reached our miserable room, which turned out to be only one room, to find the four women facing the problem of how to make us all fit horizontally into the space. There were only two rickety cots for all of us to sleep on. Rima and the twins' nanny took to the floor along with the landlady and her child. The rest of us shared the cots by sleeping at right angles to the normal position, supporting everything below the waist on suitcases.

In the morning I sent a telegram to Andrei saying we were doing everything possible to release him. Then I sat down and thought what we could possibly do. There seemed to be nothing. The idea of appealing to Nemirovich tempted me, but this was even more distasteful than appealing to Vesnin, with whom I had no claims of friendship to exploit. No, I could not do it. Surely some other solution would present itself.

It did not; neither to me nor to any other member of our group. We only thought and talked and roamed the streets.

Through arched gateways we caught glimpses of courtyards with fountains set in cobblestones, with rickety steps connecting galleries strung with bright wash. Skull-capped Georgian peasants drove their donkeys through steep, winding streets, peddling onions and *matzoni* (milk curds) from rug saddlebags. We longed to stay here and absorb the atmosphere of Tbilisi; and at any moment we might be expelled to that god-forsaken Hatch Mas where Andrei was hostage.

Rima had a remarkable encounter on one of our first days in the city. She met Mikhail Smirnov in full battle dress on Rustaveli Prospekt. Mikhail Smirnov was the widowed owner of a dacha we had rented in the summer of 1939 in the little town of Istra, famous for the icy waters of its river and the seventeenth century monastery on a hill overlooking the Moscow countryside. That summer Rima and Mikhail (Misha) had formed a romantic attachment that seemed to have petered out when the summer was over. Now, meeting him in such unusual circumstances and in a city at the other end of the globe, all Rima's former feelings flared up.

"Has he changed?" I asked.

"Yes."

"For better or worse?"

"Better," she said, blushing.

The two met after that whenever their separate duties made it possible. I could see that Rima was becoming deeply involved, and perhaps I foresaw the consequences, if any consequences can be foreseen in the fluctuating fortunes of war.

On the evening of the fourth day I again had dinner with the Kurikhins at Tito's apartment. Malyavin felt that we had no alternative but to join Andrei at Hatch Mas and set out for a city in Central Asia. Reluctantly, as a last resort, I agreed to appeal to Nemirovich. I would speak to him the next day.

So depressed was I as I left Tito's house later that evening that I did not notice the boy who stopped his bike at Tito's door. The night was as dreary as my mood; but I shamed myself with thoughts of Andrei out there all alone, without friends to support him.

Hardly had I taken fifty steps when I heard a chorus of voices calling my name. I looked back to see a head at every window of Tito's apartment and twice as many arms waving for me to come back. I did so on the run. An excited group of friends waved a telegram at me:

> EVERYTHING ARRANGED STOP LEAVING FOR TBILISI ANDREI.

I flew back to the children through the cheerful night. Not even the gummy air that hit me in the face as I opened the door could daunt me.

"Father's coming!" I cried. "Father's coming!"

At six o'clock in the morning I was plowing my way to the railroad station against an icy gale thrown down from a snow-topped peak. The train from Hatch Mas, I was told, would be in at four o'clock in the afternoon. Andrei was not on it. The next morning I was told there would be a train from Hatch Mas at ten A.M. Again he was not on it. On the third morning the twins' mother went to the station with me. This time we were told the train had just arrived. Seeing no evidence of train or Andrei we went out to the train platform and asked a porter, who told us the train was due at twelve. We decided to go shopping. As we were about to step into a streetcar a familiar voice said, "May I come along?"

It was Andrei, very gloating and secretive. Only that evening when all of us were gathered around a table in the restaurant of the Hotel Tbilisi did he give us the denouement. It was a flat story.

After spending days in ineffectual attempts to reach authorities in Baku, Tbilisi, and Moscow by telephone, Andrei had the good luck to meet an official from the Tbilisi Commissariat of Internal Affairs who was returning from Moscow. He listened attentively to Andrei's story, examined his papers and passports, then went in and had a row with the local official. When he emerged from the office he handed back all the documents to Andrei and invited him to share his train compartment to Tbilisi.

"We talked mostly about theater," said Andrei. "That was his hobby, theater. He apologized to me profusely. Guys like that are always fouling things up, he said. Bureaucrats. But, he said, the fellow had a point: your papers should have been issued by Baku or Tbilisi, not Nalchik."

It didn't matter what should have been now. The only thing that mattered now was that we had our passports and could live as legitimate citizens in Tbilisi.

The first thing we did was to move into a room belonging to Tito's mother. It was a tiny room stuffed with antimacassared sofas, with highboys and wardrobes whose doors and drawers were all securely locked. Our baggage lay piled in corners, under chairs and tables. If Rima and I wanted to exchange places in the room, we had to go out into the corridor and return in reverse order. Rising from the dinner table was a process of untangling legs like a game of jackstraws.

Once moved in, we began adjusting to our new environment. We had expected to live in Nalchik until the end of the war; now we wondered if we should be able to do this in Tbilisi. The city seemed secure.

But signs of the times had appeared. War posters were displayed in store windows and there were many more uniformed men on the streets. The most poignant reminder of war was the presence of gaunt, ragged, homeless teenagers, *bezprizorni*, who had drifted from occupied areas into this southern city. There were too many of them for authorities to cope with. Some of them deliberately evaded militiamen whose job it was to register and send them to children's homes. Those who evaded were the wayward in spirit who preferred precarious independence to an institutional regime. They could be seen clustered over the pavement gratings of a bathhouse on Rustaveli Prospekt, warming their bones in the steam the windows exhaled. They wandered from store to store, hung around railroad stations and any public place where they could absorb a little warmth before their loitering attracted attention.

Soon after our arrival Andrei resumed rehearsals of Gloomov, and became a member of the concert ensemble organized by evacuated members of the Moscow Art and Maly Theaters.

I received an appointment to the staff of a scientific research institute connected with Georgian schools. My task was to investigate how English was being taught in Tbilisi, and on the basis of my findings to write a methods handbook for teachers.

The Research Institute hung on a byclimb ("bystreet" is inadequate for Tbilisi) off the Rustaveli Prospekt. The professors received me with the cordiality which invariably attended the discovery that I was an American. The antiforeigner sentiment cultivated at the time of the Stalin purges in 1937–1938 died a natural death after the German invasion of the Soviet Union. Invariable too was the question asked by anyone meeting me for the first time: "When are we going to have that second front?"

Our day at the Institute began with discussing the latest events and tracing on a wall map the movements at the front. In December the professors were stunned by the news of Pearl Harbor, and were immediately sympathetic. They felt that the thrusting of the United States into combat brought closer our alliance in this war. The signing of pacts, the sending of food and munitions, were one thing. Blood was another. Blood was the great common denominator. Blood was binding.

In December came Soviet victories at Moscow, and on the thirty-first of December Professor Kiparidze pinned a little red flag to the Crimean city of Kerch, wrested from the Germans by Black Sea sailors.

These successes created a holiday spirit for the New Year.

Our own celebrations were physically and economically cramped. For the first time in the life of the children we had no tree. The tables and chairs, the sofas and cupboards, would not hear of it. Nor would our finances.

So New Year's Eve was spent at home after a concert for the armed forces in which Andrei participated. There were just the two of us. "A jug of wine and a loaf of bread and thou." We sat in the glow of an oil lamp with Rima and the children sleeping in the shadows behind us.

Rima was in no mood to participate in a celebration. Only a few days earlier Misha's unit had been dispatched to the Leningrad front. This was a blow, but hardly an unexpected one. Rima, always undemonstrative, accepted it with the fortitude a life of meager enjoyments and lavish disappointments had taught her. Inwardly she grieved.

One day I asked if Misha knew anything about the fate of Istra, which had been occupied by the Germans during the Battle for Moscow.

"Most of the town was razed," she said. "His house was burned to the ground."

"And the monastery?"

"They blew it up before they left."

But they left. They did not take Moscow, although they came to within an inch of it. And now Misha was going to see that they didn't take Leningrad.

Soon after the New Year I began to observe English lessons in Tbilisi schools. The teachers were so delighted to find a native speaker among them that they requested the city Commissariat of Education to finance a course of study for raising their qualifications. The request was granted and I began a series of lectures on English phonetics.

They, who had no right to travel abroad, looked upon my presence as a special dispensation. They were so grateful that they brought me gifts of fresh vegetables and fruit, and one of them found us a new room to live in. In January our family of five had moved into a room no bigger than the first one but cheaper and emptier. It was in the very last house on Chavchavadse Street, which climbs with decorum for a block or two, then suddenly stands on its head. The final stretch to our house was up a flight of twenty stone steps. The adjacent mountain funneled the wind against the house in freezing drafts. The room might have been heated by an old iron stove standing in one corner if we had

had wood. Having none, we lived in discomfort that became panic when Andrei found a louse on Dasha's nightgown. Lice are carriers of typhus, and Tbilisi was full of typhus.

It took us little more than an hour to roll our things off the mountain. The new room we found wanted painting, had to be passed through by anyone entering the rest of the apartment, and was heated inadequately by a kerosene stove. But it had innumerable advantages, such as more space, an inside toilet, and the Simoyans who owned it.

The Simoyans were three generations of women: the elderly mother, her daughters Vera and Asya, and Vera's nineteen-year-old daughter Lilly. Vera was actually the head of the family. The old mother was Russian, but her husband had been Armenian, and Vera had inherited the beauty of the two peoples. She had black hair, deep-set violet eyes, and a high-bridged nose suggesting Armenian contact with ancient Greece. Her husband had been an American doctor who worked with the American Relief Administration in Armenia after World War I. He died of typhoid fever. We moved into the Simoyans' apartment on Sunday while Vera was at church. Her mother and sister received us like old acquaintances, inconveniencing themselves to make us comfortable.

"Comfort" was a word with little application that winter. It was a cold winter, and a winter during which the food shortage grew. Undernourishment and unheated buildings kept people in a state of permanent refrigeration. At the Institute we sat in winter coats and fur hats with hands tucked in armpits. Unable to concentrate on scientific work, we talked about two things, the war and food.

Spring came as a relief to everyone. It comes early in Georgia. To be in Georgia in April is a bit like being in Pennsylvania. At least more like it than being in Moscow. There are the warming sun and the springing buds, and the whole process lengthening gently into summer, instead of leaping to it belatedly as in colder climes.

Andrei and I spent the second half of April along the Soviet Riviera. The Ensemble went on a tour of Black Sea health resorts: Sukhumi, Gagri, Sochi. They took me with them as a mark of favor to the United States. The Art Theater had spent several months on tour there and cherished kindly memories of my native land.

The train brought us to Sukhumi at noon and we stopped at a hotel at the edge of the sea. A few of us set out to inspect the town. Before we had gone three blocks we heard the familiar shots of anti-aircraft guns and the drone of a plane. We instinctively turned to the hills.

"No good," said a stranger who had seen us turn. "They're full of training camps."

We turned again, this time into a wide boulevard leading to the sea, but defense guards whistled us off the street. In a bystreet we joined a group of people gathered in the yard of a cottage. They were staring into the sky.

"Another German scouting plane," said one of the women.

"So we can expect the bombers any day now," replied her neighbor.

They didn't come while we were there. After four days in Sukhumi we went by car north up the coast to Gagri and Sochi. Further evidence of German activities along the coast lent excitement to the journey. We got a glimpse of what was actually happening in the Caucasus. Living in Tbilisi we had felt beyond the war zone. Here we were in an armed camp. Everywhere were soldiers. Barracks lined the road. Columns moved along it singing the grim theme song of this period,

> Then let our righteous wrath uprise
> Like waves that lash the shore,
> For our united people wage
> A sacred, people's war.

For the first time we saw the army in tin hats, and such a detail made the front seem very close. Our documents were constantly being verified, and no nonmilitary cars but ours were on the road.

After a few concerts in Gagri we started out on the last lap of the trip, the gorgeous, perilous, nauseating arabesque from Gagri to Sochi.

Sochi is the most famous resort in the Soviet Union. For those who knew it as well as Andrei did it was painful to see the changes wrought by the war. No songs and laughter came from the windows of hotels and sanitoriums. Instead, these windows offered glimpses of white-clad nurses moving between rows of cots.

It was mostly in these improvised hospitals that the Ensemble gave concerts. In one of them we met a captain with a smashed left arm who had been serving in Sevastopol.

"Will the Germans take Sevastopol?" we asked.

"Not if we can keep our one line of communication open," he said.

"Will it make much difference if we have to give it up?"

"Much. Morally, politically, strategically."

"We'll still have Kerch."

"We've got to have both of them to keep the Crimea."

"How did you get wounded?"

"Blown off my cruiser."

"And swam with that arm?"

"The arm wasn't so bad. I had on a fur-lined leather jacket."

"How long were you in the water?"

"Two hours."

"It's a wonder you didn't drown."

"I didn't want to drown."

The will to live explains many survivals in war. Certainly it explained how many people came through the Leningrad blockade. It was in Sochi that we first met some of these survivors. They were actors from the Leningrad Theater of Comedy, evacuated to Sochi in March 1942. The Art Director, Nikolai Akimov, told us how, when even the streetcars stopped running in Leningrad and exhaustion made walking impossible, the starving actors had moved into the theater. They lived and died there, continuing to work as long as they had strength to move about. The entire male chorus of the Leningrad Musical Comedy Theater died. Men succumbed sooner than women. Old people showed their love for children in a special way: they committed suicide by giving up their bread rations to their grandchildren. But more about the Leningrad blockade later.

We left Sochi for Sukhumi in the evening of the last day of April.

The car swerved to a sea dappled with moon. It was surprisingly warm and still, except for the motor and the driver's shifting gears for a hill. We drove all that night, reaching Sukhumi in the early hours of the morning.

At noon of that day we took the train to Tbilisi. The journey back was not important. The only important thing was that at the other end were two little children who for a month and a half had been living on scant portions of beans and black bread. Here in this suitcase was loot. There were four pastries and ten cookies and half a pound of butter and four pounds of prunes and bits of cheese and bologna and even sugar, extra lunch portions slipped surreptitiously into napkins.

The ten-minute drive from the Tbilisi station seemed endless. But there at last was Adya running out and Rima in the background looking startlingly thin and pale.

"Mother. Father. What did you bring us? Dasha's sick. Is there anything sweet?"

"Dasha's sick?"

"Pneumonia," said Rima.

She had fallen ill on the day after our departure. Rima had not summoned me back, at first because she did not think the child was seriously ill, later because she expected us to return sooner than we did. For six days Dasha had had a temperature of nearly 104.

If ever my faith in human nature had wavered, this experience gave me cause to be ashamed. Rima watched over our child night and day. Vera Simoyan came home from work to give her camphor injections, apply compresses, get in touch with her old child specialist who long since had stopped making private calls, but who for Vera's sake came to treat Dasha. Lilly, who worked in an army hospital, managed to get medicines not to be found in drugstores. All the neighbors, even people whom I would not have known had I met them on the street, brought little gifts of rice and fruit to help the child battle for her life.

When we arrived, her temperature had been normal for some time.

WE WERE IMMEDIATELY STRUCK with the changes that had taken place in Tbilisi during our absence. What had seemed a refuge was now the very center of martial activity. American military trucks drove with swift concentration through the Rustaveli Prospekt. All day long the air was filled with reverberations of artillery practice in the mountains. The blackout had come to Tbilisi, and a twelve o'clock war curfew. Column after column of soldiers marched from barracks to drill ground. Again we heard their portentous song:

Then let our righteous wrath uprise
Like waves that lash the shore,
For our united people wage
A sacred, people's war.

Newspapers on May twenty-eighth announced that the Germans had retaken Kerch.

The loss of Kerch was accompanied by a worsening of Turkish relations. One of my teachers who had been visiting her husband in a training camp near the Turkish border returned unexpectedly. All civilians had been sent out of this zone.

"The Germans are coming here for sure," Professor Tenishvili said to those of us who were sitting in the Institute office on a day in May.

"What will you do then?"

"They'll let me back in the army then," said Tenishvili.

"And your family?"

"I know what to do with my family. I was born in these mountains."

It was easier for the Georgians, all of whom had relatives or friends tucked away in mountain fastnesses. The only resort for the Russians was evacuation, and that meant going to lands east of the Caspian Sea. Already many of them were thinking of doing just that.

Actors from the Moscow Art Theater expected to rejoin their troupe evacuated to Saratov, on the Volga; those from the Maly Theater to join their troupe in Cheliabinsk, a city in the Urals.

Kurikhin and Elena received an invitation to work for the Kiev film studios evacuated to Ashhabad, Turkmenia. They were considering the question when I visited them one evening.

"What do you think?" asked Elena.

"I think it's a break," I said.

"But the heat? Kurikhin will never be able to stand that heat."

"Nonsense," said Kurikhin. "That was before the war. The war has taught me a lot about what I can stand."

He didn't look as though he were standing it any too well. He had caught up with his age, which was well on in the sixties. Formerly he hadn't looked fifty.

Andrei and I had a word about our own future just before he left with the Ensemble on a trip to Kirovabad, a city one hundred and fifty miles southeast of Tbilisi.

"We must head east," said Andrei. "But not just haphazardly. While I'm gone you think about a way. I'll do the same. Maybe one of us will get an inspiration."

I tried as I waited my turn in the bathhouse the next morning. Certainly I had time enough. It was an hour before a free locker enabled me to undress and make a hazardous descent down wet stone steps to the room where ablutions were in process. This was an oriental bath. Shafts of light from a vaulted ceiling cut the vaporous air in which feminine forms lounged and bathed. I chose a faucet where an old woman and her granddaughter seemed about to finish. But I waited another hour while they washed and rinsed and washed and rinsed, the girl washing her own back and then the grandmother washing it for her, then return courtesies, then washing hair for the third time, then fine-combing it under the water, then just resting under the warm stream, then the whole thing from the beginning. I had already been in the bathhouse for nearly two hours and still belonged to the great unwashed. When I finally got under the faucet I made the drops fly and splashed out of the room in such record time that the languid ladies thought a mistake had been made.

I am told that in old Tbilisi, bath day was holiday. You came with the family and brought your lunch.

But I had no inspiration to take home with me. Nor did I think of anything during the next three days, and when Andrei returned we were as unsettled as before he left.

Then came the telegram.

The Radakovs had dropped in as I was scrubbing the children and putting them to bed. Something serious was happening to Radakov. His collar hung on his neck like a wall whose foundations had crumbled. He did not pay any attention to it. He talked about Thomas Hardy. The doorbell interrupted him. It was a telegram for Andrei:

> CHUVASH STUDIO EVACUATED CHEBOKSARY STOP INVITE YOU RESUME WORK ART DIRECTOR.

"There you are," said Andrei, smiling. "We shall go to Cheboksary."

A few days later I met a representative from the Moscow radio.

"Do you want to return to Moscow?" he asked me.

This was too good to be true.

"If you do, send a telegram of agreement to the Radio Committee and a request for a permit to return."

When I told Andrei he said, "What about the children?"

"Children are not allowed back in Moscow yet. They would have to go to Cheboksary with you and Rima until fall. Then I would manage to get permits for them to come to Moscow."

So Andrei sent his telegram to Cheboksary and I sent mine to Moscow, and we waited.

Return to Moscow had never entered our minds. We wanted it too badly, like all the rest of the Moscow exiles. Along the Volga, the Kura, the Amur, the Lena, along all the great rivers of the Soviet Union sat Muscovites pouring tears of homesickness into waters that carried them indifferently to the Arctic Ocean, the Black Sea, the Caspian. . . .

So it was easy to understand the joy with which evacuees received news of the massive British bombing of Cologne and Essen. The information that the Germans were making a headlong evacuation of industrial centers brought a vengeful tightening of lips to Russian mothers whose children, if they had survived the horrors of attack and flight, had been subjected to the maladjustments of life in exile. They had endured hunger and cold. They had also endured childhood's deepest grief, the loss of Kiska the cat and the doll Marusya.

People took this bombing of the Ruhr as harbinger of the imminent opening of a second front in Europe.

"It won't be long now," they said.

Meanwhile the Germans opened a vicious third attack on Sevastopol, and on the third of July we learned that they had taken it. That same day Andrei received a reply to his telegram:

> STUDIO PLANNING REMOVAL TO SARATOV STOP WILL COMMUNICATE FURTHER DEVELOPMENTS.

That was bad. By the time we learned whether the studio would move to Saratov or not, by the time it moved, if it did, the summer would be over. I could not think of leaving the family and going to Moscow under such circumstances. The children were run-down, undernourished, susceptible to contagion in this hot, crowded, festering city. We had to get them away.

This we did by moving to Baghebi, where we lived in a Georgian peasant's house on the side of a mountain five miles of climb from Tbilisi. There life was an idyll to the accompaniment of tom-toms. Our house was one of two wooden ones built wall-to-wall with a long veranda on the second floor overhanging the dark dirt-floored rooms in which peasants take shelter from summer heat. Babo was our landlady. She dressed always in black with a black kerchief tied over her head.

"Ello!" she would call early in the morning. "Ello!"

Ello, one of Babo's three daughters-in-law left in her care when her three sons went off to the war, would emerge sleepy-eyed and the two of them would go down to work in the orchard until evening. Ello had recently given birth. From the room under the veranda came such persistent crying that I asked Babo one day if the infant was sick. She gave me a sharp look and walked away without answering. The crying went on day after day with diminishing force until it became a fitful wail. Then even that stopped. Very early one morning as I was brushing my teeth over the porch rail I saw Ello slip out of the dark room carrying a long box that she took down to the orchard. She came back without it.

I got dressed and went to meet Suliko, another daughter-in-law. She had brought me a pint of milk which I paid for in bread.

I was alone with the children that day, for it was Rima's turn to go to Tbilisi for bread and Andrei was in the North Caucasus. The trip was risky in view of German advances, but it was made expedient by the food problem.

Now, for example, I had to give the children breakfast. The best I could do was to take a third of the day's ration of black bread (minus what I had traded for milk), toast it on our little kerosene stove to give it flavor, and offer it butterless, with sugarless tea. The milk had to last all day, so we would not have it for breakfast.

Perhaps Rima would be able to borrow some money in Tbilisi and bring us something for dinner.

"Mother, where's my caterpillar?"

"Hush, Adya. You'll wake up Dasha."

"But where is it? It was on these flowers."

The day had begun. All morning was spent in doctoring the sores with which Adya and Dasha had become infected. Water for hot permanganate baths had to be carried from the spring half a mile up the mountain. A candle was the only means I had of sterilizing the instruments with which I cut away proud flesh. Torn-up sheets and underwear supplemented the meager supply of bandages obtainable on doctor's prescription. In lieu of soap, boiling had to suffice to remove pus and salve from used dressings. In spite of everything, the sores showed improvement.

After a lunch consisting of another third of bread, this time with milk, the children had a nap. These days they did not object. Their instincts knew that air and sleep were the best compensation for undernourishment.

As I began to wash the lunch dishes, I heard someone call.

"Ah-oo! Margarita!"

It was Svetlana, wife of the Moscow writer Boris Cherni. They, too, had rented a house on this mountain. Her golden hair was blazing with sun as she climbed the path.

"Come along to town with me," she said.

"I can't. Rima's there. Why are you going?"

"To get the news. One day of mountain is enough to set me squirming. Things are too exciting these days."

"Have Boris and his mother returned from their trip to Moscow?"

"Last week."

"What do they say?"

"Awful things about the road through Central Asia. That's the way they returned, all the way around, through Samarkand and Tashkent and across the Caspian. They were coming west, so it wasn't so bad. There are simply millions of refugees going east."

"That's what terrifies me when I think of leaving Tbilisi."

"But you had better. Things are getting sticky here."

"What are you planning to do?"

"Go away. But Boris and his mother are tied up with the films. They won't finish their scenario for another month at least."

"And by then?"

"Anything may happen. But Boris says nothing will. He's positive the Germans won't reach Tbilisi." Svetlana swung her long legs off the porch railing. "And if they begin bombing and tearing things up, Boris says we'll evacuate along with the film studio."

"Aren't you satisfied?"

"After the way we walked out of Moscow on the sixteenth of October, I've lost taste for last-minute evacuations."

I walked her down to the road.

"I'll try to find some bandages for the kids in Tbilisi," she said, and set off with a free stride and a slim body that were nice to watch going down the mountain.

Rima hadn't come back yet, and it was time for me to start foraging for the third meal.

There is a wild grass native to Georgia which resembles spinach. It grew near our house, and I took my basket and began to gather the dinner. Soon Adya and Dasha came pattering out after their nap and helped in a hunt which led us down the valley path. Old Babo spied us from her porch and came hurrying after.

"*Ginensvali! Ginensvali!*" she called, which is a common Georgian form of address.

She caught up to us and kept on going, motioning that we should follow. We crossed a field and climbed a stone fence leading into her garden. Here the wild grass grew more abundantly. With a wave of her hand she invited me to help myself. Then she went over to an ancient mulberry tree, picked the white berries, and brought them to my basket.

"*Pinti* (bad)," she said, indicating the gunfire coming from the mountains. "*Pinti.*"

When we came back I washed and picked over the greens. By the time they were ready Rima came home, hot and perspiring from her climb. In her knapsack were potatoes, bread, cornmeal, a quarter of a pound of butter, and some peaches for the children.

"Where did you get the money?" I asked.

"From Misha," said Rima, enjoying my look of surprise.

"He's back?"

"Wounded."

"Really? Badly?"

"His left hand's been amputated."

"Oh no."

But Rima was happy that he was alive and in Tbilisi.

The war kept coming down from the north. It was coming along that very railroad that had brought us to Nalchik. And it was approaching Nalchik. It was just over the mountains where Andrei had gone with the Ensemble.

On one of my days at the Institute I took time off to visit the Simoyans. Vera was at home.

"Radakov has died," she said. "It was in yesterday's paper."

This was awful. My life on the mountain had kept me out of touch, and so I could not have expected it. Radakov had died. He who had been so resistant, cleaving through obstacles, ignoring them. It would be unbearable to see Radakov dead. He had been florid and massive. He would be yellow and wasted. His deep voice would be silent. His Bacchanalian locks would lie stringy.

I hurried to find Yevgenia Lvovna. She was at home, a mere shadow of herself.

"The last thing he said was that we should never have left Moscow," she said. "It was hard to die away from home." Radakov was the third of the group of noted actors and artists to die in the last few months. First was the painter Yakovleff. Then Klimov, of the Maly Theater. Now Radakov. For each of them life's final moments were made bitter by exile.

Everyone wanted to go home, and instead everyone was leaving for more distant places. In the middle of August Andrei came back and told us about the gigantic exodus from the north. The Ensemble had played closing concerts to almost empty houses. Everybody had left.

With Andrei's arrival Rima told us that Misha needed her and she would like to stay in Tbilisi. I could not protest even though I had come to think my life depended on her. She was a beloved member of our family. Now she would have her own family. The winds of war had brought her happiness.

Later that day Dasha took a bottle, Adya the teakettle, Andrei and

I took pails, and we climbed the mountain for water. The spring was also a watering place to which bearded old men wearing skullcaps came jogging on their donkeys. They would step off of them at the water trough, letting the animals go for their drink while they flung themselves in the shade of a fig tree.

We filled our vessels and started down the path. Suddenly we heard the booming of anti-aircraft guns and looked up to see silent blooms of cotton springing in a blue sky. They were the explosions of shells, and their appearance seemed to have no connection with the delayed booming. Among these sudden puffs appeared a swift white parabola of smoke in the wake of a black dot zooming to the horizon.

A German scouting plane had made its first visit to Tbilisi.

We watched the shells chase the vanishing dot and tried to explain to the children what it meant.

Enemy scouts came the next day and the next, and this aspect of war became the latest feature of bristling, martial Tbilisi.

A few days later I went to the Institute to explain that I could no longer work now that Rima had left me. I found the secretary's office littered with archives, which were being packed for shipment.

"Is the Institute planning to evacuate?" I asked.

"We have to be ready, in case," said the secretary.

On leaving the Institute I walked up the Rustaveli Prospekt to the Simoyans'. Guards were checking documents at every corner. I passed three truckloads of refugees. Their faces were inflamed by sun, grimy with dust. They sat dejected among a heterogeneous collection of blankets, mattresses, pails, and saucepans.

Suddenly there came a burst of gunfire. The radio warned, "*Citizens, take cover from shrapnel.*" I stepped into the doorway of a store and found myself beside Ira Tuzhanskaya, daughter of one of the evacuated artists.

"We're leaving tomorrow," she said.

"Where are you going?" I asked.

"East of the Caspian."

"All the artists?"

"Yes. For better or for worse. They say traveling is frightful."

"What about Kurikhin and Elena?"

"They've already left for Ashkhabad."

"And Malyavin and his wife?"

"Gone to Tashkent."

"What about Yevgenia Radakova?"

"She is going with us."

It seemed that we were the only ones staying behind.

Nights can grow dark very early in late August. It was on such a dark night as we sat talking on our veranda that I noticed a darker blotch scuttle across the floor. Andrei saw it too: "A slipper or something. Quick!"

He struck the blotch and we brought a candle. To our horror we saw a tarantula almost the size of a man's hand. The blow had not killed it. As we brought the candle close, it struck out viciously, fighting the flame.

The tarantula seemed symbolic of the odious swastika creeping down on us. And we had no means of leaving. Weeks of sending wires and waiting had brought no news from the Chuvash studio. Every day Andrei went to Tbilisi to discover possibilities. Every day I waited for the news he would bring back.

Then one afternoon as Adya, Dasha, and I were returning from the spring, Andrei met us on the mountain. There was good news in his eyes.

"We are leaving," he said as he took the pails from me.

"For where?"

"For Tomsk, Siberia."

"With an organization?"

"With the Leningrad Theater Institute."

"How did it happen?"

"A representative from the Art Committee arranged it. The Institute is here in Tbilisi. After being rescued from the Leningrad blockade over the ice of Lake Ladoga they were brought here, to the North Caucasus—you know, sun, mountain air, food. But the Germans caught up with them. The students and their professors escaped by walking a hundred and fifty miles over the mountains. They've lost everything. I found the woman who is head of the Acting Department taking a nap with a block of wood under her head. Maybe you can find her a pillow?"

After it was dark we went inside because it seemed safer from the tarantulas. While the children slept we made plans.

"We must begin by selling things to get money for the trip," said Andrei.

"How long will it take?"

"Who knows? Troop and munition trains have right of way, so it may take a month. Maybe more."

"They say traveling is dreadful."

"Don't worry. Everything will be all right."

"What if we get stranded in Krasnovodsk?"

"We won't."

"And the heat? And no water?"

"There you are. All summer we've been racking our brains to find out how to get to the studio. Just when we find a way you begin worrying about maybe there won't be enough water."

"No, I don't. There'll be enough water. Tomorrow I'll get right after the suitcases."

"We'll need a lot of money, so sell everything."

"Everything. We'll be as stripped as the people from Leningrad."

At that time I did not know much about the blockade and siege of Leningrad. In the first years of the war the Soviet media (and we had access to no other) were sparing of news (all of it bad), limiting it to succinct statements of fact: "After a heroic defense, Red Army forces withdrew from. . . ." True, rumors of the terrible fate of Leningrad seeped through the blockade but it was not until the war was over that the whole story became known, and not until after Stalin's death that it was made public.

It seems that the capture of Leningrad was an obsession with Hitler, a central feature of his Operation Barbarossa aimed at the acquisition of eastern lands. According to his plan of operations it was to be accomplished in four weeks (i.e., by July 21, 1941) by having his northern armies advance in a *blitzkrieg* from Prussia through the Baltic states to the approaches to Leningrad, there to be joined by his Finnish allies. After taking the city they would sweep south and east to assault Moscow from the rear while his main forces assaulted it from the west in a gigantic pincers movement.

His timing turned out to be wishful thinking, but by early September all of Leningrad's road and rail connections with the rest of the world were cut off. The blockade was complete and the siege of the city, which went on for almost three years, was in full swing. Day and night the Nazis blasted Leningrad with bombs and shells, destroying its infrastructure, depriving its citizens of light, heat, water, communications, transportation—and this in a northern city where in winter darkness sets in at four in the afternoon and the temperature goes down to thirty degrees and more below zero (centigrade).

As soon as Hitler's intentions became clear, Leningraders sprang to the defense of their city. A Municipal Defense Committee was appointed, Workers' Battalions were organized, as were People's Volunteer Divisions. Every factory formed its own fighting detachment. Brigades consisting mostly of women set out with picks and shovels and built 450 miles of antitank ditches, 18,000 miles of open trenches, 22 miles of barricades, 4,000 bomb shelters. Even the children helped build fortifications.

What Leningraders failed to do was to ensure the safety of their food stores. On September eighth the Badayev warehouses, outmoded wooden structures containing practically all of Leningrad's food supplies, were set on fire by German incendiary bombs and burned to the ground. From that moment on food rations were cut again and again until by November 1941, the bread ration was 250 grams for workers and 125 grams (about two slices) for everybody else. And bread, if what became a mixture of wheatdust and sawdust can be called bread, was all that most people got. Death by hunger began in November and by December some 53,000 civilians had died.

The only way of getting any food into the city was over Lake Ladoga, north of Leningrad. Few boats ever plied its waters, which were often whipped into treacherous waves by fierce and prolonged storms. The insignificant ports on the lake's edge had primitive facilities and poor land connections. Yet at the height of winter in 1941–42 Lake Ladoga became the Road of Life for Leningraders. On November twentieth the first horse-drawn sledge trains crossed it and brought back a few tons of food. Later, when the thickness of the ice grew to more than eight inches it could support caravans of trucks, hundreds of which were lost either by Nazi strafing and shelling, or by sinking through spots of thin ice, or, after crossing the lake, by accidents on forest roads made impassable by rough terrain and towering snowdrifts.

The Road of Life did not stem the tide of death engulfing Leningrad, but it enabled the city to evacuate some 554,186 survivors from January 22, 1941, to April 15, 1942.

At the end of his definitive study of the Leningrad blockade, *The 900 Days*, Harrison Salisbury wrote (and the italics are his):

> *More people had died in the Leningrad blockade than had ever died in a modern city—anywhere—anytime.*

During the days of preparation to leave Tbilisi I was consumed with curiosity about the Leningraders who were to be our companions. They had seen suffering without precedent. The ghoulish winter in blockaded Leningrad. The flight from the Germans in the Caucasus.

I wondered what traces such extraordinary trials would have left on ordinary character. Would they be able to laugh? Could they live beyond their memories?

The first person I met from the Leningrad Theater Institute was the director. As I came out of a store on Rustaveli Prospekt I found Andrei in conversation with a man and a woman.

"Meet Nikolai Serebriakov, Director of the Institute, and his wife," said Andrei.

The man was long and thin with deep-set blue eyes, a soft hat slightly awry, a pipe impeding his articulation. A slouch went with the pipe and the hat.

I must have shown the strain of packing, for he took the arm of his big blond wife and said, "Lucky, aren't we, Maya? No packing to think about. Just step on the train and off we go."

"When?" said Andrei.

"As soon as possible. Maybe tomorrow. We're not going directly to Baku."

"Then how?"

"Through Armenia."

"Why?"

"More important things to transport over the Tbilisi-Baku road than us. The Germans are just on the other side of those peaks. They're in Nalchik."

In Nalchik! Our Nalchik! Maybe they were living in our apartment, sleeping in our beds!

"They say fighting is going on in Stalingrad," said Andrei.

So the Nazis had reached the Volga. Like reaching the Mississippi in the United States.

"If they take Stalingrad, that means they take Baku oil," said Serebriakov.

"And that means they can cut north and attack Moscow from behind," said Andrei. "In other words, zero hour."

We hurried to finish up our sell-out and the conversion of money into tea for barter, having been told the Turkmenians, through whose republic we would pass, valued tea above most other worldly blessings. The following morning a messenger came to say we were leaving that evening.

My next encounter with people from Leningrad was while sitting in our compartment waiting for the train to pull out of the station.

Andrei introduced me to a small woman in glasses with white hair combed back smoothly and held in place by a black velvet band. She stood hesitantly in the doorway.

"This is Elizavyeta Dmitriyevna, head of the Acting Department. It seems we have taken her compartment by mistake."

"Stay right where you are," said Elizavyeta Dmitriyevna. "You'll need more room with the children. There'll be a place for me next door when the train starts."

She sat down, taking out a cigarette and a piece of gummy candy. "Thank you so much for the sheet and the pillow, Margarita Danilovna. I never knew they were such a luxury." Then she talked about how long the trip would take.

She, like the Serebriakovs, seemed perfectly normal. It disappointed my expectations. Where were the twitching lips, the haunted eyes? Had these people emerged from their trials as ordinary as the rest of us?

We shared our compartment with a middle-aged woman and her son Tolya, a tall boy of about seventeen. Her name was Margarita Emilovna and she had been a teacher of English at the Leningrad Institute of Foreign Languages. Now she had joined the faculty of the Theater Institute to be with Tolya, who was a student there. She spoke English with the perfect Oxford pronunciation that marked her a product of the Leningrad School of Phonetics. Naturally we talked about our profession, but this did not last long. An inner compulsion made her tell me the story of the winter. During the following days I came to realize that with her it was a necessity to relive again and again those experiences by recounting them to anyone she met. She told me that at night she would suddenly wake up and struggle to grasp reality. There seemed no nexus joining her living before the autumn of 1941 with the phantasmagoria that followed.

"February was the bitterest month," she said. "In February I lost my husband. For weeks before he died everything connected with our daily living fell on my shoulders. He, and Tolya too (turning her eyes to her son listening from an upper berth), was too weak to help me at all. The old nanny who had been with us for fifteen years came to me in tears some weeks before my husband died. Through her muttered apologies and justifications I gathered she wanted to leave and go to her own people. She thought it would be easier with them—thought they had some food supplies. One couldn't deny anyone the right to existence in those days, so of course I agreed to her going. A few days after my husband's death I found her body on the stairs leading to our apartment. Apparently either it was no easier living with her relatives or she was driven back by remorse. I dragged her body to one of our abandoned rooms until I could secure help to bury her. Only three weeks later did I find two emaciated boys from a vocational school who helped me carry her frozen corpse down the four flights of stairs to the street. We finally placed her on two child's sleds tied together, and it remained for me to haul her to one of the spots designated by municipal authorities for the accumulation of corpses. I did not get the whole way. The sleds were so narrow that at every few steps I had to adjust the body. When I had almost reached the pile where I was to leave it, a rut in the road jerked it off. For some time I struggled to put it back but finally I had to give up and leave it where it lay."

All this was told dispassionately, as though it did not touch her, and indeed as though she did not believe it. The darkness of the train conveyed the impression that we were even now in a gruesome dream-world. Occasional matches momentarily lighted the groups of people whose disembodied voices formed a soundtrack for Margarita Emilovna's story.

"By that time my boy was in hospital. The food ration for those dying of starvation was scarcely higher than for the rest of us, and every morning when I went to see him I was afraid to enter and learn whether he had survived the night or not. He lay white and apathetic, not swollen like most of them.

"My days were entirely taken up by the sordid tasks of housekeeping. Early in the morning I took my place in the water queue at the river. For hours we stood in the bitter cold and darkness waiting our turn, and when it came there was the question of whether today we should have the strength to lift the bucket of water through the hole in the ice. Every time a bucket was drawn out some of the water spilled over, creating a high ice barrier. I could lift only half a bucketful over it. The task of carrying it to the fourth floor took me more than an hour. That half a bucketful of water, the result of hours of labor, had to suffice for the entire day.

"At the very beginning of winter the four of us had moved into one room—the smallest in the apartment—for the sake of economizing heat. Winter days in Leningrad are so short that until ten o'clock in the morning and after four in the afternoon it is dark. The dirt of ordinary living was increased by the soot of the *koptilochka*,* which

*Koptilochka: a "sooter," a lamp made by thrusting a wick into the top of a small bottle containing kerosene.

burned all the time. People in Leningrad went about with faces smudged like miners from these lamps whose light is less than that of an ordinary candle.

"Sanitary measures were very strictly enforced by city authorities, and since the sewage system was frozen, all waste had to be carried out of the houses. We kept the bucket for such purposes in one of the empty rooms. The room was unheated, the bucket froze, and in order to empty it we had to thaw it.

"All of these details turned life into a nightmare that went on and on without respite. People became so hardened to horror that I, for example, could pass a pile of corpses every morning on my way to see Tolya at the hospital and even take a detached interest in the changes the last twenty-four hours had brought to it."

Margarita Emilovna relapsed into silence and darkness, and I sensed that she was still grappling with the incomprehensible, the incredible, that would not find logical place in her life's sequence.

At the other end of the car a group of young people were gathered around Nikolai Serebriakov, the director. In the flare of a match I caught sight of his lean figure slouched on the seat, one arm thrown carelessly over the shoulder of his Maya, the other grasping the bowl of his pipe.

I said to Andrei, "I think he and his wife must be newlyweds."

"They are. They met in Pyatagorsk this summer." Then Andrei leaned over to add softly, "His first wife died in Leningrad. A beautiful girl, they say. An actress. Quite a tragedy. Be careful what you say."

The next morning we were traveling along the Turkish border. As usual, it seemed strange to find the boundary between countries undetectable. There should be a color differentiation, as on the maps, or at least some striking contrast in houses and people. But here was Armenia stretching in brown hills to the left and the same hills marking Turkey on the right, with nothing to show the difference.

At noon we arrived in Yerevan, capital of Armenia, where we changed trains for Baku. It was a pity not to have time to see this ancient city lying on the rich plains from which Mount Ararat thrusts abruptly as though specially stuck there for Noah's convenience.

I went out on the train platform after we left the station. It was cooler in the breeze. Ksenia Borisovna, accompanist for the Institute, came out and joined me. We stood watching the scenery go by.

"You must seem very far from home," she said, a smile shifting the color of her eyes from violet to purple.

"Very far," I said.

She was silent a while. Then, very quietly, "But you are not alone. You have Andrei Andreyevich. My husband lies in a cold, nameless village in the north. He died on the way to food."

She looked at a hot mountain and saw a bleak village. "It's silly, I suppose," she added, "but I envy Elizavyeta Dmitriyevna because her husband is buried in Leningrad."

"Did Elizavyeta Dmitriyevna's husband die too?"

"Oh, yes. So did Anna Vasilyevna's, the history professor. So did Marina Nikolayevna's, the dancing teacher. But all of our women have lost their husbands."

The journey to Baku was not a long one, and on reaching it we waited only four hours before boarding a boat to cross the Caspian Sea. This was not luck but special privilege accorded citizens of Leningrad, a mark of homage for the sufferings they had endured. Ours was the last passenger boat to leave Baku for five days.

I call it a passenger boat because it carried passengers, not because it was meant to. It was a small oil tanker with accommodations for a crew of not more than thirty. Now its decks were crowded with eight hundred people. Fortunately the weather was fair and warm, though a rough sea on the first night swept the decks, soaking people and baggage and making sleep impossible.

In general it was a happy passage. During these two days people relaxed and lashed their thinking to the present, letting it go neither forward nor backward. Here was sun and air and companionship. Everyone was off to the unknown. Everyone had put the greatest evil, the enemy, behind him. This was a hiatus to be enjoyed. The boat's chief engineer, a rugged sailor who had been plying the Caspian for thirty years, offered the children and me his cabin to sleep in. He told us that German scouting planes were already visiting Krasnovodsk, the port toward which we were heading.

"Why not?" he asked. "It's the natural thing to do, to bomb Krasnovodsk. All Soviet oil goes through Krasnovodsk now that the fighting at Stalingrad has closed the Volga. It's a tiny port, hills pushing it right into the sea. A couple of bombs is all it wants."

Toward the end of the second day we came in sight of land. But we discovered it was no simple thing to enter the port of Krasnovodsk. All night we stood at anchor waiting for a signal to go ahead. Early the next morning we were still waiting. It was noon before we steamed into port.

The sight that met my eyes when we drew near was the first breathtaking shock I received on this trip. Our boat was wedged into a long line of steamers whose bridges and funnels rose out of a solid mass of human beings. Here was the human avalanche that had given rise to the fearful stories we had heard about Krasnovodsk. Formerly the town could not have had a population of more than ten thousand. On the day of our arrival twenty thousand refugees landed. Altogether there were sixty thousand people waiting to be transported to the east, and this despite the fact that approximately twenty trainloads of refugees were evacuated daily.

We waited while boat after boat was unloaded. Finally our turn came, and after disembarking we made a temporary halt on a bystreet, awaiting instructions as to where we should go. The blazing streets were thick with the dust stirred up by thousands of alien feet. Almost as thick as the dust were the flies that attacked us venomously in their old age. Truckloads of munitions passed us on the way to the docks, for this port represented not only the sole outlet for Baku oil at the moment, but lay on the main artery for bringing up troops and supplies to stem the invasion of the North Caucasus.

Within an hour we were told to collect our things and set out for a given address. With difficulty we found a man with a pushcart who agreed to transport our baggage for an exorbitant sum. We followed the cart through streets lined with people who had set up temporary habitation. Some had improvised tents with blankets. Others hung sheet partitions between themselves and their neighbors on the sidewalk. Others simply sat obdurately on their bags, refusing to admit the possibility of long waiting by physically adjusting to it. Every family had placed two bricks in the gutter on which they boiled water and prepared food if they were lucky enough to have any.

Our camping ground was a yard surrounded by small frame houses. The Leningrad Institute assumed a monopoly over this yard and each of us selected a spot to "build his house." This we did with duffles and suitcases, making "corridors," "bedrooms," "dining rooms," much as children might do with blocks. "Hey!" cried Nikolai Serebriakov. "Take your feet off my dining room table!"

Some of the residents of the real houses objected to our intrusion. You could hardly blame them. After all, one hundred people setting up housekeeping in your backyard was something! But nothing could be done about it. We tried to convince them they were lucky to get nice refined people who were careful where they threw their potato peelings.

We laughed and joked and made light of the situation. But our hearts sank when we realized how long such an existence might last.

On the first morning, one of the other wives and I got up early and set out for water. There was no difficulty in knowing where to go for it, we just followed the stream of people with empty buckets and bottles. They led us to a water tank where a long line was waiting until the supply should be turned on. A hollow-eyed woman beside us said she had been in Krasnovodsk for ten days.

"The worst thing is the dread of an air raid. Scouts come over every day. We'd be wiped out like flies."

In an hour's time an announcement was made that there would be no water. The line broke up as though demagnetized and rushed to another tank where hundreds of people were already in queue. Since we had a small supply back in camp, we decided to wait until later in the day.

This day and the next Andrei and I took the children to the Caspian Sea to avoid the crowd. Comparative isolation was the only attraction of a seashore along which a railroad carried its constant freight to and from the port. We stayed there until sunset should bring a cool evening to walk back in.

As we came in sight of our camping ground on the second evening we were greeted by cries of "Hurry, hurry! Where have you been so long? We're leaving tonight!"

We could hardly believe such good fortune, but the turmoil in camp confirmed it. This was another favor bestowed on citizens of Leningrad. There followed wild packing, dressing, eating. Then we waited. We waited until the children fell asleep. We waited until we ourselves fell asleep.

At one o'clock someone came and told us to go to the station. The commotion of dressing children and assembling baggage began all over again, and it went on in a blackout that barred even matchlight.

Finally I found myself with Adya in one hand and Dasha in the other running after the blacker patches on the night that were the men carrying our bags. To lose them would mean to lose ourselves in this midnight and multitude. I dared not even contemplate the consequences of such a calamity. They led us out to the rails behind the station where our train was being shunted. There we waited among roaring engines until Andrei came and took us to the car reserved for professors of the Institute. Krasnovodsk was over.

Inside the car we found Elizavyeta Dmitriyevna already lying on a bench with a cigarette in one hand and a lump of sugar in the other. Never had I seen anything like this railroad car. It was "hard," with wooden benches instead of upholstered seats, and this proved an advantage in the dust and heat of the journey. The benches could be folded out at night, making wide berths on which mattresses and blankets were spread. There were no partitions between the compartments, so we all lived together in one huge room.

The first few days took us through the desert of Kara-Kum, down to the border between the Soviet Union and Iran. Strangling waves of heat blew into the car from the wastes of sand billowing to the horizon. There was no escaping the hot air which dried our throats and left our bodies dripping. We saw a group of refugees at the edge of the desert huddling under blankets strung between scrubby bushes. Any limitless expanse is appalling—night skies, the ocean, Siberian steppes. But nothing is as appalling as the desert. We were thankful when patches of green heralded the return of fertile land.

And the fertility of the country we now entered was in direct contrast to the barrenness of the desert. Everywhere were trees, gardens, orchards. Our diet from now on until we reached Alma-Ata in the foothills of the Ali Tag Mountains, consisted almost exclusively of fruit.

It was a friendly sort of life in this railroad car. We meandered along, giving way to troop or freight trains. We took advantage of the frequent stops to wash ourselves and our clothes at whatever station offered hot water. We stretched our muscles by walking up and down the rails. We built bonfires along country tracks for frying eggs or boiling cereal. At stations or from passing trains we got the news: "Severe fighting at Stalingrad." It had been going on for a month now.

Our chief sport was seeing who could get the best bargain in bartering combs, thread, matches, tea, for melons, grapes, and milk.

One day as Dasha stood drooling in anticipation of a slice of Andrei's latest melon, I saw Anna Vasilyevna, history professor, watching her strangely.

"My Natasha would be the age of your Dasha if she had lived," she said.

"Was it hunger?" I asked.

"No. She died before the hunger. She was killed by a bomb. She and my mother."

Hour after hour Adya sat at the window drinking in the colorful impressions of this slow-flowing country of oriental fable bearing such magic names as Ashkhabad, Bokhara, Samarkand. Here again we met the lowly ass with whom we had become so familiar in Georgia. We saw cud-chewing camels lunge lazily through sun-bright streets. We saw low, edgeless clay houses whose pyramidal walls suggested the architecture of ancient Babylon. We wanted to leave the train and go off to those trees and houses and to those people with their proud, graceful walk. We wanted to visit the tomb of Tamerlane in Samarkand and reconstruct the days when this city was the capital of that fourteenth-century Mongolian conqueror.

The reconstruction of history is easier in the East than in the West. It is much simpler to relive the days of Tamerlane in Samarkand than the days of Washington in Philadelphia. For the essential rhythm of the East has better withstood the changes of six centuries than the rhythm of the West has withstood two. I felt this keenly in our mountain home of Baghebi. There it seemed that we lived in the very atmosphere of the Bible—the wells, the watering places, the groves of fig trees, the wine skins. In Philadelphia I never felt the proximity of powdered wigs and crinolines, not even in the very shadow of Independence Hall.

Radio news remained terse: "*Severe fighting at Stalingrad.*" But people knew what was happening. They knew that Stalingrad was the crisis of the war. Perhaps of the century. They knew that history would take its course from the outcome of the Battle for Stalingrad. They knew how fierce it was, the forces that the Germans had concentrated there, and that we had concentrated there. "If only the Allies would strike in the west now!" said a man on the station platform at Alma-Ata.

After Alma-Ata we turned north to Siberia. Workmen prepared us for a change in temperature by boarding up broken windows. Day after day the weather grew colder. Most of these Leningraders had nothing to wear but the summer clothes on their backs. We shared, but there were not enough things to go around. Everyone lived in dread of the Siberian winter.

As we proceeded north the scenery changed to typical Russian woods. People clustered around the windows, sighing with homesickness and going into ecstasies at this almost-return. Though they were thousands of miles east of their native city, these mild forests of oaks and birches and evergreens were poignant reminders. Nikolai Serebriakov stood alone at a window, sucking his pipe, lost in thought. He snapped out of it when Maya came up to him. He reached for her shoulder and said: "Lots of forests around Tomsk. We'll have some skiing this winter, won't we, *podruzhka*?"

The last lap of our journey was marked by the switching of our train to a branch line connecting Tomsk with the Trans-Siberian trunk line. It brought us to our destination on a cold dreary afternoon. Darkness had descended before a truck came to pick us up. We piled into the back of it in such a crush that we could see nothing but our neighbors' shoulders until we got out at a big building occupied by the All-Union Art Committee, evacuated here from Moscow. We were given temporary lodging on the top floor. The building was unheated. The rooms were unfurnished. We felt unwanted.

thirteen

Siberia

SIBERIA IS BIG. It has big forests and big rivers and big snows. The people are not big, they are stocky and muscular; they had played a major role in turning the Germans back from Moscow, and now they were fighting them in Stalingrad. More of them were going out, and before they did they were marching here in Tomsk. They, too, sang the theme song, and it sounded even more grim when they sang it because Siberians are a taciturn people:

> Then let our righteous wrath uprise
> Like waves that lash the shore,
> For our united people wage
> A sacred, people's war.

Tomsk seemed very far away. It was isolated in the vast expanse of forest called the taiga, shunned even by the Trans-Siberian railroad with its comforting grip on Moscow in the west and Vladivostok in the east. But these boys going out were vital reinforcements for the depleted columns in the west.

In Tomsk we were assigned a room in the apartment of a shoemaker whose son was studying in an army radio school in Novosibirsk. Samson Danilovich, the shoemaker, had just returned from visiting him when we moved in.

"He's changed," he reported to his wife Axinia. "He's taller and broader. There's no talk yet about sending them off. He'll be there at least until spring."

"Does he get enough to eat?"

"Who'd get it if the army didn't? Here, he sent you his picture." Samson Danilovich handed his wife a photo of a uniformed blond boy, very serious, very much resembling his mother. Axinia was touched. Her beady eyes were stung to red and her sharp nose sniffed into the ends of the kerchief tied around her head. For that dry, crackling body harbored a nest of maternal affection which was the good that dwells in even so hard a nature as Axinia's.

She hated us for intruding upon her family privacy. Her family was the universe to Axinia. Besides the son in the army there was Vanya, sixteen, who had left school with the coming of the war to join his father in making army boots in a Tomsk shoe factory. There was daughter Nina, twenty-one, who had a baby by son-in-law Alyosha, twenty-four, just finishing dental school. Alyosha was the only member of the family diverging into intellectual pursuits, and his studies were revered with the awe attributed to the new and the unknown.

When he was not studying, he was one of the workers in this hive. He went with his father-in-law to the river to capture logs torn from lumber-camp floats. They sawed them and chopped them up for winter fuel. Alyosha brought the daily water supply from the public pump. Axinia and Nina sorted the summer's crop of potatoes. They shredded and salted a mountain of cabbages. They pickled cucumbers. The war stopped a normal flow of food products, but tradition had taught Siberians how to stock up for the winter. Here they had the advantage over untutored and unequipped evacuees. The people from Leningrad, for example, did not even have shoes for their feet, let alone the pails and axes and shovels and *koromysli* (shoulder yokes for carrying pails of water) which were essential implements to life in Siberia. Fortunately, most of our companions lived with families who shared. We drew Axinia.

Axinia was mean. She was contemptuous of my ineffectual efforts to turn wood into fire, but she offered no suggestions. She kept Adya and Dasha in a state of constant terror with her tantrums. She wrenched my pots and pans off the stove to make way for her own.

Nina and her father had slightly wider horizons. If I took the harpy's attacks meekly, they would come in with a remonstrative, "Oh, Mama. . . ." But if I struck back, then this monolithic family snapped to common defense.

We were intruders. We were indeed. But so had we been in Tbilisi. Now as never before I appreciated the Simoyans.

It was good to avoid the house, so we often walked to the Tom

River. The Tom is an insignificant Siberian river, not like the Ob into which it pours, or the Lena, or the Yenesei, rivers of colossal proportions.

The Tom steals grayly through the clearing where the city stands in forest encirclement. The market is held on its bank. Before the winter freezing, crude heavy rowboats bring bearded old men and their wrinkled wives from villages in some remoter Thule. They draw their barques up on the bank and customers cluster about for the bargaining.

"Good milk, Grannie," I remarked on tasting the wares of a raw-boned woman swathed in shawls. "Couldn't you bring me a supply every day?"

"Goodness no, dearie, I don't even know how much longer I'll be coming until she freezes. She'll be closing up any day now. Then you'll not be getting any milk till she makes a road for the sledges."

On the way back from one of our river walks, we stopped in at the Institute.

The people from Leningrad had found it difficult to adjust themselves to Tomsk. Nikolai Serebriakov had been sick from the day of arrival—first with an attack of stomach ulcer, then with boils, finally with the jaundice which struck three out of five of the students. We found him lying on a divan railing at a student who had come late to a lecture. This was no longer the jolly companion of our journey. He had become formidable. But people understood and didn't hold it against him. One week the students sacrificed their entire sugar ration (a special ration for evacuees from Leningrad) to help make up the dietary deficiency wreaking havoc with Nikolai Serebriakov's health. Maya stood by, silent and weary.

"You ought to go to the hospital," I said to him.

"It's November," he said. "It's November in Siberia. Look at those kids' feet. I must get them shoes." He swung off the divan and reached for his hat. Maya would have stopped him.

"I could go wherever you're going," she said.

He did not answer, just slouched his hat on at the same angle as his pipe and went out.

The Leningrad Institute tried hard to go on with its studies, but the ache to be elsewhere robbed them of intellectual powers. No inner fire sustained them. Nor had they the hearths and clothes and simple things that make people at home in life.

Andrei and I had the prospect of moving to Cheboksary to cheer us.

In early November a telegram came from the studio saying we were expected there. We would turn back now, thousands of miles in the direction of home. It would be almost home. To me, who wanted so badly to leave Axinia and wood-chopping and water-carrying, the Volga seemed next door to New York.

Then Adya and Dasha got the chicken pox, so we had to wait. The waiting was insufferable, but it was too full of household chores to allow me to mope. Sometimes I would run away from it all and go to the Tomsk library, a famous library on the campus of the no-less-famous Tomsk University.

One day I spoke to a student sitting beside me at a walnut table in the reading room. She was eager with questions on learning that I was an American. When I had answered, she said:

"Naturally I want to see Moscow and Paris and New York. But I don't think there could be any better place than Tomsk."

I was so taken aback that I stopped to consider. True, my impressions of Tomsk were Axinia-flavored. And we whom the war had made flotsam and jetsam cast up on this unfamiliar shore could not judge fairly of its virtues. There were this library and this university. They were enough to save anyone to whom they were important from provincialism. Here were opportunities for scholarship in an environment of peace and seclusion. Here one would never know the neurasthenia of a Western metropolis. Even the chores of fire-building, salting cabbage, and sorting potatoes might contribute to peaceful Tomsk life the same atmosphere of comfort and domestic security that we associate with American farmsteads of a former era. Tomsk offered the delights of winter sledding and skiing, of summer berrying and mushrooming. And it offered the opportunities of those close friendships that grow up in a limited environment. I was not an unprejudiced judge.

Ever since the end of August the battle had been raging at Stalingrad. Everyone awaited the outcome as an issue determining his own destiny. Still the radio said only *"Severe fighting at Stalingrad."*

In November Andrei and I celebrated our anniversary. We invited Nikolai Serebriakov and Maya to share it in our tiny room with the chicken-poxers blacked out by a newspaper over the light bulb.

Illness had left Serebriakov cadaverous. His blue eyes gleamed from such deep eye sockets and over such prominent cheekbones that his face became a grotesque of the quick and the dead.

He sprawled angularly across the table, sucking his pipe with the usual lust. Maya sat ready with matches to keep his pipe going, ready to remove dishes from the path of his broad gestures, ready for the spasmodic caresses which were her reward.

Maya was expedient in his life. From her he sought compensation for all he had lost. But that she could not suffice was evident from those attacks of spleen and dejection with which we now became familiar. His nervous jocularity, his unrepressed spasms of affection for this girl, could not conceal the mourning of his spirit.

On that night he mentioned Galya, his deceased wife, for the first time in our acquaintance. He mentioned her casually, among other things.

"The Institute sent me a birthday present last December: a quarter of a pound of butter, a can of sardines, four rolls. In Leningrad last December, that was the miracle of the loaves and the fishes. Galya and I invited guests. One of them was Tanya, a senior student. She was an ethereal creature at all times. She had gone pure spirit from hunger. I knew exactly what she'd had to eat that day—two slices of black bread and a bowl of hot water flavored with cabbage. But she took no notice of my food. Not a single covert glance gave her away. If I made a point of passing things, she looked shocked, as though I was being rude.

"There were others who were different. There was that actor friend who came to see us. It was evening, and Galya and I hadn't the strength to keep awake after eight P.M. But he couldn't seem to pull himself away. He kept sitting on, I don't think he even noticed when we left.

"The next morning when Galya reached for the piece of bread she always left on her desk for breakfast, it was gone.

"You couldn't blame him, I suppose, although he knew that Galya was living on the same one hundred and fifty grams of bread a day that was starving him. But hunger had eaten up everything except his stomach. He was just one yawning stomach, and one stomach doesn't give a damn how another stomach survives. He died the next week."

Nikolai Serebriakov refilled his pipe.

"So did Galya. You wouldn't have believed it possible if you had seen her at my birthday party. She was the jolliest one there. We even danced a little. Of course she had grown thin. But so had everybody. She didn't complain of feeling bad. She did her work as well as any of us. She never forgot her lipstick. And then one day she just stopped, like a watch. It didn't matter that I kept on going.

"I took her on a sled far away, not to one of those wretched city piles. I took her to a quiet spot where there were a couple of trees.

"When I came back to the apartment the students had set up a Christmas tree. They thought it would cheer me up. They didn't know that Galya had had a passion for Christmas trees."

Nikolai Serebriakov sat sticking his fork into a cold potato pancake for a minute, then turned instinctively to his blond. When he saw that she was finding these reminiscences hard to take, he reached back with a long arm and drew her to him.

"*Nu, nu,*" he said in affectionate remonstrance. "Don't forget that you're a Leningrader too."

It was harder to live up to that reputation here in Tomsk. Here there was not the challenge to sacrifice that had inspired people during the Leningrad blockade. There was only gnawing uneventfulness, rasping nonadjustment.

The monotony of it was broken toward the end of November. Andrei and I were still in bed on that morning when the radio began its unusual announcement. It was no terse communiqué. The announcer's agitated voice was reading figure after figure. The radio stood in the room where Axinia's family album lay on a starched doily, but Andrei invaded with the recklessness of a man of principle.

"*Soviet counteroffensive on the Stalingrad front. . . . German forces encircled . . . thirteen thousand German prisoners . . . fourteen thousand Germans killed. . . .*"

Andrei called from the other room. "Margarita! Do you hear?"

"Yes," I said.

"Alyosha! Do you hear?"

"Yes, I hear. Papa! Do you hear?"

The shoemaker left the kitchen table with his mouth full of potatoes. "*Nu?* You see? It's the Siberians who did it. It's our fellows at Stalingrad. Didn't you know that? Yes indeed, Siberians."

The whole day became holiday, subtle holiday caused by the lifting of a pall. Life went on with the same work, same food, same friends, same memories, same snow, river, taiga. But nothing was the same. The crisis of the twentieth century was ending in our favor. The war stretched on ahead with no end in view, but the war had about-faced. Now it would be a pounding to the west, a pounding to tangible victory, however remote.

This happened just before our departure for Cheboksary.

The date of our leaving had been set for the tenth of December. A letter from Andrei's brother Dmitri discouraged this move. "You must wait until spring," he wrote. "Don't forget that you will have to change trains three times under the severe conditions of a Siberian winter. This is too much of a risk with baggage and children."

But we were taking the risk.

Until December the weather had been mild for Siberia. True, we had already known months of snow and fur coats. And we had been buying milk at the market by the hunk; if what the milk lady offered was too big, she took an ax and chopped it up and you took your piece home wrapped in newspaper. But there had been few days with the thermometer lower than ten degrees below zero (centigrade). Now that we were about to take to the road again, the Siberian winter arrived, hitting twenty, thirty, forty degrees below.

I cut up old woolen underwear to make additional pants for the children and padded their mittens with cotton. We might have to spend nights waiting for trains on station platforms. For such an emergency I would keep blankets handy.

It was difficult to take farewell of our Leningrad friends. Our friendship had been brief but close. We would never forget them. On the evening of the ninth of December the students held a farewell party at which Andrei performed. Even I appeared with him in a sketch we had written together on Soviet-American friendship.

The next day the girls from the Institute came and finished pants and mittens. The boys did the packing (not much to do with our diminished possessions). And even Axinia, in her joy to be rid of us, fired up the great Russian stove to bake *piroshki* for our journey.

At seven o'clock in the evening Andrei rushed into the house to say that horse and sledge were waiting at the door. In fifteen minutes bags were tied on to the sledge, children were wrapped in blankets and perched on the bags, and Andrei and I with an escort of students set out on foot behind the sledge like a Georgian funeral procession.

The night was beautiful. Glittering stars and a horned moon struck sparks off the snow. We walked the three miles to the station quickly to keep warm, and because we were glad to be going somewhere. But the horse was more eager than we. We couldn't keep up with him and when we finally reached the station it was to find both the children in tears because they thought they had lost their father and mother. And because they knew they had lost their blankets. This, before we had left Tomsk!

The first impression of comfort in the spacious "soft" compartment for the overnight trip to Novosibirsk was deceiving. The temperature was approximately that of out-of-doors, and no huddling would help. We thought enviously of the nice overcrowded "hard" cars steaming with body heat.

Early the next morning we arrived at Novosibirsk.

"What news from Stalingrad?" asked Andrei of a young flight lieutenant striding past.

"Everything's fine."

"How many new German prisoners?"

"Don't remember. Enough. How many would you like?"

I ran the youngsters up and down the station platform while the bags were being checked, for the weather was living up to its Siberian reputation.

The train to take us to our next change at Sverdlovsk in the Urals would arrive only at midnight, and there was no guarantee that we would get accommodation on it. We climbed to the second-floor waiting room of a station in the proportions of the Grand Central and considered what to do. The chill of these vast marble halls made waiting here impossible. Suddenly I spied a sign reading: *Room for Mother and Child.*

"The very thing," said Andrei. "I'll leave you and the children there while I see about tickets."

The "Room" occupied an entire wing of the station. From an office where a nurse gave us a medical examination and filled in a questionnaire, we were led into a locker room, then upstairs to the playroom. There we found children building boats of blocks, putting dolls to bed, playing games, and reading books. It was warm and bright and cheerful. A kindergarten teacher supervised activities while mothers who had nothing to do until train time (which might be in three hours and might be in three days) sat in a corner comparing stories of evacuation.

I left Adya and Dasha with the toys and went to the sanitary bureau for a bath.

These sanitary bureaus were a war measure to prevent epidemics, especially of typhus. Therefore they provided not only baths, but also the disinfecting of clothes. No train tickets were sold, no one was admitted to a hotel or public lodging without a paper certifying that he had undergone the "sterilizing" of a sanitary bureau.

It was dinnertime when I returned to Adya and Dasha, and we joined the mothers and children who went to the dining room on the second floor. For a nominal sum we had a meal consisting of watery cabbage soup, white buns, and mashed potatoes. The money we paid for this food was the only payment made during our stay. Everything else, including lodging, playroom, supervision, services, was free of charge and extended to anyone who applied.

Soon after dinner I saw Adya and Dasha to bed. Dasha's room, being for younger children, was furnished with little white cribs. Adya's with beds. Both rooms had bright pictures on the walls, plants and curtains at the windows.

This was a far cry from camping on station platforms. It was somebody going along that hard road with you, figuring what you would need and seeing that you got it regardless of your means. I was grateful, and wanted to say so.

I made my way back to the playroom and found the supervisor sitting with a little boy whose mother had not yet returned. She was a sharp-eyed middle-aged woman with brusque manners.

When she learned I was an American she hastened to say, "In the old days my husband was a teacher in the gymnasium." There should be no mistake about her social position. One felt reservations in her support of this new world, yet the big thing she was doing had her in tow.

"Oh, you can't judge our Room now. You should have seen it in peace times. Then it was bursting with toys. The parquet floors shone so you could see your face in them. And the food—what is it now? No, no. This is only an excuse for a Room.

"All kinds of mothers come to us, and they all react differently. Sometimes simple peasant women make us presents. Sometimes they shed tears of gratitude. But not all of them appreciate what is done for them. Some are crude, and then I think, Oh, Lord, is it worth trying to do something for such thankless people? But of course it is. People are like stones; not all of them take to polishing. But the unappreciative are only one in a thousand, and in 1941 we served nearly two hundred thousand mothers."

The girl on duty came to tell me that Andrei was waiting downstairs. He brought the news that tickets were secured and we would leave at two o'clock in the morning. Until then the soft-hearted *dezhurnaya* (girl on duty) gave us permission to sit in the kitchen. Here we drank tea and ate Axinia's *piroshki* while cleaning women scrubbed tables and polished copper kettles.

It was a pity to rouse the children from warm beds and take them, heavy-eyed, to the cold waiting room. We sat there for an hour until our train arrived. Finally Andrei disappeared behind one porter, leaving me with the children to follow a second. These men had no sentiments regarding women and children. It was rush, rush, rush for them. Get rid of one job as quickly as possible, pocket as much money as possible, take on the next sucker as soon as possible. We raced blindly down steps and through tunnels, spilling scarves, my pocketbook, the basket of food, Dasha's mitten.

Finally we found ourselves in a crush of people on a narrow platform between two panting trains. Andrei was inside one of them finding places. The battle to board the train became so furious that I had visions of having the children crushed to death, or at best, simply all three of us being left behind. But finally a disheveled Andrei appeared at the door of the car and pulled us up.

We were off on our second lap of the journey. Our fellow passengers were mostly women and children returning from evacuation, for already the reverse migration had set in. They were returning to Moscow. Everyone knew that the winter in Moscow would offer little comfort: there was a fuel shortage and a food shortage and the danger of air raids. Yet with inexpressible joy these travelers announced that they were returning to Moscow.

People were willing to undergo any risk to get home.

It was particularly difficult to get permission to take children back to Moscow. So people smuggled them in. "One woman tied up her two kids in potato sacks whenever the inspector came through," a neighbor in our compartment chuckled.

At Sverdlovsk we immediately applied to the Room for Mother and Child. The quarters were less elaborate than in Novosibirsk, but just as clean, the attention as solicitous, and the food better.

At eleven o'clock of the second night we left Sverdlovsk for the junction of Kanash, which we reached in another two days. Again we got there at night. Kanash was not even a town, only a lonely junction obliterated by the blackout. Andrei left in search of a baggage room. I crouched over the children to cut the two-edged wind tearing through darkness. I wondered where we would spend the night in this hole.

Suddenly some instinct prompted me to turn around; it was just in time to see one of our suitcases and our basket of food walking off in the night.

"Stop him! Thief! Stop him!" I cried.

A long-legged figure loomed from behind a pillar. The thief dropped the bag and basket and the long legs picked them up.

"Here."

"Oh, thank you!"

"What's your nationality?"

"American."

"I thought Americans were practical people."

In a few minutes Andrei returned.

"I've found it," he said.

"The baggage room?"

"No, the Room for Mother and Child."

"In this wilderness?"

"Come on." And he led us to a small frame building beyond the station. To be sure, it bore little resemblance to the establishments of Novosibirsk and Sverdlovsk. It was a family boarding house in contrast to the Ritz. But it offered warmth, water, beds, and the cheerful smile of Lola from Leningrad who was in charge.

At seven o'clock the next morning we were on the train to Cheboksary, and a few hours later we arrived at the Cheboksary station, three miles outside the city.

At first we found nobody to meet us. Then Andrei was caught in the embrace of Vasili Danilovich, manager of the studio. Students came with smiles and helping hands. We all climbed into the back of the truck along with our baggage and a dozen other travelers, and set out at giddy speed over the icy road to Cheboksary. The town was blue and white, up and down, with a final rise to the high bank of the Volga where the hotel was situated.

Now the river was a broad ribbon of ice sweeping away in an expansive curve to the south. A blue blur on the opposite bank marked the conjunction of river ice and steppe snow. Down below, the Volga was crossed with roads along which moved the black strings of sledge trains.

The truck jerked, then skidded to a halt in front of a rather pretentious but unattractive building.

"Get out!" said the driver impatiently.

fourteen

Chuvashia

IT WAS NOT EXACTLY A HOTEL we entered. It was the "Peasant House," built a few years before the war to accommodate collective farmers of this agricultural republic of Chuvashia on their trips to Cheboksary, the capital.

The tower on the building looked fine so high above the Volga. But the best things were inside. Inside there were electricity and steam heat and showers and a room for us with four beds in it. We had not enjoyed a bed a piece since we had left Nalchik. There were also chambermaids who made beds and changed linen without my knowing it. In general, I felt restored to ladyhood, and began to powder my nose.

We had nothing to eat with us and the restaurant was closed, so students came with bread and other little offerings. Vasili Danilovich sat and told us the studio gossip. All but one of the original male students were in the forces. The studio had replaced them with new and younger boys.

Andrei felt skeptical about these new students. He had picked the old ones himself. When in 1939 the Chuvash Republic had applied to have a drama studio trained at the Moscow Theater Institute, Andrei had been sent to Cheboksary to select students, as earlier he had been sent for the same purpose to Mongolia and Kabardinia.

As soon as we knew that we were going to Cheboksary, I had looked the city up in a Russian encyclopedia published in czarist times. Not a word was mentioned about the Chuvash, only about the Russians. Apparently the author had found this Finno-Turkish people unworthy of notice. That was understandable. The Chuvash were backward, illiterate, disease-ridden, well on the decline. A painful eye infection called trachoma was the blight of the land. The years of war and famine from 1914 to 1920 cut the population from something over half a million to two hundred thousand.

Vasili Danilovich, manager of the studio, was a Chuvash patriot. He had graduated from Moscow University with a major in literature, and ever since had been working among his people. At first he taught literature, then he became so interested in the theater that he gave up teaching to manage the young studio.

All the talk that first evening centered about this studio. When Vasili Danilovich left for home, we fell into our soft separate beds in happy sleep. My last wink of thought was, if I feel this way about Cheboksary, how shall I feel about Moscow?

In the morning I took the children and set off to buy a meal at the market.

"To your left to the crossroad, then to your right and follow your nose," they told me. Not your nose, but the train of sledges hugging the ground on thick wooden runners. Their drivers were mostly women. They half-reclined on the straw and flicked their whips, bawling warnings at pedestrians unless a set of bells jangling to the rhythm of the horses made it unnecessary.

It was clear that these were not Russian peasant women because they perched a round fur hat on top of the shawls over their heads. The Russian peasant wears only the shawl.

We followed a frozen stream until a turn in the road showed us the market a block ahead. Both sides of the road were lined with sledges from which their owners peddled potatoes, flour, onions, dried peas, salted cabbage, then potatoes, and again potatoes. There had been a bumper crop of potatoes that year, and while other products were expensive, the market was flooded with potatoes. We were happy and bought a whole pailful. Then I spied carrots on one of the sledges.

"How much?" I asked a round-cheeked woman with dark, oblique eyes revealing a Tatar strain in Chuvash blood. She snapped out something unintelligible and returned to sorting her vegetables with an indifference that stung my pride. I forewent her carrots.

Between the rows of sledges walked people with towels, dresses, lengths of ribbon and embroidery thread hung over their arms to be sold or bartered for food. These were the evacuees in Cheboksary.

Like the poor, they were with us always. And they were the poor. And we were of them.

But people had developed an indifference to things. No *thing* was important. Only life was important. It gained added importance with the break in events brought about by the victory at Stalingrad. Everything would go easier now. The crisis was over. That did not mean the suffering was over. The finish would not be soon or simple. The important thing was to come in at the finish. Dresses could go, furs could go, watches could go, shoes could go, everything formerly cherished could go without so much as a hanging on with the eyes. People would come in naked to the finish. And they did not care. They did not care in the least.

The following day was the last in December, and Vasili Danilovich invited us to spend New Year's Eve with his family. He called for us at eight o'clock, a benign Mephistopheles with black eyes above high cheekbones in a pointed face. Wisps of thinning hair suggested horns.

Even Adya and Dasha were to share this outing, for which they had been prepared by a special nap. We climbed a long hill to Vasili Danilovich's frame house where his Russian wife, Anna Pavlovna, opened the door.

Electricity was being economized to supply the factories, so the room we entered was lighted by an oil lamp. An old man was bending in front of a Dutch stove, the fire illuminating his lean features and long white beard in flickering chiaroscuro.

"This is my father," said Vasili Danilovich. "In his day he was a famous *gusli* player. The Chuvash people in all the countryside knew him well for his music and tales."

The old man straightened up and met us with a frank, friendly glance, though the words we exchanged were few since he knew little Russian. "Let the children come in here and play with our Vasya," said Anna Pavlovna from the other room. Six year-old Vasya and five-year-old Dasha sidled up to each other, glancing and sniffing like two strange kittens. Then they both pounced on the same picture book and were friends.

"A fine library you have here," said Andrei.

"I've left a good part of my books in Moscow," said Vasili Danilovich. "Do you know that we may return there with the studio soon?"

"Really?"

"When I was in Moscow last month, the Art Committee decided it would be better for us to return to the Institute than to continue working here alone."

I did not allow myself to clutch this prospect too eagerly. There would be changes of decisions, complications, delay. That is what I kept convincing myself. But the thought of return kept flicking through the back of my mind like bright stitches while we sat over Anna Pavlovna's potato and cabbage soup followed by fried potatoes and salted cabbage with hot *piroshki* stuffed with cabbage and potatoes.

At twelve o'clock Vasili Danilovich opened a bottle of vodka and we toasted Stalingrad, victory, peace. The New Year stretched ahead of us with promise of new triumphs. You could not stop an army which had done Stalingrad.

And then for us the New Year might bring Moscow.

So we felt wonderful when we stepped out into the cold air. Other people coming up the hill were feeling good too, talking and laughing in the brightness of moonlit snow.

"Do you think we shall go back?" I whispered in Andrei's ear when we were outside.

"Wait and see," he said, with an arm-squeeze that meant he thought we might.

I could hardly get the children up next morning after such unaccustomed debauchery. But there was another party to be attended. It was a "New Year's Tree" held at the Red Army Club for the town's children. At two o'clock we again climbed last night's hill. In the daylight I saw that the house and buildings on either side were hung with blood-and-thunder war posters. Most of them were bad enough, but even so the world looked cheerful.

When we arrived, the auditorium on the second floor of the local club was squirming and squealing with three-to-seven-year-olds. In the center stood an enormous Christmas tree. The young sergeant who was master of ceremonies lined up the children and led them in a chorus of "Grandfather Frost, Light the Tree." Immediately it blazed into varicolored lights showing the British, American, and Soviet flags with which it was trimmed. A young girl made a speech about the recent successes at the front. It was over the heads of her audience, but it was brief. Then there were games and dances around the tree and volunteer songs and recitations. Prizes consisted of pencils and notebooks and boxes of tooth powder. Later a children's chorus performed and then a toy bomb was thrown from the balcony down to the stage. The bang was what was to happen to the Nazis.

As they went home, each child was given a bag full of cakes and candy. All the way back our conversation centered upon the bomb. Dasha was not sure whether it had been a bomb or an airplane. Adya was puzzled as to why the building didn't catch fire when it exploded.

The New Year was in, the year of 1943. It was the third year of Russia's ordeal, a year born in triumph through the travail of Stalingrad.

IN JANUARY, Andrei went to Moscow. It was a great moment for him. He had not seen Moscow for a year and a half. That would have been a long time under any circumstances. Under these circumstances it was the equivalent of half a lifetime. Across that long time, Andrei went back to Moscow. The children and I waited in Cheboksary. They entered a kindergarten, and every morning and evening I took them and brought them back along the high bank of the Volga. For the most part they were friendly walks, but sometimes barbed winds swept down the river valley and then we could hardly get to where we were going.

Throughout January the news was good. Besides the completion of the Stalingrad operation there was the expulsion of the Germans from the Caucasus. They must have run out, fearing a bottling-up as at Stalingrad. Nalchik was free, so was Prokhladny and towns as far north as Salsk and Armivir. But the biggest news was that in January the Leningrad blockade was broken. People could not help being happy. In the Peasant House all this was discussed in the kitchen, not the big kitchen connected with the restaurant, but a little spare kitchen designed for special servicing. The war had given this little kitchen prominence because now only one meal a day was served in the restaurant, and that a skimpy one. So people brought their potatoes to the stove in this little kitchen. Nobody cooked anything but potatoes. They boiled them, fried them, roasted them. They made potato cakes, potato soup, potato pancakes. But every attempt to disguise the potato's outer form left its soul unchanged. You could see this when someone paled on biting into the latest deception. In addition to the stove, there was a Titan in this kitchen. The Titan was the boiler that supplied the Peasant House with its morning and evening tea. The Titan's mistress was Glasha, a Ukrainian girl whose temperament was well suited to the job. She just sat on the floor in front of the Titan, stuffing its gullet with fresh wood to make it hiss and crackle with pleasure. On having enough, it would shoot off steam from a head nodule, and then people waiting with teakettles and glasses would open the spout and get their drinks.

You could usually find Dora Isaakovna brooding in some corner of this kitchen. During evacuation from Odessa Dora Isaakovna had lost her teenage son, and none of her efforts to find him had as yet been successful.

"Such a son," she said to me. "How he would not eat, my Abrasha, but only bend himself into a book. And his dark hair, you should see, so much and so curly. And how good he was at his music. Do I know how I lost him? So you know how the sun slips out of your room? Bombs, and running for the train, and nobody knows nothing, but when we leave, my Abrasha is not there. Then somebody saw him, how he worked in a factory in Tashkent, but no answer I get from my letter."

Men gathered at the Titan too, mostly men on furlough or recuperating from wounds. In the middle of February I heard them discussing the official report of the Stalingrad victory.

"How about capturing a field marshal in a department store basement!" gloated an infantry captain with a decoration pinned to his chest. "How do you think he felt?"

"How about taking 330,000 prisoners!" said another. "Poor slobs, I saw pictures of them. No boots, feet wrapped in rags, ladies' shawls on their heads. Boy! Did they take a beating!"

"We've come a long way since 1941," said a young boy with his arm in a sling.

"I'll say we have," agreed the captain. "Kalinin must be feeling good. When he handed out awards after the Moscow operations, all the fellows who got medals made silly speeches like 'We're sure gonna win this war!' and 'We'll show the bastards!' Kalinin said, 'Instead of boasting you'd better study tactics, learn how to beat Fritz at his own game.' "

"Looks like we've done it," put in another man. "At Stalingrad we beat him with our own tactics, not his."

The Russians were beating the Germans, but it was costing a lot of blood. Stalingrad meant a run on the blood bank, and people were urged to make new deposits. One morning after seeing the children to the kindergarten I stopped in at the Blood Transfusion Station to see if I would do.

The Station was located in what had formerly been the Cheboksary

Trachoma Institute. In the waiting room I found women who were donating for the fifth, sixth, eighth time.

When my turn came, technicians gave me a Wassermann test for syphilis and a test determining my blood type. They told me to come back in two days.

When I came back I was given the results of the tests and sent into another office where two doctors examined me. Having been approved as "donorable," I was treated to two glasses of tea and milk and as much bread as I wanted. Then I was outfitted in white coveralls and a cap which left only my eyes exposed.

When I entered the operating room, I saw four other people lying on tables with their arms extended, clenching and unclenching their fists to quicken the flow of blood into the glass jars to which their veins were connected by needle and rubber tube.

When it was over I was invited along with the others to have a substantial meal, after which we were issued certificates as donors, and cards entitling us to extra rations.

I left the station glad that I had sent my first installment of American blood to Russian battlefields. The test tubes showed no difference between my blood and that of the Russians. It would flow very nicely in the deflated arteries of some wounded Ukrainian or Siberian. It was the same blood.

A few days later Andrei returned from Moscow. I could see from his face that he was satisfied. He had not been disappointed.

"Moscow is beautiful," he said. "I think I had forgotten how beautiful. The city is sterner, very modest, engrossed in the work of the war. But Moscow is beautiful."

"When shall we go back?" I asked.

"I don't know when."

Andrei had arrived at night when the children were already asleep, so they could not get their presents. Andrei Nikolayovich, back from evacuation, had sent four candies, a glassful of dried fruit, and a package of saccharine (a coveted luxury). Andrei had saved some butter and crackers and cheese from his Moscow rations. We made a dazzling display of all these delicacies, topping it with two cardboard bunnies. The children would have their supplies on waking.

Everything was splendid except that Andrei had said he did not know when. I suppose it had been foolish to think he would come back and say, "In three weeks we shall leave for Moscow." But this was what I had hoped for.

* * *

IN FEBRUARY the kindergarten held a party in honor of Red Army Day. It almost turned out a tragedy for us, and all my fault. I got the time wrong.

"Why are you so late?" Dasha's teacher said when we got there. "I had given up hope of your coming. We've had lunch already. Cakes today. Don't cry, Dasha, I've saved yours for you. Hurry out of your things. It's time for the parade to begin." Adya had gone upstairs to join the older group. When I found him he was full of bitter recriminations. We skinned him of his leggings in a hurry and thrust him into his bright green suit with a soldier's hat and a rifle and dried his tears.

Three Red Army officers were the honored guests. One of them led the parade of fifty soldiers, pilots, and Red Cross nurses, ranging from three to seven years of age. They were awed by their captain, especially when he looked back to see how they were marching. They kept step to their song,

> A few more years and we shall stand,
> The brave defenders of our land.

Another one of the officers made a speech telling the children the reason for the war. He said the Germans had fallen on their country and wanted to take it away from them. He said they could not do it, and they knew it now, after Stalingrad.

The third officer stood at the back of the room with a set smile that needed constant jerking in place, especially after the first hour of poems and songs and dances.

Anna Constantinovna, as wife of the director of the Peasant House, was in charge of the party. She flitted from one place to another, keeping the kids in order, seating them in proper places, prompting them as they performed. No sign did she give of the despair elicited by a letter she had received a few days earlier. Anna was from Briansk in Belorussia, and the letter had been brought from there by a plane that contacted guerrillas in the Briansk woods. Anna sometimes came to visit me in our room, and on this day she came and read the letter to me.

> Dear Anna and Mikhail,
>
> I am writing to you from the woods. Maybe my letter will never reach you, and if you answer, yours may never

> reach me. But I shall try. Of course you learned from *Pravda* of 23rd July that our village of Kokerovka no longer exists. ("I didn't see it in the paper," said Anna. "I read that some of the people from our village whom I knew had been killed by the Nazis, but I didn't know that our village had been destroyed!") All of us fled to the woods where we live in caves and dugouts. During an attack on guerrillas all the members of the Kosterin family living in Altukhov were killed. ("That's my uncle's family," said Anna. "The awful thing is that one of my cousins was living with us near Minsk when the war broke out. She evacuated here to Cheboksary with us, but she couldn't find any peace. She was always worrying about her people back home. At last she took her baby and went to them. We begged her not to, we knew it was dangerous. But she was too unhappy. Now, you see, she and her baby have been killed.") Your Shura is alive. ("Shura's my fifteen-year-old brother.") He and your uncle have both joined a guerilla attachment. My husband and older son are also guerrillas and I live here in the ground with little Valeri. Your parents are with us, Anna; so are Mikhail's. We only hope and pray the end will come soon. I am only forty years old but my hair is white and my face is black. Every night I dream about my daughter Nina. When the war began she was studying at the Moscow Pedagogical Institute. In the name of our friendship, I beg you to try to find her. It should be possible there on the Mainland. It is especially difficult with food. For more than six months we have not tasted salt. As for soap, people have forgotten what it is. Again I beg you to try to find Nina. I shall be forever grateful.
>
> Yours,
> Irina Sobolyeva

Anna folded the letter. "I was worried about my people before I got this. I thought that nothing could be worse than uncertainty. This is worse. If I could only do something to help them. But they are out there in a different world. They talk about us as being on the mainland, as though they were on a desert island. How long can it last?" she asked in a little explosion of feeling. "Couldn't somebody do something about it? Couldn't somebody help to end it soon? Soon is what is important. Do you think people understand what an extra day of war means?"

People began looking toward America and England again as spring brought the nearness of summer. Most people thought the Allies would open the second front that summer. The Russians had fought furiously all winter, following Stalingrad with significant victories, such as the taking back of Rostov and Voronezh. Then at the end of February came a lull. Everyone assumed that the year's offensive was over, that a new one was in preparation. The new one, to come in spring or summer, they expected would be in collaboration with the Allies. Not all people believed this. One of the guests at the Peasant House expressed a growing opinion as he held his tin cup under the Titan.

"Why all this speculating?" he said. "The best thing we can do is to count on ourselves. The Allies will come in sometime. They can't help it. But they'll come in when it's convenient for them, so we may as well stop worrying about it."

One evening as I issued from our room with a frying pan full of potato cakes to be heated up, I collided with a man in uniform. He was a big fellow with wings on his shoulder tabs. He was bigger because the bookkeeper's three-year-old Lusya was straddling his neck.

"Is this your daughter?" he asked.

"No. That's Lusya. She lives near the stairs."

"Are there any other kids here?"

"Two in there."

"May I play with them?" It sounded silly coming from this big fellow in uniform, but he looked serious.

"It will probably make it easier for them to wait for supper," I said. I called Adya and Dasha, and went down to the kitchen. When I came back I found Adya in his lap, Lusya and Dasha on his shoulders. He was telling them a story. "The good little boy looked just like the bad little boy, so . . ."

"Why?" asked Dasha.

"Because they were twins," said the pilot. "So when the wolf saw the good little boy go into the woods he thought it was the bad little boy and was going to eat him for being bad to his brother."

"The wolf's brother?"

"No, the good little boy's brother . . . I mean, the bad little boy's brother. So the wolf . . ."

"Why was the good little boy bad to the bad little boy's brother?"

"Oh, shut up, Dasha," said Adya.

"Aren't you getting a little mixed up?" I asked the pilot.

"I never got mixed up before."

"Do you often tell stories to children?"

"Whenever I get a chance."

"Have you any children of your own?"

"I don't know. I had one six months old when I went away. That was in Dniepropetrovsk. I haven't heard anything from my family since the Germans took the city."

"How long have you been in the air force?"

"Since the first day of the war. I was a pilot before the war."

"Have you been at the front all the time?"

"Without a break. Not even for a wound."

"Oh, Mother," burst in Adya. "You're worse than Dasha." Then, to the storyteller, "Did the wolf eat the bad little boy?"

"How have you been so lucky?" I asked, ignoring my son.

"I'm a bomber pilot," he said. "The Germans don't often take us on. Only if we're without escort, and that rarely happens."

"Do you think the war will end soon?"

"Yes I do. Things have changed. Now we have the advantage in men and machines."

"I've seen the reserves of men," I said. "I didn't suppose there were so many. They're all young and well trained. And machines enough to go around. The Germans haven't anything to compare with it now. If they fill in their losses with foreigners they're only making trouble for themselves."

"*Nu*, mother," pleaded Adya. "Let him alone. Let him finish the story."

So I left for the Titan, and when I came back the pilot was gone.

The February lull gave men like this pilot a short rest. It did not last long. Andrei left for a second trip to Moscow at about this time, and scarcely had he gone when news reports again became lively. The first big news after a ten-day interim came late one night. I lay in bed conjecturing on the future when suddenly I heard the sedate gentleman who was my neighbor running down the hall. He reached his room and slammed the door. We had never done more than nod to each other so I had not suspected him of so volatile a disposition. He made a lot of noise that night. The nurse across the hall heard it and called out, "What's the matter?" He said there ought to be good news on the final broadcast. I strained to hear it through the wall, but unsuccessfully. When the voice noises stopped I sneaked out into the hall and knocked at the nurse's door.

"Did you hear the news?" I asked.

"Yes, oh yes," she said, opening the door wide. "We've taken back Rzhev. That means we're pushing the Germans away from Moscow."

From Moscow. The news could not have been better. Later the Soviets took back other cities to the west of Moscow and to the south. In fact they came to within twenty-five miles of the key city of Orel.

If they were pushing the Germans away from Moscow the studio would surely be permitted to go back. Maybe Andrei would return and say we were leaving for Moscow. That is what I kept praying for through March when the children and I took our walks along the Volga. Now the river was preparing for *le sacre du printemps*. It was spotty blue, the color of dead flesh, and it would not be beautiful again until the miracle of its breakup. One day, when it had absorbed enough warmth, it would shudder, then crack with detonations like cannon shots, then climb floe upon floe in headlong escape to the sea. People waited to see the spectacle, standing in excited groups along the riverbank.

On a day full of spring sun, Andrei came back from Moscow.

"Are we going home?" I asked him before he could say a word.

"This month," he answered, full of smiles.

fifteen

Home Again

THE MOST EXCITING MOMENT of our journey back to Moscow was when we recognized familiar suburbs, Ramenskoye . . . Ilinskaya . . . Malakhovka. . . . The ice cream booths on station platforms were sealed and weather-worn. Dachas looked neglected. But trees were greening and the stream near Malakhovka sparkled like cut glass.

Then rose the solidity of the city. We left the train, passed through document inspection, and found ourselves standing on the square in front of Kursk Station. This, then, was Moscow, so long desired, so hard achieved. We stood silent, receiving it, being received by it. The city looked swept and bare. There was little traffic and few people. Some of them stood beside us, returned voyagers like ourselves, stopping in salutation before setting out for their homes.

A blur of houses and streets swept us toward 7 Vorotnikovsky Lane. We saw the wall gone at the end of the driveway and remembered the bomb. Two little girls were chasing each other in the yard. I recognized the mother of one of them when she smiled at me, so the child must have been the infant in go-cart we had left two years before.

I found my trembling fingers missing the key I felt for in my bag. Andrei, loaded with bags and bundles, stood behind encouraging me, the children stood beside me, tense for the charge into home. My fingers finally closed on the key and I slipped it into the lock. The opened door revealed everything: the bookshelves, their empty spaces, the red-lacquered Mongolian chest, the nail hole where the picture had been blown down, the table with the broken leg. I saw it all, and it was home.

We tried out the chairs and dust stuck to us and it was home dust. We went into the children's room where the sun was trying to get through dirty windows. There was a dark patch on one corner of the floor and I knew why: the chest of drawers that belonged there had been left at the dacha. And I knew why the paint was scraped off the windowsill: Andrei had pushed flower boxes along it. And I knew when Adya had drawn that face on the wall. And I knew when Dasha had dug that hole in the plaster. I knew everything about this room because it was full of our living, because it was home.

But now it was not home as home should be. It was a dirty, abandoned home, and it should be hospitable, with color, with the chair waiting and the table inviting. And I was the mother. That was my task. So I put on what remained of a dress and began. The orgy lasted four days and four nights, and on the morning of the fifth the four of us sat down to breakfast at our own table. The tablecloth was patched and there were no others in the linen closet, just as there were no clothes in the clothes closet. But we were home.

Soon we made our first sallies into the city. We walked about sniffing its good familiarity, like sniffing coffee and bacon on waking up in the morning.

Spring in Moscow was marked by phenomena as recurrent as the seasons themselves. Little girls were jumping rope, little boys were riding bikes. Lilies of the valley were on sale at the market. Couples monopolized the parks in the evening, babies with their nannies in the morning. The smell of gasoline rose pungent in sun-warmed air. Old crones sat basking on sunny doorsteps. All this was natural, it came once a year to Moscow. And to New York and London and Paris and Rome.

But besides these constant phenomena, Moscow in the spring of 1943 presented signs extraordinary. It was stripped of frivolity like a woman of her rings when engaged in one of the more sordid jobs. Pleasure cars and taxis had withdrawn in favor of trucks and jeeps. Sometimes the air vibrated to the grinding of tank treads. Trucks hauled sausages of gas to replenish barrage balloons lurking among budding trees. Curbs were whitewashed to make them visible in the blackout. Signs read "Bomb Shelter," "Gas Shelter," words that would have frozen the blood in prewar days but meant little more than "Bakery" or "Bus Stop" to war-conditioned Moscow.

Sometimes we met acquaintances on our walks and every meeting was a new celebration of return. People we scarcely knew embraced us because each familiar face was part of that newly recovered home.

"It's good to be home," they said. "It's so very good to be home."

Soon after we got back to Moscow Andrei was asked to form a Front Line Theater. Most of the actors were young people, and this was their officially recognized way of serving their country in wartime. They rehearsed in Moscow, then took their play to wherever the boys were most exhausted by fighting, whether it be in a temporary encampment in the woods or in a beleaguered city. This is how Andrei, twice rejected, got his experience of the front.

That spring was a waiting for the new offensive to begin. The Russians knew it would be terrific when it did begin, and throughout March, April, May, June, they stood in queues and taught school and pounded typewriters and forged steel and made bombs, and all the while they were thinking, it will be tremendous when it comes and why doesn't it come soon so that we can stop waiting.

It was during this ominous lull that Andrei came home one day to tell me that Nemirovich-Danchenko had died.

"I'm glad he died at home," he said. "Survived Nalchik, Tbilisi, and Saratov, to die in Moscow. He wanted that, but he didn't want to die at all. He was working on Hamlet. And he wanted to see how the war would end."

I thought I could read this in Nemirovich's face as he lay in state in the Art Theater. It lacked the peace that might have lent death grace, revealing rather his protest at being expelled from a life in which he had been such an eager participant, to which he had made such a rich contribution.

Meanwhile, fierce battles were being waged in North Africa. Following the course of the fighting there lessened the strain of expectation here. One early morning Andrei's father rang the bell. The door of his apartment was next to ours, and he stood in his bathrobe. "Children," he said, "I think the Allies have taken Tunis and Bizerta. I'm not sure, but I think that's what the radio said."

"Hardly both at once and so soon," said Andrei. He dressed and went for the paper.

"That's right. They've taken both," he said when he came back.

One article quoted a German war prisoner as saying, "We were overwhelmed by the driving power of the Americans." That made me feel good. The Russians admired Americans for technical skill; they were not sure of them as soldiers. Operations in North Africa won their respect.

On the fourth of July Moscow honored the American holiday by holding a concert of American music at the Moscow Conservatory. When I tried to buy tickets at a box office in the subway I was told "All sold out." At the Conservatory: "All sold out." Andrei and I took a chance and went to the Conservatory half an hour before the concert began. The entrance was filled with people who accosted everyone who approached with: "Have you an extra ticket by any chance?" We found an acquaintance with management connections and got passes.

In the lobby the public was enjoying the typically Russian before-concert and during-intermission parade. Uniforms were plentiful but were outnumbered by summer dresses. Most of the uniforms had the bright shoulder boards and insignia marking them as Soviet, but the more sober American and British uniforms were well represented.

On every hand you could hear people discovering each other returned from evacuation. The State Symphony opened the concert with Roy Harris's overture on the theme "When Johnny Comes Marching Home Again." Then Natalia Spiller, star of the Bolshoi Theater, sang American songs. Among them was "My Old Kentucky Home." It ripped me more painfully this night in this land than it had as a child at Mother's Sunday evening musicales. Suddenly I heard my neighbor remark to her companion:

"Sentimental, isn't it?"

Of course it was. Why else had it made me cry at the age of six? Gershwin was next and *Rhapsody in Blue* was far from being sentimental. My neighbor applauded it enthusiastically. So did everybody else. They liked this number best.

It was raining when we came out, and so chilly that it might have been October. Everybody forgot the music and thought how rotten the weather was and how it would spoil their only pair of shoes, and when, if ever, would this war end.

There would have to be a lot more fighting before it ended. They did not know it would begin the next day.

It did not begin as people had expected. They had expected the Soviets to take the initiative. Instead it was the Germans who opened up. Operations started on the Orel-Belgorod front, right in the middle of the country. It was a spot the Soviets had been bombing, so people had thought the Russians would begin here. But the Germans began. They began like crazy, throwing in everything they had. It was so terrific that people were very quiet. They couldn't talk when their sons and husbands were caught in this mighty assault and were fighting back, smashing four hundred Nazi tanks a day and two hundred planes a day.

Orel withstood the blow, but Belgorod did not. The Germans pushed the Russians back at Belgorod. Still, the force of the impact was diminishing.

This all happened when Adya and Dasha were coming down with the measles. Adya took them hard. He lay in delirium, panting with fever. It looked as though his lungs were affected, and the doctor ordered cupping and sulphur drugs. This clipped the temperature, and at last the fever-venting rash appeared. Then one evening when I was busy with sick kids and Andrei was at a rehearsal, someone rang the doorbell. Again it was Andrei Nikolayevich and he was more excited than I had ever seen him. "We've opened up a counteroffensive," he said, coming in quickly. He walked into the middle of the room and spoke as to an assembly: "We've opened up a counteroffensive and broken through the German lines. In one place we've advanced forty-five kilometers, in another twenty-five. We've smashed ten German divisions. Not regiments, divisions! Ten!"

Now people talked. They talked all that night and all the next day and they kept on talking for a long time. Very soon after that Sicily surrendered to the Allies, and that made things look even better. For the rest of the month the Russians pushed the Germans back inch by inch. At 10:30 in the evening of August fifth a radio announcement told people to stand by for a special news broadcast at 11:30. The question debated during the tension was whether it would be news from Orel or from Italy. The news was that the Soviets had taken both Orel and Belgorod, and that the victory would be hailed by a salute from one hundred and twenty guns. When it came at midnight, Sasha (yes, our old houseworker who had lovingly taken charge of Adya as an infant was back with us) ran into the room, her eyes starting out of their sockets: "*Akh, Bozhe moi, Bozhe moi!*" she cried, which is, "Oh, my God, my God!" "Wake up the children, quick," she said as she pulled on clothes to go to the bomb shelter.

"It's not a raid, Sasha," I said. "It's victory. Two of them."

We woke up the children and went out to see what this would be like. The night sky burst into flower at every salvo. And at every salvo of the big guns came the yapping of the rocket throwers sending blossoms of light cavorting into the sky. Neighbors laughed and congratulated and kissed, as Russians are wont to do. It was a big victory and the opening of the season, so to speak.

The season was one long celebration of victory. The Soviet offensive fanned out to embrace a vast front from Smolensk to the Azov Sea. At the end of August the Soviets took back Kharkov, and for this salute I woke up the children abruptly, roughly, rushing them to the window with a physical jolt to clamp the memory. History would never forget these days. I didn't want them to.

Daily life went on, but subordinately. Even such a major event as Adya's first day of school was relatively unimportant. But we tried to start him out right in spite of the war. His grandfather made paper covers for the paper covers of his textbooks. His mother ruled and sewed paper into notebooks. His father gave him an old briefcase to take the place of a schoolbag.

I walked with him to the school around the corner. The yard was perilous with small boys, but soon the bell brought them in line. They filed past the teacher on duty at the entrance. If one of the boys forgot, she reminded him to pull off his cap and say "Good Morning."

There were only boys, because that year coeducation was abolished in Soviet elementary and secondary schools. "For various reasons," explained the principal of Adya's school at a parent-teacher meeting. "For one thing, the boys will have greater specialization in manual and physical training; and for another, there is the problem of discipline. The war has lessened possibilities of supervision by taking teachers and parents away to front and factory. With larger classes and decreased staffs, separating boys and girls will make it easier for us."

In early September of Adya's first school year the Russians took back the entire Donets Basin; that meant they took back coal. This was most important for factories and railroads, but people felt more keenly its significance when they thought what lack of coal had done to them personally. Not a house in Moscow had been heated by coal during the winter of 1942–43; had scarcely been heated at all because firewood was also unobtainable. Everyone had squeezed his living into the smallest possible space and heated it with a little tin stove fueled with torn-up books and chopped-up furniture. The chimneys of these little stoves still stuck out of some windows, and as you walked down the street you could see the smoke coming out of them and the smudges they left on the outside walls.

While the Soviets were driving the Germans back along all that long front, news came of Italy's capitulation. "The enemy is cracking up," said our neighbor Kolya, thrusting his head in the door as he left for work.

That September victory followed victory like tracer bullets. The Soviets took Mariupol on the Azov Sea, Novorossisk on the Black Sea, Briansk in Belorussia, Poltava in the Ukraine, Smolensk in central Russia. They also made that unbelievable crossing of the Dnieper River.

The blows jumped from north to south to center. They were sure and unabating. In October they took Kiev, the most important city in the Ukraine. The recapture of Kiev was announced on the eve of the great Soviet holiday of the seventh of November. People celebrated to the pounding of three hundred and twenty-four guns in twenty-four salvoes.

Russia was riding her troika. Russia was making a dazzling display of that combination of skill and daring which is the essence of her genius. Russia was releasing the fury coiled into two years of retreat.

It was not so simple, like pressing a button and having the power pour. It wasn't romantic. It was hard and dirty work. Three men came from the army which had taken Briansk in Belorussia to tell us about it at a holiday celebration held at The Actors' Club on Pushkin Square.

"We had to chop our way through the Briansk woods," said the young lieutenant who did most of the talking. "We had to fell forty-million square feet of forest. And we had to pull out the stumps of all those trees to let the motorized divisions through. Whenever we called a halt we had to dig ourselves in, and that meant digging in horses and machines too; then when everything was ready, an order to advance would come and we would have to leave our diggings and begin all over again at the next halt."

That is how these victories were won, as were the victories in North Africa and the Pacific and in Italy. Through hard and dirty work and bloodshed and lifeshed.

Nowhere were so many lives shed as in Russia. As early as June 22, 1943, the second anniversary of the Nazi invasion of the Soviet Union, the Soviet Information Bureau published figures of Soviet war casualties:

FOUR MILLION TWO HUNDRED THOUSAND DEAD

And that was before the big drive had begun.

Adya's eighth birthday fell on November eleventh. I left Andrei in charge of the party while I went to a war hospital to take gifts from our Institute of Foreign Languages.

The hospital visit took more time than I had expected and I was met by an agitated Andrei when I got home.

"Thank goodness you've come. Now you can mop up," he said.

"Mop up what?"

"I've mopped up six times."

"Mopped up *what*?"

"And you can hang the kids up to dry, and face their mothers, and explain to Sasha, who's gone away, she couldn't stand it."

"What's that noise?"

It was a swishing, swashing, splashing noise. I guessed what it was. It was ducking for apples, with carrots as a wartime substitute. "No sensible person leaves children alone in a room to duck for apples," I said crisply.

I stopped the flooding by calling the kids into our room for tea and I made them run around to dry off before sending them home. They thought it was a wonderful party.

People expected things to quiet down after the November holidays, with the coming of winter. But they did not. On the contrary, they crescendoed to the opening of a great December offensive in the Ukraine. The results of this offensive were broadcast on New Year's Eve. The Soviets had made a breach seventy-five miles deep along a two hundred mile front. They had freed more than one thousand towns and villages. Such an avalanche of victory placed New Year 1944 at the edge of the end. People thought this would be the last war New Year, and they celebrated with all the extravagance war rations would allow.

Before the holiday Andrei had taken two months off from his Moscow activities to stage a play in Saratov. At eight o'clock on New Year's Eve he arrived as a surprise.

"Happy New Year!" he said, handing out presents: a doll's sled for Dasha, crayons for Adya, and a pound of onions and a jar of honey for me.

All of us trimmed the tree while Sasha made the first cake since June 1941. After the children had had their meal and gone to bed, Sasha and I laid the table, made the salad, and cut the bread.

Everything was ready by eleven o'clock when an unexpected guest arrived. He was our friend and neighbor Pavel Andreyevich. We had not seen or heard from him since the beginning of the war. Now he entered, six feet of captain, with a long face, long eyes, and a boyish stammer.

"D-didn't expect me?" he said.

"All the better," said Andrei. "How did it happen?"

"Furlough."

"From the front?"

"From the front."

"How long have you been there?"

"Ever since I left you. Ever since August 1941."

"Been wounded?"

Pavel laughed. "I'm invulnerable," he said. "A m-month after I got to the front a b-bullet hit my breast pocket, was deflected by a cigarette case, and went out through my coat sleeve. My colonel said, 'C-congratulations, boy. If that bullet didn't get you, nothing will.' And nothing has, not even a foot of shell splinter that nailed me to the door of our dugout through the back of my coat. Here I am. H-happy New Year."

The wineglasses stood waiting as we listened to Kalinin's New Year's greeting over the radio, then to the chiming of midnight by the Kremlin clock and the first broadcast of the new Soviet anthem.

Then we drank our toasts.

"To victory," said Andrei.

"In 1944," added Pavel.

And it was 1944.

THERE WAS NOT THE SLIGHTEST ABATEMENT in victory after the New Year. January added successes on the Leningrad front to all the others. The January drive pushed the Germans out of reach of this Baltic city. The Germans and their Finnish cohorts had done their incredible worst, but Leningrad had survived.

The freeing of vast areas was not mere history and geography for Russians. It was drama. People like Anna Constantinovna, whose relatives had been hiding in the Briansk woods, would find out now who had survived. It was not just land returned. It was a father, or a wife, or a child. Now that we were back in Moscow we heard more and more about the fate of people we knew.

Andrei and I were especially curious about Nalchik. We found out about it from Simon, one of the Kabardinian actors who was now a captain of tank troops. He had been decorated for distinguished service and sent to study at a Moscow military academy. When we saw him he had just flown back from a visit to Nalchik.

"Has the city been badly damaged?" Andrei asked. "What about the hotel?"

"Burned down."

"And the theater?"

"Burned down."

"And the building of the Art Committee where we lived?"

"Burned down."

"And the new post office?"

"And the new post office, and the new government building, and the other hotel, and the Pedagogical Institute, and every single building that was big and new and worth anything. The only thing they left was the old section of the town with its little wooden houses."

"What about the actors?"

"Some of them are back. An old movie house was fixed up to serve as a theater."

"Djibal, is he back?" Djibal was the actor who had played Figaro; he was a great favorite of Andrei.

Simon paused before answering.

"Was he . . ." asked Andrei hesitantly, fearing to hear that the boy had been killed at the front.

No, he had not been killed. He had gone with the Germans when they retreated from Nalchik. This was the first story of defection we had heard and it struck very close to home. Andrei was too shocked to talk about it. He just got up and took a turn around the room with his hands behind his back. A little later he said, "Any others?"

"No."

"What about Temirkanov, head of the Art Committee?"

"Shot by the Germans. As a Communist. One of the first."

Stories about defection were suppressed. We did not hear until years later about the Red Armymen who, under General Vlasov, went over to the Germans and fought under them in the hope that their example would lead to an uprising against Soviet power. General Vlasov was caught by the Soviets and executed and the entire venture made but a ripple on the waters of history. After the war we did, however, hear of any number of people who left the country with retreating German forces. For those of us whose allegiance was all on the side of the Soviets this seemed a cynical sellout, for this war was exactly what the

Russians called it, a Patriotic War, in which battles were fought not for communism but in defense of people's homes, their land, their culture and traditions, and even—yes, even their Orthodox Church, to which the war had brought a new lease on life.

By the time the spring hiatus came, most of the country had been freed. The rebound had been as powerful as the thrust. In a year and a half the Germans had reached Stalingrad in the east. In a year and a half the Russians had reached Rumania in the west.

Now people were not so obsessed by the idea of a second front. They knew it must come this summer, for the war was already in Europe. The second front no longer meant for Russians the pulling out of this knife. They had borne the worst. But it meant getting the whole thing over with soon.

On a day in early June the air was split by a radio announcement: "*Stand by for a special broadcast at 1:45.*"

We knew what it would be. Everybody knew.

"*Today, June 6, 1944, early in the morning, General Eisenhower's forces began landing operations on the northern coast of France.*"

There it was, that long-awaited second front. The English and Americans were right in with the Russians. People laughed and slapped each other on the back and treated each other to cigarettes. I was standing in a grocery line when the news came.

"It sounds funny, after so much waiting," said a tired-looking woman with a child by the hand.

"Things should move fast now," said a workman. "Maybe everything will be over by fall."

Indeed, final victory seemed so close that behind the bright vision of peace loomed the shadow of reconstruction to spoil dreams of an easier life after the war.

Andrei and I got an idea of what reconstruction would mean when we visited Stalingrad in May. My going was tacked on to Andrei's being sent to make a report on the work of the Stalingrad Theater. I was jealous when I learned of his going, and I said so.

"Couldn't you come with me?" he said.

I thought I could. Sasha would take care of the children. Andrei Nikolayevich was there in case of bumps and rashes. My students were preparing for exams, so could spare me. And I even found a mission. The Ambijan Society in New York had assumed patronage over five hundred Stalingrad orphans. The USSR Society for Cultural Relations with Foreign Countries asked me to visit the children and see how they were getting along, so that we could write the Ambijan Society about them.

We left Moscow late at night. Most of the people in the train were going to Stalingrad on jobs connected with reconstruction; one of those we met was Stalingrad's chief architect; another was the representative of a trade organization; a woman was being sent to see how work on restoring hospitals was advancing. We became most friendly with a news photographer, and with an actor who was to give a series of recitals in Stalingrad. The news photographer had been a guerilla for two years. Now he had an artificial leg. "Funny," he said, "I always expected to get killed. I never expected to get a wooden leg."

The actor was a striking-looking young man with heavy black hair and black eyes and red cheeks. He wore a decoration for services in entertaining at the front. His name was Samson, and he showed us a picture of his little daughter whom he confessed to having named Delilah. "She can change it when she's older if she wants to," he said.

The two-day journey passed quickly. We spent most of our waking hours exchanging war stories and commenting on the destruction seen through the train windows. Both sides of the tracks were strewn with the carcasses of bombed locomotives lying on their sides and trailing the vertebrae of charred cars. They were like skeletons of prehistoric mammals from an Iron Age in which creatures as well as tools were made of metal.

We arrived at Stalingrad in that early morning hour when the world is bathed in the diffused light preceding sunrise. Andrei and Samson and I stood on the station platform waiting for someone to meet us. Nobody did. Gradually the other passengers went off and left us there alone. It was very quiet. The station was not a station at all, but only broken walls, brick dust, and twisted beams. The windows were ripped, as though a finger had torn them from corner to corner. A sign read, "Baggage Room," and pointed to a heap of ground bricks. We waited some more, then picked up our bags and went out through the gate. We went down ten steps, feeling with our feet because our eyes were looking up. Around the large square stood the mutilated city, holding its stumps and blind eyes to the sky. We crossed the square where a ring of stone children were dancing; one of the children was decapitated, others were maimed, but they smiled as they went round and round in their dance without a sound.

We walked ahead for a block and came to a large corner building with a columned entrance opening into the rubbish of crashed stories.

"The cellar under that building is where German Field Marshal Paulus surrendered," said Samson. "There should be a hotel here to the left."

We turned left and found half a house conspicuous for having glass in its windows, and a roof. It was the improvised hotel for people like us. We left our bags there and went for a walk, drawn back into this eerie city.

We again passed the building where Paulus had surrendered and we crossed a little park. It was carefully tended. Beds of flowers bloomed at the feet of rough-crafted memorials to war heroes. The paths were well laid out and there were benches to rest on. Above us gaped the ruins, with a horse laugh for human logic. Three tall stairways stood in a row leading to nowhere. Pipes held a lone radiator over a three-story leap. An elaborate wrought-iron gateway stood delicately intact without a wall, without a yard, without a house. A toilet guffawed from a piece of the fifth floor. A caryatid hunched under a weight of sky. The city grimaced and contorted in the morning silence.

We knew how long and thin Stalingrad was and that the Volga should be near. We turned east from the park and came to trolley tracks where twenty cars had been lined up to serve as a barricade. They had stood here ever since their agony. They were bent and twisted and roofless and every square foot of their bodies was sieved with bullet wounds.

Beyond the trolley tracks flowed the river, merging with mist. It was edgeless and unscarred. During the siege the river had been no less an inferno than the city. Its whole skin had been eaten by flames of burning oil. It had been asphyxiated by smoke. All the hundreds of thousands of troops who defended Stalingrad had crossed to the city on its shoulders. Missiles had plunged shrieking into its liquid flesh, rending it with explosions.

But no sign remained. Whole and unperturbed, it moved to the sea on its mission of replenishment. We stood watching the river craft cut little ripples to catch the flash of rising sun. Morning sounds grew with the light, and when we turned back the first people had already appeared on the streets. Janitors were sweeping broken pavements. They were sweeping up dust and grains of sand in a city of crumbled houses. They did it naturally, seeing no incongruity.

We saw smoke rising, and traced it to a chimney poking through a cellar window. Then a girl with a market basket climbed out of a hole in the ground. We saw other chimneys and began to detect signs of habitation under the ruins. Now that we were more used to the scene, we recognized that parts of these houses had been restored—a basement, a corner, sometimes an entire floor. The number of people on the street increased, and they were all going somewhere. We walked to the station, and it was crowded with citizens traveling to and from jobs at various points along the forty-mile length of Stalingrad.

We went back to the hotel. It was two-storied, makeshift, with no private rooms. Every room contained no less than three little iron cots salvaged from wreckage. Even the half-inch bars of the bedsteads had bullet holes in them. In one bar a bullet had become wedged and was white-enameled along with the bedstead.

I was anxious to connect with the children sponsored by the Ambijan Society, so after breakfast I went to a municipal building to find the man whose name I had been given. He was portly, in shiny black, and he looked at me through rimless spectacles as I introduced myself.

"I was told these children are at the Silver Lake Home," I said to him.

"Did you think that Home was located in Stalingrad?" he replied. "It's a hundred miles north of Stalingrad at Archeda, and thirty miles off the railroad."

"What shall I do?"

"We'll help you if you want to go to Archeda," he said. "Here, I'll put you in touch with Maria Semyonovna. She's in charge of children's homes and kindergartens in the Stalingrad Region."

He called in a woman with gray hair smoothed back plain.

"You want to go to Archeda?" she said to me.

"I do."

"We could take the Moscow train tonight. It passes through Archeda early in the morning."

She met me at the station at ten o'clock that evening. As we waited for the Moscow train a group of German war prisoners walked down the platform. Everyone stared and the Germans half ran, dropping their eyes, uneasy under Stalingrad glances. I thought they had no guard at all, but soon a Red Armyman sauntered up with relaxed rifle.

"They look healthy, don't they?" said Maria Semyonovna. "It's hard to see."

It was not so much "more food" as "less work" that made the Germans look better than the people of Stalingrad.

"We came back to Stalingrad from across the Volga on February fifth," said Maria Semyonovna, "three days after Paulus surrendered. You couldn't take two steps in the city without climbing over corpses. There were no streets. They were buried in debris, jammed with tanks, smashed machines, howitzers. Worst of all were the corpses. We had to clear away tens of thousands of corpses before spring if we wanted to avoid epidemics. It was up to us women, all the men were off to the fighting. And we did it. By spring there wasn't a corpse left on Stalingrad streets."

We arrived at Archeda in a cool dawn. Even here, one hundred miles north of Stalingrad, all the buildings along the railroad had been destroyed. Behind the crumbled station women of the town were selling milk, eggs, cottage cheese. We bought our breakfast and had it under the trees of the new frame station. Then we sought out the local official in charge of children's homes.

"Why has it been so long since we've seen you, Maria Semyonovna?" he said.

"I've been busy," she answered. "We need transportation to the Silver Lake Home."

"I'll arrange it."

"Could it be horses?" I ventured.

"Couldn't be anything else," he said genially.

He left to get the horses. While we waited a woman came in whom Maria Semyonovna introduced as a social worker.

"How are the adopted children getting on, Anna Alexandrovna?" she asked her.

"All right. But Vera Popova is worried. You remember she's adopted Kolya. She heard Kolya's father had turned up. Is it true? She's afraid he'll take the child away from her."

"I don't know whether it's true or not: we got a letter from a man who says he's Kolya's father but we haven't verified it yet."

"These letters are very upsetting," said Anna Alexandrovna. "I go around looking at the children, thinking: maybe she's Sergeant Ermolov's daughter; he wrote that she was fair-skinned with dark eyes. Or maybe this little boy is Lieutenant Ermak's son—there's that birthmark on his neck. Not long ago we identified a little girl whose father had written that her left earlobe was smaller than her right."

"How many children have been adopted in this small town?" I asked.

"Sixty-five."

Later on, Anna Alexandrovna brought Kolya and Vera Popova, his adopted mother, to meet me. Kolya was a chubby five-year-old with fair hair tending to curl at his neck. He had large gray eyes struck by the shadow of memories.

"Would you like to go back to Stalingrad?" I asked him.

"No," he said solemnly. "There's bombs there."

"Not any more, Kolya."

"There's Germans. The Germans killed my mama."

"Here's your mama, Kolya," said Anna Alexandrovna, linking her arm through Vera Popova's.

"Yes, but she had blue eyes before she was killed."

The horses were brought to us. We climbed into an old-fashioned spring buggy behind a fourteen-year-old coachman who was tow-headed and freckled-faced and named Petya. He turned the horses down past the crashed station, past all the crashed buildings, and out across the steppe. The horizons were like sea horizons, level and remote. Everything was vividly green and red in teeming sun. Twice we passed tractors plowing. Groups of women were sowing. Sometimes we swept through hamlets of thatched huts with a mill and a forge and a little river. In an hour and a half we came to a woodland fragrant with wild cherry. We passed a sawmill and forded a stream, and when we climbed the opposite bank Maria Semyonovna said, "See those red roofs through the trees off there to the left? That's the Silver Lake Home."

The children spied us from a distance and gathered to see whether we would turn in or drive past. When we turned in, they ran to meet us, shouting Maria Semyonovna's name.

When the greetings were over and treats distributed, Ivan Ivanovich, director of the home, showed us the premises. We saw children in a carpenter's shop making three-legged stools, and in a shoe-repair shop mending shoes, and in a sewing shop making pants for the little tots.

We ended our tour of buildings at the infirmary. The doctor was a short, clear-eyed young woman with hair in a boyish bob.

"I have only six patients left," she boasted. "When I came here a year ago, there were forty-seven children in the infirmary. Of the two hundred children originally enrolled—here, let me see," and she took a notebook out of her desk: "eleven had typhus, nine had meningitis, seven were wounded, seventeen were swollen with hunger, twenty-three had scurvy, seventy-nine had skin diseases. With the exception of one little girl whose brain had been injured by shrapnel, we haven't lost a single child."

In the evening the children gathered on benches in front of the boys' dormitory for a concert of songs and dances. It was dark by the time the concert ended. "You mustn't go home tonight," said the children. "You haven't told us about America yet."

But we had to go. Petya brought the buggy at half past ten and we started back over the steppe. Nightingales poured their silver into the moonlight. Petya kept losing the way and blaming the horses for it. "What kind of horses are you if you don't know the way home?" he grumbled. The few cottages we passed were dark and silent. When we reached the woods, Petya said, "Have you got any matches?"

"Yes," I said. "What for?"

"For the wolves. They don't like matches."

But there weren't any wolves. There were neither beasts nor men until at the edge of Archeda we saw a tractor plowing by night to speed sowing. At three o'clock in the morning Maria Semyonovna and I boarded the train back to Stalingrad and on the following day Andrei and I set out for Moscow.

Throughout the long train journey I kept thinking about those children at the Silver Lake Home and how lucky my own children were. Yet when I saw Dasha and Adya after being separated from them I remarked how very pale they were with their tallness and thinness. They needed apples, and there were no apples. They needed sugar, and there was no sugar. My children and all children needed the end of the war. Yet it went on, although the fighting was in the west now, in Germany and Prussia and the Baltic States. It went on for another whole year before Berlin was taken. Oh, what a celebration of victory lighted Moscow's night sky when that epochal event occurred! What pride and jubilation filled every Russian heart! And what mourning.

TWENTY MILLION DEAD.

Twenty million. How much is twenty million? If you placed twenty million bodies head to toe, how far would they reach? From Philadelphia to San Francisco? From Paris to Beijing? From the earth to the moon? It could be calculated. But however far they would reach, each individual reaches as far into life as he himself knows he reaches.

Each single one of those twenty million individuals was to himself as I am to myself. That is immeasurable. That is awesome.

On a June Sunday in 1945, four years after the invasion of Russia by the Germans, I turned from Gorky Street into a quiet lane. I saw the crosses of a church gleaming in morning sun. There was a constant stream of people coming and going through the open doors and there were people standing in groups in the street outside. I heard the chanting of a choir. When I joined the people in the entrance they drew me inside with them. There they stood in such closeness that they crossed themselves with difficulty. Everything was heavy. The air was heavy with incense. The icons were heavy with gold filigree. The priest's voice came heavily from the altar. Heavy were the hearts of the people.

"Our Father," prayed the priest, "Our only source of solace. . . ." A groan rose from the congregation, and it was like a choral response in Greek tragedy. Twenty million. Here was the humanity behind the statistics. I looked at the faces around me. Mostly they were the faces of elderly women framed in kerchiefs, seamed and hardened by too much experience of life. But there were also many younger women with children. It was a congregation of wives and mothers desperately seeking support in their hour of need.

Somebody tapped me on the shoulder and handed me a note, indicating that I was to pass it up to the altar. Then I noticed that everybody was passing up these notes. Each note named someone for whom a prayer was to be offered for the repose of his soul.

On another Sunday, Andrei and the children and I took an electric train to the dacha where we had been living when the war began. It was all so familiar. We crossed the tracks and walked along dirt roads lined with cottages. Many of the windows were boarded up, but even around such closed houses people were working in gardens. We came to a crossroad and turned right. Up ahead was our dacha. The shutters were barred. We tried the gate and found it padlocked. We entered a neighbor's yard and climbed over the fence.

"Do you remember, Margarita?" asked Andrei.

Through ages of mountain and desert and steppe and sea and taiga, I remembered. We stood there remembering, Andrei and I, listening back to the tumult of voices that had sounded the tocsin of war.

"What is war, Mother?" Adya had asked excitedly, running from the sandpile.

Now I knew what war was.

PART THREE

Postbellum

sixteen

The Enemies Return

> Therefore the individual who wishes to have an answer to the problem of evil, as it is posed today, has need, first and foremost, of self-knowledge, that is, the utmost possible knowledge of his own wholeness. He must know relentlessly how much good he can do and what crises he is capable of, and must be aware of regarding the one as real and the other as illusory.
>
> —C. G. Jung,
> *Memories, Dreams, Reflections*

A NEW PAGE IN SOVIET HISTORY was to be written after the war, a page unblotted by underground conspiracies and the reprisals they elicited. We found reminders of that sad past when we got back. Antonina Zhurvelova, our neighbor, who had been snatched away from little Tanya in 1937, was still in a labor camp, but Tanya, now ten years old, was living with her Leningrad grandmother in the third room of our apartment. We found Tanya's Leningrad Aunt Liza and Uncle Lonya sharing this little room with them. Liza and Lonya had survived the Leningrad blockade, but their little girl and Lonya's mother had not, and so the couple had fled that city of awful memory as soon as flight was possible.

The boy Tolya, he who had so stubbornly refused to leave his home when his mother and father were arrested, had been mobilized into the army during his last year in high school. He had been killed at the front. His father had died in camp. His mother, the buxom frau who had treated me to *piroshki* that day so long ago—his mother . . . well, one day after our return from evacuation I came into our yard to see a cluster of women encircling a bony, toothless hag who seemed to be telling a horrendous story. I hastened on my way, too full of horrendous stories to hear another. Later I was told the hag was Tolya's mother. She had been released from camp but denied the right to live within one hundred kilometers of Moscow. She had come here illegally (she could have been arrested again if discovered) to get news of Tolya and collect any of her old belongings that might be turned into a few rubles.

One might think the news of Tolya would have struck her dead on the spot, but life is not so merciful. She shuffled away dragging a portable sewing machine, the only thing left of her home and family. We never heard anything more of her.

But these terrible wounds would heal now, in the new era following on victory.

I had taken copious notes of our experiences in evacuation with the intention of making a book out of them. But I could not just sit at home and write a book, I had to work somewhere in order to get ration cards. A friend of mine, head of the Press Department of VOKS (the All-Union Society for Cultural Relations with Foreign Countries), persuaded me to take a job there as translator, assuring me my duties would leave me time for the book.

Working at VOKS opened my eyes to a number of things. At VOKS I saw what a top-echelon Soviet organization with sights trained on the Western world was like. It was housed in a mansion that had once belonged to an industrial tycoon, even though located in the working class district described by Pasternak in the first part of *Dr. Zhivago*. Some of its halls remained handsomely decorated with carved oak or gilded plaster for the reception of foreigners, but most had been roughly cut up into small cubicles in which journalists, translators, typists, and artists turned out propaganda to be sent abroad. At the head of VOKS stood Kemenov, a protégé of Molotov. He was brought here from IFLI, the most prestigious of Soviet institutes devoted to humanitarian studies, and he brought with him a flock of young people of his own school, raised to intellectual arrogance and ideological bigotry. Kemenov was the cold type of academic, with hair slicked down on a well-shaped head, with eyeglasses that lent an air of scholarship, with two-dimensional blue eyes; tall and well built, he was a thoroughly European gentleman in conversation and appearance. His field was art history and criticism in which he proved to be a staunch defender of Socialist Realism. Quite unexpectedly I once happened to come upon an album of dazzling watercolors by the nonconformist artist Fonvizin; they were about to be sent abroad as part of an exhibit of Soviet art. Great! thought I, now people will see that not all Soviet artists are cut to one pattern. But Kemenov vetoed the Fonvizin watercolors. He sent Kukreniksi war posters in their stead.

Kemenov followed the Stalin style of work, arriving at the office in the middle of the day in his long black limousine with a chauffeur at the wheel. The car would come back for him at five o'clock to take him home for dinner and a nap, after which it brought him to the office again for the whole night. He could not be blamed for the regime he followed. It was required of top officials in all fields—ministries, factories, plants, offices—so that they would be on call by Stalin at any hour of the night. It did not take us long to learn that Kemenov spent most of the night playing chess with his first assistant. As to how Stalin spent the midnight hours, we have a fine description of his carousing in Khrushchev's memoirs. The gullible public, however, was fed songs and stories creating the image of Stalin as a helmsman at the wheel twenty-four hours a day (well, let's make it twenty: no mysticism in Soviet Russia!). There was that touching symbol of the light ever-burning in the window of his Kremlin office.

At VOKS there were three translators into English: Gertrude Klivens, an American; Mikelson, an Englishman; and I. When I was shown to the translators' room on my first day, a girl sitting at a typewriter with her back to me swung around at the sound of my voice and said, "My! I haven't heard an American *r* like that in years!" Her enormously dark eyes flashed a smile at me. She was Gertrude—and she came from Youngstown, Ohio. She pronounced her *r*'s as broadly and unfailingly as I did mine, so between us we supplied two ripe round *r*'s for every one the English Mikelson dropped. We were a congenial trio. We laughed a lot and smoked a lot and accepted with good humor the pariah status VOKS bestowed on us owing to our lowly birth—i.e., our foreign birth, for now foreigners were again shunned. This distrust, so undisguised, was a shattering revelation to me, who still clung to my faith.

Gertrude's red-haired son, Jimmy, was ten, two years older than Adya. Together we would take our kids to the children's parties VOKS held on state holidays, and Gertrude would bring Jimmy to our house for Adya's and Dasha's birthday parties. She never invited us to her house, because she and Jimmy lived with her sister-in-law in one room.

As our friendship developed I learned Gertrude's story. Her parents were affluent enough to send her to Radcliffe College and then on a trip around the world. She went in a westerly direction, first to Japan and China, then on the Siberian Express across Russia. When she got to Moscow, she was offered a job teaching English to a group of Soviet engineers about to be sent to study in American universities. She accepted the offer and became beloved of her pupils in general and of Gramp in particular. From then on it was "Gertrude and Gramp."

When the English course was over they all set out for the States where the group dispersed among various universities and technical institutes. Gertrude began teaching high school in Youngstown. Gramp chose a university far enough away from Gertrude to be able to study, and near enough to join her for weekends, when she drove him around the country, showing him the light and the dark of it. They both went back to Moscow when his studies were over.

I met Gramp in afteryears. He was big and handsome, more blond than brunette, despite his Armenian blood. Superficially easygoing, the record of his dealing with others shows that he always demanded of them their best and always got it, because he himself always gave of his best. He would dismiss little annoyances with a deprecating smile, saving his great stores of energy for serious problems.

An ardent Communist, he had left his home in the Caucasus in early youth and come to Moscow where, in Moscow's working-class Krasnaya Presnaya District, he founded a branch of the Young Communist League. Once settled in Moscow, he brought the other members of his family to be with him. He was most concerned about the education of his younger brother, whom he wished to see inspired with the same vision of his country's future that motivated him.

When Gramp returned from the States, the Party, recognizing his exceptional gifts as a leader, appointed him head of the faculty of Railroad Engineering at the Moscow Institute of Communications. He and Gertrude were given an apartment on the campus and soon thereafter their son Jimmy was born.

1936 was the year of the descending ax. It fell on Gramp. He was arrested. Gertrude and her baby boy were thrown out of their apartment and out of Moscow. She found a miserable room in a village hut. With the help of Gramp's family she eked out a meager existence until the war. The crisis of a country invaded diverted attention from Enemies of the People, and Gertrude dared to creep back into Moscow under the protection of her in-laws. She couldn't get appropriate work, nothing better than pasting cigarette boxes in a factory near her illegal home, but it gave her food-ration cards that kept her and Jimmy alive. She tried to better her lot but was everywhere rejected because of the stigma of Gramp's arrest. VOKS was among the organizations that turned her down. Kemenov, that elegant hypocrite, knew what she had to offer, but he dared not accept it until the precarious situation of the country required an intensification of propaganda aimed at winning support from the West, especially from the

United States. Then he found it possible to employ her as a typist in English, later as a translator.

Gertrude was neither bitter nor dejected. She steadfastly worked at the daily task of supporting herself and her son for the single purpose of being united with Gramp again. And so I was not surprised when she told me she was going to apply for permission to join him in the far north. This she did as soon as she found out he had served his sentence and was no longer a prisoner but an exile in Norilsk.

She told me the news in a most matter-of-fact way, as if there were nothing exceptional about a Radcliffe graduate going off to join an ex-convict husband in Norilsk. Norilsk. Has anyone ever heard of Norilsk? Only if one has had cause to hear of such dread places as Kolyma and Karaganda. Norilsk is north of the Arctic Circle, north of Iceland, north of almost everything. Gertrude's dark eyes lighted up with joy when she told me she had received permission, though her voice was as matter-of-fact as ever. "Are you taking Jimmy with you?" I asked.

"Of course."

Of course. If Gramp couldn't come to them, they would go to him now that they had the chance. They had only to wait for official papers to be drawn up.

I was by then thoroughly fed up with VOKS. More and more the atmosphere was charged with fear and distrust. In the two years I worked there I witnessed three casualties among the members of our small staff: one suicide and two instantaneous dismissals under the aegis of the KGB.

Whenever a reception for foreign journalists and diplomats was to be held in the VOKS mansion, "boys" from Lubyanka (headquarters of the KGB) came swarming into it; they opened doors and peered into chinks and crannies to see that no one was in hiding. All of us who were not among the few chosen to be present at the reception (on the basis of dossiers) were hustled out of the building. When the building had been "fumigated" by the "boys," the caterers came to lay a feast that the authorities would hardly have wanted the half-starved population to get wind of. This venial crime affected me more strongly than more heinous ones—it was so bourgeois in character, so like putting on face, keeping up with the Joneses. How much more dignified it would be, I thought, to make no secret of the country's poverty, an honorable poverty, a wound received in gallant fight. It would be gracious to allow foreigners to share it if but for a day. So I thought. I did not yet see that the little world of VOKS was a miniature of what

Soviet society had become, governed as it was by a tyrant, stratified into the privileged and nonprivileged, based on false standards, hypocritical and bureaucratic. I looked upon VOKS as a hideous excrescence on the body politic and wanted nothing so much as to terminate my association with it.

I turned in my resignation. It was ignored. I asked to be allowed to speak to Kemenov. His pretty secretary, who had been a clerk in the Soviet Embassy in Washington, D.C., and went about in American plumage, told me she could only make an appointment for me at 11 P.M. It was, perhaps, of no moment that I had to be at the office at 9 the next morning, and how was I to get to the appointment, having no car, to say nothing of a black limousine, to take me through the blackout at midnight in the Tyshinsky market district, notorious for thieves and thugs? Of course I did not go. Andrei, who was in the Volga city of Saratov at the time, kept insisting that I join him there with the children. When I told him what the situation was he dropped everything and came rushing back to Moscow. As a result of his interview with Kemenov, the children and I were in Saratov in a month's time. Shortly after I left, Gertrude and Jimmy set out to join Gramp in Norilsk.

Andrei's association with the Saratov Theater had begun before the war, with his staging of *Anna Karenina*. On our return from evacuation he was invited to put on Alexander Ostrovsky's *Dowerless Bride*, which he did so successfully that he was awarded a National Prize for the best production of a Russian classic. Subsequently he was called to become Art Director of the Saratov Theater where, in the years from 1945 to 1948, he did the best work of his life. Saratov supplied him with the one thing he needed: an ensemble of outstanding actors who accepted his artistic platform and responded like a sensitive instrument to his direction. His production of Gorky's *Lower Depths* made him a candidate for a Stalin prize, the highest the country had to offer; he did not win it because the judges disagreed with his interpretation of the character of Luka, a pious hypocrite.

Happy in the theater, Andrei was unhappy in Saratov. His qualifications were not those demanded of a public figure in Soviet Russia. His position was made precarious by his not being a Party member despite the pressure put upon him to become one. I blush now to think that even I censured him for this. He was too much the individualist to succumb to the demands of the Party, which kept a vigilant eye and guiding hand on the theater. If he had been a Party member he would have had no choice but to obey. His individualism led him to be rashly defiant of authority. I was left aghast at times by the crude way in which he challenged those on whom his position depended. Tact and diplomacy were not in his arsenal of weapons. Indeed, he seemed devoid of that sense of what others are thinking and feeling that guides most people in their human relations. He had no "feelers."

Before the public could see any new production it had to be "passed" by the Party organization to see that it contained no harmful or heretical political elements. Andrei habitually disagreed with the opinions and judgments of these people, and if they dared to extend them to artistic matters he was like a bull aroused by the picadors. He neither chose his words nor modified his contempt. As a result his professional life became a constant collision with the powers that be. It ended in a fierce encounter in which Andrei "put them in their place" (as he thought) and won a tremendous victory (as he thought). But he could not go on working in Saratov. He rode out of it on his Rosinante with head and lance held high, happy to be shaking the dust of this philistine city off his feet.

NOW ANDREI WAS INVITED to head the Russian Theater in Riga, capital of Latvia. At that time Riga was a town seething with conflicting passions. Between the two World Wars, Latvia had been an independent country, as had her neighbors Estonia and Lithuania. Whatever antagonism for Russia the 1940 annexation inspired in Latvians was swept away by its German occupation from 1941 to 1944. I was assured by Latvian friends that when Soviet forces marched into the capital in 1944, the bulk of the population met them with cheers and flowers. They had supposed their independence would be restored to them. Any hope of this was rapidly dispelled. Russians were put in all key positions of state as shadow rulers (behind the Latvian nominal ones) to ensure the implementation of Soviet policy. But this was not enough. Stalin proved to be a worthy pupil of Machiavelli who, in *The Prince*, recommends that conquered territory be made secure by having citizens of the conquering state settle there. That is what was taking place in Latvia when we arrived.

Russians were encouraged to move there, and they were only too glad to do so. It was a land flowing with milk and honey to those who had been suffering deprivation ever since the revolution and had been reduced to the direst need by the recent war. In 1948 Riga stores were still full of what seemed fabulous luxuries: china dinner sets, soft woolen goods, leather shoes, silk stockings, and underwear. Little wonder if Russians whose homes had been razed to the ground, whose children had been half starved and had never enjoyed a new toy, who themselves had forgotten or never known what it meant to wear things bright and beautiful—little wonder if they threw themselves on the goodies and gobbled them up with a voraciousness that not only offended the Latvians' taste but left them nothing for themselves. By the time of our arrival in Riga the ordinary Latvian looked right through a Russian who approached him on the street and asked how to find a certain address.

But this was not the only reason for their hostility to Russians. Machiavelli also recommends deporting the native population. Stalin was doing this too. Deporting Latvians by the thousands. Gathering them in trucks at night and sending them away to Siberia and other eastern lands.

Into this cauldron Andrei leaped with the eagerness he brought to any new undertaking, for his joy of life was inexhaustible. He should not, however, have turned to the West. If it is true that our souls undergo reincarnation, then Andrei's soul emerged into this life from the East. India held irresistible attraction for him, and in those first days when we were still communicating with the aid of dictionaries, he assured me we would visit it eventually. His tastes were not Western tastes. He did not like bright lights, swept paths, highly polished surfaces. He would gaze entranced at a sagging wattle fence enclosing a littered barnyard, or at dilapidated wooden steps rich in sepia tones. He might appreciate the neat pattern of the woodpiles in Latvian backyards, but they did not touch his heart as did the disorderly woodpiles in Russian villages. Years later, when Ivy Litvinov was showing me the Heath in London where she first met her husband, we came upon a ragged patch of lawn which I said could stand a bit of mowing. "Oh, I don't know. I rather like it that way; you can overdo this mowing business, Peg," said Ivy, and once again I perceived a kinship with Andrei which he and she were both deeply aware of. Andrei might have been amused by the welter of New York, but he would have been bored by the smooth lawnscapes of American suburbia.

I do not find the Russian soul as enigmatic as Western readers of Dostoyevsky would make it. But the Russian outlook on life differs in many ways from the Western one. The Slavophiles in nineteenth-century Russia recognized this difference and would have made it basic in determining the country's further development. Those who were for Russia's following in the steps of the West won the day, and this, it seems to me, accounts for many of the difficulties the modernization of the country has run into. Russians are not inclined to see in efficiency the virtue Westerners make of it. Russians find the importance of punctuality greatly exaggerated. Russians look upon appointments as guidelines rather than anchor chains. Applied to dinner engagements, this is exasperating for the hostess, as I have experienced more than once; as applied to business, it is disastrous. In a word, Tolstoy's theory as expressed by Levin in *Anna Karenina*, that any project for the advancement of Russian economy must take into account the character of the Russian worker, has proved to be correct.

Perhaps the Soviet attempt to force the Russian workforce and nation into Western methods is one factor that has given rise to such ugly deformities as alcoholism, sloth, and deceit. The Japanese, on the other hand, have devised a pattern of industrialization better adjusted to the national character. "Know thyself" applies to nations as well as individuals. Who can estimate the unique influence Russia might have exerted on human destiny if her version of the revolution had remained true not only to the underlying principles of revolution—liberty, equality, fraternity—but also to her own nature, essentially unpragmatic, noncompetitive, and acutely sensitive to the mystery of life. This latter quality explains why the Orthodox Church was no less a governing force in old Russia than the state, the Patriarch no less revered than the Czar, with all the good and the bad this implies. The inflicting of godlessness upon the whole people overnight, by decree, by repressions, by the razing of temples and smashing of icons, was a savage operation that bred savagery. Who knows whether Russia will ever regain the spiritual values that so impressed Rainer Maria Rilke when he twice visited Russia at the end of the nineteenth century?

The understanding of these things was a slow process that in 1948 had hardly begun for me. Andrei took his unruly temperament into this neat little Latvia whose inhabitants until yesterday had been small farmers and shopkeepers, in the hope of effecting, through the theater, a revaluation of values. He did not believe he could rely on the old actors whose acquaintance he had made on a preliminary visit to support him in this. Many of the actors, and those the leading ones, were emigrés or the children of emigrés from Soviet Russia. It seemed improbable that people who had run away from a regime which had now overtaken them would feel at home in a Soviet repertory or would sincerely work for the success of a Soviet theater. Andrei was as certain that they would not as he was certain of most things. And so he took with him to the Riga Theater a group of young people who, he believed, would form the core of the company. They were recent graduates from Moscow's Vakhtangov Theater Studio and of the studio to which Stanislavsky had devoted the last years of his life. Andrei chose and cast his plays to the advantage of these young actors. This caused a cleavage in the troupe that brought him endless trouble. The tension caused by jealousies and animosities frustrated his artistic efforts. With the exception, perhaps, of a stage version of Turgenev's *Nest of Nobles* that exactly fitted his delicate taste and spiritual aspirations, he produced nothing outstanding in Riga. He was made to pay heavily for his failure. He never recovered from it professionally.

But if Riga was a scene of tribulation for Andrei, it was doubly so for me.

Although I had given up teaching for translating after the war, I missed students and lecture halls so acutely that I could not resist an invitation to conduct a course in English at Riga's State Pedagogical Institute. Had I sat quietly at home translating Gorky's novels I would not have made the social contacts that caused the security men to turn their eyes on me once again.

I was alone in the classroom after a lesson when two young men appeared in the doorway. I recognized them at once and knew what they had come for. If their dark clothes, meant to make them inconspicuous but actually setting them apart, had not given them away their faces would have: young, ordinary faces. Faces that in different circumstances I happily associated with my students, I now found to be a bland blur, but smiling genially to put at ease those whose hearts sank on seeing them. I instinctively cringed from the task they would offer me even though I still believed it to be an inevitable function of this capitalist-encircled state. My attitude had changed from the night I had been taken to the Lubyanka and come home feeling that a medal had been pinned to my chest. Now I knew it was a sordid task, but many are the sordid tasks that have to be done. The young men's attitude to me was like that of one fraternity brother to another: we were the initiated. They did not doubt that I would go on from where I had left off before the war. I did not disappoint them.

I was assigned two persons to report on, one of them Tamara, a younger colleague at the Institute with whom I had made friends. She was a dedicated teacher and born scholar who has since won eminence as a professor of European literature. In early youth, when Latvia was a bourgeois republic, she and her brother Joe were Young Communist

League members and took an active part in revolutionary activities. Joe was arrested by the bourgeois government and given a jail sentence. Tamara went to England, and when he had served his term he joined her there. That is where they were living when the war began. As soon as Hitler attacked the Soviet Union they came to Russia so that Joe could enter the Red Army as a volunteer. He was rejected, of course; the taint of having lived abroad canceled out whatever else was on the record. So they lived in Moscow until the war was over, when they returned to their homeland, now the land of their youthful dreams, a Soviet Latvia.

I could report nothing but good of Tamara: her loyalty to communism sprang from a conviction for which she and her brother had paid heavily. But neither this nor my testimony in her favor saved Tamara and Joe from arrest in the early fifties when Andrei and I were back in Moscow.

After Stalin's death, when both of them were "rehabilitated," I told Tamara about my secret relationship. I saw a little quiver go through her as from an electric shock, but she quickly came back with, "If it hadn't been you with me, it might well have been me with you." I don't believe it. I think she said it impulsively because, seeing my distress, she felt sorry for me and wanted to console me.

The other person assigned to me was an American woman who called herself Mrs. Davis. She too was teaching English at the Institute, although she had no qualifications for doing so. She hated teaching and seemed incapable of learning the theoretical aspects. She was an uneducated woman with no interests outside of the working-class struggle. As soon as I put in an appearance at the Institute she attached herself to me as one American to another. I could see she was famished for companionship. She had no family and made no friends. There was a sharpness and bitterness about her that staved people off. With me she was less sharp, but we had nothing to talk about. She had dark eyes that looked at you with an hysterical fixity. We might be discussing the most casual things—clothes, say—and suddenly she would turn those piercing eyes on me and ask peremptorily, "Why are you in Riga?" There were moments when I suspected we were colleagues not only at the Institute; moments when I could have taken her remarks for provocation, as when, walking together down Brevibas Street, she abruptly announced, "I hate Stalin." (Oh God, may the earth open and swallow me up!) Then, challengingly, "Do you like Stalin?" I did not. Andrei and I had had words about this. He had tried to convince me it was not Stalin who was responsible for having his picture on the front page of every issue of every paper and magazine and his hallowed words quoted in every article, be it on art, science, or philosophy. It was the Party using him as a symbol for uniting a population that had always been united by a symbol: the Czar or the Patriarch. I did not buy this banal and widely circulated argument, but I made no such admission to Mrs. Davis. I quickly turned her attention to some pastries in the window of a coffee shop we were passing and drew her inside.

In this instance I violated my resolution to be a flawless mirror. I pushed her denunciation of Stalin outside the frame; it was too egregious a crime to be mirrored. It was not without trepidation and inner gnawings that I did so.

Much worse was to come.

I was more concerned about Andrei than about Mrs. Davis in those days. I could see things were going badly with him and knew our sojourn in Riga would soon come to an end. It was toward the end of it on a late afternoon in spring that the phone rang. Mrs. Davis said she must speak to me.

"Come on over," I said reluctantly. I would turn a boring visit into a coffee klatch (we were both coffee addicts).

"Would you please make us some coffee, Mrs. Edwards?" I called out to the kitchen. Mrs. Edwards, of English forebears, was a plump, middle-aged woman, motherly looking but stepmotherly acting, who resented having to run other people's households now that her means were insufficient to run her own. The effort she made to be affable ill-disguised her contempt for Russians, all of whom she considered dirty as part of their general inferiority. I could take it temporarily for the sake of the order and good food she provided.

We lived in a big old four-storied apartment house on the far side of the Daugava river. You reached it by trolley car, crossing the bridge and a swampy stretch that offered such poor support for tracks that once when I was riding on the outside platform I was suddenly pitched against the wall, the floorboards rose up and splintered, and the car screeched to a halt two feet off the tracks.

There was no architectural design to the apartments in our house, just a string of rooms, one after another, well lighted by tall windows and well heated by tile stoves that rose from floor to ceiling, offering a warm expanse to warm your back against when you came in from the cold. Our second-floor apartment was quiet. An old couple lived below us, and above? Well, one Wednesday evening when I was sitting at my typewriter I suddenly heard a chorus singing "Rock of ages cleft for me/ Let me hide myself in thee./ Let the waters and the flood . . ." I did indeed let the waters and the flood sweep over me in a tidal wave of nostalgia. How many years had passed since I had heard that hymn, so much a part of my childhood and youth? It was as good as proscribed in this little Protestant Latvia under its Soviet masters. That is why a band of the faithful, no longer having a church to worship in, rented the upstairs apartment for services on Sundays and prayer meetings on Wednesday evenings.

I answered Mrs. Davis's ring of the doorbell. I was struck by her pallor. As she took off her things she glanced into the kitchen.

"Who's that woman?" she asked under her breath.

"Mrs. Edwards, the housekeeper."

"Let's go," and she walked swiftly past the kitchen door, through the dining room with Andrei's plants filling the bay window, through the living room where Andrei and I slept on daybeds, into the children's room at the far end of the apartment. She shut the door behind us and turned to me with a movement as swift as a cry.

"They're after me," she said. "They're out to get me."

"Who's *they*?"

"Soon," she said. "Maybe tonight, maybe tomorrow. Don't make those big eyes like you don't understand. It's not the Party, it's not Lenin—Lenin should know what's going on! It's *him*, him and his henchmen. The bastards! The bastards!" she moaned. "What shall I do, Margaret? Where can I go? Where can I hide?"

"Calm yourself. Sit down. Let me get you some coffee." How could I keep this woman from telling me things I didn't want to hear?

"If I could only reach somebody at the top. There must be somebody up there who'd listen to me. But I can't. They won't let me. All channels closed. Closed to me, *me*!" She was overcome. Between sobbing and raging she told me her story.

As an active member of the American Communist Party, she had allowed herself to become involved in espionage for the Soviets. No doubt she had accepted the offer with the same pride, the same sense of having been "chosen" I had felt in the Lubyanka that night twelve years earlier. She had become a foreign agent—not an important one, surely. She lacked the qualifications for that. She was probably just a link relaying information from one agent to another. But it had cost her years of perilous living in foreign countries, mostly Mexico and China.

"I never had a home, never had a child, never lived like everybody else, in one place, in one country, always here and there, doing the work I had to do, scared to death of getting caught, always saying to myself 'one more year, just one more year of this and I'll go home.' And you know where home was? The Soviet Union. That's what I dreamed of. Going to Moscow for good. They'd take care of me. I'd make myself a family. Adopt a war orphan. I had friends there, people I'd worked with abroad."

And instead? Instead she had been banished to this backwater where again she felt herself surrounded by enemies, where she had to go on living the same secret life with no hope of being understood, let alone appreciated.

"I was sent here like to prison," she murmured bitterly; then, with rising terror, "They're out to get me, Margaret. They're coming for me. Maybe tonight. What'll I do? What'll I do?" She almost shook me for an answer. "In God's name, what'll I do?" Her eyes were not piercing now. They were black holes. I knew what she *would* do. She would hang herself or go mad.

But what was *I* to do? I certainly had not bargained for a situation like this.

Hours later, after having expostulated with her, quieted her, given her food, and taken her home, I walked the streets struggling with my own problem. There should have been no problem. Instinctively I knew what I ought to do. I ought to bury the secrets confided to me as I had buried her denunciation of Stalin. I did not dare to. I was afraid for Andrei, for the children, for myself. Nobody wants to be bad, so if our goodness is in question we begin to rationalize. The human mind displays uncommon ingenuity in using self-deception in self-defense. As an advocate it usually wins its case.

In the Lubyanka twelve years earlier I had had no need of an advocate to prove my innocence. Such was my dedication that I accepted the necessity of using duplicity to serve it. I suffered no qualms of conscience. Since then things had happened to modify without destroying my allegiance. And so this time I did need an advocate. My pusillanimous mind did not fail me. It came up with excuses for betraying this miserable woman's confidence that appeared to be sound, some even noble.

What if she were testing me with this story? What if she had been sent to report on my reliability as a witness? Subterfuge was her stock in trade. Could she be putting on an act with me? I found this argument preposterous. There could be no doubt that her terror and despair were genuine. She was on the brink of mental collapse.

That was the point: if in her extremity she could tell me her secrets, she could tell them to others. My chief had warned me that Riga, a comparatively obscure northern port, was a convenient place for slipping foreign agents into the Soviet Union. The cold war was on. The spy scare was at its height. The things Mrs. Davis had revealed came as a shock to me. I had believed official declarations that the socialist state did not engage in international espionage. Mrs. Davis was blabbing. She was exposing herself to the danger of blackmail. Had I a right to wash my hands of her by pretending to know nothing? Perhaps through my connections she could reach "somebody at the top." Perhaps I could help her (my most eagerly clutched straw). How would I feel if she committed suicide or were taken away in a straitjacket and I had done nothing to prevent it?

My chief at that time was an intelligent, educated, middle-aged man. The name he gave me was Semyon Semyonich. I think I pleaded Mrs. Davis's case well—certainly with feeling and sincerity. And he listened well—gravely, rarely interrupting, showing sympathy and concern. When I finished he considered the matter for some time before he said, "What do you think we ought to do, Margarita Danilovna?" I said she must be gotten out of Riga as quickly as possible. It was unsafe for her to remain here. She must be given medical treatment to keep her from having a complete mental breakdown, and when she was well she must be allowed to live in a congenial environment and make the life for herself she had hoped to make.

I came away from the interview with a sense of relief. My chief's earnestness and sympathy convinced me that even if the measures taken were not those I recommended, something would be done to get her through this crisis.

A week later Tamara and I happened to run into Mrs. Davis on the street. We stopped to speak, but before we could utter a word she fixed me with wild eyes and said fiercely, "So you told them!"

My heart shriveled as under a blowtorch. Nothing was left of it but a charred and squirming thing.

Tamara pulled me away. "Come along," she said. "The woman's crazy. She suspects everybody, even me."

Not long after this our family moved back to Moscow. Tamara came to see me in the summer and told me Mrs. Davis had been arrested. Tamara herself was arrested soon afterward.

Had Semyon Semyonich fooled me? Had his earnestness and sympathy been a mask? I thought so at the time. I no longer do. Like myself he had entered into this service with the best of motives. In doing so he voluntarily became part of an enormous, impersonal, diabolical machine built, like a beehive, of countless cells, wall to wall, but each securely isolated from all others except for thin metal wires (so unlike sentient nerves) over which communications were despatched. Information fed into one of the cells was processed by first paring it down to bare facts; these facts were then directed to appropriate inner cells as securely isolated as the outer ones were; here the facts were sorted and passed on to central cells which spat out resolutions. In the initial period of the process (Mrs. Davis–me–Semyon Semyonich) the information was contaminated by human feelings. Once it was inside the machine it was sterilized of such contamination.

My experience with Mrs. Davis made it clear that I must extricate myself from the machine. I was given the opportunity in Moscow. Once more I was summoned, this time not to Lubyanka but to a second-floor room in an ordinary office building on Arbat Street. As I climbed the stairs I passed, coming down, a leading Soviet poet who spent most of his life abroad. Each of us pretended not to see the other on the stairs.

The man at the desk welcomed me in the fraternal spirit I was familiar with.

"Welcome back to Moscow."

"Thank you."

"We need you here."

"I'm sorry, I can't help you."

"How's that? Has someone offended you?"

"No, I just don't believe in what we're doing anymore."

"Why?"

"Where is Mrs. Davis?"

"Mrs. Davis? Who's Mrs. Davis?"

"Exactly. Good-bye."

That was the gist of it, though other words were spoken: the man pointed out that I had saved innocent people from arrest: Oh, had I? What about Tamara? What about Mrs. Davis whom he didn't even know? We on lower levels are incapable of seeing the whole picture, he said. I thought I could see the whole picture now and I wanted to be no part of it. I wanted to get out. For good. Whether the troubles Andrei suffered after this were connected with my getting out or not

I cannot tell. I doubt that they were. He himself had given ample cause for his troubles.

So I was out. And I was different. I had changed. Without having given it undue consideration, I had always assumed I was upright, not particularly virtuous perhaps, but decent. It took this shattering experience to make me see not only myself but all that was going on around me in a new light. I saw the evil of it, and that I was supporting evil. How had I the presumption to decide what was better for the world when I myself was on a moral level so low that I could adopt as a rule of conduct the infamous precept: the end justifies the means? Between bright moments of seeing the light I had traveled down tunnels of self-deception.

Well, no more. Riga had set me free. Riga had very painfully ripped the scales off my eyes.

seventeen

Darkening Days

Will all great Neptune's ocean wash this blood
Clean from my hand? No. This my hand will rather
The multitudinous seas incarnadine.
—William Shakespeare,
Macbeth (Act II, sc. 1)

IT WAS PAYDAY at the publishers. I was standing in line at the cashier's window chatting with one of the other translators when a lively voice behind me called out in a British accent, "And who might *you* be?" I turned around to look into the smiling brown eyes of a rather portly middle-aged lady with strands of gray hair drifting out from under a wide-brimmed straw hat that called for something more elegant than the crushed gingham dress below it. "Dowdy," Ivy once called herself. The word does not fit Ivy. Careless of clothes she was, jamming any old hat down on her head that would keep her ears warm or the sun out of her eyes, pulling on the first stocking that came to hand, hole or no hole in the heel. The dresses made for her by the lady down the street were designed to be ample for comfort and button-up for convenience. But once you got past her clothes (if you were vulgarly apt to linger) you never went back. The warmth shed by her dark eyes, the wit they flashed, commanded all attention. There was withal an imposing expanse of brow, a masculine curve of nose in arresting contrast to a feminine sensitivity of mouth, and an imperial set to a flawlessly domed head. Indeed, Ivy's natural attractions were merely enhanced and given distinction by her Olympian disregard for the accepted in clothes.

And so "And who might you be?" was my introduction to Ivy Litvinov some twenty years after this was to have been accomplished by a letter of introduction given me by Philadelphia's eminent educator Dr. Lucy Wilson.

I was lucky not to have found Ivy in Moscow at that time. She was in Geneva with her husband, Maxim Litvinov, Soviet Commissar of Foreign Affairs (a title reduced today by a deflation of pomp and change of circumstance to the more wieldy Soviet Foreign Minister). Taken up as she was at that time by the many duties devolving upon the wife of so prominent a husband, she would doubtless have dismissed me with an apologetic note, and that would have been the end of it. Now, with Litvinov in Stalin's disfavor, she was no longer the wife of the Soviet Foreign Minister nor even the wife of the Soviet Ambassador to the United States, as she had been during World War II, but a translator for the Progress Publishers just as I was, she doing Pushkin's prose at the time, I doing Gorky's *Childhood.* When she learned who my author was she let out a whoop of laughter and said, "Oh, Peg, if I was on a desert island and had my choice of two books, Gorky or the telephone directory, I'd take the directory, you bet!"

When both of us had been paid, we climbed into the old-fashioned black limousine the government still supplied the Litvinovs with and she took me home with her.

"I want you to meet my daughter, Tanya," she said.

The Litvinovs lived in the Government House, a modernistic aggregate of gray concrete cubes dumped upon the Moscow River embankment without grace of tree or grass, exactly opposite the Kremlin whose golden-domed cathedrals and belfries have sweeping lawns and sumptuous trees as their setting. The front door of the Litvinovs' fifth-floor apartment opened into a wide hall running the length of the building. So cluttered was this hall with skis, skates, sleds, scooters, bikes, and all the paraphernalia including coats and hats and scarves and overshoes belonging to growing children and sporting adults that it looked as if a kindergarten and a sports club had combined in disgorging their inventories here. A blast of air at my back as I hung my coat over a heap of other coats drew a cry from Ivy, "Get off that thing, Pavel! Can't you take your bike outside?"

"That's where I'm taking it, Gamma," was the gentle reply as the boy and his bike whisked past me onto the stair landing.

Doors in the right-hand wall led into rooms, large and small, accommodating a family comprising Ivy and husband, son Misha with wife and two children, and daughter Tanya with husband and two children.

"Tanya," called Ivy as she sailed into the dining room with me behind her. Tanya rushed out of an adjoining bedroom holding a peeled orange which she had been feeding to her little girls Masha and Vera. "This is Peg," said Ivy.

Tanya grinned at me as she made for the door into the hall. "Proskovia!" she called. "Won't you please come and take over?"

A cushiony nursemaid with a wart-riddled face came at once to relieve Tanya of the orange. "This is Peg," Tanya said to her.

Proskovia nodded as she drew Masha and Vera away from the doorway to which they had crept to ogle the stranger.

There were bookshelves on the right-hand wall of the dining room, and there was a grand piano with a children's songbook of English nursery rhymes on the stand ("That's how I teach them English," said Ivy) and there was a big white Frigidaire beside the piano ("Maxim brought it from America," said Ivy as if Frigidaires and their ilk were none of her business), and there was a big round dining room table between the two windows on the far side of the room, and the wall between the windows was a marvel ("Don't you *love* it?" asked Tanya, seeing my eyes fixed on it. "Sara Lebedeva did it.") What artist Sarah Lebedeva (sculptor of Pasternak's gravestone) had done was to join the many spots and stains on this neglected wall with a single flowing line that described a lovely lady with billowing skirts and wind-blown hair—or was it a garden hat? Ivy and Tanya and I sat at the big table under this lady's gaze and ate cheese and crackers and talked about the book Tanya had been reading. It was Boswell's *Journal of a Tour of the Hebrides with Samuel Johnson*.

"Have you come to the place where Boswell tells the story of how Prince Charles escaped to France by disguising himself as Flora Macdonald's maid?" asked Ivy.

"Oh, yes," said Tanya, "and almost got caught by pulling his skirts up too high when wading across a stream."

"That gave Flora a fright but she, brave lady, escorted him in an open boat to the Isle of Skye under the very eyes of the naval vessels in the harbor on the lookout for him. Look, here's a nice word: *whinrock*," said Ivy, who was leafing through the book as she talked.

"What does it mean?"

Ivy reached for the ever-present dictionary: " 'Collections of stones like the ruins of the foundations of old buildings.' And then there's the word *dour*. You Americans pronounce the vowels as in 'our' or 'sour,' but we English pronounce it 'd$\overline{oo}$r,' as in 'moor.' " Then, still leafing, "How do you like this as one of the doctor's deathless observations? Boswell: 'I said, I believed mankind were happier in the ancient feudal state of subordination, than they are in the modern state of independency. Johnson: To be sure the *chief* was; but we must think of the number of individuals. That *they* were less happy seems plain; for that state from which all escape as soon as they can and to which none return after they have left it, must be less happy; and this is the case with the state of dependence on a chief or great man.'

"Hard to put it simpler," said Ivy.

Presently Proscovia came out of the bedroom with empty dishes in her hands and made for the hall with the children clinging to her skirts.

"Masha! Vera!" said Ivy. "Let's sing for Peg," and she went over to the piano and the girls took up their places on either side of the stool and charmingly rendered "Polly pud de kettle on."

"You could easily get them to articulate *th*," I offered from my experience of teaching phonetics.

"Of course I could," retorted Ivy, "but what kind of life would it be for them?" Having thus dispensed with the science of phonetics for little girls, she swept back to the table, releasing Masha and Vera to the scooters and roller skates waiting for them in the hall.

This, then, was our first encounter. Those that followed were not all in such a light vein.

Once when we found ourselves alone at my place, she put her hands on my shoulders and looked deeply into my eyes in a way I was to become familiar with and said, "These are bad times, Peg."

Never worse. At the end of the forties and beginning of the fifties arrests mounted to prewar level. The high hopes all Russians had cherished of returning to normal life after the war were cruelly blasted. Russian prisoners of war who had spent time in Nazi concentration camps were sent to Soviet concentration camps when they came home, as punishment for having let themselves be taken captive—they should have shot themselves. With maniacal ferocity Stalin attacked everything vibrant and viable in Soviet culture. Besides the irreparable damage he did to Soviet science by denying the validity and prohibiting the practice of such branches as genetics and cybernetics, he rang the death knell of Soviet art by dubbing any work beyond the comprehension of the simple-minded, "formalism." Original literary talent was squelched by newspaper denunciations (couched in lurid language) of the poet Akhmatova and the humorist Zoschenko, scapegoats for the entire literary fellowship. These were followed by similar denunciations of the country's greatest composers: Shostakovich, Prokofiev, Khachaturian, Myaskovsky.

It was also the time of Stalin's despicable campaign against "Cosmopolitanism," allegedly to promote national patriotism by attacking the growing admiration for things Western evoked by the view of them caught when Russian armies invaded Europe toward the end of World War II. Essentially, however, it was an antisemitic campaign, ill masked by the euphemism "Cosmopolitanism."

"These are bad times, Peg," said Ivy, her eyes deep in mine. "Tanya's husband is not only a sculptor with his own ideas about art, he is also Jewish. As for my husband . . ."

So sure was Ivy that members of her family were marked for arrest that she asked me to go with her to buy suitcases. "When they come for you, you're not likely to remember to put soap and scissors in the bag." So we bought three suitcases and outfitted them with soap and scissors and other essentials.

The times could not have been worse for Andrei and me. After the Riga experience we were glad to be back on Russian soil. With a subconscious impulse to "dig in," we set about redecorating our apartment. Andrei and I took the sunny front room for ourselves now that the children were of an age when they spent little time at home. I sat down with a ruler to calculate how to fit bookshelves, a piano, two couches, two desks, two armchairs, and a round tea table into a longish room whose far wall was one big double-paned window. By installing daylight lamps and an electric heater, Andrei turned the space between the panes into a hothouse for his orchids. An enthusiastic handyman and I turned the room into one that looked almost spacious while answering all requirements. With linen curtains, couch covers, and pillows, in pastel shades, it was flooded with light and color in the daytime while at night moonbeams, shining through trees without and plants within, painted a mobile mural on the far wall like the one Thoreau enjoyed in his Walden cabin.

I had supposed that as soon as we were back in Moscow Andrei would pick up professionally where he had left off on going to Riga. Time passed and nothing of the sort happened. I did not urge him to tell me his plans or prospects. I waited patiently for the day when, with characteristic enthusiasm, he would name his new venture. Instead he announced, "I'm going to take time off from the theater to write a book on Stanislavsky." Andrei was going to write a book! The only thing he had ever written so far were the copious notes he kept about plays he was rehearsing or plants he was cultivating. And now he was going to write a book and leave the support of the family to me? I could handle it, but why should I? I didn't believe in him as a writer, I believed in him as a stage director. True, he had had a long and unique relationship with Stanislavsky, especially in the last years of the famous director's life. But dozens of books had been written about Stanislavsky. Anything Andrei could add had best be transmitted through a writer or researcher without distracting him from his true calling.

I was distressed. I spoke to Dmitri about it. "Can't you make him see what a mistake this is?"

"It's not easy to oppose Andrei. Once he's got his heart set on something. . . ."

Nobody knew this better than I did. Well, if I couldn't change his heart-set, I could at least let him feel my disapproval. I was cold. Disapproving. Resentful. As I sat at my typewriter on one side of the room I was distractingly conscious of him sitting at his desk a few feet away, covering sheet after sheet of paper with his minuscule handwriting, then getting up with an attempt to be soundless that grated on my nerves like the stripping of gears. Often he would leave the house for hours and come back to say cheerfully, "A good idea came to me while I was walking along the boulevard." I refused to respond. In those hard times it required swaths and swaths of translation to support our family. I lay awake nights wondering what would become of the children if anything happened to me. I took out as big a life insurance policy as I could afford and mentally told over my friends, searching for one I would want to guide the children to the age of independence without me. I chose Sonya.

This went on for months. Then one day on coming home from the publishers I found Andrei standing motionless in the middle of the room. He presented me with a face I had never seen before.

"What is it, Andrei?" I asked in fright. "Has something happened?"

He slumped down on the couch and turned cavernous eyes on me. "What am I to do—shoot myself?" he asked.

Now it all came out: how when he had gone to the Art Committee for a new appointment he had been put off time and again; how when he had persisted, the head of the committee had startled him with, "Where can I send you? Do you want to be taken off the train?"; how he had accepted this as a dire warning and had set out to confirm his suspicions by seeking work on his own, had even applied for the lowly job of Entertainment Supervisor at Gorky Park—games and things. His application was rejected. It was clear: he was being reduced to a nonperson. For what grim purpose? That was the haunting thought. We had seen it happen to others—to his friend Mick-Step for one. Mick-Step (affectionate for Michael Stepanovich) had fallen victim to

Cosmopolitanism. The purity of his Russian blood was beyond question. So was his position as a leading drama critic and professor of Russian literature. So was his loyalty to the Party, which he had joined as a young man in the early twenties. None of these things counted when it was discovered that his Russian blood was tainted by a perverse admiration for Jewish brains, as evidenced by his having appointed too many Jewish scholars to head research bureaus at the All-Union Theater Society of which he was president. For this he paid by being thrown out of the Theater Society, thrown out of his academic position, thrown out of the Party. Like Andrei, he became a nonperson. People for whom he had once done favors now crossed to the other side of the street on seeing him coming. But for the solicitude of two loving sisters he might well have starved to death. At length he was rescued by former pupils, Uzbeks by nationality, who had studied under him in Moscow and now invited him to teach in the Theater Institute in Tashkent, capital of Uzbekistan, a republic bordering on Afghanistan.

As I listened to Andrei's outpouring I blushed and blanched in turn. I had failed him terribly. The book had been a ruse to spare me the truth. Twenty years of life together ought to have made me sense disaster. Oh, I had! But not *his* disaster. How could I? He had left no chink in his carapace for me to peer through. His spirits had shown no flagging. He had attacked the book with the same energy he applied to everything else. He had accepted my moods and suffered my barbs with exasperating equanimity.

Now that I knew the truth my remorse far exceeded my exasperation. So did my admiration for his performance and the panache with which he carried it off.

Frustrated in the hope that everything would be different after the war, convinced that in this locked and barred society only time would reveal the truth, Andrei said to me on one of those bleak days, "If only we could live another fifty years and find out what it's all about!" How surprised both of us would have been had we known we would find out in less than five years.

At about this time Annushka's Jhenya died. As his wedding had suited our mood after Mongolia, so his funeral suited our mood after Riga. Annushka accepted his death stoically. Not so the year before the war when she had rushed to our house in panic and fallen on my neck sobbing, "I can't live if he dies, Margaritochka, I can't, I can't, I don't want to! Oh, God, if he dies!" He had been taken to the hospital in a diabetic coma (his diabetes induced by the murder of his father) and the doctors were not hopeful.

He came out of the coma that time; this time he did not. At the crematorium Annushka stood quietly between Kiva and Katya while friends and relatives took leave of Jhenya, kissing his waxen brow, murmuring words in parting, leaving a flower beside his hands, his head. The music played too softly to cover the pulsating hum of the flames down below. Annushka quivered when the mechanism creaked and the bier began its descent into the inferno, but when Katya pressed a sedative on her, she pushed it away, meaning no offense but wanting no intrusion.

We all went home with Annushka, where Katya had prepared a funeral feast and laid it in her own room, Anna's and Kiva's being too small. Jhenya's friend, Sergei, who had cried "Gorky! Gorky!" at his wedding (and whom the war had left with only one leg), spoke a few loving words about him as did we all, for Jhenya's had been a sad but admirable life. His other friends told anecdotes about his awkwardness and his impulsiveness, and we all laughed, Anna especially. We drank vodka but made no toasts, toasts being taboo at Russian funerals.

At first I had been shocked by the idea of feasting at a funeral. I had participated in only one funeral in America, Uncle Al's. It was very austere. He and Aunt Jessie had no children so the only people who went home from the cemetery with Aunt Jessie were Mother, Aunt Clara, Helen, and I. We talked in lowered tones and walked on tiptoe so as not to disturb Aunt Jessie, who went directly to her room to be alone. Mourning enveloped the house. I shudder at the remembrance. Funeral feasts, I learned, are the right thing. Annushka was not left alone and was given no opportunity to brood while all the brightness of Jhenya's life was summoned up in memory.

THE LIFE WE LIVED under the Sword of Damocles was punctuated by a big event: the acquisition of Leonozovo. Andrei Nikolayevich, who had Dmitri and Vyeta (now a student of Moscow University) living with him next door to us, dropped in one evening to say the government had offered his clinic some land at Leonozovo, just outside of Moscow, to be divided up into individual garden plots and given to all who wished to cultivate them. Did Andrei want such a plot? He most certainly did. This was at the beginning of the Community Gardens project, initiated as an opportunity for private citizens to raise their own fruit, which was scarce in government stores and expensive at *kolkhoz* markets.

At first Andrei's was a garden like everyone else's, from which we garnered bushels of strawberries and tomatoes, most of which we gave away, since I had neither the time nor the inclination to can vegetables and preserve fruit as other wives were doing. But over the years Andrei substituted horticulture for agriculture and then substituted wildflowers for cultivated ones until he had a collection of over fifteen hundred varieties gathered from all over the Soviet Union, a veritable annex of the Botanical Gardens, written about in journals and visited by professional and amateur horticulturists. He landscaped the ground and irrigated it with an encircling stream that trickled over rocks into a little pool at the far end. On these rocks Marfusha, a huge female frog, sunned herself surrounded by a half-dozen little suitors.

The acquisition of Leonozovo was timely. It diverted Andrei's thoughts from his troubles until the day when Mick-Step came to Moscow from Tashkent and took him back with him. He did for his friend what his students had done for him: he arranged to have Andrei invited to teach at the Tashkent Theater Institute.

So I began traveling between my husband in Tashkent and my children in Moscow. Our frequent partings and reunions added poignancy to our relationship: I highly recommend it as an antidote for the humdrum-sickness that infects many an extended marriage.

I always enjoyed joining him in that extraordinary city of Tashkent, even though it was there that Andrei's chest pains became more regular, a sure sign of the development of angina pectoris. Mick-Step, ten years older than Andrei, could run for the bus that took them to the institute. Andrei could not. But still the constrictions were not so frequent or so severe as to prevent our enjoying this hot southern city, a Muslim city, with tall trees shading the streets and manmade streams called *aryks* following the curbs to cool the air and fill it with their prattle. And we had the rare companionship of Mick-Step and Farida—yes, Farida, because Mick-Step, an exile in a foreign land, disowned and dishonored by the city to which he had given the best of his talent, found in this exotic city the love of his life. He had found her among the Uzbek students attending his course on Dostoyevsky. Although she was a modern girl, an English major at Tashkent University, who eventually defended a doctor's thesis on Howard Fast (just in time, because soon thereafter Howard Fast was denounced, his books withdrawn from all libraries, and his plays removed from all theaters owing to a public statement in which he criticized some Soviet policy or other)—although she represented the emancipated oriental Woman, she might well have stepped out of a Persian miniature. She had the grace and beauty of those dark-eyed creatures idling among birds and flowers: tall, lithesome, a small head tilted provocatively on a graceful neck, black brows arched above black eyes, a delicately carved nose, a winsome mouth, shy withal, downward-glancing. Such was Farida, thirty years Mick-Step's junior, who loved him devotedly until the day of his death thirty years later in Moscow where, after Stalin's death, he was restored to honor and academic position and to the Party, expulsion from which had been his greatest grief.

And in Tashkent, of all places, we met an American family with whom we became friends. And it was Harry Kittel, the father of this family, who spoke words that ripped into my consciousness as the ultimate definition of what I had been and done.

Harry had been an American Communist with a master's degree in chemistry. Not being an "activist" by nature, he believed the best he could do for the cause was to offer his knowledge to the Soviet Union which had just embarked on its industrialization of the country. He had married Jeanette, a pretty girl from his own University of California, who cared nothing for politics but so much for Harry that she was willing to follow him to the ends of the earth. I wonder if she would have done so had she known the consequences. He brought his bride to Moscow in 1931, refused all the privileges offered to foreign specialists, was given a job in a chemical plant near Moscow, found the job below his powers, asked for a stiffer assignment, and was put in charge of a chemical laboratory *really* at the ends of the earth—not even in Tashkent, which is, after all, a capital, but in the provincial Uzbek town of Chimkent. There he worked around the clock while Jeanette, between having babies, learned to assist him in the laboratory. Came the Stalin purges. Harry was arrested. Jeanette found herself alone in a totally alien world with two small children and the prospect of being arrested herself, in which case her children would be consigned to orphan homes anywhere in the vast Soviet Union. The man who had been Harry's first assistant and now supplanted him as head of the laboratory offered to marry her. Seeing in this her only hope of saving the children, she agreed. "But I told him I loved Harry and would join him again if he ever came back."

She insisted that they move to Tashkent where Harry was imprisoned so that she could communicate with him and take him food parcels.

Just before the war Harry was released. The man Jeanette had married went to the front and never came back.

Harry was again made head of a chemical laboratory, this time in Tashkent. His assistant was an Uzbek who gave him no end of trouble. Seeing what was going on, a friendly colleague gave warning: "This man wants your job and will stop at nothing to get it. With your background you don't stand a chance against him—an Uzbek in Uzbekistan. You'd better get out before they put you out—or . . . worse."

Harry got out. He began teaching English at the Institute of Foreign Languages where Jeanette was teaching. This was ultimate capitulation. He had struck bottom: denounced by the Party, expelled from his profession, separated from his wife. Separated because they were now man and wife in name only. Jeanette felt he could never forgive her for marrying that other man even though she had done it only for the sake of the children. That may have been so; I have heard of men being repelled by the knowledge that their woman has belonged to another. But I think Jeanette had lost her attraction for Harry. She had put on weight, her youthful freshness had been blighted by time and trials, and she admitted to me that she "was not much of a sex partner." Harry was good-looking. His students were mostly girls. They fell for him, he fell for them. "I was even glad at first," Jeanette told me. "It gave him some interest in life, he had become terribly morose." But it went on and on, one girl after another. "We were working in the same place. Everybody could see it. The gossips got busy. Our kids were old enough to understand. So one day I said to him, 'Enough, Harry. You've got to stop it.' And he did. Just like that. But it did things to him. Nothing mattered any more. He just sort of shuffled around."

It was on a night when we were visiting the Kittels that Harry spoke the searing words.

Somebody knocked at the front door. Harry went to open it.

He came back alone.

"Who was it?" asked Jeanette.

"You know him. That guy who's always trying to make friends with us." Harry gave a contemptuous little laugh. "I didn't let him in. He's a *stookatch*."

I must have heard the word before, but I'm not sure. People didn't bandy such words about in Stalin's day. They did after he died, because with the coming of Khrushchev, fear "was slinking away from Russia," as Yevtushenko put it in one of the poems Shostakovich used in his thirteenth symphony. People who had been paralyzed with fear now shook it off—not all people, and no one entirely, because twenty years of conditioning cannot be overcome in a day. But people tried to free themselves. And oh, with what withering scorn they pronounced the word *stookatch*. Knocker. *Stook! Stook!* Knock! Knock! Let me in. *Stook! Stook!* Into your house. *Stook! Stook!* Into your thoughts. *Stook! Stook!* Into your confidence. So that I can run back to my chief and whisper it in his ear. It wasn't this simple, as I have tried to show. But it boiled down to exactly this. I winced as from a painful turn of the screw when Harry pronounced the word. It meant me. That is what I had been. A *stookatch*. Up to now I had felt guilty of a great sin. Suddenly I felt guilty of a shabby one. That was more humiliating. Informing is a mean species of the same genus as spying.

The Soviets' internal system of informants did as much to disrupt their society as political corruption did. It sowed distrust like dragon's teeth. Wife distrusted husband; brother, brother; neighbor, neighbor. Can wholesome living prevail in such circumstances? The same evil attends spying on an international scale. Distrust among nations is a major factor in promoting wars. That countries should distrust their enemies and try to gain an advantage over them by discovering their secrets is natural, man being what he is. But that allies should distrust allies (Israel, for example, spying on the U.S., and undoubtedly, vice versa) is unnatural and a deplorable new page in the annals of espionage.

STALIN DIED in March of 1953. Our family will never forget his funeral. I was having a spell with the children in Moscow, and Andrei came from Tashkent to celebrate our birthdays, his on the third, mine on the twenty-fifth of March.

Did Stalin's death cause nationwide jubilation? Far from it. People were stunned. So consummately had they been hoodwinked that they could envisage no future without The Helmsman. The Soviet propaganda machine had disassociated Stalin's name from all the ills of society by assigning them to hidden enemies. His name, on the contrary, was associated with all of society's achievements: the successes of industrialization, the elimination of illiteracy, the winning of the war, the diplomatic triumph of the peace settlements by which the country annexed the Baltic States and the western Ukraine and transformed

East Germany, Poland, Czechoslovakia, Hungary, Romania, and Bulgaria into Communist states dependent upon the Soviet Union.

Few political leaders have enjoyed the adulation accorded Stalin. His body lay in state in the Hall of Columns in Union House, next to the Bolshoi Theater. Valya Sobolyeva, the Leningrad actress who had played the title role in Andrei's staging of *Anna Karenina*, was visiting us at the time. Valya and I set out for Union House, but on reaching Pushkin Square we saw such a dense mob moving down the hill from Sretenka that we turned back. Ever since Father had put me on his shoulders to protect me from the crowd celebrating Armistice Day in Philadelphia in 1918, I had feared nothing so much as the uncontrollable movement of massed humans. And right I was to fear it this time. Early in the afternoon Adya had set out for Union House with his friends. He was not home by five o'clock, nor by eight, nor by twelve. Andrei and I sat up all night waiting for the sound of a key in the lock. We didn't hear it. At seven in the morning the milk woman came. "Oi, oi, oi," she wailed. "You should see what's happening out there! Ambulances rushing about! So many people crushed to death! Oi, oi, oi!"

At eight o'clock Andrei called the emergency hospital. I heard him give our son's name, address, description. I saw Andrei's face change. "What did they say?" I asked.

"They said . . . come after nine to identify the body."

"I'm going with you."

"You are not," he said.

It was not much before nine when we heard the turn of a key in the lock, and a disheveled Adya came in.

"Andrusha!"

"I'm all right," he assured us, seeing our strained faces.

"How did you . . . ?"

"My height helped. Kept my chest above the crush."

"Did you get caught in the crowd coming down the hill from Sretenka?"

"Yes."

"My God, how did you survive?"

"We managed to work our way to the edge of the crowd and climb up on the roofs. We spent the night on the roofs."

"Wasn't anything done to stop it?"

"The stampede? How do you stop a stampede? They brought in trucks as soon as they saw the danger and parked them sideways across the street, but they just got pushed over."

No figures were ever released as to the number of casualties at Stalin's funeral. They didn't have to be given. Moscow residents compared this public calamity with that which occurred in the Khodynka district of Moscow during the coronation festivities of Nicholas II in 1896, when the distribution of free souvenirs resulted in a stampede in which thousands of citizens were trampled to death. Then it was greed. This time it was curiosity: people longed to set eyes on the mysterious, almost mystical, leader who never appeared in public except on the May first and November seventh holidays, when he waved to them from the top of the Lenin mausoleum.

Even in death Stalin was a killer.

eighteen

Ivy

Tolerant plains, that suffer the sea and the rains and the sun,
Ye spread and span like the catholic man who hath mightily won
God out of knowledge and good out of infinite pain
And sight out of blindness and purity out of a stain.

—Sidney Lanier,
"The Marshes of Glynn"

IVY AND I WERE LYING rather uncomfortably on the pebbly Crimean shore of the Black Sea at Sudak. Two men in a boat kept rowing shoreward, then out again, brazenly watching a lovely young lady, stark naked, playing on the beach with her naked little girl. The lady and her child were the only ones sharing this secluded cove with us. The October weather was tangy, the sea a gentle scintillation whose lapping at the shore was almost inaudible.

"Ah, but it's not always so docile," said Ivy, shifting her pebble-pocked thighs for relief. "A couple of summers ago when I was here with Masha and Vera I almost drowned. There'd been a storm and the waves were high with a strong undertow. Fortunately there was a young man who saw me go under and pulled me out by the hair."

"Fortunately indeed," I said.

After a little pause which she filled by watching the two men in the boat who were close to shore now, their eyes glued to the nudes, she went on, "Did I say fortunately? I'm not so sure about that. It was an easy way to die." Suddenly she cut through the pensive mood with a burst of laughter. "Those shameless brutes! They don't mind us, that's for sure!"

She and I had come to Sudak for a vacation I badly needed after a summer of seeing Dasha through the ordeal of choosing a profession and being accepted by the institute that would train her for it. Like most children brought up in theater circles, she had fallen for the romantic lure of the stage. She wanted to be an actress.

Her father was not convinced of her outstanding talent in this field:

"To become an actor," he admonished, "it's got to be either the stage or the bottom of the Volga." But he let her take her chances. When she failed the grueling entrance exam for the studio of the Moscow Art Theater she landed in my lap all of a heap. It was too late to seriously prepare for exams to another institute, nor did she have the heart for it. So I took over and did what I could to brush up the little English she had learned in school so that she could compete with the well-tutored aspiring linguists who applied for entrance to the Moscow Institute of Foreign Languages. Dasha barely scraped through the grammar test. But by the end of the first term she was head of her class and has never regretted being forced to accept a second choice.

Seeing how limp the summer had left me, Ivy said, "C'mon, we'll go down to the sea. I'll lend you the money if you need it."

We stayed in a house belonging to Ivy's friend, widow of the Moscow painter Bruni, who had bought it only a few years before the war. Nazi soldiers had ravaged and defiled it during their occupation, tearing up floorboards for firewood and leaving behind them the trash and effluvia of abandoned barracks. Since then the family had cleaned it out, the roof had been repaired and the windows replaced; as for the view—nothing could damage the view. On the south stretched the glistening sea while on the west, beyond a valley planted to purple grapes, rose the ruins of an ancient Phoenician fortress poised on a bluff that dropped perpendicularly into the bay.

Ivy and I were alone; Andrei was in Tashkent, Litvinov was dead. He had died in 1951, two years before Stalin did. Ivy was compassionately attendant during his last illness, closer to him in those months than in many of the preceding years. They had had their marital ups and downs. Once, outraged by his making a public show of his relations with a young girl whom Ivy herself had brought into their family out of sympathy for the girl's unhappiness in her own family, she, Ivy, packed her bag and took off for Sverdlovsk in the Urals where she supported herself by teaching English. Her outrage was elicited less by his infidelity—her own record was no better than his—than by his indiscretion. She stayed in Sverdlovsk until his appeals brought her back. They were, after all, deeply attached to each other, Ivy and Maxim, and each admired the other's so different talents. Ivy stood staunchly behind Litvinov in those disgraceful years when this statesman of international reputation was reduced by Stalin to a nonperson. When I first met Ivy he held an inconsequential job with the same publishing house for which Ivy and I were translators. His death was announced by a few lines on an inside page of *Pravda*.

"I wish I didn't have to go to this wretched funeral," Ivy had complained.

"Well, you do have to, Mother," said Tanya quietly.

Ivy went.

There was no funeral feast.

I might note here the little-known fact of even harsher treatment meted out to Litvinov's predecessor, Georgi Vasilievich Chicherin, the first Soviet Commissar of Foreign Affairs, a representative of the old Russian intelligentsia, a man of enviable erudition. He wrote a biography of Mozart known to most Russian music-lovers.

I heard the following from Sonya; the information is not contained in any Soviet encyclopedia or history, but that is not surprising—no victim of Stalin's purges, however eminent, has that fact included in his biography.

"I was given permission to visit Georgi in camp the first time he was arrested," said Sonya. "We weren't allowed much time together, but at our very first meeting he said, 'There's someone here I want you to meet.' I met him the next day. 'This,' said my Georgi, 'is Georgi Vasiliyevich.' I smiled at the coincidence—my Georgi is Vasiliyevich, too. That wasn't the reaction my Georgi wanted from me. He took my arm and looked at me closely and repeated with emphasis: 'This, Sonya, is Georgi Vasiliyevich, author of a biography of Mozart.' "

If this man was really Chicherin, he probably died in camp, for his death is recorded as in 1936.

This period of phantasmagoria had its hilarious moments, too. On a day after Litvinov's death but before Stalin's, Ivy opened the door to me in a state of excitement.

"Come here," she whispered, drawing me after her into the bathroom and closing the door behind me. She was choking with suppressed mirth. That was unlike Ivy. When she laughed she laughed in delighted shrieks and whoops.

"What do you think Tanya did last night?" she said when she was able.

"What?"

"She flushed seven hundred American dollars down the toilet."

"Oh, no!" Seven hundred American dollars was a lot of money in those days.

"Down that very toilet."

Having said it, Ivy let out a gust of glee that shook her ample flesh and blew away my awe. There we stood, the two of us, staring into the toilet bowl and laughing like loons in full view of the Kremlin towers framed in the bathroom window.

Suddenly Ivy was grave. "You know why she did it, don't you, Peg?"

"Of course."

"Nobody must know."

Heavens, no! Having an undeclared five-dollar bill was enough to put a person in jail, and here they had found all this U.S. money among Litvinov's effects.

THAT WAS STILL in the bad times. Our vacation in Sudak was in the good times. Stalin was dead, Khrushchev had come to power and told the truth about Stalin. This indicated we were *really* on the threshold of a new era in Soviet history. We would begin all over again, not with a clean slate—with a very dirty one, in fact—but with a better material base and much edifying experience to build on.

The reforms Khrushchev introduced were as exhilarating at that time as Gorbachev's were to be years later. Most important was his releasing of political prisoners from concentration camps. Second in importance was his launching of a huge building campaign to ease housing conditions that were driving people to insanity and suicide.

These were the reforms that won the hearts of the masses. I saw these masses greet Khrushchev and his then-partner Bulganin when they arrived in Tashkent from a visit to India. The streets were jammed with cheering crowds; the open car in which the two leaders rode—standing up to be more visible—could hardly plow its way through the throng. The two were snowed under with notes of welcome and petition. They were the new heroes of a new day. With the coming of Khrushchev to power, Hope-Which-Springs-Eternal took the leap of her life.

What was to become Gorbachev's *glasnost* was on Khrushchev's agenda too, if less widely advertised. It meant the easing up on censorship and the encouragement of telling the truth. The writer Ilya Ehrenburg called this moment in Soviet history *The Thaw*. And indeed, no sooner had the ice of repression begun to melt than honest works of art sprang up like flowers in spring, a testimony to the vitality of Russian cultural roots biding their time deep in the earth.

The works of leftist artists were included in official exhibits: Fonvisen's watercolors, Falk's oil paintings, Neizvestny's sculptures; Akhmatova was invited (and allowed to go) to Rome to receive a prize for poems Stalin had suppressed; the magazine *Novi Mir* (New World) was gobbled up in record-breaking editions for the new writing it published under poet-editor Tvardovsky. The young poets Yevtushenko and Voznesensky madc a brave start at this time; they might never have been heard of had they started earlier or later. The public threw themselves ravenously on this heretofore forbidden fare. But the most delectable dish, the richest and rarest, was the work of Solzhenitsyn. The impact on the country of his *One Day in the Life of Ivan Denisovich*, exposing the horrors of Stalin's concentration camps, can hardly be exaggerated. It was read by everybody in a land where people, even young people, still read. They read it, they discussed it, they eagerly awaited Solzhenitsyn's next work. They never got it. For suddenly Khrushchev made a right-about-face. It was as if he had opened Pandora's box and, startled by the monsters that came swarming out of it, slammed down the lid. After a memorable art exhibit at which he jeered in his boorish way at green cows and cubistic nudes, he called a meeting of prominent practitioners in every field of art—music, poetry, painting—and laid down the law to them. This alienated the intellectuals. In as high-handed a way he decreed, after visiting America and seeing its waving fields of corn, that corn was to be planted on all Soviet farms regardless of soil, tradition (favoring buckwheat, the Russian staple), climatic conditions, and know-how. This alienated the farming population. The gaffes he made in foreign policy, including the Cuba incident, alienated the Politburo. And so his much heralded reign lasted less than ten years.

Tolstoy advanced the theory that it is not leaders such as Napoleon who make history; on the contrary, it is historical movements that make leaders, throwing them up in response to the demands of the times. Accordingly, Khrushchev answered current social and political needs. This is undeniable. What is also undeniable is that he could not cope with the demands made of him. If the leader thrown up by the times is strong, he can guide the historical movement to significant achievement (Hitler, Gandhi, Napoleon). This he can do as long as he is one with the movement; the moment he diverges from it, he will be deposed by the populace or by political enemies. Khrushchev was deposed by political enemies. From the very first he was an inflated figure, not a really great statesman. His intentions were of the best and because he was able to implement them when they answered the need of the country, he overestimated his abilities and misused the power a totalitarian government placed in his hands. By reversing his policies he lost public support and played into the hands of his enemies. And so the coup that deposed him made hardly a ripple, except among those who idealized him as a rough-and-ready man of the people.

The saddest legacy Khrushchev left behind him was Hope lying lifeless on the field. When she was carried away broken and bleeding a second time (the first was after World War II), the field was quickly flooded with the waters of cynicism and apathy, turning it into the noisome swamp of the Brezhnev regime.

IVY WAS SURPRISINGLY apolitical. Apparently her life in Russia had cauterized her of the radicalism she had inherited from a Hungarian grandfather, who had taken part in his country's uprising in 1848 and had fled to England when the Russians squelched it; and from her Aunt Edith, a Fabian whose Fabian husband, Dr. Eder, was one of Sigmund Freud's first disciples in England. It was in the Eders' radical circle that Ivy met Litvinov, then a political exile from Czarist Russia.

Apolitical I call Ivy, but, involved as she was in the political scene all her life, she knew her choices in politics as definitely as she knew what sort of people she liked and what kind of food she preferred. In the sixties when her grandson Pavel was brought to trial in Moscow as a dissident protesting the Soviet invasion of Czechoslovakia, Ivy was in the Caucasus. She wrote to me, "Tanya's letters about what she calls the Try-All are historic; I wish I had more of them. I am eaten up with mortification that I didn't fly in for it. . . . It would have been so sweet if I had been there. . . . I'm sure Pavel must have looked for me, but this is mostly vanity."

Ivy did indeed make her choices, all except the one choice that was made for her at birth. She was born a writer, and her absorption in literature eclipsed all else. By the time she was married she had written two novels received by the critics as giving promise of great things to come. In that respect her marriage was a disaster. When James Joyce, who lived abroad most of his mature life, was asked if he was not homesick for Ireland, he replied that he had never left it. So was it with Ivy: she never left England. But she was so damaged psychologically by those first years of transplantation to Russia, and so caught up in a milieu alien and exhausting and baffling, that for years she could not put pen to paper.

Slowly she recovered and began writing again. Her first big effort, a detective novel called *Moscow Mystery*, served to turn her attention from the uncongenial life around her. But always, year after year, she mused over what was to be an autobiographical novel dealing largely with her childhood and youth in England. She kept making drafts of it, writing whole chapters of it, only to scrap them and turn to other enticements. At one time she began a series of portraits of English women writers of the eighteenth and nineteenth centuries. Then back to the novel again. "Everyone, especially in England, wants me to write a straight autobiography," she wrote in one of her letters, "but I don't see how that can be done. I'm only interested in intimate things and they're too painful and much too embarrassing when everyone knows the people." And so the drafts were made and scrapped, made and lost, made and remade into some of the short stories that were printed in the *New Yorker* toward the end of her life and came out later in a collection called *She Knew What She Wanted.*

That autumn in Sudak Ivy looked particularly handsome. Majestically she strolled through the vineyards, the sun making a halo of her white hair and a blue transparency of her dotted swiss dress. We made friends with the villagers and with a remarkable family whose old father had been the Prosecuting Attorney under the czar of this very *gubernia.* Now he was a watchman in the vineyards who went about with a whistle and a shotgun, for which he received a little money and a wooden house on a bosky hillside. There he lived with his old wife and a daughter once beautiful (an early photograph stood conspicuously on her mother's antique mahogany bureau), now frightening to behold. Her face had been blown away on a World War II battlefield to which she had gone as a volunteer. She had an artificial nose and patched lips, but her eyes shone courageously above the wreckage. She was admirably unabashed by her mutilations. She it was who sent Ivy into shrieks of laughter by describing how the wife of a prominent Soviet composer had hired a bulldozer to upturn the pebbly Sudak beach in search of her mother's bones.

"And how in God's name were her bones to be distinguished from those of all the others who were killed on the beach when the Germans retreated?" asked Ivy.

"She said her mother had once broken her leg."

Ivy enjoyed this most of all. "Can't you just see her going through a heap of bones looking for a scarred tibia?"

FOR A MONTH we basked in the sun and swam in the sea and ate on the open porch facing the Phoenician ruins—ate the head of cheese we had brought with us, and the Crimean version of yogurt into which we crumbled the crackers we had brought with us, and the grapes and chickens our neighbors sold us; and we drank Crimean wine, but mostly we drank Ivy's tea, brewed on a hot plate according to undeviating rules: first boil water in the kettle, then heat the empty teapot by placing it upside down on the steaming kettle, then sprinkle a generous portion of tea into the hot dry pot, then put it right-side-up on top of the steaming kettle until the dry leaves weep little brown tears, then add a drop of water, then some more, then some more, then take it off the kettle and cover it with a tea cosey and let it steep until it is as strong as brandy, then pour it into the cups with a little milk that has simmered but not boiled, God forbid!

The English, the Japanese, the Russians, all have strict rules for tea making. It was simpler for Russians in the days of the samovar, a contrivance that concentrates in itself all stages of the process—the boiling of water, the heating of pot, the steeping of tea, the filling of glasses. But efficient as it may be, I had developed a deep-seated aversion for the samovar. It was for me the symbol of "life on the dacha." Russians consider it a parental duty to get children out of the city for the entire summer. In the early years of my life in Soviet Russia this had meant a yearly migration with pots and pans, dishes, sheets, pillows, blankets, and a two-month supply of food staples. Unfortunate parents spent all their free time in the month of May (even April if they had the gumption to tackle the problem before it caught up with them) tramping the countryside in search of affordable room, rooms, room-and-enclosed porch, in somebody else's house with, like as not, an oleograph of swans and water lilies adorning the wall above the iron bedstead. Come rain, storm, and freezing weather, there you were, fixed like a moth on a pin. The city apartment with hot water and a gas stove offered no retreat; the pull-out had left it as good as ransacked. For those two awful months you were marooned on one side of a wall with landlord and wife on the other side, their ears cocked for the sound of raised voices, their eyes glued to the window to detect small feet trespassing on cabbage patch or petunia border.

As supplier of the boiled water essential to life in the country, the samovar became a symbol of this misery. I had learned the hard way about the peril of keeping a kettle steaming on an oil stove. One day I was yanked out of a volleyball game by my landlady's screams. I rushed to the porch to find the oil stove billowing forth clouds of soot that settled on dishes and chairs and hung in horrid black festoons from walls and ceiling. Half a day's scouring left me and the porch more smudged than cleansed.

The samovar came to our rescue. We carried it out under the trees, filled it with water and fed it pine cones, for which attentions it puffed away benignly early and late. Good old samovar! But for me—symbol of those hated summer migrations. Great was the day when the children graduated from dacha-age to hiking-age and I lifted our samovar off the shelf where it wintered and ceremoniously presented it to Manya, our current houseworker, "and may it serve you and your children and your children's children, aye, even unto the fourth and fifth generations."

I never cease wondering at the magnitude of that moment in a mother's life when she discovers her children can manage without her, when she doesn't have to be home to see that they eat dinner at the right time and in the right quantity, when she is not responsible for planning the use of their leisure time, when their studies are no longer any of her business. The realization that I had reached this watershed came upon me gradually and with an increasing sense of jubilation. I was free. It was like a second coming of age, opening up wonderful vistas of unencumbered activity. This, of course, is an exaggeration. The Russians have a saying: "Little children, little cares; big children, big cares." The cares and caring are with you always because you are not a loner; you have, you are, a family. But here I was in Sudak with Ivy, determined not to worry about the family. We were wholly absorbed in our sunlit life on the shore of the Black Sea. Ivy mostly prepared the food, I washed up. We helped each other.

"Help, Ivy!" I had slipped off the edge of the path leading to the sea. The drop was steep and my foot found no purchase in the crumbly wall. "Help, Ivy!" She came running, threw herself down on the path, and leaned over perilously to haul me up.

"Help, Peg!!" I ran out of the house into the sunset and saw her standing panicky in the middle of the lawn holding out the folds of her skirt. "Help, Peg! What shall I do? Too many grapes, do you think? Or sprayed with DDT? Oh, help!"

I found a watering can and filled it at the pump and ripped off her dress and poured freezing water over her legs and thighs and put her to bed and made her a cup of hot tea, and she fell sound asleep. When I got up the next morning, I found her propped up in bed with the Bible in her hands. She smiled at me roguishly.

"Poor duck, I did put you to trouble last night, didn't I? But cheer up, there's worse things than the runs, as the men of Gath can tell you. Listen: '. . . and the hand of the Lord was against the city with a very great destruction . . . and he smote the men of the city, both small and great, and they had emerods in their secret parts.' Do you know what emerods are? Of course you don't. 'And the men who died not were smitten with the emerods and the cry of the city went up to heaven.' Emerods are hemorrhoids. So I guess the Lord wasn't that angry with me last night."

We had brought some books with us (not too many, books are cumbersome traveling companions); a couple of Henry Jameses, if I'm not mistaken, and a D. H. Lawrence, and the Bible. The Bible was Ivy's old standby wherever she went.

"What a book! What snatches of speech! Could anything be more marvelous than 'Speak, Lord, for thy servant heareth?' or when Saul said, 'I have performed the commandment of the Lord' (to kill every living creature, which he didn't do), and Samuel said, 'What meaneth then this bleating of the sheep in mine ears and the lowing of the oxen which I hear?' That's calling his bluff!"

I picked up the pails and went to draw the day's supply of water. When I had put on the kettle I came back to Ivy and found her in Second Samuel.

"Oh, I do love Michal, David's wife, for despising him in her heart when she looked through a window and saw King David leaping and dancing before the Lord, the big slob, and when he returned to bless his household she went out to meet him and said, 'How glorious was the King of Israel today, who uncovered himself today in the eyes of the handmaids of his servants,' and he answered her scornfully . . . 'And I will yet be more vile than this, and will be base in my own sight.' The bed bounced under Ivy's laughter, her luxurious curves tracing the curves of pillows and mattress. She kept leafing through The Book, finding favorite bits to entertain me with. "Ah, yes, here. The awful affair of Amnon and his sister Tamar, how the minute after he 'forced her and lay with her he hated her exceedingly so that the hatred wherewith he hated her was greater than the love wherewith he had loved her,'—and God bless the expressive Perfect Tenses."

"Oh, yes," said I, "but try to teach them to Russians."

"I don't find it so hard. The aspects of Russian verbs help."

"Not always. I use diagrams to show what is 'past-er' than past."

"That only helps with the Past Perfect, not the Present Perfect. But the Present Perfect seems to be dying out of English anyway."

And so it went, our vacation in Sudak. And then one day toward the end of it, I got a letter from Andrei. It was a howl of pain.

"Why aren't you here instead of in Sudak? No words can express my loneliness, especially when I come home in the evening. I can't go on living like this. I blame myself, only myself; I alone, because of my many faults, have brought myself to this pass, to our separation. As long as we live you and I must be together."

Who was this Andrei speaking with such self-denigrating passion? Had I ever heard him speak so before? Never, not even when his fortunes were at lowest ebb. In the first days of our relationship I had been overpowered by his self-assurance. He was never troubled by doubts and misgivings, always certain of the rightness of his ways and his choices. And I followed him happily, secure in his surety.

But as the years went by, circumstances arose that led me to question the legitimacy of such overweening self-confidence. I was fully aware of his rich gifts and lofty aspirations and suspected he was prevented from giving them fullest expression by his insensitivity to the moods and responses of others. He kept banging his head against obstacles a little tact, a little diplomacy, could have removed or circumvented. People—actors, stage designers, administrators—are to a stage director what paints are to the artist, instruments to the composer, words to the writer. They are his medium and, as with all artists, achievement hangs upon mastery of the medium.

Andrei rarely had difficulty with actors. He loved them and never allowed himself to insult or humiliate them at rehearsals as I have heard so many directors do in the heat of their labors. It was an entirely different story with administrators and other "chiefs" on whom his success or failure depended no less than upon actors. If he thought they were meddling in his business, he would rudely "put them in their place" and come off with his head demonstrably unbowed, just as he had in Saratov. I could do nothing to save him from the unacknowledged injuries he sustained.

And now? "I blame myself. Only myself. I alone, because of my many faults . . ." And at another point in the letter: "In addition I have come to know the joy of humility and self-criticism."

What could have wrought such a radical change in him? Riga. Riga had led to that terrible moment when he had said, "What am I supposed to do, shoot myself?" This letter came as a natural sequence. Riga had bludgeoned him into a new image of himself, and one I found most dear. Riga had cured him of his hubris. Riga was a catalyst that changed us both. We had much to thank Riga for.

Ivy found me ruminating over the letter.

"What is it, ducky? What does he say? Bad news?"

I handed her the letter.

"Oh," she said when she had read it, "we can't have him going on like this. Let's go to Tashkent. That's one place I've never been. I'd love to see it. Our vacation's nearly over anyway. Let's go."

I needed no urging. I wired Andrei we were coming and Ivy and I set out for Moscow from where, after attending to our separate affairs, we would take the train for Tashkent.

But once in Moscow I questioned the rightness of our decision. I ought to go to Andrei alone. It was not for company he pined, it was for me. His letter was a mating call summoning me to his side. I was glad he wanted me, and grateful, and I responded with an impatience of love. I could not reach him fast enough. I told Ivy about my feelings and she, wise friend, supported them. So I went alone.

The train did not rush to its destination as I had hoped. It took me slowly, giving time for my urgency to subside as I watched the scenery go by. I spent hours standing at the window in the corridor opposite my compartment thinking about Andrei and me. My friendship with Ivy had hurt our relationship a little. I could not resist the joy of her company. Her wit, her talent, and above all her identity with literature, *English* literature, provided the stimulation needed to counteract the disillusionment of the past years. Andrei found his stimulation in the theater and his flowers. I did not share his interests with the same intensity I gave to Ivy's, and he felt it. It hurt him. It hurt me too, for anything that weakened our relationship diminished the significance of our life together.

As I stood at the train window late in the afternoon I became aware of the *Eroica*'s second movement, the funeral march, coming over the radio. We were crossing the steppe of Central Asia. Autumn was in the air and the yellow grasses bowed before the wind. The puddles nestling among the grasses shone like turquoise set in gold. The train was slow, the march was slow; slow, solemn, and sorrowful. Never before had it touched me so deeply. The hero was dead. The melody sank in despair. Shadows crept over the steppe as evening fell, putting out the little turquoise lights. The wind rose, the grasses bent lower. All was over. But no, the music would not accept this. All the instruments joined to assure us all was not over. They seized the hero in strong hands and lifted him to heights where he was esconced in glory, shedding glory all around. This was our fate, the rising and the falling, always the falling, but as surely the rising, once we willed it so.

I was roused out of my reverie by the porter, who came through the corridor turning on lights and announcing that the samovar was ready, we could have hot tea. One more night and we would be in Tashkent.

The train drew into the station on a bright and sunny morning. For a frantic moment I thought Andrei had not come to meet me. I was too excited to recognize him, so white were his southern clothes against skin so browned by southern sun. The next moment his big hands were gripping my shoulders and his radiant eyes were searching my moist ones. Suitcases banged into our shins as we stood there and gruff voices muttered, "Move on, move on!"

"We'd better," said Andrei, picking up my bag. "My landlady has breakfast waiting for us."

We breakfasted on the back porch with the bees humming in the trumpet vines and the doves cooing as they basked in the sun on the roof. I felt my spirits rising as on strong wings. Rising, rising.

nineteen

Contention

What I'm saying is simply that every totalitarian state, no matter how strict, has had its underground. In fact, two undergrounds. There's the underground involved in political resistance and the underground involved in preserving beauty and fun.

—Tom Robbins,
Still Life with Woodpecker

IF YOU WALK UP the right-hand side of Pushkin Street from Okhotny Ryad, past the big department store called Mostorg, past old brick or stone buildings with stores on the ground floor, just before you come to Stoleshnykov Lane you will pass one such building (I have forgotten the number of it) with a driveway on the far side leading into a courtyard. Inside the courtyard you will find another such brick building with no stores in it, only apartments, and a basement once occupied by an atelier making sheepskin coats for the military. Either because the basement was too dark or too damp or the enterprise too smelly for the residents, this atelier was moved out. The removal occurred just at the time when Andrei was looking for a location for a Studio Theater.

Yes, Andrei was back in Moscow teaching acting and directing, and Mick-Step was back teaching Russian literature, and even the Kittels had moved from Tashkent to Moscow to work as translators for the Radio Committee and to see that their two children got a Moscow education. The banishment to Tashkent was over. It had given us good things as well as bad, had given Mick-Step the priceless gift of Farida, and had widened our outlook through friendly living with a Muslim minority, the Uzbeks, who before this had been but an exotic name vaguely associated with the ancient Medes and the Persians.

Andrei was given the empty basement on Pushkin Street for his Studio Theater. His student actors cleaned it up, painted and varnished it, turned an adjoining hall into dressing rooms, built ascending rows of seats in an auditorium seating less than a hundred, and defined the stage by throwing a rope on the floor in a semicircle at the spectators' feet.

For the remaining years of Andrei's life this theater and his wildflower garden at Leonozovo were his consuming interests.

Our private life underwent a radical change at this time. The Vorotnikovsky apartment, however humble, had been a harmonious home until new members were added to the family. First Adya, in his last year of art school, married a classmate named Alisa. He could hardly have done so if the young man who occupied the third room of our apartment (originally the kitchen) had not moved out, allowing Dasha to move in and Adya to share with his wife the room he had always shared with his sister. By this time Dasha had graduated from the Foreign Language Institute and was teaching English. No sooner did she come into possession of a room of her own than she married Yevgeny, a friend of Adya's who had recently graduated from the same art school. A year and a half later Dasha gave birth to Fedya.

So there we were, three couples and a baby in three rooms converging on the two-by-four dinette where we gathered for meals. The cooping together of six grown people of different ages, upbringing, temperament, views, and values created an atmosphere in which one feared the lighting of a match. There were explosions, but they were less destructive than the slow growth of animosity and resentment that caused unbearable tension. The generation gap was a major cause of this, but not the only one. Jealousy crept into the young people's lives, and suspicion. I did not blame them for our family's disintegration so much as I blamed a government which, for all its declarations of dedication to the public weal, did little to further it. Our family was no worse off than many others; indeed was better off, at least each couple occupied a private room. Many newlyweds had to share a room with in-laws. I shall never forget walking with Andrei along Tverskoy Boulevard one winter evening with the temperature well below zero and seeing couples holding hands and kissing on park benches, the closest they could get to privacy.

Such flagrant indifference to the lot of the masses was harder to accept after the brief thaw following Khrushchev's exposure of Stalin. In the sixties young Russian blood was boiling with protest, as was young American blood in the States. But in Russia there could be no open expression of protest. To be effective a movement of protest must have followers as well as leaders, must be able to proclaim its platform if it is to make converts, and must be able to organize for action. The Soviet state, itself the product of a highly organized revolutionary movement, knew only too well the rules for effective protest and made certain that these rules could not be used against itself. This was soon to be demonstrated by the fate of Pavel Litvinov's "demonstration" against the Soviet invasion of Czechoslovakia when eight (eight, mind; not eight hundred, nor even eighty) brave young people, pledged to offer no resistance if attacked by plainclothesmen (which they were, and which they didn't), carried furled slogans to Red Square. Before they even had time to unfurl slogans reading "Free Dubček" and "Czechoslovakia, Your Freedom is Our Freedom," they were attacked by "indignant citizens," as the newspaper put it, were thrown into militia cars and taken to headquarters. For organizing this "revolt" Pavel spent seven years in exile. Had he not borne the name of his famous grandfather the incident would have been dismissed as of no more significance than a street brawl; since he did bear a name that might raise questions in the foreign press, it was adjudged wise to offer an explanation. So the *Moscow Evening News* came out with an article painting Pavel as a good-for-nothing. No mention was made of his being a political dissident; greed alone, it asserted, had led the young Litvinov to betray his country for thirty pieces of foreign silver with a suede jacket and a pair of American blue jeans thrown in.

Most Soviet young people answered the government's cynicism with arch cynicism of their own. They refused to buckle under to the fear that had held everyone in thrall until the short-lived semifreedom of The Thaw. They also disdained giving the authorities the satisfaction of throwing them in jails and labor camps if they shouted their views on street corners; they restricted their activities to the home, where they scoffed and sneered to their heart's content—after first putting a pillow over the telephone, just in case. Every gathering opened with the recounting of the latest jokes on the establishment, of which there was a spate at the time—wonderfully wise and witty jokes. With perverse pleasure they then proceeded to describe new outrages such as the secret building of luxurious homes for the big shots near the highway leading to the university. Workmen on the site had spread rumors of mahogany woodwork and crystal chandeliers.

Nothing could have been more foreign to Andrei's nature than scoffing and sneering. He felt sullied by it and he withdrew from it as from something unclean. This was a manifestation of what I was clearly to perceive only years later, back in America, when Andrei was gone—

that noon in Wanamaker's department store with the organ music soaring into the vault above the cacophony of trade below I saw clearly that Andrei had chosen to dwell in the upper air and never, under any circumstances, would allow himself to be dragged down into the jostling, wrangling crowd.

I did not see it that evening in Moscow when he got up angrily from the dinner table and went into the next room because the young people had grown boisterous with their joke telling and scandalmongering. In my heart of hearts I sided with them, welcoming any jibe aimed at the Brezhnev regime. But because we were a house divided I could not betray Andrei.

"What's wrong with Father?" Dasha asked with an air of innocence.

"You know what's wrong with him," I said testily. "You might have held your tongue until he left for the theater," and with that I too got up and went to Andrei.

I found him pacing the floor with his hands clasped behind his back.

"Did you have to make such a display of your feelings?" I said.

"I can't stand their yapping," he said. "If they don't like things as they are, let them do something about it, not just sit and yap."

"Do you like things as they are?"

"Sneering won't change them."

"What will?"

"Time."

"Haven't we waited long enough?"

"Who can say how long is enough? How long does it take for a glacier to move a foot?"

"You can't compare society to a glacier."

"Why not? They're both big and they both move."

"Anything else?"

"They both change."

"A lot of change we've seen in *this* society!"

"We will."

"What makes you so sure?"

"Change is implicit in movement."

"Well, those kids out there want to live now, not fifty or a hundred years from now."

"So why don't they? There are lots of things to live for besides politics. To hear them grouch you'd think everything hinged on the Politburo." He reached for his coat.

"Everything does," I said.

Andrei shot me a quick glance. "That depends on what you're looking for," he said.

"On this glacier?" I asked with a little laugh.

"Well, we're on it, we can't get off it, and we can't stop it."

"So we've got to take it with all the dirt and rubbish it's picked up on the way?"

"I didn't say that. My quarrel is with *how* we clean it up." He pulled his fur cap out of his coat sleeve. "Making faces and calling it names won't help."

"Maybe we should take a pickax to it."

"We're in a chain gang. The overseer won't let us."

I thought that was rather good. "So admit it's hopeless."

"Never. Patience is what we need. Time will bring change. Meanwhile, look for the good. You'll find it right next door to the bad. 'The good and the beautiful,' as the poets say. They are what bring joy to life. And you can communicate this joy to others. Which is what I try to do in my art." He put on his coat and made for the door. I put a hand out to stop him.

"Let's not quarrel," I said.

"Let's not," he said. "Let them do it if they like, but not us," and he kissed me good-bye.

I went with him back through the dinette to the front door. The young people were still sitting there yapping, but they stopped as if to let us pass and followed us with cold and hostile looks. The feeling seemed to be that we, their elders, were not members in full standing of this ménage. Oddly enough we had considered ourselves founding members. No longer were we at home in our home.

This was a dark passage in our family history, without light, without love. We were thrashing about emotionally within confining walls like insects in a bottle, destroying one another. All things in nature give off vibrations. The Hindus say if individuals vibrate on conflicting wave lengths they should avoid being together, there can be no harmony between them and they will suffer injury. All of us were injured by our unholy juxtaposition.

Realizing that our living conditions offered a threat to her marriage, Dasha tried to save it by buying a small cooperative apartment. The law would not allow her to; the room she and Yevgeny occupied measured fourteen square meters; the number making an application for additional living space acceptable was four square meters per person. The only way Dasha could improve her circumstances was by exchange or inheritance. Exchange would have meant putting a stranger in our midst. But by this time we were all strangers to one another.

Alisa was the first family member to move out. Through Sonya she met Petya, son of a prominent film director whose wife was soon to take Georgi away from Sonya. Alisa sensed that life as a member of such a prominent family would be better than life in ours, just as she had sensed that life with us would be better than life with the husband she had left to marry Adya. Alisa feared nothing so much as poverty, with which she had been closely acquainted in childhood. Her father had come home from World War II an alcoholic, leaving her mother to bring up two daughters on the scanty earnings of a quite ordinary seamstress.

Two years after Alisa had left us I answered the doorbell to find a white-faced Petya cowering on the threshold.

"May I speak to you, Margarita Danilovna?" he murmured.

"Of course. Come in."

For the next hour he complained bitterly to me of Alisa, now the mother of his daughter. "She wants to ruin my family," he said. "She wants to take one of the rooms of our apartment away from us for herself and our daughter, and she lays claim to half of our dacha."

"Why, have you separated?" I asked.

"Yes," he said in his timorous voice, which fell to almost a whisper as he confided the purpose of his visit. "One day in the kitchen she drove me to the point of striking her. Then she ran to the clinic across the street and got a signed paper saying I had struck her—I must have picked up a heavy spoon or something—oh, not a knife! Believe me, not a knife!—and now she's taken the case to court." He waited a moment, trying to compose himself. "I could be expelled from Moscow for this," he brought out at last with difficulty. "Will you help me, Margarita Danilovna?"

"Gladly, Petya, but how?"

"Will you write a character of Alisa I can present in court? You know what she's like. You lived with her for two years."

"It wouldn't do any good," I said ruefully. "You forget I'm the mother of the man she deserted. My testimony would hardly be considered unprejudiced. Your father can do more for you than I can."

"My father," moaned Petya. "My father hardly speaks to me."

Despite his anger, his father evidently used his influence, for Petya was not expelled from Moscow and the last I heard Alisa had a room of her own in a different apartment.

Then Adya got a room in Andrei Nikolayevich's apartment. In the spring of 1964 Andrei Nikolayevich died, leaving one room of his apartment to Adya and the other two to Vyeta. This opened up the bright prospect of Andrei's and my living with only Dasha and Yevgeny, with baby Fedya and his nurse in the room Adya had moved out of. Andrei and I felt sympathy for Yevgeny. Life had dealt roughly with him. His grandfather had been a Baltic baron and a graduate of the Russian Naval Academy outside of St. Petersburg for Sons of the Nobility. For such villainy Yevgeny's father was arrested soon after his son was born and sentenced by a Soviet tribunal to twenty-five years in a labor camp. Yevgeny's mother had to support her mother-in-law, her son, and a nephew whose father had suffered the same fate as her husband. Dasha was deeply touched by photos of the child Yevgeny, so ragged was he, so emaciated. To his credit be it said that he never forgave the Soviets and had the courage as a mere schoolboy to refuse to be promoted from the Pioneer organization for elementary school children to the Young Communist League for teenagers. This was tantamount to declaring himself an enemy of the state. He held himself aloof from the public activities other boys engaged in and grew to be a silent, sullen young man whose dark-eyed glance fell on strangers with suspicion. Suffering makes some people compassionate, others harsh. Yevgeny was harsh. That was not the sort of man Dasha needed. She was all softness, wanting love. That is why she was plagued with a nervous rash while bearing her baby and nearly died while delivering it. Ivy and I took her and her infant to Pitsunda on the Black Sea to speed recuperation. It was while we were there that Andrei wrote to tell us of his father's death. When we got back to Moscow Dasha and Yevgeny went to stay in the room of a friend who was traveling, thinking all would be well if they lived outside of the family for a while. It was not. Dasha came back alone. Yevgeny came back a year later, but it was too late. Dasha had met Vitya.

Vitya swept Dasha off her feet. He was all that Yevgeny was not: gay, debonair, attentive, a *verray parfit knight* with many followers, all topers, who gathered around Dasha's square table to provide the conviviality Vitya required at day's end. He adored Dasha and he adored Fedya, who adored him. Naturally. Vitya was six feet two inches of very macho man. He had run away as a child to become a circus acrobat and could still turn somersaults in the air; he had been a parachutist in the army and an actor in the films; he was now writing poetry and plays. Dasha was conquered. Andrei was not. He saw in

Vitya an egotist and womanizer. He tried to break up the relationship by denying Vitya our house, but I warned him not to, that Dasha would never forgive him if he caused their separation. Andrei relented but he never showed friendship for Vitya and Vitya never moved into our apartment while Andrei was alive, he only frequented it.

Meanwhile, outside the home, the Brezhnev regime was relentlessly pursuing its policy of destroying the last vestige of free thought. When the voices of even such giants as Solzhenitsyn and Sakharov were suppressed, the underground press, *samizdat*, came into being. Since no copying machines of any kind were accessible to the public (they were subjected to as tight security as nuclear weapons), the works of *samizdat* were typed at night in secret on cigarette paper, the lines single-spaced and readable only by placing a blank sheet of typewriter paper underneath. The dedicated people who performed these feats of love and labor knew exactly what the risk was. One of them was discovered by the secret police and so cruelly harassed that she committed suicide to make sure she would never, under torture, reveal who her colleagues were.

In a few short years *samizdat* was wiped out and dissidents were swept up like roaches and thrown on the dust heap. A prominent trial in the sixties, called "public" but with the courtroom filled with a selected audience, was that of Andrei Sinyavsky. Sinyavsky had been a Moscow University classmate of Vyeta and her friend Lena, who had been living with Vyeta ever since the death of her mother in the Ashkhabad earthquake. From the wild little girl who had tamed wild dogs in Mongolia, Vyeta had grown into a young woman retaining the independence of spirit Fenya's guardianship had nurtured. When Dmitri evacuated his family to a village during the war, fourteen-year-old Vyeta became head of that family. She drove a tractor on a collective farm, she helped her stepmother Tonya, now nursing an infant son, to cope with the primitive conditions of village life by doing all the hard chores, and at the same time she attended the village high school. On returning to Moscow in 1943 she was within a year of entering Moscow University. Dmitri was given an apartment of his own after the war, but Vyeta chose not to live with a stepmother. She stayed with her grandfather, next door to us, living the independent life that suited her independent spirit.

For months before the Sinyavsky trial Moscow had buzzed with rumors of a writer who called himself Abram Tertz publishing stories abroad whose exposures of Soviet reality were obviously coming from one who lived within this reality. As time went on and the writer remained undiscovered, the prevailing feeling was of wonder and jubilation: the KGB had met their match!

But nobody was a match for the KGB. It took time but, as always, they got their prey.

Tertz was Andrei Sinyavsky, a young literary critic, admired by liberals for his preface to a collection of Pasternak's poetry, admired by conservatives for his essay on Socialist Realism. The former put the hounds on his scent, the latter threw them off it.

When Sinyavsky heard the dogs barking at his very heels, he brought to Vyeta and Lena manuscripts that were irrefutable proof of his identity. They took them to Sonya. Sonya burned them in her stove in Perlovka.

By this time both Vyeta and Lena were under suspicion. One day Sonya came to town to make our regular exchange of *samizdat* and other forbidden literature. I had obtained Akhmatova's *Requiem* for her, she had brought us the writings of Vivecananda. As Vyeta, Sonya, and I sat at the dinner table making the exchange, there came a sharp ring of the doorbell. Vyeta answered it. We heard men's voices, the words "search warrant," and before we could make a move uniformed men brushed past us and entered the adjoining room, Vyeta's bedroom-living room. One of them turned in the doorway.

"Who are these women?"

"This one—my mother; she lives out of town."

"The other?"

"My aunt; she lives next door."

"Let her go home." He disappeared. With movements as casual as if gathering up used tea cups, Sonya slipped the forbidden literature under the tablecloth. I went out. The officers did not search the dining room. They shook out every book in Vyeta's considerable library, they ransacked drawers and snatched off couch covers, but confined the search to Vyeta's room, for which the warrant was issued. Vyeta summoned me back when the men had gone. Gleefully we released Akhmatova and Vivecananda from their hideout. Ruefully we surveyed the mess in Vyeta's room.

For all her tranquility Sonya was not above gloating over the smallest defeat dealt the KGB. She smiled as she picked up books and returned them to their shelves.

By the time of the Sinyavsky trial, Sonya's personal trials had reached a point beyond ordinary endurance. One might have supposed things would be easier for her after Stalin's death. They were—for a while. Georgi came back from prison camp as did her son Yuri, who went directly to the country town where he had been arrested and married Zina, his faithful high school sweetheart. Arseni, Sonya's son by Georgi, was soon married to a high school sweetheart too, but he and she lived near his parents in Perlovka, she studying to be a pianist, he to be a pilot in the armed forces. Arseni had a passion for vehicles. He rode a motorcycle, drove any car he could borrow, and was determined to pilot a plane. He went to great lengths to be accepted into aviation school despite his parents' objections, but a year's taste of military life made this strongheaded boy go to even greater lengths to get out of the military. He succeeded in doing so and entered an Engineering Institute.

The long years when Sonya and Arseni had been alone together, the terrible war years when Sonya did physical labor in a warehouse to get a worker's food ration card so that her growing boy would have more than a mere four hundred grams of black bread a day to live on—these years had made even stronger the bond that unites most sons and mothers. She was ever his good companion.

For the second time Sonya had made a home for Georgi to come back to. She exchanged her room in the country town for half a log house just down the road from the Perlovka railroad station. Around the station clustered the local stores, which dropped their debris in the mud or snow of the road leading to Sonya's house. Like all village houses, it had a tall fence of solid palings in front of it. On opening the gate one stopped in astonishment: here was an unexpected feast for the eyes. A profusion of old and neglected cherry trees cast their shade upon a round pool with a Water Idol Georgi had modeled sitting in the middle of it. On one side of the pool Arseni had erected a frame of bamboo poles over which he threw straw windowshades to make an open shelter accommodating two cots for Sonya and Georgi to sleep on in midsummer heat. A path winding through the garden was lined with Sonya's ferns, out of whose depths glanced the bright eyes of Sonya's flowers.

Twenty years of turbulence had ended in this restful garden and no less restful home, whose two rooms were dominated by the serene gaze of a bronze Buddha ensconced on top of Georgi's bureau. These were good days for Sonya and Georgi, days that moved from season to season, from Buddha to Water God, back and forth, filled with peace and prosperity.

Georgi was working with great success as a film artist. His success was due as much to his unique personality as to his talent. People were invariably drawn to him. There was something attractive in the very oddity of his appearance. An oversized bald head was supported by a wholly inadequate body. Two enormous hooded eyes gave off a green glow as of electricity, and indeed a mesmerizing flow of electricity came from within that great dome of a head.

His speech was slow and sardonic, his wit sharp but rarely caustic. There was something elfish in his looks, something whimsical and appealing, especially for women. When rumors reached Sonya's ears that a girl from the Film Institute was pursuing him, she tracked the girl down, confronted her, called her a silly fool, told her that she, Sonya, was Georgi's mate with whom he was still mating, and if the girl had any pride she would get out of Georgi's life. The girl did.

That was the first disturbance of the still waters. The next was far more serious. Georgi had a terrible seizure. I went out to Perlovka a week after it happened.

"He was meant to die, but I couldn't let him die," said Sonya. "The woman who lives in the other half of our house is a doctor. She answered my cries, and together we tried to subdue him. It was like the worst possible epileptic fit, but Georgi is not an epileptic. He flayed about with his arms with a force that almost knocked us down. We tried to sit on him, hold him down, tie him up. He was no match for us. When the fit was over, he was as good as dead."

"As bad," corrected Georgi from the next room. We went in to him. His arms lay limp on the covers but his green eyes were alight. "Those foolish doctors said I had a heart attack. So why can't I move my arms?" he asked.

"You wore out your arms," said Sonya with a little laugh.

"Nothing of the sort," said Georgi. They've come unplugged." He was right. By the time the doctors agreed with him he had to be taken to the hospital to have his arms plugged back into their sockets.

This seizure (the result of sclerosis of the brain according to a later diagnosis) marked the beginning of a steady mental decline, unrecognized as such for a long time. Its effects caused Sonya anguish of an order she had never known before.

Among their acquaintances was a well-known film director with whom Georgi worked. This director and his wife, Lola, were the parents of Petya, who had taken Adya's wife away from him. They came frequently to Perlovka, turning professional consultations into friendly visits. The two couples enjoyed these visits until it became clear that Georgi and Lola felt more than friendship for each other. Sonya's serenity was gone. She came to see Andrei and me at Leonozovo.

"I think I could take it more easily if he left me and went to her. I can't share him. Or be second best."

"You could never be second best with Georgi," said Andrei consolingly. "It's a whim. It will pass. Think what he's been through."

"Not he alone." Sonya could be snappy.

"I know. But I've seen it happen to others in his circumstances." He was thinking of Harry Kittel and what Jeanette had gone through.

"She comes to him every day, and I must get out of the house."

"Oh surely it isn't that bad."

"Would I be telling you if it weren't? Georgi tells me to get out."

"Of your own home?"

"I have no home any more."

"The man must be mad!" exclaimed Andrei.

"Don't say that," said Sonya vehemently. "I've had a horror of madness all my life. Anything but that."

Two weeks later, when we were in Moscow to buy food supplies, Georgi came to see us. "Sonya's gone," he said unhappily.

"Gone where?"

"Do *you* know where?"

"No idea. She came to see us in Leonozovo a couple of weeks ago. She didn't say anything about going away."

"I've got to find her. I've asked everybody, all our friends and acquaintances. Nobody knows."

"Why would she go away?"

"She has good reason." His big green eyes flooded with tears. "I've got to find her."

"Isn't she with Arseni?" I asked.

"No."

"And he doesn't know where she is?"

"If he does, he won't tell me."

"Maybe she's with Yuri?"

"I've been to Yuri's. She isn't there."

"Don't worry, she'll come back."

"She won't. You don't know Sonya. She'll enter a convent."

She didn't enter a convent. She moved in with the woman doctor next door. "I did that so I could keep an eye on him without intruding," she explained later. "He was behaving strangely. Sometimes I could hear him scream at her and I knew he would scream even louder at me if he caught sight of me. I saw to it that he never did. At night when he was alone I could hear him moaning and groaning, calling now for Lola, now for me, but I didn't dare go to him, he couldn't bear the sight of me."

Georgi's condition reached the stage where he required hospitalization. Sonya dared to go to him now; she would visit him one day, Lola the next, each woman careful not to meet the other. When his course of treatment came to an end and Sonya, as his legal wife, was expected to take him home, she was again faced by a dilemma. "How can I take him home? Lola will come every day and there is not room for both of us in that house. She could take him to her house, but . . . there's her husband. . . ."

Sonya took him, of course; took him for the rest of his life, which dragged on and on. She watched over him and ministered to him as he slowly disintegrated into a drooling idiot. She was afraid of him and repulsed by him, but because of the love she bore him she never left him or committed him to an asylum.

I thought his end had come one day when daughter Dasha answered the phone in the next room and I heard a sudden note of alarm enter her voice:

"Oh, no! When? How is Sonya taking it?"

Dasha came running to me after hanging up.

"Georgi has died?" I asked quietly.

"No . . . No!"

I was frightened by the look on her face. "But somebody has died?"

"Yes."

"Who?"

She didn't answer.

"Who, Dasha?"

"Oh, Mother!"

"You must tell me."

"Arseni." She scarcely breathed the name.

"Not Arseni!"

"On a motorcycle . . . standing at a red light . . . a drunk driver."

A dry-eyed Sonya buried her son with Russian Orthodox rites on the side of a hill overlooking a river and a meadow and a wide expanse of sky. She went there often after that—not to the grave, but to the river, the meadow, and the sky, from whose serenity she imbibed her own.

twenty

A Conclusion

Not in this world to see his face
Seems long, until I read the place
Where this is said to be
But just the primer to a life
Unopened, rare, upon the shelf,
Clasped yet to him and me.
—Emily Dickinson

"MARGARITA! COME HERE!" Andrei called to me from the bench beside the tiny pool in his garden. I hurried down the path and found him teasing with a little stick a big ant upraised on its hindlegs, striking out with its forelegs.

"See? He's a fighter. They're all different. I catch them to feed the goldfish. They're as different as humans. This fellow's putting up a fight; another one scuttles into the grass the minute he sees the stick: a third drops in his tracks and plays dead. Would you have believed that each of these pinheads has its own personality?"

Andrei let the fighter go and picked up one that tried to run away. It struggled when he dropped it into the water. Perhaps its struggle hastened its demise, for the movement caught the round eye of the biggest fish, and the ant was swallowed in a trice.

"I'll tell you something else you wouldn't believe. Those wild tulips I brought from Tashkent—they like alkaline soil. So last fall I thought I'd do a little experiment: I buried a lump of lime some distance away from a tulip bulb—oh, maybe a foot—and what do you think? In the spring the bulb was on top of the lime. Would you have believed that bulbs could travel under their own steam?"

On fine mornings we would eat our breakfast of crackers and *prostokvasha* (a Russian version of yogurt) on a bench that was just a wooden plank laid on stones. We would listen to the water trickling into the pool and watch Marfusha the frog, sunning herself in a puddle ringed by her suitors.

After breakfast Andrei would make his daily round of the garden and daily entry in his journal, noting which plants had begun to flower, which had just finished flowering, which were flourishing, which needed attention. Then began labors that lasted, with a brief siesta, until sundown. I would sit at my typewriter half the day, devoting postsiesta hours to weeding. I guess I'm the world's champion weeder, reduced to this humble position by ignorance of the more complicated aspects of horticulture. It hurt Andrei that I resisted his efforts to educate me. He bought me books on botany and tried to teach me, but I was not interested. I loved the garden and would help to the extent of pulling weeds, but there I stopped. Except that I would make bouquets of flowers for the house—yes, we had built ourselves a house, and such a duck of a house! Two rooms little larger than, and similar in plan to, Russian train compartments, which is to say each had a divan on either side of a table underneath a window. We had built bookshelves and closets opposite the window. Andrei's and my room was all white: tempered walls, enameled woodwork, curtains of bright flowers on a white background. The other room was all wood: plywood walls, stained woodwork, curtains of flowers on a red background. This room was mostly empty while Dasha and Adya were investigating the world on their own, but now that Dasha had a son she would come for weekends and leave her son, Fedya, with us for the rest of the week. Andrei adored his grandson and taught him gardening from the age of three.

At Leonozovo we seemed to be far away from the stormy surface of a sea whose depths were realms of quietude. Some of this quietude seeped into our souls. The joy of intimacy attending our earliest years together returned in full measure. As I sat at my typewriter I knew Andrei was within calling distance if I needed to discuss the meaning of a Russian word with him. And he in his garden knew I was within calling distance if he discovered an unexpected form or color or scent he wanted me to enjoy with him. Our separate tasks were interrupted by shared pleasures: lunch, walks to the woods in search of sphagnum, playing with Fedya, reading aloud to each other in the evenings, he from a history of Eastern philosophy, I from Birukov's biography of Tolstoy. Nothing here deterred us from living on a level we had always sought and too rarely achieved.

Over the years Andrei's interest in wildflowers centered on wild orchids, an endangered species. He became head of the Orchid Section of the Horticultural Society sponsored by Moscow University. In the fall of 1967 he and Ivan Arcadiyevich, a fellow orchid-fancier, and I set out on a wild-orchid hunt in a forest reservation on the

Oka River. Research scientists had headquarters on the reservation where we were hospitably received. We roamed the woods for three days. Quick little wide-eyed creatures rustled through the underbrush, deer and bison eyed us indifferently, having known nothing but benevolence at the hands of man. Andrei and his friend found more orchids than they had counted on, ranging from the common Lady Slipper to large blooms not unlike the mauve tropical flower American students used to send their girls as corsages to be worn at Junior Proms. There were also delicate sprays of pink and white flowers. Andrei and Ivan dug them up with huge clumps of earth to preserve the moss and nutrients they needed. Andrei had spent a month in the hospital with his heart that spring, so he couldn't help Ivan lift them. I did, and also helped bind up the clumps of earth, and we came home with a great load of treasure. For the next two days Andrei occupied himself with choosing the best location for each plant and getting them all in the ground. Soon thereafter we closed up the garden for the winter.

Andrei now turned his attention to his Studio Theater. For their first full-length play they had chosen one by Anhouilh about the conflict between philistinism and the creative life, a theme Andrei found inspirational. He was still a dynamo of creative energy and he threw every bit of it into this play, going to Pushkin Street four or five mornings a week for rehearsals. As the weather grew colder, the constrictions in his chest grew worse. He always took a nitroglycerin pill before leaving the house and even so was stopped by pain every half a block or so. For Andrei's sake, the actors insisted on coming to the house for rehearsals. This posed a problem for me. I couldn't concentrate on translating with a group of actors working on their parts in the same room. And so in December, pressed by a publisher's deadline, I ran away for a month to the Writers' House in Golitzino, half an hour by train from Moscow. Ivy went too. We made arrangements that Andrei was to join us on weekends.

Ah, bliss: alone with my typewriter in a room to myself and Ivy's incomparable company whenever she and I were free. At such times, the day's stint behind us, we would go for walks along the dirt roads of this shabby suburban town that had grown up on what in the nineteenth century had been the handsome wooded estate of Prince Golitzin. The houses belonged mostly to city workers who had added unsightly excrescences to accommodate summerfolk. Writers—elderly ones—

would rent these because of easy access to the city and, more important, easy access to the dining room of the Writers' House. Ivy had spent two summers in such rooms.

In our walks we would as inevitably talk about writing as actors talk about theater. Ivy was working on another short story, "Apartheid" I believe, whose locale was this very Golitzino.

"I wonder if my stories are as good as you say," she mused on one of our walks. "Or is it just Peg being carried away by her own eloquence? I know you like "Amabel." I do too. I even like it when you don't like a story, because that shows discrimination, but, of course, I always *want* you to like them. I must try and write one you will like again."

I liked "Apartheid" in the draft version she read to me, but not as much as "Babushka" or some of those stories crafted out of excerpts from the unfinished novel.

"So much of the novel is written," I said. "It's a pity to give it up."

"But I've retreated from the idea of writing an old-fashioned novel. That way only farces or comedies can be written, as a vehicle for types. A thing I should love to be able to do but am not. Henry Green has found a way. But I'm not sure he's *shown* a way. Joyce almost killed all novelists by seeming to have written the novel to end novels."

"I don't think he's done it. I don't think a novel, or any work of art, ought to be made difficult on purpose, and that's what I feel Joyce has done when I read *Ulysses*. Parts of it are amazing, of course, the beginning, on the tower, for instance; and Bloom at the funeral. But then those long, long passages, so obscure."

"That's a matter I asked Joyce about when I saw him in Paris."

"And what did he say?"

"He said it had taken him ten years to write *Ulysses*, so why shouldn't the reader work a little over it too?"

"Tolstoy took a different view. He rewrote *War and Peace* seven times to make sure he was reaching his reader as directly and unambiguously as possible."

"Good for him. But Tolstoy is Tolstoy and Joyce is Joyce."

"You're right. But we began by talking about *your* novel . . ."

"*My* novel. Well, I've always thought there were good things in the manuscript. But I find frequent lapses into bright old-fashioned narrative tinctured with sprightliness. Partly my mother's influence, partly too much second-rate novel reading in girlhood."

"Must girls always be reading masterpieces?"

"Why not? I feel sure that every cheap children's book or 'light' novel is a serious debilitation. Perhaps one's style will never shake off the pernicious influence."

ON SATURDAY MORNINGS we would go to meet Andrei at the railroad station at the end of a main street made slippery by the pounding of many feet on unshoveled snow. The last time Andrei came we were late for the train. I caught sight of him turning into the general store. "Andrei!" I called. He looked splendid. The frost had put color in his cheeks and his eyes were shining. "What are you going in there for?"

"Look," pointing to the window display. "They're selling hazel nuts."

"Come along," said Ivy, pulling him away. "Your teeth are no better than mine for cracking hazel nuts."

The three of us had fun on these weekends. The Writers' House in Golitzino is small, housing only about thirteen people at a time. We all sat around a single table in the dining room for our meals, but on weekends so many guests arrived that little tables were set up in the four corners of the room. We were given one of these when Andrei was there. We liked that. We didn't have to join in the general conversation.

"How can you eat that?" Andrei asked Ivy with a grimace, indicating the dripping persimmon she had brought for dessert.

"How can you eat *that*?" retorted Ivy, turning away in disgust from the dish of glutinous dessert made of fruit juice and potato starch we had been served. "At least this is natural fruit."

"*Un*natural," protested Andrei. "Is it natural to bring fruit to this state of decomposition by keeping it on the radiator? And that's what you do."

"Alex says it makes my room smell nice."

"Alex? Who's Alex?"

"You don't know Alex? He's Yesenin's son by Nadya Volpina."

"You wouldn't expect the son of a great poet to be a great mathematician, would you?" I put in.

"He's said to be a genius. Most geniuses are wacky," said Ivy.

"Is Alex wacky?"

"Oh yes, but that's not why they put him in the lunatic asylum. They did that because he was teaching dissidents what protection Soviet law offers them. The establishment has given him—and Nadya—a bad time. But he says everything will work together for good in spite of the revolution and because inherently *der mensch ist gut.* A beautiful example of the triumph of hope over experience, as the feller said about second marriages," and her ringing laugh drew all eyes to our table.

These weekend visits seemed to do Andrei good. As he was leaving this last time he said, "I don't know whether it's the air or the company, but I haven't felt like this for months," and he drew a deep breath to prove it. And so I was completely unprepared for Dasha's call three days later telling me he had had another heart attack.

I rushed back to Moscow. I found him in bed. He greeted me with a sheepish smile as if apologizing for a misdemeanor.

"But you were feeling so well," I said.

"I know," he said.

He spent two weeks in bed, his actors coming and going, bringing him news of their work. He was in good spirits. I pulled the tea table up to his bed, and we ate our meals together. By the end of January he was up and about, and in February he began going to his Studio Theater again.

Since both of our birthdays were in March, we celebrated them together. For some reason that year, 1968, I held our party earlier than usual, on the fifth I think.

Mick-Step and Farida came, and Dmitri and his wife Tonya, and Annushka of course. The young people, Dasha and Adya, Vyeta and Lena, dropped in to toast us in champagne. It was a nice party. Andrei seemed touched. "Thank you," he said to me when it was over. "Thank you."

The eighth of March is Woman's Day in the Soviet Union. Andrei got up early in the morning and went to market to buy me a bouquet of Georgian mimosa, those clusters of downy yellow flowers set off by feathery gray-green leaves, the first blooms to greet the spring. The weather was perfect.

"Let's go to Leonozovo," said Andrei when he got home.

"Let's," I said.

"And take Fedya with us."

"And Nina." Nina was Fedya's nanny, a country girl less than five feet tall, a fourthgrade dropout because she hated school and loved to keep house. Later she became the most efficient manager of our household I have ever engaged.

In an hour we were out of the city.

No day can match in splendor a March day in the Moscow countryside. A big sun in a blue sky turns snow dust to gold dust as gentle breezes blow it off the boughs. The air is as soft as a cat's paw, but with a little prick to it as of claws not quite withdrawn. Birds dart and rabbits scurry. The road with its traffic holds no charm; it is the woods that seduce; one longs to race down the paths, slide down the slopes, and plunge into the drifts. Andrei couldn't do this, so we took the bus for three stops and walked along pavements to the community gardens. When we got to our own garden we couldn't open the gate for the snow. I borrowed shovels from a neighbor, and while Nina and I sweated, throwing off first scarves, then jackets, then sweaters, Andrei walked up and down the road in front of the house and Fedya gamboled at his side.

The glory of the day was slow in fading. So reluctant were we to part with it that Andrei said when we could linger no longer, "Let's not take the bus, let's go through the woods to the station."

It was easy going along trampled paths. We dawdled, admiring the patterns woven by lengthening shadows on the snow and the filigree of oak branches against a pink sky. Here and there a dry leaf clung to a branch, dancing hysterically whenever the wind blew.

In twenty minutes the station came in sight, and here the path turned toward the road where the traffic ran. We chose to shorten the way by cutting directly across a patch of virgin snow a city block in length. Before we had gone ten yards we found ourselves foundering in deep drifts. Nina and I tumbled about up to the waist in snow. We picked Fedya up and threw him down and rolled him over and he shrieked with glee. We tossed snow into the air to see it sparkle in the rosy ambience, catching it on our upturned faces as it came down. I turned to see Andrei standing at the edge of the drifts.

"C'mon, Andrei! Catch up with us!"

His crooked smile came blurred through the brightness of the tossed snow. I waited while he plowed toward us. When he drew near I saw that his eyes had the deep dark look that always came with the pain.

The snow was fun for Fedya and Nina and me. It was fatal for Andrei. Four days later he died.

THAT SUMMER THE ORCHIDS BLOOMED in Leonozovo, bloomed throughout the garden, under the walnut trees, under the willow, beside the pool, and among the ferns under our window.

And in the fall Andrei's play had its premiere. The actors carried it to conclusion with the help of a good friend, a director of his own artistic persuasion.

Postscript

I AM BACK in the United States. Not only in the United States, but in Philadelphia. Not only in Philadelphia but in the very district of Philadelphia where I spent my girlhood and youth and from which I set out on the great adventure. In a word, my life has come full circle.

After Andrei died I did not soon consider leaving Russia—because for thirty-six radiant, stormy, disappointing, jubilant, apocalyptic years Russia was the stage on which Andrei and I played out our destinies. The play was over.

I did leave Moscow—that is, I rented a room in Peredelkino, the writers' colony in the woods outside of Moscow, and there I worked on a book Andrei had asked me to write. It troubled him that Alexander Ostrovsky, Russia's great nineteenth-century playwright, had never received due recognition in the West, and he asked me if I couldn't do something about it. I tried to by translating four Ostrovsky plays and writing a biographical preface to them. That is what I was doing with great contentment a few years after Andrei's death when suddenly one evening Adya came rushing up from the city with the news that my brother had arrived from the states. My brother Dan! I hadn't seen or communicated with him for over thirty years! He had come unannounced, as unexpectedly as Andrei had been wont to come home from trips. Adya brought me back to town in a hurry.

We sat up all night talking in our Moscow apartment—Adya, Dasha, Dan, and I. "Come back home, Peg," Dan said. "You have nothing to keep you here now." Only half a century of memories and this vast Russian land I was knee-deep in. "All your relatives are there," he went on, urging me. Knee-deep in Russia but deep-rooted in America.

If the Roman Catholic Church says, "Give us the first six years of a child's life and he is ours for good," the pull of the first twenty-five years must be even more irresistible. I have never been free of it, and with Andrei gone I felt it more strongly than ever. "That's where all of you belong; all of you with all of us," Dan said emphatically.

These words sounded sweet to Dasha and Adya. Dasha was bringing up Fedya alone now. She and Vitya had parted and she longed for a change of scenery.

Adya had always wanted to go to America. For years I saved a note sent home by his teacher in second grade complaining that he was playing truant. When Andrei confronted him with the charge he confessed that these truancies had been spent riding Moscow trolleycars on his way to America. And there was that cold, dreary, drizzly autumn day when he (now grown up) and his father and I went to the cemetery in which Andrei Nikolayevich had been buried in the spring to sign papers and fill in forms and wait in lines to see functionaries. At the most exasperating moment Adya bent down to whisper in my ear with a vehemence I would not have wanted his father to hear, "Why in God's name did you ever come to this wretched country?"

Wretched indeed. "Wretcheder and wretcheder," as Alice would have said. Less than six months after Andrei died the Soviets invaded Czechoslovakia. I wonder how this would have affected Andrei's loyalty to the new order. Probably not at all, so long-range was his historical viewpoint, so implicit his belief in inevitable change.

Well, anyway, here we were, Adya, Dasha, and I, faced with the necessity of making a definitive decision. We would begin a new life on another continent as paupers, for Soviet émigrés were not allowed to take valuables out of the country, and money only to the amount of one hundred dollars. According to Soviet standards all three of us were doing well. Translators of literature are held in high esteem in Russia; they enjoy the status of *literati* and are rewarded accordingly. Who would offer me this at my age in America? And who there needed Adya, an artist with a job as a TV settings designer that gave him plenty of free time to paint on the side? Or Dasha, a teacher of English at Moscow University? This thought gave us pause. We decided not to rush into anything. I would go on a visit first. That was my visit in 1973-74 when, on boarding that Pan Am jet a London's Heathrow Airport, I set foot on American soil, so to speak, for the first time in almost half a century.

I was overwhelmed by the reception I received on this visit. Friends and relatives gathered round as if they had been waiting for me all these years, sure I would come back. Because of so long a separation I experienced the joy of abiding friendship with a poignancy those who live with it as part of their daily lives can never know. Now they opened their arms to me and said, "Come home, and we'll see to it that you and your family will be taken care of."

This was the message I brought to Dasha and Adya who met me at the Moscow airport on my return. We could go.

But we did not go for another five years, and then only Dasha, Fedya, and I. Dasha, who had never ceased loving Vitya, went back to him. She never did learn to unlove him, but in these five years he hurt her so deeply that she learned to reject him. Eventually she said, "We've got to get Fedya out of here, Mother, and as soon as possible. I feel in my bones it's our last chance."

As for Adya, not long before I left for my visit to the states he had married a second time, an artist named Lara whose blond loveliness and quiet dignity resembled that of Dr. Zhivago's Lara in the film version of Pasternak's novel. And like Lara of the novel, Adya's Lara had a little girl by a former marriage; her name was Natasha. Soon after I got back Lara gave birth to twin boys. She was as patriotically Russian as Andrei had been and she could no more consider leaving her native land than Andrei could have. Knowing how painful the process of transplantation is, I did not try to persuade her. "I cannot go," she said. "Then neither can I," said Adya.

Ah, but the pain of that night before we parted. Adya tried to comfort me. "It will be all right, Mother. You'll come to see us. We'll come to see you." I was not deceived. How many years had passed before I had been allowed to visit my relatives? The present period of *détente* with its relaxation of laws forbidding Soviet citizens the right to foreign travel could end at any moment.

And, sure enough, hardly had Dasha, Fedya, and I left the country when the Soviets invaded Afghanistan, the United States retaliated by boycotting the Moscow Olympics, and, bang, down came the Iron Curtain again. The year after I arrived in Philadelphia I sent Adya an invitation to visit his mother. "*Nyet!*" said the Soviet government. The enormity of it shocked Lara out of her allegiance to her homeland. "If that is how it is to be, we will all go for good," she wrote, thinking it would be as easy for them to get permission as it had been for Dasha and me. Far from it. As soon as they sent in the application to emigrate both Adya and Lara were fired from their jobs and for the next seven years they were held in the country as *refuseniks*. The anxiety of these years, the insecurity, the deprivations, the indignity of being a social outcast, so undermined Lara's health that by the time Gorbachev came to power and they were allowed to join us she was virtually an invalid. American medicine soon restored her to health.

Among the friends I had visited in 1974 were Helen and Harold Minton. Helen was a college friend; she and her husband Harold were among those who saw me off to Russia in 1932. On parting in 1974 she said, "Let's write more often, Peg." Before we had a chance to do so she died. Friends wrote that Harold was inconsolable. They had no children and he was left alone in a seventeen-room house just off the University of Pennsylvania campus, a house that had rung with Helen's infectious laughter, with the voice of innumerable friends, with music of four-hand pieces played on the two baby grand pianos in their spacious living room. The living room was Helen's province: she was a musician. The enormous studio, two stories high, was Harold's: he was an artist.

Into this house, now mournful with emptiness and neglect, Harold received Dasha, Fedya, and me. Soon Dasha left for California to teach Russian at the Defense Language Institute, and Fedya took an apartment with students from the School for the Performing Arts, which he attended. For nearly ten years Harold and I offered each other companionship and consolation. This six-foot man whom grief had reduced to one hundred and thirty pounds began eating again because there was someone to talk to at the table. Together we refurbished the house and replanted the garden. We needed each other.

And then, one bright autumn day in 1988 (by which time Adya's family had arrived and were living with us until they could find a home of their own), I stepped out of the kitchen into the garden to call Harold to lunch and found him lying stark and still, his eyes closed, his face serene, the cat Kate sitting quietly beside him. There was no calling him back.

Adya and Lara now have a home of their own only two blocks away from me. They are attentive; I see them often. Even so I occasionally feel lonely in the evenings. So many have gone: Andrei, Harold, relatives, friends. It is not given to many to live from one end of the century to the other. But loneliness is not only the lot but also the privilege of old age, which is a time for reflection and preparation, occupations best served by solitude.